FAILURES OF AMERICAN METHODS OF LAWMAKING IN HISTORICAL AND COMPARATIVE PERSPECTIVES

America's 18th century founders expected that the people of the United States would establish a wise and happy government of written laws adopted with a single eye to reason and the good of those governed. Few Americans today would say that America's lawmaking fulfills the founders' expectations. Dysfunctional is the word that many Americans use to describe their methods of lawmaking.

The legal professions tell the American people that they are doing the best they can. They tell a myth of common law. They say the people should rejoice, and not complain, when America's judges make law, for such lawmaking makes America's laws exceptional. It is how America has always made law, they say. Judges make better laws than legislatures, they claim.

The historical part of this book explodes the common law myth of dominance of judge-made law in American history. Using sources hardly accessible until 21st century digitization, it shows that statutes have had a much greater role in American law than the legal professions acknowledge.

The comparative part of this book dismantles the claim that judges make better law then legislatures. It shows how the methods of American legislative lawmaking, owing to neglect, have failed to keep up with their counterparts abroad, and have thus denied the people the government of laws that the founders expected. This book shows how such a system works in Germany and would be a solution for the American legal system as well.

JAMES R. MAXEINER is the associate director of the Center for International and Comparative Law at the University of Baltimore. Among many other books, he is coauthor of *Failures of American Civil Justice in International Perspective* (Cambridge University Press, 2011) and a series editor for Ius Gentium: Comparative Perspectives on Law and Justice.

Failures of American Methods of Lawmaking in Historical and Comparative Perspectives

JAMES R. MAXEINER

With a Foreword by
PHILIP K. HOWARD

CAMBRIDGE
UNIVERSITY PRESS

University Printing House, Cambridge CB2 8BS, United Kingdom

One Liberty Plaza, 20th Floor, New York, NY 10006, USA

477 Williamstown Road, Port Melbourne, VIC 3207, Australia

314-321, 3rd Floor, Plot 3, Splendor Forum, Jasola District Centre, New Delhi - 110025, India

79 Anson Road, #06-04/06, Singapore 079906

Cambridge University Press is part of the University of Cambridge.

It furthers the University's mission by disseminating knowledge in the pursuit of education, learning and research at the highest international levels of excellence.

www.cambridge.org
Information on this title: www.cambridge.org/9781108731935
DOI: 10.1017/9781108182195

First published 2018
First paperback edition 2019

A catalogue record for this publication is available from the British Library

Library of Congress Cataloging in Publication data
NAMES: Maxeiner, James R., author.
TITLE: Failures of American methods of lawmaking in historical and
    comparative perspectives / James R. Maxeiner.
DESCRIPTION: Cambridge [UK] ; New York : Cambridge University Press, 2017. |
    Includes bibliographical references and index.
IDENTIFIERS: LCCN 2017029293 | ISBN 9781107198159 (Hardback)
SUBJECTS: LCSH: Legislation–United States–History and criticism. |
    Parliamentary practice–United States–History and criticism. |
    Law–United States–History. | United States–Politics and government. |
    Parliamentary practice–Germany. | Legislation–Comparative studies.
CLASSIFICATION: LCC KF4945 .M39 2017 | DDC 328.73/077–dc23
    LC record available at https://lccn.loc.gov/2017029293

ISBN 978-1-107-19815-9 Hardback
ISBN 978-1-108-73193-5 Paperback

To Philip K. Howard

America's finest jurists have combined practical and theoretical knowledge, dedication to law improvement, and appreciation for how legal science and foreign law facilitate better law. You stand in this tradition of Joseph Story, David Dudley Field, and Karl N. Llewellyn. Your generous support has made this work possible.

Laws for the People

The laws are not made for the lawyers but for the people.

American Law Journal (1813)

The laws are not – we mean they ought not to be – written for the lawyers, but for the people.

American Themis (1844)

Though our [government] claims to be a democratic government, our statutes are addressed to lawyers and not to the people; a layman can hardly be expected to understand their phraseology. The principal German statutes, particularly the civil code, are published in cheap, popular and handy editions, and are found in hundreds of thousands of homes. The extraordinary sense of legality of the German people is not entirely unconnected with the intelligibility of their laws.

Special Committee on Drafting of Legislation, American Bar Association (1914)

Our legal system has become extremely difficult to understand for ordinary citizens, even for smart lawyers.

Geoffrey C. Hazard, Jr. (2014)

Contents

Foreword

PHILIP K. HOWARD

The test of law is how it works. Of course, that begs the question of how law is supposed to work. A further difficulty is getting a clear view of modern law; there's just too much of it. We constantly complain about legal excesses – telling stories about red tape and lawsuits has become a national pastime. But debates about reforming law always seem like rear-guard actions, striving to avoid legal defeat instead of making law work for us.

What's needed is a fresh perspective. What is law supposed to do? Well, it supports our freedom by setting outer boundaries of reasonable behavior – by prohibiting misconduct, law liberates us to deal with strangers without undue defensiveness. Law also supports freedom by providing a legal framework to protect common resources, such as clean air and water, and providing common services. With law in place, we don't tiptoe through the day looking over our shoulders, or carry chemical kits to test the water we're drinking, or check to see if toys have lead paint. Law is supposed to be a framework designed to liberate human freedom and initiative.

How's American law doing? On the positive side, there's not a scourge of banditry (in most communities); people generally trust contracts; state power is not abusive; and common resources are okay. On the negative side, law is suffocating human initiative. Instead of a framework for freedom, law has replaced freedom. Instead of asking "What's the right thing to do here?," people ask "What does the rule require?" or "Could someone sue me?"

The stifling effects of too much law are evident in every aspect of society. It may be useful to flip through some snapshots:

- Decrepit infrastructure isn't fixed for a decade because of endless red tape. By prolonging bottlenecks, multi-thousand page environmental reviews end up harming the environment.

- Starting a business is fraught with legal costs and uncertainty. The United States ranks low in the world in ease of starting a business.
- Doctors spend up to half their time filling out required paperwork. Because of distrust of American justice, they practice "defensive medicine," raising costs and compromising patient safety with unnecessary tests. It's hardly surprising that the cost of American healthcare approaches twice as much as other developed countries, with no better outcomes.
- Candor in the workplace is basically illegal. Businesses no longer give job references. For fear of offending someone, we now make it almost impossible for people to learn from their mistakes and from the opinions of those around them.
- Government itself is legally ossified, doing what it did yesterday because the law doesn't allow anything else. The idea of a "public choice" is an oxymoron in Washington. No one is choosing anything, at least when it comes to domestic matters. Every institution is frozen. Personnel choices are not permitted; over 99 percent of federal employees got a "fully successful" rating or better in 2013 – because any negative comment would subject the supervisor to an awful legal trial. The Trump election was clearly a vote against Washington, but it remains to be seen whether Trump can remake the structure of government so that it works.
- Children are the canary in the legal mine. Children often need affection – but teachers and caregivers are forbidden from hugging a crying child. Children need to learn to take responsibility for themselves – but legal fear has eliminated free play and stripped playgrounds of anything involving modest risk, such as seesaws and jungle gyms. Young people must learn to deal with conflict, but schools instead feel a legal need to coddle and create "safe zones," even in college, to protect them from being upset by different points of view.

In all these stories, no one is doing what they think is right, or sensible. Why not? The law doesn't let them, or puts them at risk for reasonable choices.

Who designed the legal system? The answer is that no one designed it. It just grew. Nor is it a "system." It's a dense jungle of overlapping laws, regulations and rights. Most of these laws ostensibly address worthy social goals, or least plausible goals. But no one has actually gone back to see how law is actually working. Nor has anyone tried to organize it – the federal government, for example, has scores of separate teacher-training programs. Criminal law is found in thousands of federal, state and municipal statutes. The National Inventory of Collateral Consequences of

Conviction lists over 48,000 federal and state laws that impose collateral consequences for criminal convictions.

If you want to find out if something is lawful and what the consequences of violations are, you need to hire a lawyer, and even then, there will be uncertainty.

The natural consequence of this legal tangle is social paralysis. Maybe people can't cheat and pollute – a good thing – but at the cost to human initiative and freedom. Law makes lots of things unlawful, but doesn't protect conduct that should be lawful. Law is also a one-way ratchet; statutes and regulations get added every year but are rarely removed. Not surprisingly, government is unable to adapt to new challenges or, indeed, do anything other than what it did yesterday. Like sediment in a harbor, law has accumulated to the point where it's hard to get where we need to go. Political scientist Francis Fukuyama calls our system a "vetocracy" – anyone can find legal support to block almost anything. "Who governs?" is obviously an important question, political scientist Samuel Huntington observed. "Even more important, however, may be the question 'Does anybody govern?'"

What do we do about it? The answer is pretty basic: We need to create a legal structure that is deliberate, not ad hoc. Doing so requires drawing lines about risk, authority and acceptable conflict. Then we need to monitor and adapt this new system to make sure it is working as intended.

The goal of a deliberate legal system – blindingly obvious to nonlawyers – is actually not the tradition of American law. In the historical part of this book, James Maxeiner shows how the aspiration of the framers and others for organized legislative systems lost out to a kind of theology about the wisdom of the common law. Legislation was with us from the beginning, of course. It turns out that Jefferson took it upon himself to systematize most of Virginia law, and no less a personage than Madison was responsible for trying to get it adopted. But the common law ideal of doing justice case by case, and discerning law from countless judicial opinions, appealed to the individualist strain in America. Fairness would be decided case by case. The push for coherent codes such as the Napoleonic Code was demeaned as, well, European. The idea of a "civil code" was criticized as an effort to determine fairness in advance, without taking into account the circumstances.

As the agrarian society of the early republic blossomed into the industrial revolution, statutes were essential to deal with modern challenges: commerce, corporations, common schools and colleges, public lands, public health, navigation, taxation, elections, immigration and establishment of many government offices that we rely on including for police and national defense. But the ad hoc nature of the common law seems to have infected the enactment of positive law. Most statutes enacted by legislatures do not aspire to being systemic codes such as the Uniform Commercial Code. Statutes are more like Band-Aids to a specific problem. When Congress in the 1970s discovered widespread neglect of special needs students, it passed a broad law giving disabled students the right to an "individualized education." How does that law fit with other statutes dealing with K–12 education? Congress doesn't even ask. As it turns out, federal special education laws have spawned a bureaucratic monster, pitting parents against educators, consuming a high percentage of total K–12 expenditures and burdening states and local school districts with most of those costs. It's hard to find a statutory program that isn't broken in significant ways. But Congress doesn't fix them because it treats old law as immutable, not a part of a working code that must be kept up to date and evaluated by how it works in practice.

This is no way to run a society. The waste is prodigious. The ineptitude is seen in regular breakdowns, such as the Oroville Dam. The populist outrage against Washington stems, at least in part, from the mindless dictates that ordinary citizens encounter daily in the workplace, schools and hospitals. The phoniness of Washington is perhaps the best evidence that no one, in fact, is making deliberate choices on how to run our society.

Making law work is not, in fact, rocket science. But, as Professor Maxeiner persuasively demonstrates, it requires a new goal: legal codes that strive to be organized and systematic, not a hodge-podge of programs piled on top of old programs. Germany and other countries do this just fine. The benefits will be huge: People will know what the law is, and will feel free to take initiative. Legal waste will be minimized. The law will be able to adapt to new circumstances, because government officials have the job of keeping it up to date. Democratic responsibility will not be empty rhetoric, but real – because the statutes lay out clear lines of authority and accountability. In helpful detail, Professor Maxeiner describes exactly how German law is structured to achieve these goals.

Systematic codes are hardly un-American. Find any area of American law that works well and you'll find a code that people feel they can rely upon. The Uniform Commercial Code, written in the 1950s, gave commerce a boost by bringing order to the mess of forty-eight different state contract laws. As it happens, the primary draftsman of the UCC was Professor Karl Llewellyn, who knew and admired German codes.

As Professor Maxeiner demonstrates in this important book, the supposed conflict between common law and civil law is based on a misperception about how civil law systems work. Civil law systems do not dictate results in advance – like the common law, cases hinge on concepts of good faith and

reasonableness. Ironically, it is America's undisciplined approach to legislation that resembles mindless results – dictating all sorts of idiocies for no
reason other than some regulation writer forty years ago thought it might be a
good idea.

The American approach to legal organization of our society is unsustain-
able. Thousands of laws and regulations written by people long dead, piled on
top of each other and rarely reviewed or reorganized, can only result in
frustration, waste and progressive paralysis. What's needed is not broad deregulation, but a complete recodification. It's actually not impossibly hard,
because codes that focus on goals, general principles and lines of authority
and accountability are far simpler and less controversial. What's hard is to
dictate choices in advance in thousand-page rulebooks. The benefits, as with
the Uniform Commercial Code, will be immediate. As Professor Maxeiner
demonstrates, many things could work better.

Preface

America's legal system is broken. Too many people, even with the aid of lawyers, cannot know the law that governs them. They cannot apply laws sensibly.

This book, through comparative perspective, shows that Americans are not compelled to suffer a broken system. Other systems based on legislated statutes and statutory methods work better.

America's legal professionals, however, do not learn from foreign examples. America, they say, is a common-law country based principally on judge-made case law and common-law methods. Statutory methods have little place in America's past or present.

This book, relying on newly available sources, asserts new observations that show that Americans have not been wedded to case law to the exclusion of statutes.

Besides the Introduction (Part I), it has two main Parts: Historical (Part II) and Comparative (Part III).

* * *

America's legal system is hardly a system at all. It is chaotic instead of systematic. America's people do not enjoy a government of laws, but suffer a rule of men.

A legal system consists of laws, precedents and procedures organized to work together in harmony and to present a consistent whole. Comparing our rules and practices with those of foreigners makes clear that ours is defective as a system to guide and judge peoples' behavior. The differences are not incremental but overwhelming. They jump out at anyone familiar with ours and with a successful system.

America's legal professionals have given up on a government of laws. They no longer support one of the most basic expectations of people for a legal system: that law consists of rules set down beforehand to apply to facts.

In the Comparative Part of this book (Part III) I compare America's legal system with that of one of the more successful of foreign legal systems, that of Germany.[1] I identify ways in which Germany's legal system by design makes rules knowable and susceptible to sensible application in five different areas of legal methods:

- Systematization and Simplifying Statutes
- Lawmaking for the Common Good
- Federalism and Localism
- Constitutional Review
- Law Applying

In each of these areas I show how America's legal system lacks intelligent design and suffers rules that are hard or impossible to know and apply sensibly. In short, I show how Germany has a working legal system – a working government of laws – and the United States has a deficient one.

* * *

Demonstrating the superiority of Germany's legal methods will not persuade America's jurists to adopt them. America's legal professionals have persuaded themselves of the superiority of their case-law methods.

They have, as David Dudley Field told them, "a superstitious reverence for the law of precedents."[2]

America's law schools indoctrinate first-year students in common law myths. They teach that judge-made case law and common-law methods are superior to statutes and statutory method and are an adequate substitute for a government of laws. They tell students that all American law is based on English common law

---

[1]   In my generation, that of the baby-boomers, Germany's Nazi past made such a choice suspect. I try to dispel those suspicions in an appendix in an earlier book. JAMES R. MAXEINER WITH GYOOHO LEE AND ARMIN WEBER, FAILURES OF AMERICAN CIVIL JUSTICE IN INTERNATIONAL PERSPECTIVE 272 (2011). In my children's generation, that of the Millennials, the idea is not suspect at all. With the United States apparently laying down the mantel of leader of the free world, many are looking to Germany or to the European Union as leading candidates to assume that role.

[2]   *Address of David Dudley Field of New York, President of the Association*, REPORT OF THE TWELFTH ANNUAL MEETING OF THE AMERICAN BAR ASSOCIATION HELD AT CHICAGO ILLINOIS, AUG. 28, 29 AND 30, 149, 232 (1889).

and that America had little to do with statutes until the 20th century. They thus inoculate their students against statute-based law reform.

This book dispels these myths.

The idea that case law can be an adequate substitute for a government of laws – as widely held as it is – is readily dispelled. I dispatch it in Chapter 3, Common Law is not an Option, of Part I. The principal challenge is to make legal professionals aware that their legal methods are not the only ones.[3]

The idea that America has always been a country of English and American common law to the exclusion of statutes, on the other hand, is more difficult to dispel. It has been gospel for more than a century. Owing to the peculiarity of legal publishing, its provenance coincides almost exactly with the contents of America's law libraries of the 20th century: case reports, textbooks and law school reviews published after 1880 (including reprints of cases decided before then). I show that it was not always so.

Through newly available sources – not before much used – I upend this 20th century gospel and show that it is no longer tenable in the light of these new sources.

The common-law gospel rests on a blinkered view of history: case reports, textbooks and law school law reviews. These were not, however, the principal venues for legal discussion and instruction for most of the 19th century. Pamphlets, addresses, general interest journals and books, legislative debates, committee reports and so on were. These materials tell a different story from the conventional one.

Once, to find and access these materials was very difficult, although possible with perseverance.[4] With the digitization of America's historic legal literature in this century, no longer are these materials inaccessible or unusable. They refute the conventional wisdom of common law exclusivity.

* * *

I wrote this book for the many Americans who believe that their government is broken and who would like to find ways to fix it. I suggest, but do not prescribe, some ways toward solving some problems. I assume no political agenda. I hope that conservatives and liberals, Republicans and Democrats, all will find something of value here. I do assume the goal of a government of laws; I am looking for ways to make those laws function well as rules.

---

[3] *See* James R. Maxeiner, U.S. *"methods awareness" for German Jurists, in* FESTSCHRIFT FÜR WOLFGANG FIKENTSCHER, 114 (Bernhard Großfeld *et al.*, eds., 1998).

[4] *See, e.g.*, James R. Maxeiner, *Bane of American Forfeiture Law – Banished at Last?*, 62 CORNELL L. REV. 768 (1977).

I wrote this book for general readers interested in fixing America's broken legal system. By general readers, I mean people who are not in the legal professions (i.e., lawyers, judges, law professors). I assume, however, that these general readers have a keen interest and some knowledge of law and legal systems. I have tried, at least to some small extent, to bring to the book the perspective of people subject to laws.[5]

I have not written this book for experts in comparative law or in legal philosophy. They may find some of what I say simplistic or insufficiently rigorous in description. Still, I hope that they will find thoughts here that challenge them. What I have to say about German law is not controversial. I have accordingly limited my citations to German-language materials to publications that make particular points that are less commonly discussed or that help find other materials. Where English-language materials exist, I have sought to cite those that are more substantial and relatively recent.

I apologize to historians who would prefer that I had written an historical monograph. In writing about the past, I am not so much writing a history as I am working to disestablish common-law untruths and myths of today. I am not establishing an alternative statutory reality. I seek as much to show how things were *not*, as to show how they were.

I encourage historians, and their students, to investigate America's legal history anew. For their sakes, I have referred generously to primary source examples of the importance of statutes. I have not, however, tried to be exhaustive. Digitization means I am constantly finding new examples. I have hardly begun to look at newspaper accounts. I refer less generously to the growing body of secondary works in legal history since little of the new work addresses the issues on which I focus.

I apologize to law reformers who would like plans for a new legal system. I identify system failures in the United States and system successes in Germany, but I do not go on to prescribe a new system for America. I do not have strength or the political acumen to do that. Legal system changes depend on practical political possibilities. I hope here to make the environment more welcoming for such change and to encourage reformers to seek it.

Finally, I make no apology to America's law professors for encouraging a "best practices" approach to comparative law. I regret that most American law professors pay comparative law no mind and many of the few who do have turned from law reform to the milquetoast of "learning valuable lessons" from abroad. My own teacher, Rudolf B. Schlesinger, saw in best practices the first

---

[5] This idea does not come easily to the legal professions. *See* Dennis Jacobs, *The Secret Life of Judges*, 75 FORDHAM L. REV. 2855 (2007).

of all uses of comparative law. My colleagues will spot in this book my impatience with the idea of a common law–civil law divide that precludes adaption of practices that work.

As this book was in press, in the fifty days between November 2 and December 22, 2017, the United States adopted the most sweeping changes in its tax laws in thirty years, the Tax Cuts and Jobs Act, Public Law 115-97. Time did not allow consideration of the process and substance here. Readers skeptical of my criticisms of contemporary American methods of lawmaking are encouraged to read about it and its passage.

JAMES R. MAXEINER
Bronxville NY
The 500th Anniversary of the Reformation

Acknowledgements

Ordinarily acknowledgements in "star" footnotes credit legions of people who helped the author put a work together. Without diminishing my appreciation for that help, here I want to thank the stars of this book, who by steadfastly and materially supporting the very idea of this work made it possible to bring it to a finish notwithstanding substantial opposition: Andrea Bessac Maxeiner, Philip K. Howard, Mortimer Sellers, Eric Easton, John H. Langbein and John Berger.

Summary

A GOVERNMENT OF LAWS, NOT MEN: AMERICANS' EXCEPTIONAL
IDEAL REALIZED ABROAD BUT NOT AT HOME

In 1776 on the eve of the Independence of the United States of America John
Adams set out his *Thoughts on Government* on what he thought America's
new government should look like. The best of governments, Adams wrote, was
a republic, and "the form of government which is best contrived to secure an
impartial and exact execution of the laws, is the best of republics." In other
words, "good government is an empire of laws." It is not a government of men.

Adams built the ideal of a government of laws, not of men, into the
Massachusetts Constitution or Frame of Government of 1780, which he
drafted. It governs today. 125 years later in 1905 Katherine Lee Bates added
law to her iconic poem *America The Beautiful*:

> America ! America !
> God mend thy every flaw.
> Confirm they soul in self-control,
> Thy liberty in law![1]

Through the 19th century, when Americans spoke of law, they had in mind
legislatively adopted statutes. A government of laws, not men, meant laws that
men could understand. At constitutional conventions, in state legislatures, in
public gatherings and in civics instruction, law meant laws. People expected
that laws would be well-ordered and understandable statutes. All states established regular publication of their laws. All states compiled their statutes. All
states revised their statutes. Of common law, of judicial lawmaking, few

---

[1] Katherine Lee Bates, *America the Beautiful*, 78 THE HOME MISSIONARY 375 (Mar. 1905).

people other than members of the legal professions had much to say that was anything other than pejorative.

At the nation's Centennial in 1876 Americans identified the drive toward systematized law as American exceptionalism. Progress in law meant progress in getting rid of oppressive common law and substitution of modern statutes. In systematizing their laws, results were mixed. Compiling laws was not controversial. Revising laws was. Some revisions were little more than compilations. Some were nearly codes.

By the turn of the 20th century when Bates revised "America the Beautiful," the legal professions had turned the country away from modern legal methods. In the last quarter of the 19th century the legal professions established themselves. At first, many leaders of the new professions sought the government of laws their ancestors had longed for. But by century's end judges assumed supremacy over statutes and constitutional interpretation; lawyers and law professors favored litigation over legislation.

Ironically, legal professionals claimed primacy of judge-made law just as America was entering what their successors now call the "age of statutes." Instead of cultivating a government of laws, the professionals promoted a "rule of law" that they imported from Victorian England to displace Adams' government of laws.

Today the United States of America has, says Geoffrey C. Hazard, Jr., a "Rule of Legal Rhetoric: political pushing and shoving, conducted in legal terminology . . . a complicated combination of multiple public authorities and decentralized private initiatives." It amounts to, says Walter K. Olson, "The Rule of Lawyers." It is not a proper government for the people, Philip K. - Howard says, but "A Rule of Nobody."

AMERICANS DESERVE A GOVERNMENT OF LAWS

It does not have to be that way. Instead of consigning the United States to a rule of lawyers, Americans might better think about building a government of laws. The ideal has not been abandoned elsewhere, but is there embraced and achieved. Foreign examples show how that can be done.

Five German Advantages[2] in Realizing a Government of Laws
1. Germany's laws are systematized and simplified. They coordinate one with another. They are counted in scores. They present people with one consistent set of directions. America's laws are little systemized. They

---

[2]   John H. Langbein, *The German Advantage in Civil Procedure*, 52 U. CHI. L. REV. 823 (1985).

frequently conflict with one another. They are counted in thousands. They present people with inconsistent directions (Chapter 9: Systematizing and Simplifying Statutes).

2. Germany's laws are made by processes designed to involve the whole people in order to serve the common good. They are professionally crafted to coordinate one with another. They are presented for public discussion before enactment. America's laws are made by "those who show up." They reflect the interests of their sponsors and not the interests of the common good. They are adopted before the public has opportunity to critique them (Chapter 10: Lawmaking for the Common Good).

3. In federalism, federal, state and local governments share power and authority. Germany's federalism is designed to present the people with one overall government of laws. Federalism serves the common good and the people's interest in laws administered close to home. America's federalism ("our federalism") is not designed to present the people with one overall government of laws. It assumes the opposite: that different sovereigns may adopt laws at conflict with one another. States' rights, not the common good, are often thought the justification of federalism (Chapter 11: Federalism and Localism).

4. Constitutional review assures that people are subject only to laws legitimately adopted that are consistent with their respective constitutions. Germany's methods of constitutional review do this in such a way as to minimize uncertainty resulting from review. Only specially qualified judges are authorized to put laws out of force. America's methods, on the other hand, produce substantial uncertainty as to the validity of laws in time and space. Inferior judges of no special constitutional qualification put laws out of force (Chapter 12: Constitutional Review).

5. Germany's methods of crafting and applying laws facilitate sensible application by people and courts in individual cases to promote actions consistent not only with law but also with justice and policy, without upending democratic legitimacy. America's unsystematic crafting of laws leads legal professions to turn laws in their application upside down to the detriment of law, justice and policy (Chapter 13: Applying Laws).

PART I

Introduction

1

Introduction

Of Governments and Laws

For a Common-wealth without lawes is like a Ship without rigging and steeradge. *The Lawes and Libertyes of Massachusetts* (1648)

People rely on governments to order their collective affairs. Governments govern using laws. Good governments are democratically chosen and adopt laws to promote justice and the common good. In states with good governments, people voluntarily apply laws to themselves.

A. AMERICANS' LONGING FOR A GOVERNMENT OF LAWS

Americans have a glorious history of uniting government and laws. The Pilgrims on the *Mayflower* in 1620, while at anchor offshore of the new land but before disembarking, agreed in the *Mayflower Compact* to "combine ourselves together into a Civil Body Politic, for our better ordering and preservation." They pledged that they would "enact, constitute and frame such just and equal Laws, Ordinances, Acts, Constitutions and Offices, from time to time, as shall be thought most meet and convenient for the general good of the Colony, unto which we promise all due submission and obedience."

The Colony of Massachusetts Bay carried through the pledge of the Pilgrims. Its *Lawes and Libertyes of Massachusetts* of 1648, one of America's first law books, colorfully explains why the colony adopted laws: as "rigging and steeradge" are to sailing ships, laws are the means that drive and steer the state and its people into the future. Good laws make good government possible.[1]

Good laws guide people in how to act. When laws speak to the people, most people follow them. So the 1648 *Lawes and Libertyes* was an "indeavor to satisfie your longing expectation, and frequent complaints for want of such a volume to be published in print: wherein (upon every occasion) you might readily see the rule by which you ought to walke by."

Good laws protect people when they act. So the *Lawes and Libertyes* eschewed general, unspecific clauses: "It is very unsafe & injurious to the body of the people to put them to learn their duty and liberty from general rules." Good laws are clear about what they require.

Good laws are organized. So the *Lawes and Libertyes* were organized "so they might more readily be found, & that the diverse lawes concerning one matter being placed together the scope and the intent of the whole and of every one of them might more easily be apprehended."

Good laws are general rules for all for the welfare and justice of all. Thus they claim the obedience of all. So the *Lawes and Libertyes* provide that "lawes are made with respect to the whole people, and not to each particular person; and obediance to them must be yielded with respect to the common welfare, and not to thy private advantage. . . . Nor is it enough to have laws except they be also just."

Good laws rely on faithful execution. So the *Lawes and Libertyes* provide that "The execution of the law is the life of the law." Good laws look to future change and are an ongoing project. So the *Lawes and Libertyes* provide "we have not published it as a perfect body of laws sufficient to carry on the Government established for future times, nor could it bee . . . expected that we should promise such a thing. . . . the Civilian gives you a satisfactory reason of such continuall alterations, additions &c: *crescit in orbe dolus*."[2]

---

[1] THE BOOK OF THE GENERAL LAWES AND LIBERTYES CONCERNING THE INHABITANTS OF THE MASSACHUSETTS, Reprinted from the copy of the 1648 edition in the Huntington Library preface (Thomas G. Barnes, ed., 1982).

[2] The phrase is part of a longer Latin maxim that explains the multitude of laws by an ever-changing world.

Laws that people follow voluntarily make civil society possible. For every instance of application of law in a lawsuit, there are millions of instances of people applying law to themselves.[3] For people to follow laws, laws must be made for them.

The Colony of Connecticut literally gave its laws to the people: it printed, delivered and collected payment for them. In 1672, when it printed its Code of 1650,[4] it required that "every family in the several plantations in this Colony shall purchase one of our Law books, to keep for their use." Constables delivered the books and collected payment on delivery of twelve pence in silver or a peck and half of wheat, or failing in that, in two-thirds of a bushel of peas.[5]

The 1780 *Constitution or Frame of Government of the State of Massachusetts-Bay*, drafted principally by John Adams and still in force, brings these ideas of laws for the people together in the concept of "a government of laws, not men." The Constitution's preamble explains:

> The body politic ... is a social compact by which the whole people covenants with each citizen and each citizen with the whole people that all shall be governed by certain laws for the common good. It is the duty of the people, therefore, in framing a constitution of government, to provide for an equitable mode of making laws, as well as for an impartial interpretation and a faithful execution of them; that every man may, at all times, find his security in them.

I discuss in historical and comparative perspectives principally three elements of governments of laws:

1. *Laws are made for common good and justice*: Are laws made "for the common good" in an "equitable mode"?
2. *Laws are known to those to whom they apply*: Are laws clear, publicized and stable, i.e., capable of being followed? (Are laws "certain"?)

---

[3]   Cf. H.L.A. HART, THE CONCEPT OF LAW 40 (2d ed., 1997) (asking why should law not be concerned "with the 'puzzled man' or 'ignorant man' who is willing to do what is required, if only he can be told what it is? Or with the 'man who wishes to arrange his affairs' his if only he can be told how to do it?" and concluding "The principal function of the law as means of social control ... is to be seen in the diverse ways in which the law is used to control, to guide, and to plan life out of court.")

[4]   *Code of Laws, Established by the General Court, May, 1650, in* J. HAMMOND TRUMBULL, THE PUBLIC RECORDS OF THE COLONY OF CONNECTICUT, PRIOR TO THE UNION WITH NEW HAVEN COLONY, MAY, 1665, 509 (1850).

[5]   J. HAMMOND TRUMBULL, THE PUBLIC RECORDS OF THE COLONY OF CONNECTICUT, FROM 1665 TO 1678, 190 (1852).

3. *Laws are applied to realize law and justice*: Are laws interpreted and applied justly as written? (May every man "at all times, find his security in them"?)

Americans have not wavered from the ideals of a government of laws[6] although today they are more likely to speak of the ideals as a "rule of law."[7] Their exceptional ideal is now shared around the world.[8] It is universal.[9] The German-language analogue is the *Rechtsstaat*, the "law state," or "right state" or "rule-of-law state." The German term keeps the focus on governing. The "rule of law" of America's legal professions, on the other hand, shifts the focus to process and resolving disputes.

B. MAKING GOOD LAWS IS HARD

The public assumes that it is easy to make and apply[10] good laws. Many lawyers, judges and academics share that false assumption, especially scholars outside law. They dismiss decisions not to write new laws on political grounds when, in fact, technical reasons such as lack of manpower may stand in the way.

Lawmaking is more demanding than is litigating. It is harder for lawmakers to make good laws than it is for lawyers and judges to decide individual cases, for in lawmaking one is deciding classes of cases for the future. Lawyers work with one case at a time. In counseling, they advise how they see the law in one or in a handful of fact situations. In litigating, they argue for one view that they

---

[6] *Cf.*, Boddie v. Connecticut, 401 U.S. 371, 374 (1971) ("Perhaps no characteristic of an organized and cohesive society is more fundamental than its erection and enforcement of a system of rules defining the various rights and duties of its members, enabling them to govern their affairs and definitively settle their differences in an orderly, predictable manner.")

[7] Or used together. *See, e.g.*, ABA DIVISION FOR PUBLIC EDUCATION, PART I, WHAT IS THE RULE OF LAW?, http://www.americanbar.org/advocacy/ruleoflaw/what-is-the-rule-of-law.html, last visited July 20, 2016.

[8] Volker Bouffier (Minister President of the German state of Hessen and former President of the German Bundesrat), in "GESETZGEBER" UND RECHTSANWENDUNG viii (Christian Baldus, *et al.*, eds., 2013) (making and applying law are the basis of every democratic rule-of-law state).

[9] *See, e.g.*, WORLD JUSTICE PROJECT, RULE OF LAW INDEX 2015, Box 1: Four Universal Principles of the Rule of Law; ORGANISATION FOR ECONOMIC COOPERATION AND DEVELOPMENT (OECD), RECOMMENDATION OF THE COUNCIL ON REGULATORY POLICY AND GOVERNANCE (2012).

[10] Applying laws to facts well is not easy, either. *See generally* JAMES R. MAXEINER WITH GYOOHO LEE AND ARMIN WEBER, FAILURES OF AMERICAN CIVIL JUSTICE IN INTERNATIONAL PERSPECTIVE (2011); REMME VERKERK, FACT-FINDING IN CIVIL LITIGATION: A COMPARATIVE PERSPECTIVE (2010).

see as benefiting their client. Judges focus on one set of facts and the laws that might apply to it.

Good laws, on the other hand, make provision for not one case, but for all cases, even though lawmakers know that they cannot anticipate all cases. Good laws capture in a few understandable words what people are compelled to do. Good laws are consistent internally and consistent with other laws. John Austin, the famous English legal philosopher of the 19th century saw that "the technical part of legislation, is incomparably more difficult than what may be styled the ethical."[11]

Systematizing is necessary to a government of laws. In a government of laws, law must be accessible to people. Without a system, laws become unknowable, inconsistent and incoherent. Tyrants, not laws, govern. In the 19th century, proponents of systemization likened its absence to the reign of the Roman Emperor Caligula, who "published" laws in such ways that no one could read them.

C. AMERICA'S BROKEN GOVERNMENT OF LAWS

The United States falls short in realizing a government of laws. This is not controversial. Congress is dysfunctional. Thousands of articles and books document how America's legal system doesn't deliver a government of laws. It's broken.[12] Looking only to the three elements of the government of laws just discussed, it is accepted wisdom that:

- Only the gullible believe that America's legislatures make laws for the common good and justice. Those in the know realize that laws are made for those who show up.[13]
- Only the inexperienced believe that America's laws are knowable by those to whom they apply. The experienced know that America's laws are incoherent.[14]

---

[11] John Austin, *Codification and Law Reform, in* 2 JOHN AUSTIN, LECTURES ON JURISPRUDENCE OR THE PHILOSOPHY OF POSITIVE LAW 1092, 1099 (5th ed., Robert Campbell, ed., 1885).

[12] Congressional consideration in 2017 of "repair and replacement" of the Affordable Care Act must have convinced even the most optimistic of skeptics.

[13] JACK DAVIES, LEGISLATIVE LAW AND PROCESS IN A NUTSHELL xi (3d ed., 2007). Experts teach novice Congressmen this. JUDY SCHNEIDER & MICHAEL KOEMPEL, CONGRESSIONAL DESKBOOK: THE PRACTICAL AND COMPREHENSIVE GUIDE TO CONGRESS (6th ed., 2012).

[14] ORGANISATION FOR ECONOMIC CO-OPERATION AND DEVELOPMENT, REGULATORY REFORM IN THE UNITED STATES 48–49 (1999). Professors of legal research and writing teach first year law students this.

- Only the innocent believe that America's laws are applied in order to realize law and justice. The realists know that the law may be changed in any case from what it was when the case began to suit those involved in the process.[15]

What will the United States do about its unfulfilled longing for a government of laws? Unless the people rise up and insist that legislators and legal professionals, i.e., judges, lawyers and law professors, provide one, most likely, nothing.

The United States does not have a government of laws, not because it is incapable of creating one, but because its legal professionals have given up on the project. They deny that it can be done or that it is even worth doing. They avert their eyes from their own history and from successes elsewhere in the world. They pretend that the United States has a "common law" system that obviates the need for a government of laws.

D. GERMANY'S WORKING GOVERNMENT OF LAWS

Germany substantially achieves a government of laws, or, as it is called in German, a *Rechtsstaat*. In Germany, America's goals of a government of laws are recognized and pursued: laws are known to those to whom they apply; lawmaking is for common good and justice; and laws are applied to realize law and justice.

This book examines Germany as a successful example of a government of laws, not men. Most modern countries aspire to governments of law and comparison with any of them would be useful. I have chosen to examine that of Germany because, among larger countries, that of Germany is among the most admired and most successful.

Governments and laws in Germany have provided positive models to the world.[16] The development of government and of laws in Germany and the United States have had many parallels. Each country sought a government of laws and modern legal methods. Each sought to integrate many small states into one larger entity, before, and after, civil wars in the 1860s. Each sought

---

[15] Geoffrey C. Hazard, Jr., *Rule of Legal Rhetoric*, 67 SMU L. Rev. 801, 803 (2014). Professor Hazard was Director of the American Law Institute for fifteen years. Professors of first-year law classes, *e.g.*, torts, contracts, property, criminal law, constitutional law, teach this to first-year law students.

[16] *See, e.g.*, the detailed 770-page study published by the Brookings Institution only five years before the Nazi takeover: FREDERICK F. BLACHLEY & MIRIAM E. OATMAN, THE GOVERNMENT AND ADMINISTRATION OF GERMANY (1928).

modern governments and modern legal methods to deal with economic and social needs of that larger entity. German successes are worthy of note in America.

E. THE THESES OF THIS BOOK

Part III, the Comparative Part, compares the attempt at a government of laws in America today with that of Germany. It shows how Germany's methods work well and how America's methods by comparison work less well.

Part II, the Historical Part, refutes the idea of common law exclusivity in American legal history. It shows that outside the legal professions – and even within them – Americans through the 19th century expected a government of statutes and not of case law.

Part I, Chapter 2 shows that at the Centennial in 1876 Americans still expected a government of statutes. Chapter 3 shows common law is not an option now, nor was it then.

F. HOW TO READ THIS BOOK

I have written this book for sophisticated laymen, but I hope that members of the legal professions will read it too. That means there are parts that not all readers need to read. Here are my suggestions.

Pragmatists, who believe that America's legal system is broken and needs fixing, who are looking for ideas that work and who carry no baggage, can skip to Part III. It compares contemporary failures of America's methods and reports what I see as successes of Germany's methods.

Skeptics and *Exceptionalists* can skip to Part II. It will make them proud. No longer need they defend a broken system simply because it is America's. After reading Part II they can work whole-heartedly to bring to America the government of laws longed for but not gotten. No longer must they accept the lame excuses of America's legal professionals that it may be a lousy government of laws, but it is "our" system.

Lawyers, judges and law professors should continue with Part I. Chapters 2 and 3 give reasons that may allow them to suspend belief in myths they were taught in law school long enough to entertain the heretical idea that America's legal system just may not be best in the world.

2

America's Exceptionalism in 1876

Systematizing Laws

Philadelphia Centennial Exhibition, *Frank Leslie's Historical Register of the United States Centennial Exposition, 1876* at 239 (1877)

PHILADELPHIA CENTENNIAL EXHIBITION[1]

In 1876, a century after Americans met in Philadelphia to declare independence, they returned to celebrate the anniversary with "a competitive display of industrial resources, constructions, fabric, and works of use and beauty, distributed through a hundred departments of classified variety."[2] Americans invited the world to participate. France sent the Torch of Liberty that a decade later would adorn the Statue of Liberty in New York Harbor that today greets the world.

For the legal professions, participation in the Centennial Exposition of 1876 was problematic. What would be their "works of use and beauty?" Long-serving federal judge and later chancellor of the State University of Iowa Law School, James H. Love, wryly related to the Iowa bar:

> If we could exhibit at the Centennial, the burning of a witch or a heretic, at the stake; or the putting of a prisoner to the question on the rack; or the disemboweling of a traitor while yet alive; . . . the progress and amelioration of the law would be made manifest to all men. If we had any means of making a visible exhibition of what the common law, which forms the basis of our jurisprudence was even a century ago, in contrast with what it is to-day, we might venture to challenge a comparison of progress with any calling, art or profession which is displaying the evidences of its progress at the great exposition.[3]

Love presented an indictment of common law consisting of about a dozen "atrocities." He added, "if time allowed, I could give a thousand illustrations and proofs to maintain it as a 'true bill.'"

Although America's legal professions provided no exhibit at the Centennial Exposition, they did contribute to commemorative volumes published by two of the nation's leading journals, *The North American Review* and *Harper's New Monthly Magazine*. Each volume reported on American progress in the century just past. *The North American Review* presented a special issue that included an essay on "Law in America, 1776–1876."[4] *The North American*

---

[1] FRANK LESLIE'S HISTORICAL REGISTER OF THE UNITED STATES CENTENNIAL EXPOSITION, 1876 at 239 (1877).

[2] *History and the Centennial*, 8 POPULAR SCIENCE MONTHLY 630 (Mar. 1876).

[3] James H. Love, *Address of the Hon. J. M. Love, Delivered at the Third Annual Meeting of the Iowa State Bar Association, in* PROCEEDINGS OF THE THIRD ANNUAL MEETING OF THE IOWA STATE BAR ASSOCIATION HELD AT DES MOINES, MAY 11 AND 12, 1876, 7, at 17, *reprinted in* 10 WESTERN JURIST 399, 409 (1876).

[4] G.T. Bispham, *Law in America, 1776–1876*, 122 N. AM. REV. 154 (1876) [hereinafter *Law in America, 1776–1876*, 122 N. AM. REV.].

Review, then under the editorship of Henry Adams, was the premier intellectual journal of the day. Harper's *New Monthly Magazine* was a part of one of the most successful publishing enterprises of the day, Harper & Brothers. It offered a series of articles that it then combined into a Centennial volume, *The First Century of the Republic: A Review of American Progress*. The Centennial volume included a new essay on "American Jurisprudence"[5]

The editors recorded their goals for their commemorations.

Henry Adams of the *North American Review* wrote to one potential contributor that "the ultimate aim of the article should be to settle the question whether on the whole the movement of American Law has been such as ought to satisfy our wishes and reasonable expectations, or has fallen short of them, and whether we are justified in feeling confidence in its future healthy progress."[6]

Harper's, in *The First Century of the Republic's* foreword ("Publishers' Advertisement"), stated goals that, if anything, were more ambitious for its "Review of American Progress." The volume was "an indispensable supplement" to the Philadelphia exposition's display of "the material symbols of progress." The papers taken together suggested a comparison of progress in the United States with that of other countries "such as to awaken a feeling of just pride in every American citizen."[7]

The two volumes are similar. Both display a century of American progress in many fields. Their two essays on law are likewise similar. Both measure progress in law in terms of replacing feudal English law with modern American statutes: property law, criminal law, and procedure.

Such improvements were for *The North American Review* "but passing illustrations of the originality of American thought in jurisprudence." They were instances where "[t]he American mind, practical as well as liberal, brought down [an idea] from the region of speculation and applied it, through the machinery of *statute law*, to the direct and practical amelioration of mankind."[8] That is what made American law exceptional.

The North American Review elaborated: "The *great* fact in the progress of American jurisprudence which deserves special notice and reflection is its

[5] Benjamin Vaughn Abbott, *American Jurispudence*, THE FIRST CENTURY OF THE REPUBLIC: A REVIEW OF AMERICAN PROGRESS (Harper and Brothers, 1876) [hereinafter, THE FIRST CENTURY OF THE REPUBLIC].
[6] Letter of August 28, 1875 from Henry Adams to Thomas M. Cooley, Benton Historical Library, Cooley Collection, Box 1, Folder August to September. Judge Cooley, one of the century's most renowned jurists, apparently declined the invitation.
[7] THE FIRST CENTURY OF THE REPUBLIC at 437.
[8] *Law in America, 1776–1876*, 122 N. AM. REV. at 174 [emphasis added].

tendency towards *organic statute law* and towards the *systematizing of law;* in other words, towards *written constitutions* and *codification.*"[9] Similarly Harper's *The First Century of the Republic* wrote: "the art of administering government according to the directions of a written constitution may fairly be named among the products of American thought and effort during our century."[10]

Both essays saw American progress similarly: written constitutions of the people implemented by written codes and statutes of their legislatures. These differences from English common law, not affinity with it, are what defined American progress. Both essays distinguished American constitutions from earlier charters. *The North American Review* characterized American constitutions not as *"concession[s]* from a sovereign," but as expressions "of a free people, who are perfectly at liberty to form their own governmental institutions."[11] More fully, Harper's *The First Century of the Republic* explained:

> Now a 'constitution,' as we in America understand the term, is something far deeper and more fundamental than any of the state papers of past centuries. Our idea is that there is no hereditary right, but that all the powers of government, all the authority which society can rightly exercise toward individuals, are originally vested in the masses of the people; that the people meet together (by their delegates) to organize a government, and freely decide what officers they will have to act for them in making and administering laws, and what the powers of these officers shall be. These written directions of the people, declaring what their officers may do and what they may not, form the constitution. The idea, in its practical development, is American.[12]

Legislatively enacted statutes are the corollary to the peoples' constitutions. In accord, *The North American Review* wrote: "Akin to the disposition to crystalize organic law in the form of written constitutions is the disposition to codify municipal law, which has always displayed itself in the legal history of all of the States of the Union."[13] Similarly, Harper's *The First Century of the Republic* wrote: "[t]he readiness of American Legislatures to codify or revise the laws is a noticeable feature."[14]

The North American Review concluded that codification, to a greater or lesser extent must become "indispensable to any nation which draws its laws

---

[9] *Id.* [emphasis in original].   [10] THE FIRST CENTURY OF THE REPUBLIC at 437.
[11] *Law in America, 1776–1876,* 122 N. AM. REV. at 176, 177 [emphasis in original].
[12] THE FIRST CENTURY OF THE REPUBLIC at 437.
[13] *Law in America, 1776–1876,* 122 N. AM. REV. at 176.
[14] THE FIRST CENTURY OF THE REPUBLIC at 451.

from varied sources ... and which designs or attempts to make the progress of those laws keep pace with the growing wants of the times without developing into a mass of unmanageable contradictory rules." The practical administration of law, the essay argued, depends on its simplicity, and "this end can only be attained ... by resorting to the expedient of codification."[15] *The First Century of the Republic* agreed with qualifications: "Codes are useful; but immediately relieving the lawyer of his library has not been their strong point."[16]

Whether the Centennial Writers were right, particularly in their conclusions, might be questioned, but that their point of view is to be taken seriously, cannot. Part II shows how serious it was. But before I address the role of statutes, I discuss the greatest failure of American lawmaking: the myth that common law and common law lawmaking could ever be satisfactory substitutes for a government of laws and for good lawmaking.

---

[15] *Law in America, 1776–1876*, 122 N. AM. REV. at 179.
[16] THE FIRST CENTURY OF THE REPUBLIC at 436.

3

Common Law Is Not an Option

Ours is not a government of precedent, so much as a government of statute.

Cornell University Board of Trustees in establishing a Department of Law (1886)[1]

This book is about lawmaking, i.e., about making good statutes that can be routinely applied and that taken together provide people with a government of laws. Some readers from America's legal professions may protest that their common law already provides that. Common law, they may say, is an alternative that makes this book unnecessary.[2] What difference does it make if America's statutory methods are poor? America is a common law country. This chapter is for them.

In this chapter, I ask America's legal professionals to suspend their common-law faith as they read the rest of this book.

Make no mistake: common-law precedents and common-law methods are not an alternative to a modern government of statutes. Judicial decisions can supplement statutes, but cannot supplant them. Americans should demand a government of statutes.[3]

---

[1] CORNELL UNIVERSITY, REPORT OF A SPECIAL COMMITTEE ON THE ESTABLISHMENT OF A DEPARTMENT OF LAW TOGETHER WITH A PRELIMINARY ANNOUNCEMENT OF THE ACTION OF THE TRUSTEES ESTABLISHING SUCH A DEPARTMENT 6 (1886).

[2] *Cf.* GUIDO CALABRESI, A COMMON LAW FOR THE AGE OF STATUTES (1982). Lately, in what is known as "legal origins" theory, legal economists have claimed superiority of common law systems over French civil law. Often the claim is not that common law systems make better rules, but that that they make fewer of them. This book assumes rules; it does not address minimalist approaches. For a critique of legal origins theory, see NUNO GAROUPA, CARLOS GÓMEZ LIGÜERRE & LELA MÉLON, LEGAL ORIGINS AND THE EFFICIENCY DILEMMA 5, 11 (2017).

[3] So *New York Times* columnist David Brooks did: "In our system, change means legislation. It starts with the ability to gather a team of policy experts who can craft complex bills." David Brooks, *The Banality of Change*, N.Y. Times, Nov. 4, 2016, at A29.

Suspending faith in common-law precedents and in common-law methods asks much of America's legal professionals. For more than a century America's law professors have told their students that the United States is a "common law" country where substantive law is better made by judges as they decide cases.[4] They have belittled statutes and a government of statutes. Harvard Law School's contracts law icon, Samuel Williston, himself the drafter of one of America's more successful statutes (the Uniform Sales Act), said that early in the 20th century: "We have been trained to believe that no code can be expressed with sufficient exactness, or can be sufficiently elastic to fulfill adequately the functions of our common law."[5]

Common-law precedents and common-law methods may serve legal professionals in dispute resolution, but they fail the public when they are allowed to dominate the legal system. Three truths show that:

1. Common-law precedents cannot make a structure of government.
2. America's common law is unknowable.
3. Common-law rules fail as rules of law.

A. THREE COMMON-LAW TRUTHS

1. *Common-Law Precedents Cannot Make a Structure of Government*

America's judge-made law *could not* be the basis of a government of laws. No matter how one feels about common law, judicial precedents cannot do the job people expect of law in a modern world. They cannot make a structure of government and they cannot provide for governing.

Judge-made law is necessarily incomplete. It consists of rules borne of litigation; it is law created by judges to decide cases that parties bring before them. It arises out of and settles disputes among a limited number of parties about a limited number of issues. Only parties participate in common-law lawmaking. Judge-made law looks backward.[6] A matter not litigated does not create common law.

Judge-made law could not be the basis of a government of laws because the structures of government do not ordinarily lead to litigated disputes. If every

---

[4] *See,* Frederick Schauer, Thinking Like a Lawyer: A New Introduction to Legal Reasoning 104 (2009).

[5] Samuel Williston, The Uniform Partnership Act with Some Other Remarks on Other Uniform Commercial Laws, an Address before the Law Association of Philadelphia Dec. 18, 1914, 1 (1915) *reprinted in* 63 U. Pa. L. Rev. 196 (1915).

[6] *Cf.* Schauer, *supra* note 4, at 36.

instance of applying law were concerned with the structures of government, governing would come to a halt.

When disputes in government structure do arise, they need to be resolved today and not tomorrow. They need to be resolved for general application and not just for the jurisdiction of one court. A structure of government is concerned with all the people all the time. It does more than resolve disputes; it authorizes governing. It is future-directed.[7]

2. *America's Common Law Is Unknowable*

Common-law methods make rules in judicial precedents. Precedents lack authoritative rule texts. Common law is unknowable.

America's legal professionals know that. Nearly all have taken a course euphemistically called "legal research." It used to be that these courses taught "how to find the law." Today they teach students how to create a "research strategy." They show how to look for all of the relevant "sources of law," i.e., cases, statutes, regulations, "legislative history" and secondary materials.

Follow-on courses, labeled "legal writing" or "advocacy," teach how to "synthesize" these separate sources into rules.[8] Even with such training, lawyers may be unable to synthesize applicable law. Laymen, who lack such training, cannot themselves synthesize applicable law. Some of America's law teachers now say they teach, not how to find the law, but how to argue it.

All of this confounds people unfamiliar with America's legal system. They expect to find law in minutes, not in hours, not in days or not ever. They are interested less in knowing the law and more in understanding how it applies to them. Legal professionals familiar with America's legal system, on the other hand, are accustomed to *not* finding the law, so that they hold it as normal and do not find it a failure. Finding the law in minutes they suppose to be fantastical.

---

[7]   Judge-made law finds the strongest place in private law and its weakest place in public law. *See, e.g.*, JAMES C. CARTER, ARGUMENT OF JAMES C. CARTER IN OPPOSITION TO THE BILL TO ESTABLISH A CIVIL CODE: BEFORE THE SENATE JUDICIARY COMMITTEE, ALBANY, MAR. 23, 1887, at 26 (1887); JAMES MAXEINER, POLICY AND METHODS IN GERMAN AND AMERICAN ANTITRUST LAW: A COMPARATIVE STUDY 122 (1986).

[8]   Relevant recent textbooks include LARRY ALEXANDER & EMILY SHERWIN, DEMYSTIFYING LEGAL REASONING (2008); DANIEL L. BARNETT & JANE KENT GIONFRIDDO, LEGAL REASONING AND OBJECTIVE WRITING: A COMPREHENSIVE APPROACH (2016); STEVEN J. BURTON, AN INTRODUCTION TO LAW AND LEGAL REASONING (3d ed., 2007); SCHAUER, *supra* note 4; KENNETH J. VANDEVELDE, THINKING LIKE A LAWYER (2d ed., 2010). Textbooks on finding and synthesizing law are practically unknown in Germany.

Rarely are America's rules found in a single authoritative statute or in a single precedent. Commonly multiple statutes and multiple precedents compete and conflict. Every statute is counted uncertain until construed by a court in a judicial precedent ("statutory precedent" or "statutory *stare decisis*"). Finding a relevant statute is an invitation to search for precedents interpreting the statute.

Central to contemporary American legal methods is the doctrine of *stare decisis*. It applies whether the basis of law is in statute, the more common situation today or only in judicial precedents. Only a legally trained professional can confidently apply *stare decisis*.

Under the American doctrine of *stare decisis* some precedents are binding, that is, mandatory, while others are nonbinding, that is, persuasive. Only those precedents issued by courts superior to the court in which cases are being conducted are binding. This means that until one knows in which court a case is to be brought, one cannot know which precedents are binding. In applying federal law, since the Supreme Court decides fewer than 100 cases a year with precedents, usually the binding precedents are of the intermediate appellate courts, the United States Court of Appeals for thirteen different circuits. That means, in effect, federal law has thirteen different manifestations. Similar problems arise in state systems.

To determine whether a precedent is binding requires substantial legal knowledge about the interrelationship of statutes and precedents, about the hierarchy of statutes and precedents in the American federal system, and about the continued validity in time of statutes and of precedents. Some precedents found will be binding, most will be persuasive, but all should be found and considered.[9]

Saying a precedent is binding, or even persuasive, however, is not finding the law. A statute sets out a rule that is to apply to future cases. It is so stated. A precedent, on the other hand, decides a past dispute and only incidentally suggests a rule for future conduct. It is written as a narrative to justify that single decision. The rule that it incidentally states is necessarily tied up in the facts that the decision judged.

To understand a rule of case law, one must understand the case itself, both its facts and its law. One reads the case repeatedly to extract the rule from the opinion. The opinion necessarily contains much that is relevant to deciding the case before the court that is not, however, part of the rule of law that the precedent creates ("dicta"). Analysis is necessary to distinguish the rule or

---

[9]   *See, e.g.*, BARNETT & GIONFRIDDO , *supra* note 8, at 95–96 ("While in some legal problems you'll find that a court in the jurisdiction will have fully articulated in a single case its analysis on a given legal issue, most often you will encounter situations where the courts have not clearly set out their entire analysis in any single case.").

"holding" from "dicta."[10] To do that one must understand all of the opinion, that is, facts, procedural history, procedural and substantive decision. If different judges give different opinions (majority, plurality, concurring and dissenting), one must note how those opinions affect the asserted rule.

Since there may be no single authoritative statute, and since there cannot be a single authoritative precedent, there is no obvious stopping point in the search for authority. Today's legal research manuals advise students to stop when they keep coming across the same stuff. One advises: "you will know that you have come full circle in your research when, after following a comprehensive research path through a variety of sources, the authorities you locate start to refer back to each other and the new sources you consult fail to reveal significant new information."[11]

Armed with multiple statutes and still more interpretative precedents, the legal professional now is ready to engage in the "synthesis" of legal sources learned in the legal argument or advocacy course.

I won't even try to summarize how different instructors go about teaching synthesizing. It would be a Sisyphean labor. The process is "a beginning." It requires "good sense," even if at times one later finds "a different process would have been more efficient." One must be "ready to cycle through this process several times."[12]

3. *America's Common Law Fails as Rules of Law*

Justice Antonin Scalia famously wrote: "The Rule of Law is a Law of Rules."[13] America's judicial traditionalists such as Scalia doubt "that common law is 'law' in any conventional sense."[14] They say that American common

---

[10]   *See* MAXEINER, POLICY AND METHODS IN GERMAN AND AMERICAN ANTITRUST LAW, *supra* note 7 at 27–31 (discussing with further references precedent and stare decisis in the United States). This is historic common law method, long threatened by search for authority rather than principle thanks to the multitude of American cases, may in the digital age fall altogether. *See, e.g.,* Allison Orr Larsen, *Factual Precedents,* 162 U. PA. L. REV. 59, 62 (2013) ("The new digital mode of research often leads directly to language in a decided case that is perfect for an argument in a new one – regardless of whether the language was central to the case in which it was offered or whether the holding of the cited case has any relevance to the one at hand.").

[11]   AMY E. SLOAN, BASIC LEGAL RESEARCH: TOOLS AND STRATEGIES 300 (6th ed., 2015).

[12]   BARNETT & GIONFRIDDO, *supra* note 8, at 100–102. Barnett devotes all of chapter 7 to "Synthesis of Judicial Opinions." Vandevelde devotes chapter 3 to "Synthesizing the Law." VANDEVELDE, *supra* note 8, at 39–56.

[13]   Antonin Scalia, *The Rule of Law as a Law of Rules,* 56 U. CHI. L. REV. 1175 (1989).

[14]   Robert P. Young, Jr., *A Judicial Traditionalist Confronts the Common Law,* 8 TEX. REV. LAW & POLITICS 299, 303 (2004). Young, the Chief Justice of the Supreme Court of Michigan, observes that everyone tries to ignore the contemporary common law, as one would ignore "a

law – substance or method – is incompatible with a government of laws or a rule of law.[15] They are right. Look just to the three elements of a government of laws highlighted in Chapter 1.

Common Law Is Undemocratic

Litigation does not involve the people, but only those who are permitted to participate: the parties to the case. There is only the most limited of opportunity for public participation in this kind of lawmaking. Judges are not authorized to make law for the future. They are institutionally incapable of making law. They have neither the knowledge nor the legitimacy to do so.[16]

Common Law Is Inaccessible to Laymen

In a government of laws people can find, read, understand and apply the laws to which they are subject. Laymen cannot search hundreds of thousands of cases for possibly relevant precedents, synthesize them into a rule, suppose which facts are relevant and then prophesize how a court might find.[17]

When people apply rules to themselves, they normally follow a syllogistic process: a legal rule is the major premise, facts are the minor premise, and these facts are subsumed logically under the legal rule to reach a correct legal decision. Syllogistic application of law to facts brings law and facts law together.[18] Common law court procedures require first the opposite: they separate law and facts.[19]

---

drunken, toothless ancient relative sprawled prominently and in a state of nature on a settee in the middle of one's genteel garden party."

[15] *See, e.g.,* GORDON TULLOCK, THE CASE AGAINST THE COMMON LAW 2 (1997); FRANK UPHAM, MYTHMAKING IN THE RULE OF LAW ORTHODOXY 17 (2002), *reprinted in* PROMOTING THE RULE OF LAW ABROAD: IN SEARCH OF KNOWLEDGE 75 (Thomas Carothers ed., 2006).

[16] *See, e.g.,* H.L.A. Hart, *American Jurisprudence through English Eyes: The Nightmare and the Noble Dream,* 11 GA. L. REV. 969, 971 (1977); ANTONIN SCALIA & BYRAN A. GARNER, READING LAW: THE INTERPRETATION OF LEGAL TEXTS 4 (2012); Young, *supra* note 14, at 304. *Contra,* RUGGERO J. ALDISERT, LOGIC FOR LAWYERS: A GUIDE TO CLEAR LEGAL THINKING 9 (3d ed., 1997) ("... there had to be consent and endorsement by the people and institutions affected by judicial decisions."); Matthew Steilen, *The Democratic Common Law,* 2011 J. JURISPRUDENCE 437 (finding elements of democratic legitimacy).

[17] *Cf.* Oliver Wendell Holmes, Jr., *The Path of the Law,* 10 HARV. L. REV. 460–461 (1897).

[18] *See* Lynn M. LoPucki, *Legal Culture, Legal Strategy, and the Law in Lawyers' Heads,* 90 NW. U. L. REV. 1498, 1498 (1996) ("Most lawyers and judges experience law as a process of logical deduction. They believe they apply the law laid down by legislatures and appellate courts to the facts of cases and generate answers. Most law professors at elite schools (and many of the best trial lawyers) hold this 'Formalist' view of law in contempt.").

[19] *See* Chapter 13 *infra.*

Common Law Is Unreliable

Because common law makes law as laws are applied, whatever is the law is always subject to change. The classic warning to novice lawyers is to check whether the cases they are relying on are not overruled before they present them to the court. Although common law jurists have labored for years to show that results are foreseeable, they have been unable to overcome the fatal challenge that laws should be known beforehand.

B. FIVE COMMON-LAW MYTHS

HENRY II ATTEMPTS TO
INVENT THE COMMON LAW

Stephen Morillo, used with permission.

How is it that legal professionals ignore these truths? Students studying America's laws for the first time sometimes suspect them. They wonder how, from individual cases, can people find rules to follow in their own lives? Few are the students, however, who demand explanations from their teachers. Fewer still are the teachers who give serious answers. America's law schools avoid the truth. They instill in their students common-law myths that squelch troublesome consideration of common law failures and statutory successes.[20]

1. Myth: The United States Is a Country of Common Law[21]

The first-year curriculum of America's law schools, introduced by Harvard's Christopher Columbus Langdell in 1870–1871, inculcates common myths in its students. It is able to instill faith in common law because it avoids considering whether there might be anything else. Unlike law school curricula proposed by Langdell's competitors, by his later critics and in use abroad, it omits instruction in law as a legal system.[22] Instead, from the first day of class it focuses on a handful of common law subjects, e.g., property, contracts and torts, and on teaching common law methods to argue law and decide specific cases.[23] In its earliest incarnations, it considered cases exclusively. Still today that is its focus.

The first-year curriculum ignores reality. Law schools teach property, contracts and torts as if there were no state statutes or local ordinances, but only an amorphous national common law of cases.[24] They teach constitutional law, civil procedure and criminal procedure, as if those subjects consisted of U.S.

---

[20] *See* Richard A. Cosgrove and John H. Langbein, who speak of "the cult of the common law." RICHARD A. COSGROVE, OUR LADY THE COMMON LAW: AN ANGLO AMERICAN LEGAL COMMUNITY, 1870–1930, at 1 (1987); John H. Langbein, *The Influence of Comparative Procedure in the United States*, 43 AM. J. COMP. L. 545, 551 (1995). For a similar review of common-law myths, which makes many of the same points more from a law and economic perspective, *see* Nuno Garoupa & Andrew P. Morriss, *The Fable of the Codes: The Efficiency of the Common Law, Legal Origins, and Codification Movements*, 2012 U. ILL. L. REV. 1443, 1448–1450.

[21] *See* Calvin Woodard, *Is the United States a Common Law Country?*, *in* ESSAYS ON ENGLISH LAW AND THE AMERICAN EXPERIENCE 120 (1994).

[22] This has been a recurrent criticism of American legal education since the case law method achieved hegemony at the end of the 19th century. *See* JAMES R. MAXEINER, EDUCATING LAWYERS NOW AND THEN: AN ESSAY COMPARING THE 2007 AND 1914 CARNEGIE FOUNDATION REPORTS ON LEGAL EDUCATION 32–33 (2007). The first major report on American legal education called for "the abandonment of the present method of teaching law mainly by distinct topics, at least during the first year of the course, and the substitution for it of a careful and systematic study of the system as a whole after the European method." *Report of the Committee on Legal Education*, REPORT OF THE FIFTEENTH ANNUAL MEETING OF THE AMERICAN BAR ASSOCIATION HELD AT SARATOGA SPRINGS, NEW YORK, AUG. 24, 25 AND 26, 1892 317, 360 (1892).

[23] *See* M. Stuart Madden, *The Vital Common Law: Its Role in a Statutory Age*, 6 UALR L. REV. 555, 558 (1996).

[24] *E.g.*, BRIAN A. BLUM & AMY C. BUSHAW, CONTRACTS: CASES, DISCUSSION, AND PROBLEMS 5 (3d ed., 2012) ("contacts is a common law subject because most of its rules are not found in legislation, but have been developed by courts"). *But see* James R. Maxeiner, *Costs of No*

Supreme Court cases. They justify this teaching of cases as something more important than rules: "the method of legal reasoning." They deprecate the "frantic quest of the new law student to learn the 'rule.'"[25]

Of late, law schools have moved still further from teaching law as systematized rules to "doing law." American Bar Association accreditation standards mostly eschew specific course requirements, but now mandate that all students take the equivalent of two "experiential courses" (defined as simulation, clinic or internship courses), two "writing experiences" and one course on the legal profession.[26] The requirements are reminiscent of Karl Llewellyn's lament of the 1930s: "one learns from experience. ... But little thought is given to *what* one is learning."[27] It is as if physicians today insisted on teaching medical students bloodletting experientially.

America's law professors know that common law does not exhaust legal rules. For more than a generation in their writings for other law professors they have acknowledged that America lives in an "age of statutes." They know, moreover, that to teach state statutes and state precedents as if they were national law is misleading. They realize that to teach federal civil and criminal procedure as if it were valid in all states is no less misleading.

Pretending that subjects such as property, contracts and torts are a kind of national common law permits law schools to ignore variations in statutes and precedents from state-to-state. Looking principally to federal law in procedure permits the same simplification. It is a fiction that permits law schools to claim that they teach a national curriculum. It is a fiction thought better left unsaid. Privately, Roscoe Pound, perhaps Langdell's most distinguished successor as Dean of Harvard Law School, acknowledged that a "composite of the law of [then] forty-eight American states cannot, in the nature of things, be the logical unity in which Langdell believed."[28] Even before Pound, Herbert

---

Codes, 31 MISSISSIPPI COLLEGE L. REV. 363, 382–396 (2013) (identifying thousands of contracts statutes).

[25] *See, e.g.,* TRACEY E. GEORGE & RUSSELL KOROBKIN, K: A COMMON LAW APPROACH TO CONTRACTS, Preface (2012).

[26] Standard 303 Curriculum. ABA STANDARDS AND RULES OF PROCEDURE FOR APPROVAL OF LAW SCHOOLS 2016–2017 (2016). Ironically the ABA does not mandate that practitioners provide practical training outside of professional school such as is usual in most other legal systems and in America's medical system.

[27] KARL N. LLEWELLYN, THE CASE LAW SYSTEM IN AMERICA 2 (M. Ansaldi, transl. 1989, first published in German in Germany in 1933).

[28] Roscoe Pound to Frederick Pollock, May 22, 1934, in Roscoe Pound Papers, Harvard law School Library) as *quoted in* COSGROVE, *supra* note 21, at 37 (1987). *See* James R. Maxeiner, *United States Federalism: Harmony without Unity, in* FEDERALISM AND LEGAL UNIFICATION: A COMPARATIVE EMPIRICAL INVESTIGATION OF TWENTY SYSTEMS (D. Halberstam &

Pope, a lawyer in Chicago, called the fiction out: "There can be no doubt that the present organization of the courts in this country makes the development of a general and uniform common law an impossibility."[29]

Law professors knew that when Pope wrote a century ago. They could not entirely ignore statutory law. Their casebooks in the 1920s morphed into books of "cases and materials."[30] Long before that development, however, law professors readied other myths to deflect doubts in common law.

2. *Myth: Common Law Is Superior to Statutory Law in Individualizing Justice*

The legal professions claim common law methods are superior to statutory methods in individualizing law application. Introspection calls the myth into question. Comparative study, including that in this book, destroys it.

The myth has a distinguished pedigree. Already in 1870 Oliver Wendell Holmes, Jr., as a youthful commentator who had yet to assume judicial office and status as judicial icon, asserted anonymously: "It is the merit of the common law that it decides the case first and determines the principle afterwards."[31] More recently the late Judge Ruggero Aldisert, in a textbook used by the National Institute of Trial Advocacy, elaborated:

> The heart of the common-law tradition is adjudication of specific cases. Case-by-case development allows experimentation because each rule is ree-valuated in subsequent cases to determine if the rule did or does produce a fair result. If the rule operates unfairly, it can be modified. . . . The genius of the common law is that it proceeds empirically and gradually, testing the ground at every step, and refusing, or at any rate evincing an extreme reluctance, to embrace broad theoretical principles.[32]

M. Reimann, eds., Ius GENTIUM: COMPARATIVE PERSPECTIVES ON LAW AND JUSTICE, Vol. 28, 2013).

[29] Herbert Pope, *The Federal Courts and a Uniform Law*, 28 YALE L. J. 647 (1919). *Accord* Herbert Pope, *The English Common Law in the United States*, 24 HARV. L. REV. 6 (1910). *See* COSGROVE, *supra* note 21, at 19.

[30] *See* MAXEINER, EDUCATING LAWYERS NOW AND THEN, *supra* note 24, at 36–37.

[31] [Oliver Wendell Holmes, Jr.], *Codes, and the Arrangement of the Law*, 5 AM. L. REV. 1 (1870).

[32] RUGGERO J. ALDISERT, LOGIC FOR LAWYERS: A GUIDE TO CLEAR LEGAL THINKING 8 (3d ed., 1997). Aldisert was Chief Judge of the United States Court of Appeals for the Third Circuit. Abroad he defended judicial lawmaking. RUGGERO J. ALDISERT, GRENZLINIEN: DIE SCHRANKEN ZULÄSSIGER RICHTERLICHE RECHTSSCHÖPFUNG IN AMERIKA (1985). *See also* P.S. ATIYAH & ROBERT S. SUMMERS, FORM AND SUBSTANCE IN ANGLO-AMERICAN LAW 91 (1987) (common law permits "open modification of the rule to allow purposes or policies to be taken into account"); FREDERICK SCHAUER, PLAYING BY THE RULES (1993) (asserting that rules apply only so long as their reason applies).

But does this make sense? Is a rule that is subject to being changed as it is applied still a rule? English legal philosopher H.L.A. Hart called it a "noble dream" that is a "nightmare" for those subject to it.[33]

Hart's "noble dream" is one way of dealing with an eternal problem of enacted law: how to reconcile written law and justice. Rules are adopted to apply to the future by legislators with imperfect knowledge of both present and future. In some number of cases, applying the law may lead to unjust or unintended decisions. One can understand how those charged with applying law would nobly dream of a law that they can change. It lets them change the law to reach a solution that they think is better than that which existing law provides.

For the people, however, the possibility that laws might be changed as they are applied by courts is a "nightmare." On the one hand, in court they experience the most unpleasant of surprises: condemnation for what they thought deserved, if not commendation, at least acceptance. Out of court, how can they plan their actions? Until judges decide, how can they know what the law will require of them? Laws that change as they are applied (e.g., punishment by analogy) destroy a government of laws.

Modern statutory methods in use abroad individualize justice without undermining laws. In the United States, on the other hand, Frederick Schauer shows how "rule-based and precedent based decision making often require legal decision-makers to do something other than the right thing."[34]

3. *Myth: Common Law Is Superior to Statutory Law in Adapting to Changes in Time*

This sales pitch is probably the best-seller in defending common law today. The idea is that common law is more adaptable than statutory law. "Judicial rules evolve slowly as a flexible response to the actions and preferences of individuals and institutions involved in disputes."[35] "The common law is not static; its life and heart is its dynamism—its ability to keep pace with the world while constantly searching for just and fair solutions to pressing social problems."[36] Otherwise intelligent judges, lawyers and law professors recite this

---

[33] Hart, *supra* note 16.

[34] *Compare* FREDERICK SCHAUER, THINKING LIKE A LAWYER: A NEW INTRODUCTION TO LEGAL REASONING 212 (2009) *with* James R. Maxeiner, *Thinking Like a Lawyer Abroad: Putting Justice into Legal Reasoning*, 11 WASHINGTON U. GLOBAL STUDIES L. REV. 55 (2012).

[35] Frank Partnoy, *Synthetic Common Law*, 53 U. KAN. L. REV. 281, 297 (2005).

[36] Harrison v. Montgomery County Bd. of Educ., 456 A. 2d 894, 903 (Md. 1983), *quoted in* M. Stuart Madden, *The Vital Common Law: Its Role in a Statutory Age*, 18 UALR L. REV. 555 (1996).

myth without thinking about it. More than 180 years ago Justice Story discounted it as no argument at all: "for the same could be said of any provision of a systematic code. No code is supposed to be inalterable."[37]

There are two claims that this myth makes: that common law consistently evolves usable judicial rules in response to encounters with new situations and that it does this better than do statutory methods. Introspection explodes the former and comparison the latter.

It is true that litigation often encounters new legal issues before legislation. Whether judges' resolving these new issues routinely produces usable rules is disproven by introspection. The features of common law that make it unknowable likewise make its efforts at law reform second best.

Case-by-case decision making leads to what are admired as "incremental reforms," but incremental reforms often are little more than unsystematic or idiosyncratic exceptions to general rules. Who can know of them if one is not a lawyer familiar with precedents? Who can rely on them if one's case is not "on all fours" with the exception? Go to litigation – already an exceptional burden – and one may find the court limiting the precedential exception to its facts.

Case-by-case decision making also means, at best, jurisdiction-by-jurisdiction law reform. What is a good precedent in another judicial district may not be good precedent in this district. Sometimes it is necessary to go through two levels of appeal only to find out that it is not good![38]

Could there be a better example of common law's inability to reach usable changes in law than the various contract doctrines of consideration? One of the greatest accomplishments of the American Law Institute's statute-like *Restatement (Second) of Contracts* is its attempt to bring order to cases on consideration. To do that it takes 38 of its 385 sections! More than 35 years later, it is hard to say it has been a great success.

The claim that common-law methods work better than statutory methods to reform law cannot be conclusively demonstrated here. Advocates of judge-made law, however, are hard put to cite real-life instantiations of such salubrious consequences of common law. Reforms they typically assert are belied by history or by comparison or by both. For example, one advocate of common-law methods points to inroads made on the employment-at-will doctrine,[39] which otherwise permits an employer to fire an employee for no reason. Yet, although marginally weakened, it remains the rule in the United States. More

---

[37] [Joseph Story], *Law, Legislation, Codes, in* 7 ENCYCLOPÆDIA AMERICANA 576, 588 (1831).

[38] *See, e.g.,* Keltner v. Washington County, 310 Or. 499, 800 P.2d 752 (1990).

[39] Madden, *supra* note 24, at 604.

than a century ago the German Civil Code provided otherwise. Laymen who are not captivated by common-law myth of legal professionals see plainly that change requires legislation. That's what Chapter 10 is about.

4. Myth: America's Judges Have Always Freely Made Law

Common-law myth holds that America's judges today make law much as America's judges did in the 19th century when they are said to have dominated lawmaking.

America's first judges were reticent to make law. James Wilson, the first Associate Justice of the U.S. Supreme Court, famously wrote that "every prudent and cautious judge ... will remember that his duty and his business is, not to make the law, but to interpret and apply it."[40] Through the 19th century judges asserted that they were not making law.[41]

Justice Story described common law as "a system of rules ... fixed, certain, and invariable."[42] Most of the time, it was not changing. When making law, judges asserted that they were only "discovering" law that had always been there.[43] Judges were appliers of law and were not legislators. Fitting new facts in old law was not making law.[44] In the early 20th century Justice Benjamin N. Cardozo acknowledged that judges might make law, but minimized its impact: judges were just filling in the interstices between established points of law.[45]

The system of common-law pleading in use in 19th century litigation discouraged judicial lawmaking. The parties were required to make a single

---

[40] *Lectures on Law, Chapter V, Of the Constituent Parts of Courts—Of the Judges*, 2 The Works of the Honorable James Wilson, L.L.D. 299, 303 (Bird Wilson, ed., 1804).

[41] Scalia and Garner nicely captured both the continuity and discontinuity when they wrote: "It used to be said that judges do not 'make' law—they simply apply it. In the 20th century, the legal realists convinced everyone that judges do indeed make law. To the extent that was true, it was knowledge that the wise already possessed and the foolish could not be trusted with. It was true, that is, that judges did not really 'find' the common law but invented it over time." Scalia & Garner, *supra* note 16, at 5.

[42] Joseph Story, *Law, Legislation, Codes, in* 7 Encyclopædia Americana 576, 588 (Francis Lieber ed., & trans., 1831).

[43] *See* Stephen B. Presser, *The Development and Application of Common Law*, 8 Tex. Rev. Law & Politics 291 (2004). *See also* Zechariah Chafee, Jr., *Do Judges Make or Discover Law?*, 91 Proceedings of the Am. Philosophical Soc. 405 (1947).

[44] *See* Ezra R. Thayer, *Judicial Legislation: Its Legitimate Function in the Development of the Common Law*, 5 Harv. L. Rev. 172, 181–182 (1891).

[45] Benjamin N. Cardozo, The Nature of the Judicial Process 113–114 (1921). *See* James R. Maxeiner, *Legal Indeterminacy Made in America: U.S. Legal Methods and the Rule of Law*, 41 Valparaiso L. Rev. 517, 538 (2006).

point of law or a single fact determinative of the case, but not both. To change the law required that the point of law be determinative. By doing that, however, the opportunity to dispute a point of fact and to involve a jury was lost.[46]

America's 20th century "legal realists" thought they knew better: "the common law is not a body of rules, it is a method. It is the creation of law by the inductive process."[47] That it may be, but it may not claim the mantel of 19th century history. Proponents of a more modest role for judges in law-making challenge it for the same reasons as advocates of statutory law might.[48]

5. *Myth: England's Common-Law Tutelage*

On the first day of law school otherwise excellent professors tell their students a much-loved common-law myth: "All American law is based on the common law of England, transplanted to America by the colonists and used by the colonies – and later by the states – as the basis of their legal systems."[49] That is not true.

In Chapter 4, I deal with the enigmas of reception of British law in America, that is, both of British statutes and of English common law. Both were important, but neither was wholesale. Statutes and common law were adopted for practical reasons, selectively as suited local conditions, and varied from state-to-state. The cult of common-law law creation was not part of the reception.[50] It is a development of the late 19th century. Its ascendency parallels the demise of a government of laws.

There was little love and much criticism for English common law in the first century of the Republic.[51] At the Centennial in 1876 its demise was

---

[46] *See* text at Chapter 13, note 33, *infra*.

[47] See, already, Arthur L. Corbin, *What Is the Common Law?*, 3 AM. L. SCHOOL REV. 73, 75 (1912)

[48] *See* Allan C. Hutchinson, *Work in Progress: Evolution and Common Law*, 11 TEX. WESLEYAN L. REV. 255, 257–258 (2005) (quoting Chief Justice McLachlin of Canada: "Generally speaking, the judiciary is bound to apply the rules of law found in the legislation and in the precedents." In just over 300 words she gives a good explanation of a contemporary conservative judge's view of judicial lawmaking.).

[49] BRIAN A. BLUM & AMY C. BUSHAW, CONTRACTS: CASES, DISCUSSION, AND PROBLEMS 4 (4th ed., 2017).

[50] *Accord*, Eric Hines, A CONSERVATIVE'S TREATISE ON AMERICAN GOVERNMENT 247 (2012).

[51] See text at Chapter 4, notes 59 to 83, *infra*. It wasn't loved by everyone in England either. For example, one critic in 1837 wrote: "In flash language, Common Law – in honest English, judge-made law—is an instrument, that is to say, Judges are instruments – for doing the dirty work of Parliament: for doing in an oblique and clandestine way, that which Parliament would at least be ashamed to do in its own open way." WILLIAM CARPENTER, PEERAGE FOR THE PEOPLE 239 (1837). Earlier, Jeremy Bentham had famously assailed common law as "dog law":

celebrated. The cult that developed in the years after 1876 was not based on reception of English common law but on affinity of English and American elite lawyers and a wish to promote Anglo-American friendship more than shared law.[52] When law became the topic, not everyone cottoned to English common law. In the 1880s, love of common law was challenged as "myth"[53] and a "fetish-like worship."[54]

The supposed common-law affinity, however, served the needs of Harvard Law School. Among other things, it nicely supported Harvard's choice of teaching cases to the exclusion of teaching statutes. Harvard professors not only taught a law of precedents rather than statutes, they taught a law of *English* cases.[55] After English professor Albert Venn Dicey in 1885 coined the term "rule of law," it was from Harvard that the litigation-focused term spread over the United States largely to supplant Adams' century-old governing-focused government of laws.[56]

The fin de siècle political environment that culminated in the First World War led to an ever-increasing worship of common law and its ideal of an

---

"When your dog does anything you want to break him of, you wait till he does it, and then beat him for it." Jeremy Bentham, *Truth versus Ashhurst; or, Law as It Is, Contrasted with What It Is Said to Be* (1792), *in* 5 THE WORKS OF JEREMY BENTHAM, published under the superintendence of his executor, John Bowring, 231, 233 (Bowring ed., 1843), available online at http://www.ucl.ac.uk/bentham-project/tools/bentham-textsonline-online/truthvash.

[52] *See generally* COSGROVE, *supra* note 21.

[53] *E.g., Our Common Law*, 19 CENTRAL L.J. 60 (1884) (quoting Judge Campbell, "They tell you ... that the English common law is our inheritance. I am sorry we fall heir to any such myth.").

[54] W. Morton Grinnell, in debate in REPORT OF THE NINTH ANNUAL MEETING OF THE AMERICAN BAR ASSOCIATION HELD AT SARATOGA SPRINGS, NEW YORK, AUG. 18, 19 AND 20, 1886 23 (1886).

[55] The casebook that started it all begins *every one* of its twenty sections with an English case (presumably on chronological grounds). Sometimes the case postdates American independence. C.C. LANGDELL, A SELECTION OF CASES ON THE LAW OF CONTRACTS WITH REFERENCES AND CITATIONS. PREPARED FOR USE AS A TEXT-BOOK IN HARVARD LAW SCHOOL (1871). The other books are similar. *See also* Chapter 7 and the Appendix, *infra*.
To this day American law professors make free use of 19th century English cases in their casebooks. That free use contrasts with the antagonism they give use of other foreign legal materials.

[56] Dicey first used the term in 1885. A.V. DICEY, LECTURES INTRODUCTORY TO THE STUDY OF THE LAW OF THE CONSTITUTION, Lectures V to VII (1st ed., 1885) *reprinted in* 1. J.W.F. ALLISON (Ed.), THE OXFORD EDITION OF DICEY 95–184 (2013) (introducing the term "rule of law." Dicey visited Harvard and found a boundless enthusiasm for English common law. A.V. Dicey, *The Teaching of English Law at Harvard*, 13 HARV. L. REV. 422, 424, 429 (1900) ("The Harvard Law School is a professional school for the practical teaching of English law. [sic!] ... The teachers at Harvard are saved from the unreality and vagueness which are apt to infect speculative jurists [German professors?] ... by their intense enthusiasm for the Common Law of England, or rather of the English people. They are apostles of English law [sic!].")

Anglo-American legal community. In the aftermath of the First World War, the American Bar Association (ABA) assembled in London and celebrated the common bond with England. The Second World War, the Cold War and other wars created a myth of a political "special relationship" between the United States and England,[57] which gave and gives a declining common law legal community new vitality.

In 1957, a large contingent of the ABA (including three members of the Supreme Court) again went to England to dedicate the ABA's own monument at Runnymede, England, to the historic English document Magna Carta. At the Bicentennial in 1976 in two special volumes the ABA celebrated *Political Separation and Legal Continuity (Common Faith and Common Law: A Declaration of Kinship of the English and American Legal Profession)*. At the millennium in 2000 it co-sponsored a volume with the Bar Society of England and Wales on *Common Law, Common Values, Common Rights: Essays on Our Common Heritage By Distinguished British and American Authors*. The volume proclaims "the strengths and vibrancy of the Common Law System for the new century" and ignores statutes. It dotes on "Our Shared Legal Tradition."[58] In 2015 the ABA refurbished the Monument at Runnymede at the 800th anniversary of Magna Carta.[59]

Thanks to common-law myth, despite a paucity of historical evidence, it has become "axiomatic" that English common law has had unqualified "tutelage" on American law. It is usual to address American legal issues assuming that they are sourced in English common law.

The myth of English tutelage leads all too many of America's legal professionals to divide the world into two unequal parts, the smaller Anglo-American world, and the larger civil law world, to praise the former as better and to ignore the latter as inferior.

---

[57] GUY ARNOLD, AMERICA AND BRITAIN: WAS THERE EVER A SPECIAL RELATIONSHIP? (2014).

[58] AMERICAN BAR ASSOCIATION, COMMON LAW, COMMON VALUES, COMMON RIGHTS: ESSAYS ON OUR COMMON HERITAGE BY DISTINGUISHED BRITISH AND AMERICAN AUTHORS vi (2000). The lead American contributor was Justice Anthony Kennedy.

[59] *See* ABA Magna Carta Commemoration: Magna Carta Icon of Liberty, http://www .americanbar.org/groups/leadership/officeofthepresident/magnacarta.html (last visited Nov. 1, 2016). Among the few naysayers is Judge Posner. *What Is Obviously Wrong with the Federal Judiciary, Yet Eminently Curable, Part I*, 19 GREEN BAG 2D 187, 188 (2016).

PART II

Historical Part: Americans' Longing for
Laws for the People

You and I, my dear friend, have been sent into life at a time when the greatest lawgivers of antiquity would have wished to live. . . . When before the present epoch, had three millions of people full power and a fair opportunity to form and establish the wisest and happiest government that human wisdom can contrive?

John Adams, *Thoughts on Government* (1776)

When I left Congress in 76, it was in the persuasion that our whole code must be reviewed, adapted to our republican form of government, and, now that we had no negatives of Councils, Governors & Kings to restrain us from doing right, that it should be corrected in all its parts, with a single eye to reason, & the good of those for whose government it was framed.

Thomas Jefferson, *Autobiography*

It will be of little avail to the people, that the laws are made by men of their own choice, if the laws be so voluminous that they cannot be read, or so incoherent that they cannot be understood; if they be repealed or revised before they are promulgated, or undergo such incessant changes that no man, who knows what the law is to-day, can guess what it will be to-morrow. Law is defined to be a rule of action; but how can that be a rule, which is little known, and less fixed?

James Madison, *The Federalist No. 62* (1788)

This Part II draws on my article, *A Government of Laws Not of Precedents 1776–1876: The Google Challenge to Common Law Myth*, 4 Brit. J. Am. Legal Studies 137 (2015).

4

Founding a Government of Laws

Great Seal of the United States of America, Out of Many One (obverse), He/She Approves of the Undertaking (reverse), New Order of the Ages (1782)[1]

The founders of the United States believed that they were creating a new order of the ages. It was to be an order built on statutes, not on common-law precedents.

---

[1] *Great Seal of the United States*, [1782], 8 FAMILY MAGAZINE: OR, MONTHLY ABSTRACT OF GENERAL KNOWLEDGE 36 (1840–41). The reverse today is ubiquitous on the one-dollar bill. In 1840 this was apparently only the second printing of it. This illustration predates by seventeen years the Department of State's candidate for that honor. *See* U.S. DEPARTMENT OF STATE BUREAU OF PUBLIC AFFAIRS, THE GREAT SEAL OF THE UNITED STATES (pamphlet, 2003). Available at https://www.state.gov/documents/organization/27807.pdf

A. THE FOUNDERS' VISION: A GOVERNMENT OF LAWS
FOR A NEW NATION

In the world of John Adams and Thomas Jefferson, law was about legislating and government was about governing. Written laws were supposed to state principles beforehand and to authorize governors and governed alike to judge according to those principles. Democratically selected legislatures were to be supreme and not judges. States were governments of laws and not of men.

Lost in clouds of common law myths is American leadership in statute law in the 18th century. Americans have long taken pride in their leadership in the world of written constitutions – that of Massachusetts of 1780 is the oldest still in force – but few know that America, for a time, was a leader in written statutes as well.

The nation's founders were not captives of the hoary English common law; they believed in written law. Of English law, they made selective interim use, and dispatched much to the dustbin of history. For American statutes, they labored. Against judge-made law, they cautioned. They relied on right-minded judges to refrain from making law in the guise of interpretation. Their aspirations ran to written law of legislation and not to unwritten common law.[2]

The Declaration of Independence of 1776 was about legislation and legislatures. Its first charge against King George was that "He has refused his Assent to Laws, the most wholesome and necessary for the public good." That and the next seven charges related to legislation and legislatures. Thirteen of the twenty-seven charges in all dealt with some manifestation of legislation. Of common law, there was no mention.

More than any other two people, Adams and Jefferson brought the Declaration of Independence into being. They acted to make the republican ideals of the Declaration reality in law. For Adams, it was a frame of governing and making laws: the constitution. For Jefferson, it was the nuts and bolts of governing itself: the laws.

1. *Adams' Massachusetts' Constitution or Frame of Government of Massachusetts*

In fall 1779, Adams drafted the *Constitution or Frame of Government of the Commonwealth of Massachusetts*, which is still in force today.[3] In writing the

---

[2] *Cf.* Charles Abernathy, *The Lost European Aspirations of U.S. Constitutional Law*, in 24 Februar 1803: Die Erfindung der Verfassungsgerichtsbarkeit und Ihrer Folgen 37 (Werner Kremp, ed., 2003).

[3] *See* James R. Maxeiner, *Building a Government of Laws: Adams and Jefferson 1776–1779*, in Legal Doctrines of the Rule of Law and of the Legal State (James Hickey & James Silkenat, eds., Ius Gentium: Comparative Perspectives on Law and Justice, Vol. 38, 2014).

Constitution, Adams relied on his 1776 pamphlet, *Thoughts on Government: Applicable to the Present State of the American Colonies*.[4] There he wrote that "the very definition of a republic 'is an empire of laws, and not of men'" and that "a republic is the best of governments." He took the term from James Harrington's 1656 *Oceana*. For Massachusetts, Adams wrote of a government and not of an empire of laws.

Adams wrote *Thoughts on Government* to give to other Americans advice on how they might create governments for the new states coming into being in 1776. He began by rejecting Pope's famous aphorism "The forms of government let fools contest: That which is best administered is best." Adams said no: "Nothing is more certain, from the history of nations and the nature of men, that some forms of government are better fitted for being well-administered than others." And so, Adams asked: "As good government is an empire of laws, how shall your laws be made?" Three years later, he gave his answer in his draft of the Massachusetts Constitution.[5]

Adams' Constitution is about a government of laws and not about precedents of judges. The preamble begins by stating that government balances common good and individual rights: "The end of the institution, maintenance, and administration of government is to secure the existence of the body-politic, to protect it, and to furnish the individuals who compose it with the power of enjoying, in safety and tranquility, their natural rights and the blessings of life."

The preamble's second paragraph states the means to accomplish this end: "certain laws for the common good." So it is "a duty of the people ... *to provide for an equitable mode of making laws, as well as for an impartial interpretation, and a faithful execution of them*." [Emphasis added.] It is through these written laws, "that everyman may at all times, find his security in them."

Adams' Constitution provides a frame for statute law and for governing. Chapter I, Section I, Article IV of Part the Second, the Frame of Government, gives the legislature authority "to make, ordain, and establish all manner of wholesome and reasonable orders, laws, statutes, and ordinances, directions and instructions, either with penalties or without, so as the same be not repugnant or contrary to this constitution, as they shall judge to be for the

---

[4] It, together with *The Report of a Constitution, or Form of Government, for the Commonwealth of Massachusetts* (1779), are conveniently reprinted in THE REVOLUTIONARY WRITINGS OF JOHN ADAMS, SELECTED AND WITH A FOREWORD BY C. BRADLEY THOMPSON (2000) at 287–293 and at 297–322 respectively.

[5] References here are to the final language of the adopted 1780 constitution and not to that of Adams' 1779 draft. Differences between the two with respect to specific sections cited are believed minor.

good and welfare of this commonwealth, and for the government and ordering thereof, and of the subjects of the same, and for the necessary support and defence of the government thereof." Article XXII of Part the First, the Declaration of Rights, calls on the legislature frequently to assemble "for address[ing] of grievances, for correcting, strengthening, and confirming the laws, and for making new laws, as the common good may require."

Adams' Constitution does not contemplate judge-made law or judicial supremacy. Article X of Part the First, the Declaration of Rights provides: "In fine, the people of this commonwealth are not controllable by any other laws than those to which their constitutional representative body have given their consent." Article XX adds: "The power of suspending the laws, or the execution of the laws, ought never to be exercised but by the legislature, or by authority derived from it, to be exercised in such particular cases only as the legislature shall expressly provide for."

Adams' Constitution commands "standing laws" to protect the people from rapid changes in law. Article X of Part the First, the Declaration of Rights provides: "Every individual of the society has a right to be protected by it in the enjoyment of his life, liberty, and property, according to standing laws."[6]

Adams' Constitution anticipates laws that are coordinated one with another.[7] Chapter VI, Article VI of Part the Second, the Frame of Government, avoids a gap in law by continuing in force existing laws. To assure consistency Chapter III, Article II gives executive and legislative branches "authority to require the opinions of the justices of the supreme judicial court upon important questions of law, and upon solemn occasions." Article XXIX of Part the First, the Declaration of Rights calls for "an impartial interpretation of the laws, and administration of justice."

Adams' Constitution looks for a government that will govern according to law. It comes close to anticipating a requirement of statutory authority for government action, i.e., a principle of legality. Article XVIII of Part the First, the Declaration of Rights, provides that the people "have a right to require of their lawgivers and magistrates an exact and constant observation of them [i.e., fundamental principles of the constitution], in the formation and execution of the laws necessary for the good administration of the commonwealth." It allows for exceptions to rights, such as search warrant may issue, and soldiers may be quartered in homes, but only "with the formalities, prescribed by the

---

6   *See* JOHN ADAMS, A DEFENCE OF THE CONSTITUTIONS OF GOVERNMENT OF THE UNITED STATES OF AMERICA ... VOL. 1 (3d ed. 1797) at 141 (viewing negatively frequent changes in law).

7   On the idea generally, *see* Karl Riesenhuber, *English Common Law versus German Systemdenken? Internal versus External Approaches,* 7 UTRECHT L. REV 117 (2011).

laws" or "in a manner ordained by the legislature."[8] Government officers are to swear to carry out their duties "agreeably to the rules and regulations of the constitution and the laws of the commonwealth."[9] Carry laws out they must. Later Adams explained: "The executive power is properly the government; the laws are a dead letter until an administration begins to carry them into execution."[10]

Adams' Constitution sets out a frame of a government of laws and not of men, i.e., a legal state. But what would an American legal state look like? Jefferson's legislation suggests one such state.

2. *Jefferson's Revisal of Virginia's Laws*

From fall 1776 through spring 1779, Jefferson wrote the laws for a new republican government of Virginia. He provided legislation for reformation of the laws of the nation's then most populous state. James Madison described Jefferson's reformation as "a mine of legislative wealth, and a model of statutory composition."[11] One modern scholar sees in Jefferson's legislation, "a rare and comprehensive view of how a founder envisioned an actual republican society."[12]

Jefferson's lawmaking from 1776 to 1779 is without parallel in American history. No American legislator before or since has accomplished so much of such importance in such a short period of time. In three weeks in June 1776 he drafted the Declaration of Independence. Then he already had in mind as much building a government of laws as declaring rights and independence. In May in Philadelphia for Congress, he wrote a friend back home that the government to be established was "the whole object of the present controversy."[13] In the three years that followed, he drafted the laws for a republican government.

No work had more substance for Jefferson than building a government of laws. He wrote in his autobiography, "I knew that our legislation under the regal government had many vicious points which urgently required reformation, and I thought I could be of more use in forwarding that work. I therefore

[8] Declaration of Rights, Arts. XIV and XXVII, respectively.
[9] Frame of Government, Chap. VI.   [10] ADAMS, *supra* note 117, at 372.
[11] James Madison to Samuel Harrison Smith, Nov. 4, 1826, *in* THE WRITINGS OF JAMES MADISON, VOL. 1819–1836 at 256, 257–258 (Gaillard Hunt, 1910).
[12] RALPH LERNER, THE THINKING REVOLUTIONARY: PRINCIPLE AND PRACTICE IN THE NEW REPUBLIC 62 (1987).
[13] Jefferson to Thomas Nelson, May 16, 1776, *in* 1 THE PAPERS OF THOMAS JEFFERSON (VOL.1, 1760 TO 1776) 292 (Julian P. Boyd, ed., 1950).

REPORT

OF THE

COMMITTEE of REVISORS

APPOINTED BY THE

GENERAL ASSEMBLY

of *VIRGINIA*

In MDCCLXXVI.

49358

PUBLISHED BY ORDER
OF THE
GENERAL ASSEMBLY,
AND
PRINTED BY DIXON & HOLT,
In the CITY of RICHMOND,
NOVEMBER, MDCCLXXXIV.

Jefferson's Revisal: Commissioned 1776, reported 1779, and published for Public Review 1784. Of 118 bills introduced, 58 bills were adopted.

retired from my seat in Congress on the 2d. day of Sep., resigned it, and took my place in the legislature of my state."[14] When a messenger reached him in Virginia with a Congressional commission to join Benjamin Franklin on the critical mission to France, Jefferson took three days to think it over – keeping the messenger waiting – and finally declined the appointment.

From October 1776, when Jefferson joined the state legislature, until June 1779, when he became governor, he did little else than work on legislation. His work took two forms: (1) drafting bills on particular subjects, e.g., civil justice, property law, the established church, importation of slaves, and naturalization; and (2) systematic review and reform of Virginia law.[15] The latter is known as the "Revisal." The Revisal was literally two bundles of 126 bills that the Virginia House Committee on Revision under Jefferson's leadership prepared from October 1776 to June 1779.[16] The bills of the Revisal alone were printed in ninety oversized folio pages in tiny type (over three hundred pages in a standard type face in a large octavo book).[17] Other legislation he wrote or sponsored was of comparable extent. He was, as the editor of his papers said, "a veritable legislative drafting bureau."[18]

Jefferson reviewed the whole of Virginia law to adapt it for a republican form of government "with a single eye to reason, & the good of those for whose government it was framed." He scripted statutes that struck at the heart and soul of common law: land law, inheritance and criminal law. According to one biographer, Jefferson intended to "completely overthrow the English legal system that had chained Virginia for 170 years."[19] Jefferson's legislation abolished primogeniture and completely changed rules of descent. He proposed a new penal law "to proportion crimes and punishments in cases [previously] capital." It failed of passage by a single vote. Jefferson drafted legislation that would end forever the idea that common law made Christian doctrine a part of law. His legislation disestablished the Anglican Church in

---

[14] The Autobiography of Thomas Jefferson, 1743–1790, Together with a Summary of the Chief Events in Jefferson's Life 67 (Paul Leicester Ford, ed., 1914; *New Introduction* by Michael Zuckerman, 2005), at 57.

[15] The Papers of Thomas Jefferson (Vol. 2, 1777 to 18 June 1779, Including the Revisal of the Laws, 1776–1786) 306 (Julian P. Boyd, ed., 1950).

[16] *Id.* at 306–307.

[17] Report of the Committee of Advisors Appointed by the General Assembly of Virginia in MDCCLXXVI (1784) (available best at Google books). The following paragraphs do not cite to individual bills from the Revisal. They are found in the Committee's Report and in Boyd's analysis of the Revisal, *in* 2 The Papers of Thomas Jefferson (Vol. 2, 1777 to 18 June 1779), *supra* note 15.

[18] The Papers of Thomas Jefferson (Vol. 2, 1777 to 18 June 1779), *supra* note 15, at 306.

[19] William Sterne Randall, Thomas Jefferson: A Life 285 (1993).

Virginia. His bill establishing religious liberty is the best-known of all his legislation. Jefferson sought to organize and rationalize common law institutions. His legislation restated and reorganized court institutions and procedures both civil and criminal to make, writes one historian, a "mantel of procedural safeguards for all."[20] Jefferson's legislation reorganized government in all its branches. It provided for a state militia and navy, a board of war, a board of trade and a board of auditors. It districted the legislature and provided for elections and appointments. It created a public land office to administer claims to the western lands.

Although Jefferson's Revisal did not banish common law altogether, it did not promote 18th century common law methods as a path to the New Republic. It gave no hint of approval of judicial legislation that characterizes contemporary common law method. To the contrary, Jefferson opposed judicial rendering of law "more incertain under pretense of rendering it more reasonable."[21]

Jefferson's Revisal promoted legislative methods; it *was* legislation. Jefferson could hardly have proceeded in any other way. Only statutes can root out old laws, rationally refashion remaining institutions, create new institutions, and provide direction to governors in how to govern. Jefferson sought to use legislation to do all these things. His success was limited by his own methods. In a democratic republic, Jefferson could not decree a new society and new laws. He had to get assent of the democratically elected legislature.

3. *Madison's Adoption of Jefferson's Revisal*

The British invasion of Virginia in 1779 delayed the Virginia legislature's consideration of Jefferson's Revisal. By the time the British were expelled

---

[20] LERNER, *supra* note 12, at 64.

[21] In a letter about Lord Mansfield's free revisions of law contemporaneous with legislative consideration of his Revisal, Jefferson wrote an Italian friend: "Relieve the judges from the rigour of text law, and permit them, with pretorian discretion, to wander into it's equity, and the whole legal system becomes incertain." Jefferson stressed the importance of system, of fixed rules, and of definition and explanation. The opposite, legal chaos, he wrote his friend, "would be a monster whose existence should not be suffered one moment in a free country wherein every power is dangerous which is not bound up by general rules." Letter From Thomas Jefferson to Philip Mazzei, November 1785, FOUNDERS ONLINE, National Archives, last modified Oct. 5, 2016. http://founders.archives.gov/documents/Jefferson/01-09-02-0056. Perhaps the myth of common law tutelage is today coming undone. Instead of assuming common law, as have so many scholars in the past, contemporary scholar Professor Matthew Steilen explains how common law could fit into the Founders' statutory world. *See* Matthew Steilen, *On the Place of Judge-Made Law in a Government of Laws*, 3 CRITICAL ANALYSIS OF LAW 243–260 (2016).

and the legislature able to take up the work, Jefferson was on a mission in Europe. James Madison took Jefferson's place as legislator leading the Revisal. In the years just before Madison managed to bring the country together in 1787 for a constitutional convention and draft a constitution, he presented Jefferson's anti–common law revision to the Virginia legislature. He introduced 118 of the Revisal's 126 bills and achieved adoption of fifty-eight.[22]

4. *Madison's and Wilson's Constitution*

The Founders designed a government of written laws. That made America exceptional in 1787. Contemporary common-law myth claims the Constitution for common-law tradition but its "true family affinity," writes Professor Charles Abernathy, "is that of the written law of the great codes of France and Germany that followed in the nineteenth century."[23] The Founders were much influenced by Continental legal thought, by Montesquieu, Locke and Beccaria and classical Roman ideas.[24] That meant written laws. The Constitution is about making and applying written laws.

Article 1, section 1, grants Congress "legislative power." Article 1, section 8 lists specific powers and concludes with a general grant "To make all laws which shall be necessary and proper for carrying into execution the forgoing powers." Article II vests the "executive power" in the President. Article II, section 3, provides that the president "shall take care that the laws be faithfully executed." Article III, section 1 vests the "judicial power" in "one Supreme court." Article III, section 2, provides that that power extends to an assortment of controversies, but first to cases "arising under" written law, i.e., "arising under this Constitution, the Laws of the United States, and Treaties made, or which shall be made, under their Authority." Article VI provides for the supremacy of written laws and binds all judges to that written law: "This Constitution, and the Laws of the United States which shall be made in Pursuance thereof; and all Treaties made, or which shall be made, under the Authority of the United States, shall be the supreme Law of the Land; and the judges in every State shall be bound thereby . . ."

---

[22] THE PAPERS OF THOMAS JEFFERSON (VOL. 2, 1777 TO 18 JUNE 1777), *supra* note 15, at 322–323.

[23] Abernathy, *supra* note 2, at 37.

[24] *See, e.g.,* DAVID J. BEDERMAN, THE CLASSICAL FOUNDATIONS OF THE AMERICAN CONSTITUTION: PREVAILING WISDOM (2008); Matthew P. Bergman, *Montesquieu's Theory of Government and the Framing of the American Constitution,* 18 PEPPERDINE L. REV. 1 (1990); JOHN D. BESSLER, THE BIRTH OF AMERICAN LAW: AN ITALIAN PHILOSOPHER AND THE AMERICAN REVOLUTION 332 (2014); M.N.S. SELLERS, AMERICAN REPUBLICANISM: ROMAN IDEOLOGY IN THE UNITED STATES CONSTITUTION (1994).

The Federalist Papers confirm the commitment of James Madison, Alexander Hamilton and John Jay to written law. They address issues of statute law and statute lawmaking. These include quality of legislation, uniformity of laws throughout the nation and worries that constitutional review of statutes might lead to judicial superiority over legislatures. For example, *Federalist No. 62, The Senate,* by Madison, saw in the Senate (as contrasted to the House) a body with "due acquaintance with the objects and principles of legislation." It would protect the people against "so many monuments of deficient wisdom" that were "are all the repealing, explaining, and amending laws, which fill and disgrace our voluminous codes." It would provide "a knowledge of the [legislative] means by which that object [of the happiness of the people] can be best attained." It would secure that laws are not "made for the FEW, not for the MANY." [Emphasis in the original.]

5. *The First Supreme Court Justices and Written Law: Legislating for Legislatures and Applying Laws in Court*

The first Supreme Court of the United States was not a third legislative chamber that made law through precedents. Probably its most enduring act was not a judicial decision, but a 1793 letter to President Washington declining to give an advisory opinion.[25] It decided only a few cases. It delivered its decisions in a way structurally not conducive to creating precedents: seriatim. There was no opinion of the Court.[26] There was no provision for reporting decisions of the Court.[27]

The first Supreme Court justices were not judicial legislators. The first Chief Justice, John Jay, resigned his position to become governor of New York.[28] Three associate justices – John Rutledge, William Cushing, and John Blair, Jr. – today would be counted "textualists"; one is said to have invented

---

[25] *See* Stewart Jay, Most Humble Servants: The Advisory Role of Early Judges 179 (1997) (reprinting the letter in full). The letter is the origin of the case or controversy requirement.

[26] *See* Seriatim: The Supreme Court Before John Marshall (1998).

[27] The proceedings of the Court were not reported until 1798 in a privately prepared collection of decisions of courts sitting in Philadelphia. 2 A.J. Dallas, Reports of Cases Ruled and Adjudges in the Several Courts of the United States, and of Pennsylvania, Held at the Seat of the Federal Government 399 (1798) (now cited as 2 U.S.).

[28] In his first speech as governor of New York in 1796 Jay stressed that "One great object of which a people, free, enlightened and governed by laws of their own making, will never lose sight, is, that those laws be always so judiciously applied and faithfully executed, as to secure to them the peaceable and uninterrupted enjoyment of their rights." John Jay, *Speech of January 6, 1796, in* The Speeches of the Different Governors, to the Legislature of the State of New York 47, 49 (1826).

textualism.[29] Two – James Wilson and James Iredell – were better known as drafters of written laws.

Associate Justice James Wilson (1789–1798) was *the* first justice of the Supreme Court to take office. He was one of only six men who signed both the Declaration of Independence and the Constitution. He is considered to have been second only to James Madison as principal drafter of the Constitution. While he was on the Court, in March 1791 the Pennsylvania House of Representatives engaged him "to prepare bills, containing such alterations, additions and improvements as the code of law, and the principles and forms of the constitution then lately adopted might require."[30] Wilson accepted the challenge. He proposed that he would work to make law "a plain rule for action" and through a commentary reduce common law into "a just and regular system." He intended to write laws "level to the understanding of all."[31] Had Wilson brought the work to completion, it would have rivaled Jefferson's revisal. His attempted revisal is forgotten, but he is remembered for his counsel, that "every prudent and cautious judge … will remember that his duty and his business is, not to make the law, but to interpret and apply it."[32]

Associate Justice James Iredell (1790–1799), who died prematurely at forty-eight, is remembered as reviser of laws in the model of Jefferson and Wilson. In 1776, he served on the North Carolina Commission established to recommend which statutes should continue in force as "consistent with the genius of a free people."[33] In 1787 the State Assembly appointed him to revise and compile the legislative acts of the state and former colony. He completed the work in 1791 after joining the Court. It is known as "Iredell's Revisal" and long was the basis for North Carolina law.[34]

---

[29] Scott Douglas Gerber, *Deconstructing William Cushing, in* SERIATIM, *supra* note 26, 97, 106–113. Rutledge, best known as a Chairman of the Committee of Detail of the Constitutional Convention of 1787, resigned from the Court to become Chief Justice of South Carolina, where his judicial philosophy is said to have been to "leave legal innovation to legislators." James Haw, *John Rutledge: Distinction and Declension, in* SERIATIM, 70, 89. For Blair, *see* Wythe Hold, *John Blair: "A Safe and Conscientious" Judge, in* SERIATIM, *id.*, at 155.

[30] 1 THE WORKS OF HONORABLE JAMES WILSON, L.L.D. Preface (Bird Wilson, ed., 1804), *reprinted in* 1 COLLECTED WORKS OF JAMES WILSON 417 (Kermit L. Hall & Mark David Hall, eds., 2007). On Wilson's role in drafting the Constitution, *see* William Ewald, *James Wilson and the Drafting of the Constitution,* 10 J. CONST. L. 901 (2008).

[31] 1 WILSON, *supra* note 30, at 419–421.   [32] 2 WILSON, *supra* note 30, 306.

[33] JAMES IREDELL & WILLIAM H. BATTLE, *Preface, in* 1 THE REVISED STATUTES OF THE STATE OF NORTH CAROLINA v, x–xi (1837); Willis P. Whichard, *James Iredell: Revolutionist, Constitutionalist, Jurist in* SERIATIM: THE SUPREME COURT BEFORE JOHN MARSHALL 198, 203 (1998). *See generally* WILLIS P. WHICHARD, JUSTICE JAMES IREDELL (2000).

[34] *See* IREDELL & BATTLE, *supra* note 33, at xii.

B. THE ENIGMAS OF BRITISH LAW IN AMERICA

Common-law myths inflate the extent of reception of British law and mischaracterize what America did receive. Not America generally, but individual American colonies and states, received not all of British law, but some British statutes and some English common law.

Such common-law method as American judges of the colonial and early Republican eras claimed, was not the method of contemporary common law, where judges make law, but the more modest judges-discover-law method of classic English common law.[35] American scholars have known for years that "The legal philosophy dominant when [the American] government was established did not contemplate judicial legislation in any form."[36]

The reception of British law in America has been one of the most researched and debated issues of American legal history. According to Professor William E. Nelson, who has tried to read all of the colonial sources, the reception of common law is "the central focus of colonial legal history."[37]

For all the discussion that it has engendered, I find it flawed in three respects.

First, the discussion invariably assumes that there is a reception of "common law." The issue of *when* can obscure the issues of *whether*, or of *what*. Without knowing which common law the discussant has in mind, one may go off track.

Second, the discussion is addressed to common law in the courts and not to common law in society generally. That makes it a discussion of reception of law for lawyers and not of law for people.

Finally, discussions of reception can be difficult to follow because discussants do not always distinguish among sub-issues. Does the discussion refer to British statutes or to English common law? If to common law, to common law substantive law or to common law method? If to common law method, to the classic method of discovery or to the contemporary method of making law? And then, to which colony or state or the nation does the discussion relate?

---

[35] *See* Stephen B. Presser, *The Development and Application of Common Law*, 8 Tex. Rev. Law & Politics 291 (2004). *See also* Chapter 3, text at notes 42 to 50, *supra*, and this chapter, text at notes 79 to 81, *infra*.

[36] Fred V. Cahill, Jr., Judicial Legislation: A Study in American Legal Theory v (1952). *See also* 21 and 151.

[37] The Common Law in Colonial America: Vol. 1, The Chesapeake and New England, 1607–1660, 13 (2008).

Although reception is a confusing issue for writing history, it need not be for law reform. The myth of contemporary common law is in any case de-legitimatized.

1. *English Common Law and American Colonies*

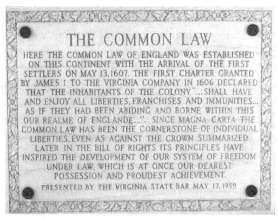

THE COMMON LAW

HERE THE COMMON LAW OF ENGLAND WAS ESTABLISHED ON THIS CONTINENT WITH THE ARRIVAL OF THE FIRST SETTLERS ON MAY 13,1607. THE FIRST CHARTER GRANTED BY JAMES I TO THE VIRGINIA COMPANY IN 1606 DECLARED THAT THE INHABITANTS OF THE COLONY"...SHALL HAVE AND ENJOY ALL LIBERTIES, FRANCHISES AND IMMUNITIES... AS IF THEY HAD BEEN ABIDING AND BORNE WITHIN THIS OUR REALME OF ENGLANDE...". SINCE MAGNA CARTA THE COMMON LAW HAS BEEN THE CORNERSTONE OF INDIVIDUAL LIBERTIES, EVEN AS AGAINST THE CROWN SUMMARIZED LATER IN THE BILL OF RIGHTS ITS PRINCIPLES HAVE INSPIRED THE DEVELOPMENT OF OUR SYSTEM OF FREEDOM UNDER LAW, WHICH IS AT ONCE OUR DEAREST POSSESSION AND PROUDEST ACHIEVEMENT.
PRESENTED BY THE VIRGINIA STATE BAR MAY 17, 1959

Common Law Myth. Commemorative Plaque at Jamestown VA, presented by the Virginia State Bar May 17, 1959.

In contemporary common-law myth the 17th century colonists well-nigh brought "the common law" over in the holds of their ships. A plaque placed in 1959 by the Virginia Bar at Jamestown says as much: "Here the common law of England was established on this continent with the arrival of the first settlers on May 13, 1607." No. That's wrong. [38]

Ironically, when the settlers of Jamestown were at sea on their way to America, the settlement's namesake, King James I, was telling the British Parliament that it should replace common law with statute law: "leave not the Law to the pleasure of the Judge, but let your Lawes be looked into: for I desire not the abolishing of the Lawes, but onely the clearing and the sweeping off the rust of them, and that by Parliament our Lawes might be cleared and made knowen to all the Subjects.

---

[38] Legal historian and common law specialist, William E. Nelson rejects the myth without equivocation: "The English settlers who arrived in Jamestown, Virginia, in 1607 did not bring the common law with them." THE COMMON LAW IN COLONIAL AMERICA: VOL. 1, THE CHESAPEAKE AND NEW ENGLAND, 1607–1660, 13 (2008).

Yea rather it were lesse hurt, that all the approved Cases were set downe and allowed by Parliament for standing Lawes in all time to come."[39]

Reception of English law was enigmatic in Colonial America. In 1774 loyalist John Dickenson, repeating a grievance from New York, complained that law in the American colonies was in a state of "confusion" and "controversy"; no one knew when English law applied. He argued that "passing an act for settling the extent of the English laws" was "absolutely necessary for the public security."[40]

Today's scholars see common-law carryover differently than the legal professions did a century ago. Professor William E. Nelson, concludes, "England's common law was not the initial foundation of [the] legal systems." Instead "the English legal heritage ... constituted a set of background norms to which [colonies] turned when convenient."[41] Professor James R. Stoner sees as "a serious error" the assumption "that the Americans of the Revolutionary era simply accepted the dominant understanding of common law in contemporary Britain . . . ."[42] Already a half century ago, in a comprehensive study of British statutes in America, Elizabeth Gaspar Brown, warned against the "utter folly" of presuming an identity of law between law as practiced in individual colonies and in England.[43]

It could hardly have been otherwise. English laws, legal institutions and legal methods were so complex as to make it practically impossible for even the most sophisticated colonials to know, let alone import and recreate them.[44] The first modern systematization of English common law – Blackstone's *Commentaries*

[39] King James I, *Speach [sic] to Parliament of 31 March 1607*, KING JAMES VI AND I: SELECTED WRITINGS (Neil Rhodes et al., eds.,) 307, 310–311 (2004). *Accord, King James I, Speech [sic] to Parliament, March 1609, id.* at 325, 332–333, and partly quoted in SAMUEL ROBERTS, A DIGEST OF SELECT BRITISH STATUTES, COMPRISING THOSE WHICH, ACCORDING TO THE REPORT OF THE JUDGES OF THE SUPREME COURT, MADE TO THE LEGISLATURE, APPEAR TO BE IN FORCE, IN PENNSYLVANIA, WITH SOME OTHERS xv (1817) ("I would wish both these statutes and reports, as well in the parliament as common law, to be once maturely reviewed, and reconciled").

[40] [JOHN DICKINSON], LETTERS FROM A FARMER IN PENNSYLVANIA TO THE INHABITANTS OF THE BRITISH COLONIES 90–91 (Philadelphia 1774). Dickinson wrote for Pennsylvania, but he took (with attribution) most of his criticism from New York's WILLIAM SMITH, THE HISTORY OF THE PROVINCE OF NEW YORK, FROM THE FIRST DISCOVERY TO THE YEAR M.CDD.XXXII 243 (London 1767).

[41] WILLIAM E. NELSON, THE COMMON LAW IN COLONIAL AMERICA, VOL. 1, THE CHESAPEAKE AND NEW ENGLAND, 1607–1660, 8 (2008).

[42] JAMES R. STONER, JR., COMMON-LAW LIBERTY: RETHINKING AMERICAN CONSTITUTIONALISM 13 (2003).

[43] ELIZABETH GASPAR BROWN, BRITISH STATUTES IN AMERICAN LAW 1776–1836, at 20 (1964).

[44] *Cf.*, PAUL SAMUEL REINSCH, THE ENGLISH COMMON LAW IN THE EARLY AMERICAN COLONIES 7 (1899), *reprinted in* 1 SELECT ESSAYS IN ANGLO-AMERICAN LEGAL HISTORY 367, 369 (1907).

on the Laws of England – came too late to enable a colonial reception; it was not published until the very eve of the Revolution, in England in 1765–1769, and in the United States, not until 1771 to 1772. While a masterful improvement, it is not short. It consumes four thick oversized volumes. It was intended only as an introduction![45] Brown, in her path-breaking work, concluded that, "However much the colonists may have wished that they possessed the full body of the common law of England, they did not."[46]

English law, even leaving to one side the laws of other legal systems subject to the King of Great Britain in 1776 (e.g., Scotland, Ireland, Hanover on the Continent), was a potpourri of national and local laws.[47] The common law was the law of the King of England's common-law courts at Westminster (principally, the Court of Common Pleas, the Court of King's Bench, and the Court of the Exchequer). The "common law" those courts applied consisted of statutes and of statute-like writs, as construed by the courts in oral opinions taken down in unevenly edited and privately published books of reports. Alongside these common courts sat "civil law courts" (the Court of Chancery, the Court of Admiralty, the Court of Chivalry and others). They applied a law of conscience of their own-making or a law of more international origin. Local courts outside the royal capital remained and continued to apply local laws.

Common law even in early modern England did not enjoy the overwhelming dominance that contemporary common-law myth supposes. Written laws always had a role. Already in the early modern era statutes made major inroads on common law in England. A "deluge of parliamentary legislation"[48] in the mid-18th century led the Lord Chancellor to complain that "our statute books are increased to such an enormous size, that they confound every man who is obliged to look into them."[49]

---

[45] *"Sullivan's Lectures,"* 3 MONTHLY ANTHOLOGY & BOSTON REV. 438, 439 (1806).

[46] Brown, *supra* note 43, at 20–21. Owing to the unwritten constitution of the United Kingdom, statutes were British, for they generally applied in Scotland, but common law was "English," for it applied only in England and Wales.

[47] *See, e.g.,* HUGH H. BRACKENRIDGE, CONSIDERATIONS ON THE JURISPRUDENCE OF THE STATE OF PENNSYLVANIA, No. 1, at 6 (1808) ("Even in the country of its origin the common law is not a *national,* or a *uniform* system. . . . As a part therefore of English jurisprudence the common law is intricate, and too much embarrassed with exceptions and distinctions to be a subject of ready comprehension to the public mind.")

[48] DAVID LEMMINGS, LAW AND GOVERNMENT IN ENGLAND DURING THE LONG EIGHTEENTH CENTURY: FROM CONSENT TO COMMAND 3 (2011).

[49] *Quoted in id.* at 9 and *in* 18 THE SCOT'S MAGAZINE 476 (1756).

Reception of English law varied throughout the colonies. Law in one colony cannot rightly be assumed to have been law in another.[50] The new world was a land of "many legalities."[51] Each colony must be investigated separately.[52] Their differing origins, as settlements of previously uninhabited territories or as lands obtained by cession, and their differing constitutional statuses, led to debate about differing legislative authority.[53]

That there might have been an indigenous and dominating American common law in the colonial era does not seem plausible. The rudimentary nature of courts and law practice, the lack of lawyers, as well as the lack of law reporting made even limited adoption of new law wherever sourced difficult. Before the Revolution, there were no published books of American precedents. Books of English decisions, on which an American common law would have built, were hard to come by and imported.[54]

There were, however, statutes in large numbers to guide governors and governed alike. Digitization permits perusal of the many volumes of indigenous colonial statutes. In some colonies there were already revisals of statutes.[55] A case might be made that colonial Americans lived already in an "age of statutes" or even of codification.[56] Indeed, a reviewer of one of the first volumes of American precedents to appear in the first decade of the 19th century wrote: "In America the popular sentiment has, at times, been hostile to the practice of deciding cases on precedent, because the people and lawyers too, have misunderstood their use. Precedents are not statutes. They settle cases, which statutes do not reach."[57] For the reviewer, himself a proponent of precedents, law meant first statutes and only second precedents.

---

[50] *See* Brown, *supra* note 43, at 20.

[51] *See, e.g.,* The Many Legalities of Early America (Christopher L. Tomlins & Bruce H. Mann, eds., 2001); William E. Nelson, The Common Law in Colonial America, Vol. I, The Chesapeake and New England 1607–1660 (2008), Vol. II, The Middle Colonies and the Carolinas, 1660–1730 (2012).

[52] Brown, *supra* note 43, at 20.   [53] *Id.* at 1–15.   [54] *Cf.* Brown, *supra* note 43, at 19–20.

[55] For an extensive guide to prestatehood law in the several states, *see* Prestatehood Legal Materials: A Fifty-State Research Guide, Including New York City and the District of Columbia, 2 vols., (Michael Chiorazzi & Marguerite Most, eds., 2005).

[56] *See* Reinsch, *supra* note 44, at 53; Erwin C. Surrency, *Revision of Colonial Laws*, 9 Am. J. Legal Hist. 189 (1965).

[57] Book Review, *Art. 17. Vol. I. part I., Feb., term, 1806-Reports of Cases Argued, and Determined, in the Supreme Court of Judicature of the State of New York. By William Johnson, Esquire, Counselor at Law.—New-York, I. Riley & Co., 1806,* 4 The Monthly Anthology and Boston Review 206, 207 (1807).

2. British Law in the First Century of the Republic

THE HUMORS OF LAW.

Law – *ignis fatuus* ("fleeting fire," i.e., illusion)[58]

Contemporary common-law myth would have it that the United States, by 1800, was a land where common-law substantive law and common-law method as known today applied. Neither is true. The suspicion of both just seen at the turn of the nineteenth century did not abate.

In 1826, a half century into the New Republic, satirist and later Secretary of the Navy James Kirke Paulding in a popular satire quipped: "That it is the

[58]   FREDERICK SAUNDERS, SALAD FOR THE SOLITARY AND THE SOCIAL, ILLUSTRATED WITH FIFTY-TWO ORIGINAL DESIGNS BY EMINENT AMERICAN ARTISTS 423 (Popular ed. London 1883 & New York 1886).

common law is certain. But nobody can tell exactly what is the common law."[59] Eleven years later in 1837, in what was soon the most popular one volume student's introduction to American law of the 19th century, Professor Timothy Walker made the same point: "The only certainty, therefore, is that we have something which we call common law, scattered at random over a vast surface. But precisely what it is, or how far it extends, is hidden in the breast of our judges, and can only be ascertained by experiment. I need hardly to observe, that this uncertainty is a vast evil."[60]

The uncertainty was self-inflicted. British law, including English common law, had no force in the new states except as the states themselves adopted it.[61] When in 1776 the American colonies became "free and independent states" with full power "to do all the other acts and things which independent states may of right do,"[62] among those powers was the power to legislate for themselves without royal interference. And legislate they did. But it was thought expedient to carry over British statutes and to adopt some English common law.[63]

When a legislature enacts a specific foreign statute, or continues one in force, with or without modification, lawgiving is not problematic. For a formerly occupied state to carry on law of the erstwhile occupier is common. Legal systems are complicated and are not easily created. So German states on which Napoleon imposed his codes, for one example, continued his codes in force after French troops departed, some for nearly a century.[64] Korea, for

---

[59] James Kirke Paulding, *The Perfection of Reason, in* The Merry Tales of the Three Wise Men of Gotham 144, 166 (1826) (2d ed., 1835; 3d ed., 1839).

[60] Timothy Walker, Introduction to American Law, Designed as a First Book for Students 56 (1837) (11th and last edition, 1905). The final sentence Walker deleted already in the second edition. The rest of the quotation was retained through to the last edition in 1905. *See also* Paul Samuel Reinsch, The English Common Law in the Early American Colonies 8–9 (1899), *reprinted in* 1 Select Essays in Anglo-American Legal History 367, 370–371 (1907) (". . . on the basis of this indefinite notion there has been claimed for the courts an almost unlimited power, under the guise of selecting the applicable principles of the common law, of fixing really new and unprecedented rules and, by their adjudications, legislating in the fullest sense of the word.").

[61] St. George Tucker, *Note E, Of the Unwritten, or Common Law of England, and Its Introduction into, and Authority within the United American States, in* 1 Blackstone's Commentaries with Notes of Reference, to the Constitution and Laws, of the Federal Government of the United States; and of the Commonwealth of Virginia 378 (1803). In their introduction to the 1996 reprint of the St George Tucker's edition of Blackstone, Paul Finkelman and David Cobin explain that Tucker "placed much greater emphasis on legislation than Blackstone had." *Id.* at x–xi.

[62] Declaration of Independence.   [63] Brown, *supra* note 43, at 23–24.

[64] *See, e.g., Abolition of the Code Napoleon in the Rhenish Provinces,* 1 Jurist: Q.J. Juris. & Legisl. 246 (1827).

another example, continued Japanese law in force long after Japanese troops were expelled in 1945.[65] Although some states adopted by legislation specific British statutes, others did so by less precise means. Some legislatures just continued in force existing law. Others adopted English law specifically, but wholesale, by reference and without enumeration. Others did the same, but placed limits on which laws applied, of time (e.g., of a certain date or event) or nature (e.g., "general nature," "applicable" or "suitable" to America conditions).[66] All of these general measures left it to whoever applied the law – subject, governor or courts – to decide in particular cases whether English or British law applied.[67]

The *raison d'être* of the first volume of American reports of cases, Ephraim Kirby's reports in 1789 for Connecticut, a state where there was no reception statute, was the identification of which British statutes applied in the state.[68] Kirby acknowledged that his reports would not have been feasible had the Connecticut legislature in 1785 not required superior courts to give written reasons for their decisions when pleadings closed in issues at law.[69] Jesse Root, Connecticut's other reporter in the 18th century, likewise thought reports would help show which "laws of England and the civil law ... have been incorporated into our own system, and adapted to our own situations and circumstances."[70]

---

[65] *See* JAMES R. MAXEINER WITH GYOHOO LEE & ARMIN WEBER, FAILURES OF AMERICAN CIVIL JUSTICE IN AMERICAN CIVIL JUSTICE 276–281 (2011).

[66] BROWN, *supra* note 43, at 25–26 lists these in tabular form for the first years of the New Republic and then details them all through her book.

[67] *Cf.*, SAMUEL ROBERTS, A DIGEST OF SELECT BRITISH STATUTES, COMPRISING THOSE WHICH, ACCORDING TO THE REPORT OF THE JUDGES OF THE SUPREME COURT, MADE TO THE LEGISLATURE, APPEAR TO BE IN FORCE, IN PENNSYLVANIA, WITH SOME OTHERS xvi (1817) (noting that the judges' report was not determinative in later legal proceedings whether a particular English statute was in force in Pennsylvania).

[68] EPHRAIM KIRBY, REPORTS OF CASES ADJUDGED IN THE SUPERIOR COURT OF THE STATE OF CONNECTICUT FROM THE YEAR 1785 TO MAY 1789 WITH SOME DETERMINATIONS IN THE SUPREME COURT OF ERRORS iii (2d ed., 1898) (1st ed., 1789) ("Our courts were still in a state of embarrassment, sensible that the common law of England, 'though a highly improved system,' was not fully applicable to our situation; but no provision being made to preserve and publish proper histories of their adjudications, every attempt of the judges, to run the line of distinction, between what was applicable and what not, proved abortive: For the principles of their decisions were soon forgot, or misunderstood, or erroneously reported from memory.— Hence arose a confusion in the determination of our courts; — the rules of property became uncertain, and litigation proportionately increased.") *See* Alan V. Briceland, *Ephraim Kirby: Pioneer of American Law Reporting, 1789*, 16 AM. J. LEGAL HIST. 297, 302–305 (1972). Briceland also describes the difficulties Kirby had financing, producing and distributing the book.

[69] *Id.* at iii–iv.

[70] 1 JESSE ROOT, REPORTS OF CASES ADJUDGED IN THE SUPERIOR COURT AND SUPREME COURT OF ERRORS ... PREFACED WITH OBSERVATIONS UPON THE GOVERNMENT OF LAWS OF CONNECTICUT ... xiv (1798).

Such piecemeal adjudicatory determination was inadequate for the public. Some states simply repealed all British statutes. In other states, where British statutes were too numerous to repeal *in toto* or to adopt specifically, jurists, sometimes with legislative sanction, and sometimes without, compiled volumes of British statutes that they considered applicable to American conditions.[71] The purpose of these volumes was the same as that of compilations of the states' own statutes. So, wrote the author of a Georgia volume: "Now [the laws] are placed within the power of every man, and all may know the *statute* law of Georgia who chose to read it."[72]

Identifying and applying English common law presented greater hurdles still. In 1837 Justice Story, as Chair of a committee reporting to the state legislature, listed five prerequisites for applying a rule of English common law in Massachusetts: (1) was it was in force at the time of emigration; (2) had it since then remained unmodified by English statutes; (3) was it "applicable to the situation of the colony"; (4) had it been "recognized and acted upon"; and (5) "with this additional qualification, that it ha[d] not been altered, repealed, or modified by

---

[71] Georgia: WILLIAM SCHLEY, A DIGEST OF THE ENGLISH STATUTES OF FORCE IN THE STATE OF GEORGIA (1826);

  Kentucky: *Appendix. A Collection of All the Acts of Parliament Acts of Virginia, of a General Nature, Which Remain in Force in the State of Kentucky, in* 2 THE STATUTE LAW OF KENTUCKY; WITH NOTES, PRÆLECTIONS, AND OBSERVATIONS ON THE PUBLIC ACTS 493 (William Littell, Compiler, 1798);

  Maryland: WILLIAM KILTY, A REPORT OF ALL SUCH ENGLISH STATUTES AS EXISTED AT THE TIME OF THE FIRST EMIGRATION OF THE PEOPLE OF MARYLAND, AND WHICH BY EXPERIENCE HAVE BEEN FOUND APPLICABLE TO THEIR LOCAL AND OTHER CIRCUMSTANCES .... (1811); JULIAN J. ALEXANDER, A COLLECTION OF THE BRITISH STATUTES IN FORCE IN MARYLAND ACCORDING TO THE REPORT THEREOF MADE TO THE GENERAL ASSEMBLY BY THE LATE CHANCELLOR KILTY: WITH NOTES AND REFERENCES (1870) (2d revised ed. in two vols. by Ward Baldwin Coe, 1912);

  North Carolina: FRANÇOIS-XAVIER MARTIN (ED.), A COLLECTION OF THE STATUTES OF THE PARLIAMENT OF ENGLAND IN FORCE IN THE STATE OF NORTH-CAROLINA (1792). [It was said to be "utterly unworthy of the talents of the distinguished compiler, omitting many import statutes, always in force, and inserting many others, which never were, and never could have been in force ...." IREDELL & BATTLE, *supra* note 33, at xii];

  Pennsylvania: THE REPORT OF THE JUDGES OF THE SUPREME COURT OF THE PENNSYLVANIA OF THE ENGLISH STATUTES, WHICH ARE IN FORCE IN THE COMMONWEALTH OR PENNSYLVANIA; AND OF THOSE OF THE SAID STATUTES WHICH, IN THEIR OPINION, OUGHT TO BE INCORPORATED INTO THE STATUTE LAWS OF THE SAID COMMONWEALTH REPORTED ON THE 19TH AND 20TH OF DECEMBER 1808 (1808); SAMUEL ROBERTS, A DIGEST OF SELECT BRITISH STATUTES, COMPRISING THOSE WHICH ... APPEAL TO BE IN FORCE, IN PENNSYLVANIA (1817) (2d ed. by Robert E. Wright, 1847). *See also,* HUGH HENRY BRACKENRIDGE, *Note: Introductory to the Report of the Judges on the British Statutes in Force, &c.* [By an act of Assembly of April 7, 1807] *in* LAW MISCELLANIES .... 39 (1814).

[72] SCHLEY, *id.* at xvii (1826) ("hence the ignorance of many in regard to this branch of our laws, which was as much out the reach of the people, as were the laws of Caligula.")

any of our subsequent legislation now in force."[73] From this long checklist one might assume that little English common law was applied in Massachusetts.[74] Without an exhaustive examination of early court records and printed records, it is difficult to reach definitive conclusions. Suggestive that there was not much is the absence of English common-law volumes counterpart to the collections of applicable British statutes.[75] On the other hand, the absence may be indicative only of uncertainty.[76] In any case, by 1841 the *United States Magazine and Law Review* had had enough of the common law. It regretted any carryover of English law: the Founders "should have declared their independence not only of the government, but of the laws of the mother-country."[77]

Whatever was the extent of carryover of English 18th century common substantive law, that carryover does not validate contemporary common-law myth of lawmaking judges. At the beginning of the New Republic, common law, whether English or American, if there was such, was understood to be a preexisting body of rules that judges *discovered* and did not *create*. Judges declared law; they did not make it, so the judges said. Judges found law in long-existing customs, in statutes and in statute-like common-law writs. They

---

[73] REPORT OF THE COMMISSIONERS APPOINTED TO CONSIDER AND REPORT ON THE PRACTICABILITY AND EXPEDIENCY OF REDUCING TO A WRITTEN AND SYSTEMATIC CODE THE COMMON LAW OF MASSACHUSETTS OR ANY PART THEREOF 7 (1837).

[74] Professor Stoner quoting this passage observes: "To the modern reader, this sounds so qualified as to sever all relation, but Story is merely writing with his customary precision." JAMES R. STONER, JR., COMMON-LAW LIBERTY: RETHINKING AMERICAN CONSTITUTIONALISM 14 (2003).

[75] According to Cook, "Regrettably, no one has attempted to compile a list of received common law rules." CHARLES M. COOK, THE AMERICAN CODIFICATION MOVEMENT: A STUDY OF ANTEBELLUM LEGAL REFORM 12 (1981). Thanks to digitization, I found one exception: CHARLES HUMPHREYS, A COMPENDIUM OF THE COMMON LAW IN FORCE IN KENTUCKY, TO WHICH IS PREFIXED A BRIEF SUMMARY OF THE LAWS OF THE UNITED STATES (1822).

[76] *See* SCHLEY, *supra* note 72, at xvii–xviii (1826). Schley lamented that he could not provide the same service for common law: "But the common law is still in some measure unattainable by the people, being as it is, a collection of immemorial customs which are not written like the statute law, but handed down from one generation to another, by the decisions of the court of justice, which are said to be the evidence of the common law, and preserved in the various books of reports and elementary treatises, written by men who have made this subject their particular study. This branch of law then, from its nature, is not susceptible of being placed in a *tangible* form and handed to the people like the statute law; and therefore the General Assembly by giving us the following statutes, have done all they have power to do, unless, indeed, they should be disposed to new model our whole system of jurisprudence, and present us with a new code, *a la mode du code Napoleon.*" [Emphasis in original].

[77] *Edward Livingston and His Code, Second Article,* 9 U.S. MAG. & DEMOCRATIC REV. 211, 212 (1841). The article continued: "In consenting to adopt the Common Law as the rule of their civil existence, they brought upon themselves a vast and complicated system, which every year would render more cumbersome and intricate, and demonstrate its utter want of congeniality with the institutions they were about to establish, and the popular spirit and manners destined to grow up under their influence." *Id.*

"pretended" that common law consisted of statutes "worn out by time, their records having been lost."[78] The reports of their decisions were merely evidence of the law and not the law.[79] What Professor Stoner calls "the Great Transformation" to today's world of judges as lawmakers did not come until the second century of the Republic. Stoner dates it to the publication in 1881 of Oliver Wendell Holmes, Jr.'s book, *The Common Law*.[80]

Development of contemporary common law could hardly have come much sooner. The prerequisites were lacking. Common-law pleading and the lack of modern common-law bibliographic tools stood in the way. The system of common-law pleading used in England, and when copied in America, discouraged lawyers from urging judges to make law. Pleaders had to make a single issue of law or of fact determinative of the court's decision. If they sought to make new law through interpretation and failed, they lost the case.[81] Wise pleaders would seek to make new law only when absolutely necessary and then still describe the decision sought as applying old law. Moreover, much "new law" that courts made worked not to reform substantive law and justice, but to expand their own jurisdiction.[82]

C. EULOGIES OF ADAMS AND JEFFERSON

On July 4, 1826, the fiftieth anniversary of American Independence, the two men most responsible for drafting and adopting the Declaration of Independence, John Adams and Thomas Jefferson, both died. The coincidence was taken as a sign from heaven blessing the American enterprise. Across the country there were

---

[78] See WALKER, *supra* note 60, at 53.

[79] See generally, *id.* at 53; WILLIAM G. HAMMOND, *Not Delegated to Pronounce a New Law but to Maintain and Expound the Old One*, (note 30) in 1 WILLIAM BLACKSTONE, COMMENTARIES ON THE LAWS OF ENGLAND ... EDITED FOR AMERICAN LAWYERS 213–226 (William G. Hammond, ed., 1890); EUGENE WAMBAUGH, THE STUDY OF CASES 75–80 (2d ed., 1894); *see also* STONER, *supra* note 74, at 3 and 11.

[80] STONER, *supra* note 74, at 25–29.

[81] *Cf.*, THEODORE F.T. PLUCKNETT, STATUTES & THEIR INTERPRETATION IN THE FIRST HALF OF THE FOURTEENTH CENTURY 3–4 (1922) (observing of 14th century pleading, "there were circumstances under which a clever pleader would offer up ... puzzling points, for the simple reason that he had no better matter to advance. Judges, however, were men of plain common sense, and not infrequently put an abrupt end to such attempts to 'embarrass the court,' whereupon the ingenious pleader would immediately offer to take issue on some simple matter of fact.").

[82] *See, e.g.*, 3 WILLIAM BLACKSTONE, COMMENTARIES ON THE LAWS OF ENGLAND 43, 103, 107 (1768) (accepting as irrebuttable plea that contract was made in England in order to give common law court over jurisdiction of civil law court). *See* Louisa Harmon, *Falling Off the Vine: Legal Fictions and the Doctrine of Substituted Judgment*, 100 YALE L. J. 1, 5–9 (1990).

joint eulogies. Nineteen of these were collected and issued in a single volume the same year as *A Selection of Eulogies Pronounced in the Honor of Those Illustrious Patriots and Statesmen, John Adams and Thomas Jefferson*. What do those eulogies suggest?

The book has only two mentions of common law and a like number of mentions of civil law. The former are negative or neutral, while the latter are positive. The first mention of common law in the collection of eulogies is that of the young Caleb Cushing, who later would be Attorney General of the United States, commissioner charged with revising the federal statutes, and President Grant's nominee to be Chief Justice of the United States. Cushing in his eulogy remembered that Adams and Jefferson were both educated to the bar. But they were not educated in law as they would have been in England, "to the barbarous technicalities of the common law," but in the American way "where the study is more a study of principles."[83]

The first mention of civil law in the collection is that of the lawyer, editor and author Samuel L. Knapp. He reported that Adams's mentor, Jeremy Gridley, Attorney General of the Province of Massachusetts Bay, told Adams that the secret of his eminence was his "collection of treatises on the civil law, with the institutes, of Justinian, whereupon "Mr. Adams spent his days and nights, until he made himself a good master of the code."[84]

The second and last mentions of both common law and civil law are by William Wirt, then the Attorney General of the United States and to this day the longest-serving Attorney General ever. Wirt referred to the common law as the mundane part of Jefferson's law studies: "The study of the law he pursued under George Wythe; a man of Roman stamp, in Rome's best age. . . . Here, too, following the giant step of his master, he travelled the whole round of the civil and common law."[85]

Most of the nineteen eulogists remembered Adams and Jefferson for the government and the legislation that they created. John Tyler, then governor of Virginia and later President of the United States, rejoiced of Jefferson: "The

---

[83] Caleb Cushing, *Eulogy, Pronounced at Newburyport, Massachusetts, July 15, 1826, in* A SELECTION OF EULOGIES PRONOUNCED IN THE HONOR OF THOSE ILLUSTRIOUS PATRIOTS AND STATESMEN, JOHN ADAMS AND THOMAS JEFFERSON 19, 29–30 (1826).

[84] Samuel L. Knapp, *Eulogy, Pronounced at Boston, Massachusetts, August 2, 1826, in* SELECTION OF EULOGIES, *supra* note 83, at 174, 175, 176. Adams' knowledge of civil law was extensive. *See* David S. Clark, *Comparative Law in Colonial British America*, 59 AM. J. COMP. L. 637, 663–673 (2011); Daniel R. Coquillette, *Justinian in Braintree: John Adams, Civilian Learning, and Legal Elitism, 1758–1775, in* LAW IN COLONIAL MASSACHUSETTS: 1630–1800, at 359 (1984).

[85] William Wirt, *Eulogy Pronounced at the City of Washington, October 19, 1826, in* SELECTION OF EULOGIES, *supra* note 83, at 379, 396.

statute book of this state, almost all that is wise in policy or sanctified by justice, bears the impress of his genius . . . ." Tyler recalled that Jefferson's laws abolished the common law of entails and descents.[86] Daniel Webster, then representative in Congress, orator par excellence, and the nation's most celebrated Supreme Court advocate, recounted the careers of Adams and Jefferson and noted Jefferson's "important service of revising the laws of Virginia . . . ."[87] Less well-known eulogist Sheldon Smith might have spoken for the nation when he said of Adams and Jefferson: "They formed a system of government, and a code of laws, such as the wisdom of man had never before devised."[88]; On the last page of the collection, Attorney General Wirt let Jefferson speak for himself . He quoted the inscription Jefferson directed for his gravestone: "Here was buried: Thomas Jefferson, Author of the Declaration of Independence, Of the Statutes of Virginia, for Religious Freedom, And Father of the University of Virginia."[89]

These eulogies put to rest the myth that America's founders founded a common law country.

---

[86] John Tyler, *Eulogy, Pronounced at Richmond, Virginia, July 11, 1826, in* SELECTION OF EULOGIES, *supra* note 83, at 5, 8.

[87] Daniel Webster, *Eulogy, Pronounced at Boston, Massachusetts, August 2, 1826, in* SELECTION OF EULOGIES, *supra* note 83, at 193, 223.

[88] Sheldon Smith, *Eulogy, Pronounced at Buffalo, New-York, July, 22d 1826, in* SELECTION OF EULOGIES, *supra* note 83, at 91, 94.

[89] Wirt, *supra* note 85, at 426.

5

Building a Government of Laws in the
First Century of the Republic

A government of laws rests on institutions. In the first century of the Republic Americans looked to written laws – constitutions and statutes – to build those institutions. They adopted statutes to guide society. They taught their children and each other about those statutes. They used those statutes – without judicial intervention – to apply law. There was ample justification for the Centennial Writers in 1876 to see "The *great* fact in the progress of American jurisprudence which deserves special notice and reflection is its tendency towards *organic statute law* and towards the *systematizing of law*; in other words, towards *written constitutions* and *codification.*"[1]

A. CONSTITUTIONS

Before there was the Declaration of Independence there was what Gordon S. Wood calls "the real declaration of independence:" the resolution of the Second Continental Congress of May 10 and 15, 1776 recommending the assemblies of the United Colonies create new governments as "best conduce to the happiness and safety of the constituents."[2] The Founders were serious about creating a government of laws.

By 1780 all but two states (Connecticut and Rhode Island) had followed the recommendation of the Continental Congress and had adopted written constitutions for new governments. Americans did not stop adopting constitutions

---

[1]   G.T. Bispham, *Law in America*, 1776–1876, 122 N. AM. REV. 154, 174 (1876) [emphasis in
      original].
[2]   GORDON S. WOOD, THE CREATION OF THE AMERICAN REPUBLIC, 1776–1787, 132 (1969).

Washington giving the Laws to America[3] [holding "The American Constitution"] Anonymous, ca. 1800. Washington as President of the Convention transmitted the Constitution to Congress.

[3] *Washington giving the laws to America* [ca. 1800]. Retrieved from the Library of Congress, https://www.loc.gov/item/2014645020/. (Accessed Feb. 24, 2017.)

then. In 1782 they adopted the Articles of Confederation and, when those Articles proved inadequate, in 1787 they published the Constitution of the United States. When new states joined the Union, they adopted their own constitutions. When state constitutions fell behind the times, states amended or replaced them. In 1876, coincident with the centennial of independence, the United States Senate ordered publication of the states' constitutions to that date. The collection required two over-sized volumes of more than 2,100 pages.[4] By 1887, the centennial of the drafting of the U.S. Constitution, by one count, the United States had adopted one hundred four state constitutions (including Connecticut and Rhode Island) and two hundred and fourteen partial amendments.[5] Americans in the first century of the Republic were serious about building governments of laws.

Conventional wisdom today, in the shadow of contemporary common-law myth, holds that constitutional changes are a bad thing.[6] But in the 19th century amendments were thought to be essential for improvement.[7] Legal educator and judge George Sharswood may have had that in mind when in 1860 on the eve of the Civil War he wrote: "How sublime a spectacle it is to behold a great nation ... engaged peacefully and calmly in considering, and determining by the light of reason and experience those deeply interesting and exciting questions which in other countries and

---

[4] THE FEDERAL AND STATE CONSTITUTIONS, COLONIAL CHARTERS, AND OTHER ORGANIC LAWS OF THE UNITED STATES, 2 vols. (Ben Perley Poore, compiler, 1877). Poore's collection was updated by THE FEDERAL AND STATE CONSTITUTIONS COLONIAL CHARTERS, AND OTHER ORGANIC LAWS OF THE STATES, TERRITORIES, AND COLONIES NOW OR HERETOFORE FORMING THE UNITED STATES OF AMERICA COMPILED AND EDITED UNDER THE ACT OF CONGRESS OF JUNE 30, 1906 BY FRANCIS NEWTON THORPE (7 vols. 1909).

[5] Henry Hitchcock, AMERICAN STATE CONSTITUTIONS: A STUDY OF THEIR GROWTH 13–14 (1887).

[6] *See* Lawrence M. Friedman, *State Constitutions in Historical Perspective*, in STATE CONSTITUTIONS IN A FEDERAL SYSTEM, 496 THE ANNALS OF THE AMERICAN ACADEMY OF POLITICAL AND SOCIAL SCIENCE 33, 35 (1988). Conventional wisdom may be changing: leading jurists, including Supreme Court justices, have called for constitutional amendments in light of lawmaking failures. *See, e.g.*, PHILIP K. HOWARD, RULE OF NOBODY: SAVING AMERICA FROM DEAD LAWS AND BROKEN GOVERNMENT 179–183 (2014) (proposing a "Bill of Responsibilities" consisting of five amendments); JOHN PAUL STEVENS, SIX AMENDMENTS: HOW AND WHY WE SHOULD CHANGE THE CONSTITUTION (2014). *See also* THOMAS E. BRENNAN, THE ARTICLE V AMENDATORY CONSTITUTIONAL CONVENTION: KEEPING THE REPUBLIC IN THE TWENTY-FIRST CENTURY (2014).

[7] JOHN ALEXANDER JAMESON, THE CONSTITUTIONAL CONVENTION; ITS HISTORY, POWERS AND MODE OF PROCEEDING § 81, 80 (3d ed., 1873). The first edition appeared in 1867; the 4th and last, in the centennial year of the U.S. Constitution, 1887. I cite the third edition as the one just before the 1876 Centennial. *See* Roman J. Hoyos, *A Province of Jurisprudence?: Invention of a Law of Constitutional Conventions*, in LAW BOOKS IN ACTION: ESSAYS ON THE ANGLO-AMERICAN LEGAL TREATISE 81 (Angels Fernandez and Markus D. Dubber, eds., 2012).

other ages not far remote were settled on the battle-field or in more terrific
scenes of domestic revolution."[8]

In the decade of the 1860s the United States adopted what has sometimes
been called "the second constitution," i.e, the Civil War amendments, the
13th, 14th and 15th amendments.[9] They (finally) abolished the scourge of
slavery from the country. But the United States had to settle these issues on
the battlefield.

At the end of the 19th century, in 1897 James Schouler, newly elected
president of the American Historical Association and law treatise writer, in
his inaugural address, proposed "A New Federal Convention" to change the
Constitution. Schouler contrasted the absence of "constructive statesman-
ship" in the federal constitution with amendments of state constitutions
where one could see "American ingenuity still at work." He proposed that
the convention consider, among other issues, "improved modes of federal
legislation."[10]

In the 19th century Americans used constitutional conventions to
change their framework laws. Constitutional conventions were so common –
192 by 1876 – that John Alexander Jameson wrote a 684-page treatise on
their "history, powers and modes of proceeding." His book appeared in four
editions from 1867 to 1887.[11] At a time of general legislative stinginess, the
people or their representatives repeatedly brought expensive conventions
into being.

There was a less-expensive alternative: unwritten constitutions – a mix of
judge-made law and interpreted statutes – as was the case in England. Yet in
the United States, all constitutions save two in early Connecticut and Rhode
Island have been written. Why? According to Jameson for the same reasons
that one might prefer statute law to common law. "Precisely the same distinction exists between written and unwritten Constitutions":

> An unwritten Constitution is made up largely of customs and judicial
> decision, the former more or less evanescent and intangible ...; and the

---

[8]   Sir William Blackstone, Commentaries on the Laws of England, Vol. 4, 443 n. 4, 646
      (George Sharswood ed., 1860).
[9]   *See, e.g.*, Garrett Epps, Democracy Reborn: The Fourteenth Amendment and the
      Fight for Equal Rights in Post–Civil War America (2007); James R. Stoner, Jr.,
      Common Law Liberty: Rethinking American Constitutionalism 1 (2003).
[10] James Schouler, *A New Federal Convention*, Annual Report of the American Historical
      Association 19, 24, 28 (1898), also separately printed as well as reprinted in James Schouler,
      Ideals of the Republic 289 (1908).
[11] The count is from the fourth edition of Jameson, *supra* note 7 at 655.

latter composing a vast body of isolated cases having no connecting bond but the slender thread of principle running through them, a thread often broken, sometimes recurrent, and never to be estimated as a whole but by tracing it through its entire course in the thousand volumes of law reports.[12]

"Not so with written Constitutions," he continued. Such constitutions are "statutes merely." Like well-written statutes, they can reduce the ground for interpretation; they cannot and should not eliminate all interpretation. "The field thus provided for construction," Jameson wrote, "though infinitely narrower than in unwritten Constitutions, is still ample, for a Constitution can only deal in generalities, whereas its application to particular cases is precisely that which must daily be determined."[13]

In discussing the difference between applying a written constitution and applying an unwritten one, Jameson made a perceptive point that is equally valid to the difference between applying statute law and case law. Applying unwritten law adds an extra and difficult step: "the duty of those who construe a written Constitution is merely, first, to ascertain the meaning of the general clause of it covering the case; and, secondly, to determine its application to the particular facts in question." In interpreting an unwritten constitution, "this inquiry must be prefaced by another still more difficult [task] . . .; it first inquires what the terms of the law are and then proceeds to determine their meaning and application."[14] That extra step undercuts self-application of law.

Jameson saw written constitutions as inhibiting judge-made law: "If judicial legislation is an evil, written Constitutions are clearly barriers in the way of its progress." But "how far are they advantageous on the whole?"[15] He agreed with Jefferson that an important benefit is that "they fix. . . for the people the principles of their political creed."[16] He saw the major drawback in inflexibility of amendment. Constitutions required efficient mechanisms for amendment, which are neither too restrictive nor too lax.[17]

B. CONSTITUTIONAL CONVENTIONS

State constitutions are just one place to look for American views of statute law and common law. The debates that gave rise to them are goldmines for

---

[12] *Id.* at 76. [13] *Id.* [14] *Id.* at 77. [15] *Id.* at 78.
[16] *Id.* at 78 (quoting Letter to Dr. Priestly, 4 *Works* at 441) [17] *Id.* at 80–81.

EUREKA. 1849: California Constitutional Convention's Great Seal[18]

exploring American legal culture.[19] People cared about their constitutions. In Pennsylvania they cared so much that they published the proceedings of the convention begun in 1837 in fourteen volumes in English *and* in an additional fourteen volumes in German translation![20] Use of written or unwritten law arose in disparate issues affecting legal methods, such as incorporation by

[18] Bayard Taylor, *Great Seal of California*, N.Y. WEEKLY TRIBUNE, Dec. 12, 1849, p. 1. *See* J. ROSS BROWNE, REPORT OF THE DEBATES IN THE CONVENTION OF CALIFORNIA ON THE FORMATION OF THE STATE CONSTITUTION IN SEPTEMBER AND OCTOBER, 1849, 467 (1850)

[19] *Cf.*, WILLIAMJAMES HULL HOFFER, TO ENLARGE THE MACHINERY OF GOVERNMENT: CONGRESSIONAL DEBATES AND THE GROWTH OF THE AMERICAN STATE, 1858–1891 x (2007) ("one finds a treasure trove of thinking about the nature and function of government embedded in the debates on particular pieces of legislation."). *See* James R. Maxeiner, *Bane of American Forfeiture Law: Banished at Last?*, 62 CORNELL L. REV. 768 (1977) (using Congressional debates over the Civil War confiscation acts to gain insights into contemporary forfeiture law).

[20] PROCEEDINGS AND DEBATES OF THE CONVENTION OF THE COMMONWEALTH OF PENNSYLVANIA TO PROPOSE AMENDMENTS TO THE CONSTITUTION COMMENCED AND HELD AT HARRISBURG ON THE SECOND DAY OF MAY, 1837 (John Agg, compiler, 14 vols. 1837–1839), hereafter PENNSYLVANIA 1837–1839 PROCEEDINGS, *published in German as* VERHANDLUNGEN UND DEBATTEN DER CONVENTION DER REPUBLIK PENNSYLVANIEN UM VERBESSERUNGEN ZU DER CONSTITUTION VORZUSCHLAGEN, ANGEFANGEN UND GEHALTEN ZU HARRISBURG, AM ZWEITEN MAI, 1837 (14 vols., 1837–1839).

reference of foreign law,[21] constitutional mandates for codification of state laws,[22] length of legislative terms,[23] judicial life tenure,[24] election of judges,[25] and Supreme Court judges' circuit riding.[26]

Into these debates scholars today can dig from their desktops to uncover buried gold. The California Convention of 1849 is a particularly rewarding dig because contemporaries throughout the nation saw California government as a national achievement accomplished by the tens of thousands of Americans from around the country who settled California in only two years. Looking back in 1881 legal educator William G. Hammond recalled: "That wonderful state was the first to grow up to full maturity almost in a night and to create a judiciary, a bar, and the entire organization of the state government, of men suddenly brought together from all parts of the continent."[27]

---

[21] Thoroughly researched with respect to English statutes in the pre-digital age is ELIZABETH GASPAR BROWN, BRITISH STATUTES IN AMERICAN LAW 1776–1836 (1964). Several Constitutions incorporate by reference English common law and statutes up to a particular time. Louisiana constitutions have prohibited adoption of foreign law.

[22] *See* text at notes 275–294, *infra.*   [23] *See* text at note 39, *infra.*

[24] E.g., 10 PENNSYLVANIA 1837–1839 PROCEEDINGS, *supra* note 20, at 195–204 (remarks of Mr. Read) (arguing that life tenure had not worked well, gave judges "despotic power," allowed them to "change the law according to their own caprice," at 201; permitted them to "unblushingly avow their determination to *make law*" and disregard "the plainly expressed intention of the *legislature*, at 202; and leading to "a glaring usurpation of legislative power," at 203).

[25] *Id.* at 159, 162 (Remarks of Mr. Biddle) (arguing that election of judges would threaten "that uniform and consistent symmetry, which should exist in a system of laws, and which is so essential in the administration of justice.").

[26] E.g., REPORT OF THE PROCEEDINGS AND DEBATES IN THE CONVENTION TO REVISE THE CONSTITUTION OF THE STATE OF MICHIGAN. 1850, at 640 (1850) (remarks of Mr. Goodwin) (arguing against the asserted benefits of judges of the Supreme Court holding local circuit courts to obtain popular sentiment: "The application and construction of the laws and the construction of statutes are neither of them to be determined or aided by popular sentiment and popular impulses, as has been in fact suggested. The interpretation of statutes is to be ascertained from the statutes themselves, and those rules of construction which reason and good sense have established; and the rules of the common law are to be determined by the investigation of its principles and reasons, in reports and other books of authority, and the exercise of sound judgment in their application to facts as they are presented, and circumstances as they arise in the progress of things. The judges are not to make the law, but to determine what it is, and apply it to the case presented.").

[27] WM. G. HAMMOND, AMERICAN LAW SCHOOLS IN THE PAST AND IN THE FUTURE 5 (1881). Hammond elaborated: "Its law and practice were constructed from materials gathered in every state of the union." *Id.* It modeled its Constitution on the New York Constitution of 1846 and the Iowa Constitution of 1844. CARDINAL GOODWIN, THE ESTABLISHMENT OF STATE GOVERNMENT IN CALIFORNIA 1846–1850, at 230–246 (1914). California considered adoption of Mexican civil law, but chose "American common law." *Report on Civil and Common Law*, 1 REPORTS OF CASES … IN THE SUPREME COURT OF THE STATE OF CALIFORNIA 588 (1851). In 1872 California adopted Field's five codes.

Reading the 1849 California debates one finds nuggets. One is whether the California constitution should incorporate, in deviation from the English common-law rule, the then new rule of modern American statutes of separate property for married women. Conditions in California made the issue ripe for challenge since existing law was not the English common law of coverture (no separate property) but the Mexican civil law (of separate marital property rights).

One proponent of separate property promoted it as one of "many excellent provisions in the civil law" that had been the "law of the land" under which "native Californians" had "always lived."[28] Another recommended it as a practical way to get women to immigrate to California: "It is the very best provision to get us wives that we can introduce into the Constitution."[29] Still another attacked the English common-law rule as having its origin "in a barbarous age;" in the "nice distinctions of the common law," "the principle so much glorified" was "that the husband shall be a despot, and the wife shall have no right but such as he chooses to award her."[30]

Advocates of English common-law coverture countered: "we tread upon dangerous ground when we make an invasion upon that system which has prevailed among ourselves and our ancestors for hundreds and hundreds of years."[31] They made a nationalist argument: "The great mass must live under the common law. It would be unjust to require the immense mass of Americans to yield their own system to that of the minority."[32]

Still others defended the substance of the English common-law rule itself: "there is no provision so beautiful in the common law, so admirable and beneficial, as that which regulates this sacred contract between man and wife. ... Nature did what the common law has done – put [wife] under protection of man."[33]

Opponents made the methodological argument that it would be better to try the new rule as a statute that the legislature could revise or repeal if experiences were adverse.[34] Proponents of separate property used the debate over separate property to make their own methodological arguments against

---

[28] J. Ross Browne, Report of the Debates in the Convention of California on the Formation of the State Constitution in September and October, 1849 at 258 (Remarks of Mr. Tefft).

[29] *Id.* at 259 (1850) (remarks of Mr. Halleck). Henry Wage Halleck was Secretary of State of the military government and a principal drafter of the constitution. Later he authored international and comparative law books and in the Civil War served as General in Chief of the Union Armies in the East.

[30] *Id.* at 264 (remarks of Mr. Jones).   [31] *Id.* at 257 (remarks of Mr. Lippitt).

[32] *Id.* at 260–261 (remarks of Mr. Lippitt).   [33] *Id.* at 259 (remarks of Mr. Botts).

[34] *Id.* at 258 (remarks of Mr. Lippitt).

adopting English common law of any kind. One said: "Sir, I want no such system; the inhabitants of this country want no such system; the Americans of this country want no such thing. They want a code of simple laws which they can understand; no common law, full of exploded principles with nothing to recommend it but some dog latin, or the opinions of some lawyer who lived a hundred years ago."[35]

In short, said this proponent of statute law: "They want something the people can comprehend." He explained that: "the law is the will of the people properly expressed, and that the people have a right to understand their own will and derive the advantage of it, without going to a lawyer to have it expounded."[36]

One delegate, reared in common-law faith, reacted in shock: "for the first time in my life, to hear the common law reviled; yes sir, that which has been the admiration of all ages . . . has been in this House, this night, spoken of with contempt and derision."[37]

The Convention voted with the proponents of statute law and against a substitute proposal that would have retained common-law coverture.[38]

The married women's property rights issue was not the only instance when the Convention weighed use of written versus unwritten law. It considered whether it had authority to appoint a commission of three persons to form a code of laws to be submitted to the legislature at its first session. In the end, it tabled the motion, but in consequence directed that the legislature meet every year and not every other year as the motion's proponent favored.[39]

C. STATUTES

A government of laws is a government of written laws, i.e., constitutions and statutes. Statutes are inevitable in modern government. Statutes are how modern societies democratically decide what they shall do. Statutes are how democracies inform people and guide their officials. Statutes are the people's

---

[35] *Id.* at 264 (remarks of Mr. Jones).
[36] *Id.* The speaker continued: "Where is this common law that we must all revert to? Has the gentleman from Monterey got it? Can he produce it? Did he ever see it? Where are the ten men in the United States that perfectly understand, appreciate, and know this common law? I should like to find them. When that law is brought into this House – when these thousand musty volumes of jurisprudence are brought in here and we are told this is the law of the mass – I want gentlemen to tell me how to understand it. I am no opponent of the common law, nor am I advocate of he civil law. Sir, I am an advocate of all such law as the people can understand." *Id.*
[37] *Id.* at 268 (remarks of Mr. Botts).   [38] *Id.* at 269.   [39] *Id.* at 76–82, 301–304, 322.

Amerika's Gesetze von I. Lehman[40] (America's Statutes by I. Lehman) [Justitia holding
Constitution and Statute Laws] A guide to written law for German-Americans

---

[40] I. LEHMANN, AMERIKA'S GESETZE (1857).

directions for modernization: they throw out the old and bring in the new. In the first century of the Republic statutes drove out English law; statutes gave the American people new and better rules.

1. *Necessity of Statutes*

Were there only a constitution establishing a government, but no statutes to structure the government and to guide governing, there would be a government of men. Precedents cannot create institutions. Precedents can determine who was right in the past, where there is general agreement on what is right, but not what is better policy for the future. Precedents assume existing institutions; they cannot create new ones. Precedents assume consensus; they cannot legitimate commands where consensus is absent.

Written statutes are a corollary to written constitutions.[41] American legislatures lost no time adopting statutes. Virginia led in the New Republic thanks to Jefferson, but was not alone. Legislatures passed statutes on just about any imaginable subject. By the 1840s, according to one civics text, "Almost every transaction of life is regulated by laws."[42] But making good laws is hard.[43] The Centennial Writers touched on some issues.

The "Jurisprudence" essay of *The First Century of the Republic* cheerfully characterized organized American legislation as four tones sounding together to make the "common chord" of the "ear of 1876": (1) divine authority underlying human law, (2) willingness to obey for the present existing law, (3) confidence in ability to improve the forms and modes of law as growth warranted, and (4) a resolute purpose to make that improvement in due season.[44] The "Law in America: 1776–1876" essay of *The North American Review* affirmatively concluded that three headings captured how American law in the past century had progressed to become "(1) more simple, (2) more humane and (3) more adaptive."[45]

The First Century of the Republic eschewed stating details. Even in a single jurisdiction that would be impossible in a brief and accurate epitome. "In our country such difficulty is increased by the consideration that the law in all its

---

[41] *Cf.* TIMOTHY WALKER, INTRODUCTION TO AMERICAN LAW, DESIGNED AS A FIRST BOOK FOR STUDENTS (1st ed., 1837) ("our constitutional law has been codified to the admiration of the world, while that of England still remains unwritten, a heavy mass of doubtful precedents. . . . Again, the criminal law both of the United States, and of our own state [Ohio], has been likewise codified."). The last, 11th ed., appeared in 1915.

[42] SAMUEL G. GOODRICH, THE YOUNG AMERICAN: OR BOOK OF GOVERNMENT AND LAW; SHOWING THEIR HISTORY, NATURE, AND NECESSITY; FOR THE USE OF SCHOOLS 35 (8th ed., 1847).

[43] *See* Chapter 1, Section B, *supra.*

[44] Benjamin Vaughn Abbott, *American Jurisprudence*, in THE FIRST CENTURY OF THE REPUBLIC: A REVIEW OF AMERICAN PROGRESS 434 (1876).

[45] *Law in America: 1776–1876, supra* note 1, 122 NORTH AM. REV. at 191.

details differs exceedingly in different States. . . . Hence in matters of law it is not possible to give concise, simple answers, which shall be accurate, to even the simplest questions."[46]

Each state had (and has) its own books of statutes and, eventually, its own books of case reports. In 1876, *The First Century of The Republic* estimated, that just the volumes in current use, including statutes, reports, treatises and journals, had counted more than three thousand volumes. That count made no measure of the multitude of legislative materials appearing separately in pamphlets and addressed again and again in successive revisions and reenactments.

The outpouring of legislative materials in America to 1876 already was enormous.[47] In 1906 the State Library of Massachusetts published a "Hand-List of statute law" in which it made "the effort to record every legislative session and every volume containing session laws or revisions and compilations of law." It disclaimed completeness. It chose to publish a "Hand-List" and not a catalogue to save time and money. The *Hand-List* includes only a few non-official materials, e.g., contemporaneous or historic discussions of statutes. Yet, so limited, the list is more than six hundred pages long and includes more than 10,000 entries.[48]

Behind each entry is a statute – or more commonly several or many statutes – to which a legislature devoted hours, days, weeks, months or even years of attention. One page of a statute, even a hastily drafted one, is likely to have required more human attention than one page of a case report. Yet common-law myth acknowledges only the latter and ignores the former.

2. *Statutes for Progress*

What did all these statutes address? In the first century of the Republic new statutes had two principal tasks: changing existing rules, often originating in England, and creating new rules to deal with a modern world.[49]

---

[46] *Id.*

[47] Already in 1836 James Paulding parodied the urge to legislation: "Like many modern legislators of the present time, a single fact was sufficient ground for passing half a dozen great wordy laws, which, after all, nobody obeyed." 1 JAMES KIRKE PAULDING, KONINGSMARKE: OR, OLD TIMES IN THE NEW WORLD 174 (Revised ed., 1836).

[48] STATE LIBRARY OF MASSACHUSETTS, HAND-LIST OF LEGISLATIVE SESSIONS AND SESSION LAWS, STATUTORY REVISIONS, COMPILATIONS, CODES, ETC., AND CONSTITUTIONAL CONVENTIONS (1912).

[49] Along similar lines, but asserting a dominant though not exclusive role for unwritten law, *see* E.W. [presumably Emory Washburn], *We Need a Criminal Code*, 7 AM. L. REV. 264 (1872). *See also* Thomas H. Watts, Sr., *Report of the Committee on Jurisprudence and Law Reform of the Alabama State Bar Association (1879) Jurisprudence and Law Reform*, 1 SO. L.J. & REPORTER 81, 82 (1880) ("It is rare that any changes of the common law made by statute have benefitted the public or its business.")

Replacing English Common Law with Statutes

It should be no surprise that Jefferson sought to get rid of English common law.[50] American legislatures followed Virginia's lead and by statutes overturned the heart of English common law: property law, criminal law and civil procedure. Here is a partial list:

- Statutes, not precedents, ended English common-law tenures and created modern ones.
- Statutes, not precedents, abolished English common-law coverture and created married women's property rights.
- Statutes, not precedents, ended English descents and created modern ones.
- Statutes, not precedents, ended English criminal law and created criminal codes.
- Statutes, not precedents, ended English criminal procedure and created counsel-based criminal trials.
- Statutes, not precedents, ended English pleading and created code pleading.

In other words, Americans could look at their statutes with pride, as one Ohioan did: "if our legislation has been excessively variable and fluctuating ... it has at least the merit of doing away many of the abuses which have come down to us with the common law, by introducing simplicity in the place of technicality."[51]

New Laws for a New World

Getting rid of old laws alone was not enough to create the new American order which rapid changes in life of the 19th century demanded. The first century of the Republic required new laws and new applications of old laws. Early in the 19th century America began making new laws needed for a modern economy of national travel, fast communication, mass production, national markets and national corporations, in which people could make their own choices. The Centennial Writers saw that.

Common-law myth, already in the early 20th century, held that Americans should thank judges for the "vast body of jurisprudence ... built up to meet these new and unexpected conditions of society."[52] Modern American law was, according to the myth, "the work of the judges and the lawyers, aided or

[50] Virginia by Act of December 27, 1792 ended application of British statutes that the Revisal had not included in its text. *See* HERBERT A. JOHNSON, HISTORY OF THE SUPREME COURT OF THE UNITED STATES, OLIVER WENDELL HOMES DEVISE HISTORY VOLUME II, FOUNDATIONS OF POWER: JOHN MARSHALL, 1801–1815, 562 (1981).

[51] *Ohio Legislation*, 11 AM. JURIST & L. MAG. 91, 100 (1834).

[52] William B. Hornblower, *A Century of Judge-Made Law, Address before the School of Law of Columbia University, June 16, 1907*, 7 COLUMBIA L. REV. 453 (1907).

interfered with only occasionally by statutory provisions."[53] Yesterday's myth is today's conventional wisdom. One text writes, "Antebellum judges dethroned the English common law by Americanizing it."[54] A noted monograph takes as its point of departure: "Especially during the period before the Civil War the common law performed as great a role as legislation in underwriting and channeling economic development."[55]

That was not the view of the Centennial Writers.[56] It was not the view of a leading common-law proponent a century ago. In 1908, Harvard Law School, basking in the teaching triumph of the case method, was the epicenter of emerging American common-law myth. Yet Cambridge icon Charles Warren in discussing "The New Law: 1830–1860" in his semi-official history of Harvard Law School, even as he paid homage to the role of common law, gave more credit to "the simplification of the law by codes and statutary [sic] revisions, *for the benefit of laymen as well as lawyers.*"[57]

In twenty of twenty-five pages in his *New Law* chapter, Warren cataloged changes in fifteen areas of law: mill act and watercourse law, the law of torts, telegraph law, gas corporation law, street railway law, grain elevator law, insurance law, patent law, copyright law, trademark law, insolvency and bankruptcy law, labor law, married women, criminal law and the law of evidence. In each of his entries, judges appear as handmaidens to statutes, if they appear at all. Expanding on Warren's list and considering the reports of the Centennial Writers, the following seem true:

- Statutes, not precedents, created the post office and provided for carrying the mails.
- Statutes, not precedents, created corporations.

[53] *Id.* For an extreme statement from the 20th century, *see* J.A. Corey, *Book Review,* 9 CANADIAN J. ECONOMICS & POL. SCI. 265, 266 (1953) (there was "only an infinitesimal amount of law-making by legislatures until after the middle of the nineteenth century").
[54] KERMIT L. HALL, THE MAGIC MIRROR: LAW IN AMERICAN HISTORY 109 (1989). In the posthumous second edition of Hall's work (2008), Peter Karsten deletes the quoted sentence and writes instead "To a certain extent, American jurists in the first century of the 'new nation' altered or 'Americanized" some English common law."
[55] MORTON J. HORWITZ, TRANSFORMATION OF AMERICAN LAW 1780–1860, at 1 (1977). Roscoe Pound, on the other hand, saw a common-law contribution coming to an end by the Civil War, lingering in some places to 1875. He discounted judge-made law: "Our case law is incapable of solving new problems or of meeting new situations of vital importance to present-day life. ... we have had to turn to legislation." Roscoe Pound, *Law in Books and Law in Action,* 44 AM. L. REV. 12, 22–23, 32 (1910).
[56] *See* THE FIRST CENTURY OF THE REPUBLIC at 451–452 (a "Brief Retrospect" listing many areas where America had achieved "systems of laws.").
[57] *Id.* at 234 [emphasis added].

- Statutes, not precedents, created common schools and provided for educating children.
- Statutes, not precedents, governed distribution of public lands.
- Statutes, not precedents, created state land-grant colleges.
- Statutes, not precedents, regulated trade in alcohol and explosives, sometimes controversially ("license laws").
- Statutes, not precedents, guarded the public health, *e.g.*, authorizing quarantines.
- Statutes, not precedents, regulated navigation and merchant seamen.
- Statutes, not precedents, created taxes and provided for tax collection.
- Statutes, not precedents, created new government offices.
- Statutes, not precedents, created election laws.
- Statutes, not precedents, created protections for civil rights.
- Statutes, not precedents, governed immigration.
- Statutes, not precedents, infamously constrained internal emigration (fugitive slave laws).
- Statutes, more than precedents, regulated and protected the public in steamboat and railroad traffic.
- Statutes, more than precedents, regulated and protected the public in markets.

America could and did legislate. The first century of the Republic and its *Golden Age of American Law*[58] was itself an "Age of Statutes."

D. CIVICS

Common-law myth holds that following the American Revolution, "The content and method of the common law were absorbed into American social culture and have never been displaced."[59] Modern legal historians claim that "It was as clear to laymen as it was to lawyers that the nature of American institutions, whether economic, social or political, was largely to be determined by judges."[60] Digitization challenges the idea that the American people preferred common-law rules and judge-made law over statutes.

If common law had been absorbed into American "social culture," as common-law myth claims, a digital check should disclose the common law

[58] *Cf.*, CHARLES M. HAAR (ED.), THE GOLDEN AGE OF AMERICAN LAW [1820–1860] (1965).

[59] Graham Hughes, *Common Law Systems, in* NEW YORK UNIVERSITY SCHOOL OF LAW, FUNDAMENTALS OF AMERICAN LAW 9, 12 (Alan Morrison, ed., 1996).

[60] HORWITZ, *supra* note 55, at 2 (*quoting* Mark De Wolf Howe, *The Creative Period in the Law of Massachusetts*, 69 PROCEEDINGS OF THE MASSACHUSETTS HISTORICAL SOCIETY 237 (1947–1950)).

receiving pervasive praise in popular literature for schools and adults. I find no such acceptance. Patriotic addresses and civics texts give glory, laud and honor to legislation. Common law makes almost no appearance in popular literature other than as a subject of satire.

1. *Patriotic Commemorations*

July 4, 1876: Richard Henry Lee reads the Declaration of Independence at the Centennial Celebration[61]

---

[61] *July 4, 1876. The centennial celebration in Philadelphia – Richard Henry Lee of Virginia, reading the Declaration of Independence Square, July 4th*/Hyde, FRANK LESLIE'S ILLUSTRATED NEWSPAPER (July 22, 1876). Retrieved from the Library of Congress, https://www.loc.gov/item/95507511 (accessed Feb. 24, 2017).

Americans have celebrated the 4th of July 1776 since the 4th of July 1777.[62] Long before the Public Broadcasting System began its series "Capitol Fourth" on the Washington Mall,[63] Americans gathered to fete the Nation's Birthday. The Centennial Celebration of 1876 and the Bicentennial Celebration of 1976 were only the biggest of the parties. Throughout the first century of the Republic Americans got together in public places and had notables give orations. Many of these addresses – particularly those given in New England – were published.[64] Add to the 4th of July orations addresses for similar commemorations and patriotic addresses multiply. Many have been digitized. If common-law content and common-law methods are, or were, part of the fabric of the nation, one would think that their threads would be found when the nation gathered to celebrate its nationhood.[65]

I haven't read them all – there are at least 500 published addresses for the Fourth of July alone – but reading and searching, I am yet to find tributes to common-law content or to common-law methods.[66] What I do find are commendations of the heroism of the founders. I find that only some orations address law or government. I suspect that there is a common emphasis – the United States created a government of and for the people – but I haven't conducted a study. Contemporary common-law enthusiasts should go and make such a study. They should read as many of these pamphlets as the can. Light skeptics of these claims can look at a single volume that might stand for all the celebratory addresses: the 1826 eulogies for Adams and Jefferson already discussed in Chapter 4, Section C.

---

[62] *See* Hannah Keyser, *The First Fourth of July Celebration* (in 1777) http://mentalfloss.com/article/57633/first-fourth-july-celebration-1777 (excerpting the July 18, 1777 issue of the *Virginia Gazette*. The 4th was an official holiday first in Massachusetts in 1781.). *But see* LEN TRAVERS, CELEBRATING THE FOURTH: INDEPENDENCE DAY AND THE RITES OF NATIONALISM IN THE EARLY REPUBLIC 6 (1997) ("because these orations were consistently delivered by lawyers, clergymen, college professors, and politicians ... I question their validity as representative of popular belief.")

[63] John. J. O'Connor, *TV Weekend*, N.Y. Times, July 3, 1981 reports the program. It may have begun sooner.

[64] *See* University of Missouri, Fourth of July Orations Collection, 1791–1925, http://library.missouri.edu/specialcollections/bookcol/rare/fourth/ (458 pamphlets). The Internet Archive, https://archive.org permits a search on "Fourth of July Orations" which returns about 500. *See also* TRUMPETS OF GLORY: FOURTH OF JULY ORATIONS, 1786–1861 (Henry A. Hawken, ed., 1976) (reprinting about twenty); INDEPENDENCE DAY ORATIONS AND POEMS, JULY 4, 1876, NEW YORK TRIBUNE, EXTRA No. 33 (1876) (printing the five semi-official national orations for the Centennial).

[65] And that is just as true, if not more true, if one accepts Travers' assertion, *supra* note 62, at 7, that many a celebration was intended as much "to do battle with opponents" as "to minimize the conflicts and to assert the idealized (but dubious) unity of the American people."

[66] Even the common-law jury makes only a few cameo appearances. A Google search of jury in books with title including July 4 published 1776 to 1876 identified only ten orations that even mentioned the jury. *See, e.g.*, ISAAC STORY AN ORATION ON THE ANNIVERSARY OF THE INDEPENDENCE OF THE UNITED STATES OF AMERICA, PRONOUNCED AT WORCESTER, JULY 4, 1801, at 11 (1801), which mentioned the jury in passing but focused, at 24, on measuring political doctrines against the Constitution and laws.

2. *Civics for Adults*

The spirit that led to instruction of youth in civics (next subsection), and that celebrated the government of the people in commemorative addresses (previous section), found realization too in the idea of a legally-educated people. A government of laws is not a law for lawyers: it is a law for people. Every citizen should know something of the law. So in 1834 Justice Story addressed the American Institute of Instruction, a professional group of educators, "I do not hesitate to affirm, not only that a knowledge of the true principles of government is important and useful to Americans, but that it is absolutely indispensable, to carry on the government of their choice, and to transmit it to their posterity."[67]

The civics books discussed in the next subsection were generally denominated for "use of schools." What was meant was for use of common schools for children of perhaps eight to fourteen years of age. But some were marketed to more sophisticated students. These might be older students or students in academies or colleges. At the same time, authors wrote introductory works for law students in self-study, law office study or law school study. These were works for adults to educate themselves. These works presented a picture of a whole legal system, and not just of any one corner.[68] The most distinguished of these – designed to reach all areas of knowledge – was the 13-volume *Encyclopædia Americana* which first appeared between 1829 and 1834. Justice Story provided the principal entries on American law.

Justice Story carried out his convictions in other ways. He turned his scholarly learning into popular instruction. His three-volume *Commentaries on the Constitution of the United States* of 1833 he abridged the same year into a one-volume text *for "the use of colleges and high schools."* The next year he further boiled it down to *The constitutional class book: being a brief exposition of the Constitution of the United States: designed for the use of the higher classes in common schools.* Finally, in 1840 he brought out *A Familiar Exposition of the Constitution of the United States with an Appendix and Glossary.* Never revised, it has been repeatedly reprinted and now is available in several heirloom editions.

When states systematized their laws, discussed below, and brought them out in one-to-three volumes of compiled or revised statutes, they did so for the benefit of the people at large and not for the legal profession alone. The creators of these works said that in the introductions to their books. Some went further.

[67] Joseph Story, *On the Science of Government as a Branch of Popular Education, in* THE INTRODUCTORY DISCOURSE AND THE LECTURES DELIVERED BEFORE THE AMERICAN INSTITUTE OF INSTRUCTION, IN BOSTON, AUG., 1834 [Annual Meeting of the American Institute of Instruction, Vol. 5] 234, 255 (1835), *reprinted in* THE MISCELLANEOUS WRITINGS OF JOSEPH STORY 614, 619 (William W. Story, ed., 1852).
[68] That distinguishes them from subject- or task-focused books. The former might be, for example, books on education; the latter might be the everyman-his-own-lawyer books.

To make them usable to the public they provided "practical forms ... with appropriate directions,"[69] "notes ... pointing out the principal alterations made by them in the common and statute law,"[70] and even collections for the general public of what the world now calls Frequently Asked Questions (FAQs).[71]

3. *Civics for Youth*

Civil Government.

Government of a school.

The Young American by S.G. Goodrich (Popular Civics Text in the 1840s)[72]

---

[69] MANUAL OF THE REVISED STATUTES OF THE STATE OF NEW-YORK; OR, A COMPLETE SERIES OF ALL THE PRACTICAL FORMS, OR PRECEDENTS, REQUIRED BY THE REVISED STATUTES WITH APPROPRIATE DIRECTIONS, EXPLANATIONS AND REFERENCES, TO CASES ADJUDGED IN THE COURTS OF SAID STATE, AND IN THE SUPREME COURT OF THE UNITED STATES IN FIVE PARTS. PREPARED AND COMPILED BY A COUNSELLOR AT LAW (1831).

[70] JOHN CANFIELD SPENCER, NOTES ON THE REVISED STATES OF THE STATE OF NEW-YORK POINTING OUT THE PRINCIPAL ALTERATIONS MADE BY THEM IN THE COMMON AND STATUTE LAW (1830); JOHN CANFIELD SPENCER, ABSTRACT OF THE MOST IMPORTANT ALTERATIONS, OF GENERAL INTEREST, INTRODUCED BY THE REVISED STATUTES; THE PRINCIPAL PART OF WHICH ORIGINALLY APPEARED IN THE ONTARIO MESSENGER (1830). Spencer was later Secretary of State of New York, Secretary of the Treasury of the United States, Secretary of War and first editor of Alexis de Tocqueville's *Democracy in America*.

[71] WILLIAM B. WEDGEWOOD, THE REVISED STATUTES OF THE STATE OF NEW YORK REDUCED TO QUESTIONS AND ANSWERS FOR THE USE OF SCHOOLS AND FAMILIES (1843). Wedgwood brought out a series of these books for other states besides New York.

[72] GOODRICH, *supra* note 42, at 42. *Cf.* Story, *On the Science of Government, supra* note 67 at 34 (reprint at 632) (comparing learning political philosophy to "comprehending the value of good order and discipline in a school").

America's public schools – first called common schools – are largely an innovation of the first fifty years of the 19th century. Beginning already in colonial times in Massachusetts, they gradually spread throughout the land. Jefferson made the establishment of public schools a central part of his Revisal. Slave states were slower than were free states in making public education available. Civics had a central role in the newly-established common schools. The American Revolution was about self-government. Since the Revolution Americans have taken interest in providing for the education of the people in the workings of their government. James Wilson reports that already the first assembly of Pennsylvania adopted an act "for teaching the laws in the schools."[73]

American civics texts date to the introduction of universal public education in the first half of the nineteenth century.[74] They were central to achieving the mission of the newly forming common schools, i.e., public schools: to educate youth as private citizens who would in public life take responsibility for government and administer its laws.[75] When in 1819 New York promoted public schools, the state's Superintendent of Common Schools recommended that the "course of study in every well organized common school, ought to embrace ... "the history of our own country, its constitution and form of government, the crimes and punishment which form our criminal code, and such parts of our civil jurisprudence as every man in his own daily intercourse with the world, is concerned to know."[76] In laying out his plans, he lamented that there was yet no proper book for this. He expressed hope that soon a "suitable" one would be available. It took more than a decade for his hope to be fulfilled, but by the 1830s there were a dozen or more candidates for common schools to choose from.[77] In the 1840s yet another dozen or so came

---

[73] 1 THE WORKS OF HONORABLE JAMES WILSON, L.L.D. 420 (Bird Wilson, ed., 1804), *reprinted in* 1 COLLECTED WORKS OF JAMES WILSON 417 (Kermit L. Hall & Mark David Hall, eds., 2007).

[74] Of his proposals for new legislation in his Revisal, Jefferson was especially proud of his bills for "the more general diffusion of knowledge." Jefferson wanted to establish universal public schooling. His bill for public education was an American model for a generation.

[75] INSTRUCTIONS FOR THE BETTER GOVERNMENT AND ORGANIZATION OF COMMON SCHOOLS, PREPARED AND PUBLISHED PURSUANT TO A PROVISION IN THE ACT FOR THE SUPPORT OF COMMON SCHOOLS, PASSED APR. 12, 1819, at 3, 6 (Gideon Hawley, Superintendent of Common Schools, 1819).

[76] *Id.* at 4.

[77] Authors included: Arthur J. Stansbury (1828), Alexander Maitland (1829), Andrew Yates (1830), William Sullivan (1831), Samuel C. Atkinson (1832), William Alexander Duer (1833), Edward D. Mansfield (1834), Joseph Story (1834), Francis Fellowes (attributed, 1835), John Phelps (1835), Andrew W. Young (*Introduction to the Science of Government*, 1835), Alfred Conkling (1836), and Marcius Willson (1839). Young's book had more than twenty editions.

on the market.[78] Some of these and new similar books provided America's
civics texts to 1876.

These books do not teach common-law content or judge-made law.[79]
These books do teach a government of laws, not of men. They instruct in
legislation not litigation. Their laws are statutes not precedents. One of the
first of the then new books, Arthur J. Stansbury's *Elementary Catechism on the
Constitution of the United States for the Use of Schools* (1828) boasts: "Let
every youthful American exult that he has no master but the law."[80] *The
Young American* (first edition, 1842), written by S.G. Goodrich, author of
the popular Peter Parley children's books series, uses illustrations to show
the progress from the customs of "The Savage State" to the written laws and
civil government of "The Civilized State." The book explains the illustrations:

> Among savages, there are no written or printed laws. The people have certain
> customs and if disputes arise, they are settled according to these. . . .
>
> [Barbarous states] are still without books in general use, without education
> among the people at large, without printed laws. . . .
>
> [In Civilized States] laws are enacted to secure to each individual the
> acquisition of his labor, skill and exertion.[81]

A consistent theme of the civics texts is that governments and written laws are
essential features of society. Goodrich's text is explicit already in its subtitle:
Book of Government and Law: Showing Their History, Nature and Necessity.
The other books are no less explicit in their texts. William Sullivan's *Political
Class Book* (1830) teaches that "[a]n extensive and varied society . . . *could not
go on* without established laws, and a faithful observance of them."[82] Andrew
White Young's *Introduction to the Science of Government* (first edition, 1835),
the book most frequently issued (25+ editions), teaches that "government and
laws are necessary to social beings," and warns that "[w]ithout laws, there
would be no security to person or property; the evil passions of men would

[78] Following in the 1840s came new books by James Bayard (1840), Joseph Story (1840), A. Potter
(1841), S.G. Goodrich (3d ed., 1843), Charles Mason (1843), Andrew W. Young (*First Lessons in
Civil Government*, 10th ed., 1843), Thomas H. Burrows (1846), J.B. Shurtleff (1846), Daniel
Parker (1848), and Joseph Bartlett Burleigh (1849).
[79] Because these have little entered the legal discussion, I detail them more than other primary
sources of this article.
[80] J. STANSBURY, ELEMENTARY CATECHISM ON THE CONSTITUTION OF THE UNITED STATES FOR
THE USE OF SCHOOLS 18 (1828).
[81] GOODRICH, *supra* note 42, at 14, 15, 22. The first edition is from 1842.
[82] WILLIAM SULLIVAN, POLITICAL CLASS BOOK: INTENDED TO INSTRUCT THE HIGHER CLASSES IN
SCHOOLS IN THE ORIGIN, NATURE, AND USE OF POLITICAL POWER. WITH AN APPENDIX UPON
STUDIES FOR PRACTICAL MEN; WITH NOTICES OF BOOKS SUITED TO THEIR USE BY GEORGE
B. EMERSON 19 (1830).

prompt them to commit all manner of wrongs against each other, and render society, (if society can be said to exist without law,) a scene of violence and confusion."[83]

Government is by statutes. That was textbook learning. Goodrich's text explains:

> The system or form of government of the United States, is prescribed in a written constitution, sanctioned by the people. The statutes are the laws enacted by congress, agreeably to this constitution. The administration con-sists of the president of the United States, his secretaries, &c.[84]

Other texts likewise teach that a government of laws is a rule of laws that guides ruled and rulers alike. J.B. Shurtleff's *The Governmental Instructor* (first edition 1845) instructs, "[i]n order to aid the chief ruler in ruling in accordance with the wishes of the people, most nations, in modern times, have adopted a *Constitution* and *Code of Laws*, which they have bound themselves to obey, and by which the ruler has bound himself to govern."[85]

A law is a legislatively adopted statute. Later editions of Young's text put it this way: "Law, as the word is generally used, has reference to the government of men as members of the body politic; and signifies an established rule, prescribed by a competent authority in the state, commanding what its

---

[83] ANDREW W. YOUNG, INTRODUCTION TO THE SCIENCE OF GOVERNMENT, AND COMPEND OF THE CONSTITUTIONAL AND CIVIL JURISPRUDENCE; COMPREHENDING A GENERAL VIEW OF THE GOVERNMENT OF THE UNITED STATES AND OF THE GOVERNMENT OF THE STATE OF NEW YORK: TOGETHER WITH THE MOST IMPORTANT PROVISIONS IN THE CONSTITUTIONS OF THE SEVERAL STATES ADAPTED TO PURPOSES OF INSTRUCTION IN FAMILIES AND SCHOOLS 18, 20 (2d ed., 1836). This is the version available on Google Books. The first edition's title from 1835 shows even better that it was teaching a world of written law. Its title: INTRODUCTION TO THE SCIENCE OF GOVERNMENT, AND COMPEND OF THE CONSTITUTIONAL AND STATUTORY LAW. The book went through at least twenty-five editions.

　　Young may have conquered the market. He subsequently brought out a book for younger students (age 10) and books for older students. The latter included one on comparative government and several books on political history for older ones. One book was marketed nearly twenty-five years after his death in 1877. THE GOVERNMENT CLASS BOOK: A MANUAL OF INSTRUCTION IN THE PRINCIPLES OF CONSTITUTIONAL GOVERNMENT AND LAW (1901 ed. by Salter S. Clark).

[84] GOODRICH, *supra* note 42, at 22.

[85] J.B. SHURTLEFF, THE GOVERNMENTAL INSTRUCTOR, OR A BRIEF AND COMPREHENSIVE VIEW OF THE GOVERNMENT OF THE UNITED STATES, AND OF THE STATE GOVERNMENTS, IN EASY LESSONS, DESIGNED FOR SCHOOLS (4th ed., 1846) [emphasis in original]. This is an edition available on Google Books. The first edition is from 1846; the last is from 1871. There was even an edition for German-language schools: DER KLEINE STAATSMANN, ODER, EINE KURZE UND UMFASSENDE UEBERSICHT DER REGIERUNG DER VEREINIGTEN STAATEN UND DER STAATEN-REGIERUNGEN: AUF EINE LEICHT UND FASSLICHE ART DARGESTELLT ZUM GEBRAUCH FÜR SCHULEN (New York, 1845).

citizens are to do, and prohibiting, what they are not to do."[86] John Phelps' *The Legal Classic* (1835) teaches: "Law is the work and the will of the legislature in their derivative and subordinate capacity."[87] Charles Mason's *Elementary Treatise* (first edition 1842) similarly says: "The office of the legislative department is to pass laws."[88] The people, through their representatives, make laws. The people must be able to understand laws, not only to follow them but to evaluate them. So Young's text explains the purpose of the book in its preface: "The power to make and administer the laws, is delegated to the representative and agent of the people; the people should therefore be competent to judge when, and how far, this power is constitutionally and beneficially exercised."[89] The texts worked to fulfill the goals expressed already in the Superintendent's 1819 report: "where the people are entrusted with the government of themselves, a knowledge of the constitution and form of government, under which they live, is necessary to enable them to govern with wisdom and to appreciate the blessings of their free and happy condition."[90]

It is the duty of citizens to learn the laws and the duty of the legislature to write laws that citizens can observe. So Sullivan's text teaches youth: "Our first duty then, is, to use the gift of reason in learning the laws which are prescribed to us."[91] Young's text comforts youth that they can do it: "[man's] reason enables him to understand the meaning of laws, and to discover what laws are necessary to regulate human action."[92] Mason's book stresses the importance of the legislature providing comprehensible rules: "As laws are established to be the rules of action, they ought to be expressed in the most clear and

---

[86] ANDREW W. YOUNG, INTRODUCTION TO THE SCIENCE OF GOVERNMENT, AND COMPEND OF THE CONSTITUTIONAL AND CIVIL JURISPRUDENCE OF THE UNITED STATES WITH A BRIEF TREATISE ON POLITICAL ECONOMY. DESIGNED FOR THE USE OF FAMILIES AND SCHOOLS, § 22, at 20 (19th ed., 1850).

[87] JOHN PHELPS, THE LEGAL CLASSIC, OR, YOUNG AMERICAN'S FIRST BOOK OF RIGHTS AND DUTIES: DESIGNED FOR SCHOOLS AND PRIVATE STUDENTS 27 (1835). This edition is available in Gale, *Making of Modern Law* series online in subscription or in print-on-demand.

[88] CHARLES MASON, AN ELEMENTARY TREATISE ON THE STRUCTURE AND OPERATIONS OF THE NATIONAL AND STATE GOVERNMENTS OF THE UNITED STATES. DESIGNED FOR THE USE OF SCHOOLS AND ACADEMIES AND FOR GENERAL READERS 27 (1842). There was a second edition in 1843.

[89] YOUNG, INTRODUCTION, 2d ed., 1835, *supra* note 83, at iii.

[90] INSTRUCTIONS, *supra* note 75, at 6. Fifteen years later a successor reported: "On our common schools we must rely to prepare the great body of the people for maintaining inviolate the rights of freemen." ANNUAL REPORT OF THE SUPERINTENDENT OF COMMON SCHOOLS, ASSEMBLY DOCUMENT NO. 8, JAN. 7, 1835, at 34.

[91] SULLIVAN, *supra* note 82 at 17.   [92] YOUNG, INTRODUCTION, 2d ed., 1835, *supra* note 83, at 19.

intelligible form."[93] Alfred Conkling's *The Young Citizen's Manual* (first edition 1836) lauds the New York legislature for having done so in the criminal code of the 1829 Revised Statutes: "One of the great excellencies of this branch of our written laws, consists in the brevity and precision of language in which it is expressed.[94]

Statutes are nothing to fear. Long before American lawyers spoke of "statutorification" textbook writers identified the phenomenon, its cause and its solution. Goodrich tackled the issue head on. The phenomenon was "the law is seen to be everywhere, upon the land and the sea in town and country."[95] The cause of our numerous laws is "whenever any evil arises, or any great good is desired, the law-makers seek to aver the one and secure the other by legislation, if it is within their proper reach."[96] The solution is, not to deny statutes, but to deal with them: adopt just statutes, systematize them and enforce them. Goodrich's explained:

> In a civilized society, the laws are numerous, and as each law is an abridgment of some portion of absolute liberty, would be taken away. But still, it appears that all liberty, essential to happiness, is compatible with a complete system of laws; and in fact where the laws are just, and most completely carried into effect, there is the greatest amount of practical liberty.[97]

The texts teach separation of powers. Stansbury's book states the division. "[Legislators] make the laws, while judges only explain and apply them."[98] Mason's text explains why we need judges and cannot depend on self-application alone: "To the judicial power it belongs to expound and enforce the laws. . . . Laws would be very inadequate to the purpose for which they are designed, were there not some tribunal competent to decide authoritatively upon their meaning and application, and clothed with power to enforce and effectuate its decisions."[99]

---

[93] MASON, *supra* note 88, at 27.

[94] ALFRED CONKLING, BEING A DIGEST OF THE LAWS OF THE STATE OF NEW YORK AND OF THE UNITED STATES, RELATING TO CRIMES AND THEIR PUNISHMENTS, AND OF SUCH OTHER PARTS OF THE LAWS OF THE STATE OF NEW YORK RELATING TO THE ORDINARY BUSINESS OF SOCIAL LIFE AS ARE MOST NECESSARY TO BE GENERALLY KNOWN; WITH EXPLANATORY REMARKS. TO WHICH IS PREFIXED, AN ESSAY ON THE PRINCIPLES OF CIVIL GOVERNMENT. DESIGNED FOR THE INSTRUCTION OF YOUNG PERSONS IN GENERAL AND ESPECIALLY FOR THE USE OF SCHOOLS 28 (2d ed., 1843). The first edition was published in 1836.

[95] GOODRICH, *supra* note 42, at 12.

[96] *Id.* at 35. The text continues: "The consequence is that almost every transaction of life, is regulated by laws."

[97] *Id.* at 31–32.   [98] STANSBURY, *supra* note 80, at 62.   [99] MASON, *supra* note 88, at 27.

The texts leave little room for judges to make laws. None teaches it. Shetleff's book warns: "If the *judicial* power absorbs or encroaches upon the executive or legislative, or if the *legislative* encroaches upon the executive or judicial, the result is as fatal to liberty as if the executive absorbed the judicial and legislative." Why? Because "All the legislative or law-making power granted by the constitution of the United States, is vested in a congress."[100] The elected representatives of the people make laws.

The civics texts saw that America was exceptional. But the young nation wasn't exceptional because paternal common-law judges guarded what they held to be citizens' rights. It was exceptional because the people governed according to law. Stansbury's text tells youth the story that they could see unfold in their later lives:

> In the first place, consider how happy and how highly favored is our country, in having a system of government so wisely calculated to secure the life, liberty, and happiness of all its citizens. Had you lived or travelled in other parts of the world, you would be much more sensible of this, than you can possibly be without such an opportunity of comparing our lot with that of others. But, as your reading increases, particularly in history and in travels, you will be able to form a more just estimate of what you enjoy. When you read of the oppression which has been, and still is exercised, I do not say in Africa and Asia, whose inhabitants are but partially civilized – but even in the most enlightened countries of Europe; under absolute monarchs, a proud and haughty nobility – a worldly, selfish, and ambitious priesthood – a vast and rapacious standing army, and a host of greedy officers of government; and then turn your eyes on your own happy home, a land where none of these evils has any place – where the people first make the laws and then obey them – where they can be oppressed by none, but where every man's person's property, and privileges are surrounded by the law, and sacred from every thing but justice and the public good; how can you be sufficiently grateful to a beneficent Providence, which has thus endowed our country with blessings equally rich and rare?[101]

Common schools taught liberty in laws of Americans' making.[102]

So what did common schools teach of common law – the supposed fabric of their society? If the civic texts they used are any indication, they taught very

---

[100] SHURTLEFF, *supra* note 85, at 44.   [101] STANSBURY, *supra* note 80, at 76.

[102] *See, e.g.,* CONKLING *supra* note 94, at 19 ("strictly speaking, it was not civil liberty that they achieved. It was National Independence, and it was nothing more. It was the faculty of self-government – the privilege of framing a government for themselves and of making their own laws, instead of receiving laws from the king and parliament of Great Britain. It was a change from colonial dependence to a state of independency.").

little. The texts devote pages to legislation. None devotes pages, even sentences, to common-law method of making law while applying it. There are
only a few thin threads of the common law in the nation's fabric. Most of the
texts give common law no more than a dozen or two mentions. These
mentions are of two sorts. The one is to show how Americans have overcome
common law through written law. Even Justice Story's text, which is the one
book to address common law in detail and with favor, relates how Congress
abolished the common law of treason with its "savage and malignant refine-
ments in cruelty."[103] Another type of mention is to show how Americans relied
on common law to define terms used in the Constitution or in other written
laws, e.g., impeachment,[104] murder.[105] In other words, common law provided
a kind of vocabulary. Occasionally, it filled in gaps, for example, when New
York repealed the age of consent for marriage.[106] Most texts make no more
than passing mention of the carryover of common law to the American
colonies. English common law was only an interim measure. Only three of
the antebellum texts identified address common law as a topic in any sense to
which a class might devote time; only one – that by Justice Story – provides the
foundation for a class session. And that class would have been largely
historical.

Sullivan's text asks the question: "What is the Common Law?"[107] It
answers with a paragraph of text, explains its basis in English custom, its
use to define terms and identifies as it principal role then to prescribe "the
rules of proceeding in a great majority of all the cases, civil and criminal,
which are tried in our courts."[108] This text, by a lawyer, is the only one to
even mention the concept of precedent: it does that in a single sentence.[109]
Sullivan's text is neither an endorsement of past common law nor of its then

---

[103] JOSEPH STORY, A FAMILIAR EXPOSITION OF THE CONSTITUTION OF THE UNITED STATES WITH
AN APPENDIX AND GLOSSARY. THE SCHOOL LIBRARY PUBLISHED UNDER THE SANCTION OF THE
BOARD OF EDUCATION OF THE STATE OF MASSACHUSETTS § 211, 124 ("The offender is to be
drawn to the gallows on a hurdle; hanged by the neck, and cut down alive; his entrails taken
out, and burned while he is yet alive; his head cut off; and his body quartered. Congress are
intrusted with the power to fix the punishment, and have, with great wisdom and humanity,
abolished these horrible accompaniments and confided the punishment simply to death by
hanging.").
[104] E.g., WILLIAM ALEXANDER DUER, OUTLINES OF THE CONSTITUTIONAL JURISPRUDENCE OF THE
UNITED STATES: DESIGNED AS A TEXT BOOK FOR LECTURES, AS A CLASS BOOK FOR ACADEMIES
AND COMMON SCHOOLS, AND AS MANUAL FOR POPULAR USE 89 (1833).
[105] E.g., SULLIVAN, *supra* note 82, at 31.   [106] E.g., CONKLING, *supra* note 94, at 111.
[107] SULLIVAN, *supra* note 82, at ix.   [108] *Id.* at 30–31.
[109] *Id.* at 37 (explaining why citizens should be interested in exercise of the judiciary power, it
notes that "the principle on which the case is decided, may form a precedent affecting his
interests materially.").

present direction of procedure, nor any basis for creating a new common law, substantive or procedural.[110]

The second of the three is one of Young's later civics texts, a longer and denser text than his *Introduction*. Designed for senior students and adults The *Citizen's Manual* adds materials on foreign governments, international law, practical substantive law and parliamentary procedure. It reports on sixteen areas of substantive laws under the title "Common and Statutory Laws."[111] The sections on substantive law convey what the law generally is, by statute first, and by common-law gap-fillers, second. Sometimes they show how Americans have reversed the common law (*e.g.*, allowing aliens to acquire real estate). The common law that Young's text describes is a passing gap-filler destined to disappear. As if to emphasize the demise of common law and the growth of statute law, the text adds more than twenty-five pages on parliamentary rules.[112]

Justice Story's book, alone, explains English common law, its partial adoption in the colonies, and the potential for American judge-made law. In this regard, the 1840 version of the book,[113] which appeared after the 1837 Massachusetts Code Report, is more extensive than that of the 1834 version, which appeared before the Code Report.[114] In an historical chapter on colonial

[110] *See* WILLIAM SULLIVAN, AN ADDRESS TO THE MEMBERS OF THE BAR OF SUFFOLK, MASS. AT THEIR STATED MEETING OF THE FIRST TUESDAY OF MARCH, 1824 (1825) (63 page address on history of the profession and legal methods by author of the text.).

[111] ANDREW W. YOUNG, THE CITIZEN'S MANUAL OF GOVERNMENT AND LAW. COMPRISING THE ELEMENTARY PRINCIPLES OF CIVIL GOVERNMENT; A PRACTICAL VIEW OF THE STATE GOVERNMENT, AND OF THE GOVERNMENT OF THE UNITED STATES; A DIGEST OF COMMON AND STATUTORY LAW, AND OF THE LAW OF NATIONS; AND A SUMMARY OF PARLIAMENTARY RULES FOR THE PRACTICE OF DELIBERATIVE ASSEMBLIES; WITH SUPPLEMENTARY NOTES ON THE GOVERNMENT OF THE STATE OF OHIO, AND THE CONSTITUTION OF THE STATE 173–230 (1853) There is a revised edition of 1859. Subjects addressed are rights of persons, domestic relations, minors, rights of property, wills and testaments, deeds and mortgages, incorporeal hereditaments, leases, contracts in general, contracts of sales, fraudulent sales, principal and agent, partnership, bailment, promissory notes and bills of exchange. The text explains that this part of the book gives "an abstract of the laws which more particularly define the right, and prescribe the duties, of citizens in the social and domestic relations." These laws are "first, *statute laws*, [and] secondly, the *common law*." Common law is not new law created by judges; it "consists of rules that have become binding by long usage and general custom" and is the "same as that of England. *Id.* at 173–174.

[112] *Id.* at 254–282.

[113] JOSEPH STORY, A FAMILIAR EXPOSITION OF THE CONSTITUTION OF THE UNITED STATES WITH AN APPENDIX AND GLOSSARY. THE SCHOOL LIBRARY PUBLISHED UNDER THE SANCTION OF THE BOARD OF EDUCATION OF THE STATE OF MASSACHUSETTS, Vol. XIII (1840). The book was reprinted, but not revised.

[114] JOSEPH STORY, THE CONSTITUTIONAL CLASS BOOK: BEING A BRIEF EXPOSITION OF THE CONSTITUTION OF THE UNITED STATES: DESIGNED FOR THE USE OF THE HIGHER CLASSES IN COMMON SCHOOLS (1834).

governments it answers the question how "the common law of England came to be the fundamental law of all the Colonies?" Story's text answers by explaining the differences among the Colonies, both in their legal status, and in how each chose to accept "only such portions of it, as were adapted to its own wants, and were applicable to its own situation." The text praises the common law as "thus limited and defined by the colonists themselves, in its application, the common law became the guardian of their civil and political rights."[115] The text praises common law of the past, but it makes no claims for a common law of the future such as present-day proponents do. The text does not assert, as claimed today by English and American judges alike that "common law provides the tools and flexibility to allow the law to continue to serve the needs of a diverse society in world of rapid change and technological development."[116] Instead, like the other civics texts, it records how constitutions and statutes corrected defects of the common law. Just as do the other texts, it gives chapters to legislation and on the judicial department; it has not one word on precedents or *stare decisis*.[117]

E. SELF-GOVERNMENT

The rule being prescribed, [a statute] becomes the guide of all those functionaries who are called to administer it, and of all those citizens and subjects upon whom it is to operate.

Joseph Story, *Encyclopedia Americana* (1834)[118]

Common-law myth assumes that the United States in the first century of the Republic was a "night-watchman" state where people were largely free of being governed. Only later, sometime in the 20th century, did Americans create an "administrative state." Recent scholarship challenges that assumption. It shows Americans governing and administering in the 19th century.[119] That governing and administering rested on written laws.

---

[115] *Id.* at 20–22.

[116] COMMON LAW, COMMON VALUES, COMMON RIGHTS, ESSAYS ON OUR COMMON HERITAGE BY DISTINGUISHED BRITISH AND AMERICAN AUTHORS viii (American Bar Association, 2000).

[117] More than do the other texts, Story's identifies the jury with the common law. *See, e.g.*, STORY, *supra* note 114, at 25.

[118] Joseph Story *et al.*, *[Appendix] Law, Legislation, Codes*, 7 ENCYCLOPÆDIA AMERICANA 576, 581 (1834).

[119] *See, e.g.*, BRIAN BALOGH, A GOVERNMENT OUT OF SIGHT: THE MYSTERY OF NATIONAL AUTHORITY IN NINETEENTH CENTURY AMERICA (2009); JERRY L. MASHAW, CREATING THE ADMINISTRATIVE CONSTITUTION: THE LOST ONE HUNDRED YEARS OF AMERICAN ADMINISTRATIVE LAW (2012); WILLIAM J. NOVAK, THE PEOPLE'S WELFARE: LAW AND REGULATION IN NINETEENTH CENTURY AMERICA (1996). *See also*, OSCAR HANDLIN & MARY FLUG HANDLIN, COMMONWEALTH: A STUDY OF THE ROLE OF GOVERNMENT IN THE AMERICAN

For statutes to govern, Charles Warren rightly wrote in his *History of the Harvard Law School*, they must be accessible *"for the benefit of laymen as well as lawyers."*[120] There he saw one of the great benefits of codes and revisions: laymen can read and apply the law themselves without lawyers. People in their occupations and their professions can themselves implement law. People in their daily lives can follow the rules that are imposed on them. Proponents of common-law myth claim that the public does not read laws and is not interested in statutes. Codes and revisions are of little use to them more than a listing of court decisions. An 1827 Committee Report to the South Carolina legislature by Thomas Grimké countered that argument: "Not, that the people will read a portion every day, or will even have them in their houses; but that, whenever in the course of public or private business, the people are required to read or hear the law for their guidance, it may be simple clear and concise." Thus, the report continued, "the sovereign authority, above all in a republic, [is duty bound] to prepare the laws in the best possible manner for the use of the people whenever they are called upon to act upon them." Someone charged with applying the law, the Report continued, could find his duties nowhere "concisely and clearly stated. . . . But in a Code, he would read in a few pages all that concerned him."[121]

Digitization supports Grimké's prognosis: it shows even before Grimké's report the beginnings of an occupational literature of collected statutes that continued long afterwards. By occupational I mean books intended to permit educated laymen to learn and apply the law applicable in their occupations ordinarily without legal consultation. These books give or refer lay readers to rules to apply themselves; they assume no involvement of lawyers. Readers of these books, however, may include lawyers who advise participants in the occupational field. Such books cannot easily persist where judicial precedents predominate, for laymen cannot be expected to possess, find, understand, identify as authoritative or apply precedents that would be needed to supplement the texts for current application.

Already in the first twenty-five years of the 19th century such occupational literature began to appear in a variety of fields. In numbers of publications and copies printed they may have exceeded case reports in those years. Among the first were guides to military and education law, which governments often

ECONOMY, MASSACHUSETTS 1774–1861 (Revised ed. 1969); William J. Novak, *Making the Modern American Legislative State, in* LIVING LEGISLATION: DURABILITY, CHANGE, AND THE POLITICS OF AMERICAN LAWMAKING 20 (Jeffrey A. Jenkins & Eric M. Patashnik, eds., 2012).
[120] 1 CHARLES WARREN, *Chapter XXXV: New Law 1830–1860, in* HISTORY OF THE HARVARD LAW SCHOOL AND OF EARLY LEGAL CONDITIONS IN AMERICA 234 (1908); CHARLES WARREN, *Chapter XVII: Progress of the Law 1830–1860, in* HISTORY OF THE AMERICAN BAR 446 (1911).
[121] REPORT, SOUTH CAROLINA [of the "Committee appointed 20th of December last, to report on the practicability and expediency of a Code of the Statute and Common Law of this State] 9 (1827).

distributed free to users. The War Department provided, for "the use of the army," a compilation of all the laws related thereto, including penal laws and laws related to organization and administration. State superintendents of schools provided laws and regulations for the conduct of the new common schools. These were statutes for the people and not for lawyers.[122] They continued to come up to the Centennial and beyond. Here is a sampling of such books focused on those which appeared first in the particular types referenced and which have been digitized. Included in the notes to the list are comments from some of the authors relevant to the need of the people for such books and for their systematizing:

- Military,[123]
- laws of war,[124]

---

[122] Erwin C. Surrency, A History of American Law Publishing 74 (1990).

[123] E.g., Adjutant-General of the Commonwealth of Massachusetts, Laws for Regulating and Governing the Militia of the Commonwealth of Massachusetts (1803); Isaac Maltby, A treatise on Courts Martial and Military Law: Containing an Explanation of the Principles which Govern Courts Martial and Courts of Inquiry, under the Authority of an Individual State, and of the United States, in War and Peace: The Powers and Duties of Individuals in the Army, Navy, and Militia, and the Punishments to Which They May Be Liable, Respectively, for Violations of Duty: The Necessary Forms for Calling, Assembling, and Organizing Courts Martial, and All Other Proceedings of Said Courts iii–iv (1813) (treatise and appendix of rules and regulations) ("This treatise was originally undertaken, in compliance with the solicitations of military gentlemen; and solely with a view to the militia. . . . The militia man is indeed deeply interested in *all* its details, being liable to the same pains and penalties, and to the same rules and regulations, by the articles of war, as the individual of the regular army. Besides this personal interest, which every militia officer has at stake, in these discussions, there is also a public interest involved. . . . If officers will give themselves the necessary information, those disagreeable delays, so frequently witnessed at court-martial, will be avoided. . . . The author is not without hope, therefore, that the work as now presented, will be found interesting and useful, not only to the militia, but to the army and navy of the United States."); Adjutant General's Office (of Virginia), Military Laws (1820); Trueman Cross, Military Laws of the United States; to Which Is Prefixed the Constitution of the United States (1825) (unnumbered iii: "the question of repeal is purely a *judicial* one, belonging to the competent tribunals to determine. It is, indeed, a right which they cannot surrender; one which no other power can legally exercise.") (unnumbered iv: "for the use of the army, a compilation of the acts of congress relating thereto. . . . The propriety of rendering all the *penal* laws accessible to those on whom they are to operate, is sufficiently obvious – and it is believed to be an object of some moment, that the law relating to organization and administration, though repealed or modified, should be placed within the reach of the army.")

[124] General Orders No. 100, promulgated by Lincoln, was not a handbook, but the laws themselves for the guidance of the armies. See John Fabian Witt, Lincoln's Code: The Laws of War in American History (2012). Its author was Francis Lieber, the creator of the *Encyclopædia Americana. See* Paul Finkelman, *Review [of Witt], Francis Lieber and the Modern Law of War,* 80 U. Chi. L. Rev. 2071 (2013).

- postal service,[125]
- schools,[126]
- universities,[127]
- tax and revenue laws,[128]
- bankruptcy,[129]
- mechanics' liens[130]
- farming,[131]
- land offices,[132]
- military pensions,[133]

[125] *E.g.*, POST-OFFICE LAW, WITH INSTRUCTIONS, FORMS AND TABLES OF DISTANCES, PUBLISHED FOR THE REGULATION OF THE POST OFFICE (1800); POST-OFFICE LAW, INSTRUCTIONS AND FORMS, PUBLISHED FOR THE REGULATION OF THE POST-OFFICE (1825).

[126] *E.g.*, INSTRUCTIONS FOR THE BETTER GOVERNMENT AND ORGANIZATION OF COMMON SCHOOLS, PREPARED AND PUBLISHED PURSUANT TO A PROVISION IN THE ACT FOR THE SUPPORT OF COMMON SCHOOLS, PASSED APR. 12, 1819 (Gideon Hawley, Superintendent of Common Schools, 1819); THE SCHOOL OFFICERS' GUIDE, FOR THE STATE OF OHIO; CONTAINING THE LAWS ON THE SUBJECT OF COMMON SCHOOLS, THE SCHOOL FUND, &C, TOGETHER WITH INSTRUCTIONS FOR THE INFORMATION AND GOVERNMENT OF SCHOOL OFFICERS (1842).

[127] *E.g.*, LAWS OF THE STATE UNIVERSITY: ACTS OF CONGRESS AND LAWS OF THE MISSOURI LEGISLATURE RELATING TO THE UNIVERSITY OF MISSOURI AND AGRICULTURAL AND MECHANICAL COLLEGE, AND SCHOOL OF MINES AND METALLURGY TOGETHER WITH THE BY-LAWS OF THE BOARD OF CURATORS: WITH AN APPENDIX (1872).

[128] *E.g.*, L. ADDINGTON, A DIGEST OF THE REVENUE LAWS OF THE UNITED STATES: WHEREIN ARE ARRANGED, UNDER DISTINCT HEADS, THE DUTIES OF COLLECTORS, NAVAL OFFICERS, SURVEYORS, MERCHANTS, MASTERS, AND ALL OTHER PERSONS CONNECTED WITH THE IMPOSTS (1804); ALEXANDER SIDNEY COXE, THE SYSTEM OF THE LAWS OF THE UNITED STATES IN RELATION TO DIRECT TAXES AND INTERNAL DUTIES INACTED IN THE YEAR 1813, CONTAINING THOSE LAWS AT LARGE WITH SOME EXPLANATIONS; AND A COPIOUS INDEX (1813).

[129] *E.g.*, THOMAS COOPER, THE BANKRUPT LAW OF AMERICA COMPARED WITH THE BANKRUPT LAW OF ENGLAND (1801) (reprinting U.S. and English statutes, providing a guide to proceedings)

[130] *E.g.*, PETER ARRELL BROWN, A SUMMARY OF THE LAW OF PENNSYLVANIA SECURING TO MECHANICS AND OTHERS: PAYMENT FOR THEIR LABOUR AND MATERIALS IN ERECTING ANY HOUSE OR OTHER BUILDING CONTAINING THE SEVERAL ACTS OF ASSEMBLY ON THE SUBJECT; AND THE DECISIONS THAT HAVE TAKEN PLACE UNDER THEM (1814) (statute printed followed by questions and answers explaining it).

[131] *E.g.*, JOHN M'DOUGAL, THE FARMER'S ASSISTANT, OR, EVERY MAN HIS OWN LAWYER (1813) (collection of forms, not statutes).

[132] *E.g.*, JOHN KILTY, THE LAND-HOLDER'S ASSISTANT, AND LAND-OFFICE GUIDE; BEING AN EXPOSITION OF ORIGINAL TITLES, AS DERIVED FROM THE PROPRIETARY GOVERNMENT, AND MORE RECENTLY FROM THE STATE OF MARYLAND: DESIGNED TO EXPLAIN THE MANNER IN WHICH SUCH TITLES HAVE BEEN, AND MAY BE, ACQUIRED AND COMPLETED v (1808) (the preface includes four pages of fine type on creation and use of the book, *e.g.*, "I have believed that it would not fail to engage the perusal of that respectable description of citizens for whose use it is professedly designed.").

[133] *E.g.*, THE PENSION LAWS, OF THE UNITED STATES, INCLUDING SUNDRY RESOLUTIONS OF CONGRESS, FROM 1776 TO 1833: EXECUTED AT THE WAR DEPARTMENT ... COMPILED BY

- poor,[134]
- canals,[135]

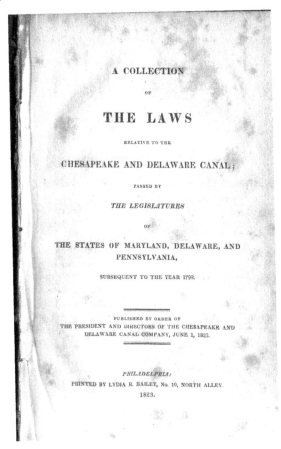

A COLLECTION

OF

THE LAWS

RELATIVE TO THE

CHESAPEAKE AND DELAWARE CANAL;

PASSED BY

THE LEGISLATURES

OF

THE STATES OF MARYLAND, DELAWARE, AND
PENNSYLVANIA,

SUBSEQUENT TO THE YEAR 1798.

PUBLISHED BY ORDER OF
THE PRESIDENT AND DIRECTORS OF THE CHESAPEAKE AND
DELAWARE CANAL COMPANY, JUNE 1, 1823.

PHILADELPHIA:
PRINTED BY LYDIA R. BAILEY, No. 10, NORTH ALLEY.
1823.

ROBERT MAYO, M.D. iv (1833) ("the Secretary of War has thought proper to charge an humble individual in the Pension Office, with the task of compiling this system of laws . . . . To dignify the Pension laws of our country, with a place in the nomenclature of systems, may seem ridiculous to those who view these laws in a detached sense, or in the order of their dates only. But he who will take a survey of the prominent enactments, connected with the minute details growing out of each as they are developed, though they were commenced and progressed under the dictates of justice and gratitude, without any view to system building, will nevertheless discover and admire therein, that beautiful symmetry and order of parts, which constitute system in any branch of science or law, natural or civil.")

[134] E.g., JONATHAN LEAVITT, A SUMMARY OF THE LAWS OF MASSACHUSETTS, RELATIVE TO THE SETTLEMENT, SUPPORT, EMPLOYMENT AND REMOVAL OF PAUPERS (1810).

[135] E.g., A COLLECTION OF THE LAWS RELATIVE TO THE CHESAPEAKE AND DELAWARE CANAL: PASSED BY THE LEGISLATURES OF THE STATES OF MARYLAND, DELAWARE, AND PENNSYLVANIA, SUBSEQUENT TO THE YEAR 1798: PUBLISHED JUNE 1, 1823 (1823).

- commerce,[136]
- maritime,[137]
- slavery laws for abolitionists,[138]
- slavery laws for slave owners,[139]

[136] *E.g.*, J. C. GILLELAND, THE COUNTING-HOUSE ASSISTANT, OR, A BRIEF DIGEST OF AMERICAN MERCANTILE LAW: EMBRACING THE LAW OF CONTRACT (1818) (statement of rules for self-application to avoid lawsuits); JOSHUA MONTEFIORE, THE AMERICAN TRADER'S COMPENDIUM: CONTAINING THE LAWS, CUSTOMS, AND REGULATIONS OF THE UNITED STATES, RELATIVE TO COMMERCE: INCLUDING THE MOST USEFUL PRECEDENTS ADAPTED TO GENERAL BUSINESS (1811) (alphabetical listing of concepts with some forms).

[137] *E.g.*, JOSEPH BLUNT, THE MERCHANT'S AND SHIPMASTER'S ASSISTANT; CONTAINING INFORMATION USEFUL TO THE AMERICAN MERCHANTS, OWNERS, AND MASTERS OF SHIPS iii (1832) ("a work of this nature has long been imperiously required by the shipmaster, the merchant, the lawyer, and the statesman. . . . [It includes] As much of the common law, relative to bills of exchange, factorage, and freight, as is necessary to guide a person in the ordinary course of business, is next presented. . . . A digest is then given of the laws of Congress . . .. The commercial statutes of the different states follow the acts of Congress. . . .. Without regarding the different legislative jurisdiction to which he is subjected at different times, a master naturally acts as if the same law was in force throughout the United States, and becomes liable to penalties, which a little acquaintance with the statutes would have enabled him to avoid. In enacting laws relative to commerce, the state legislatures have evidently seldom, if ever, consulted the provisions on the same subject in the sister states; and in this independent method of legislation, a system discordant in its provisions, overburdened with details, and incongruous in itself, has grown up with the increase of our trade, to the vexation and dismay of the owners and masters of ships."); *id.*. (1st ed., 1822; 9th ed., 1857); German edition, BESTIMMUNGEN ÜBER HANDEL UND SCHIFFFAHRT DER VEREINIGTEN STAATEN VON NORD-AMERIKA ... NACH J. BLUNT'S AMERIKANISCHEM WERKE (Carl F. Loosey, transl., 1855) (published in Vienna, but by an Austrian in New York City).

[138] *E.g.*, NEW YORK MANUMISSION SOCIETY, SELECTIONS FROM THE REVISED STATUTES OF THE STATE OF NEW YORK: CONTAINING ALL THE LAWS OF THE STATE RELATIVE TO SLAVES, AND THE LAW RELATIVE TO THE OFFENCE OF KIDNAPPING; WHICH SEVERAL LAWS COMMENCED AND TOOK EFFECT JANUARY 1, 1830, TOGETHER WITH EXTRACTS FROM THE LAWS OF THE UNITED STATES, RESPECTING SLAVES (1830); GEORGE M. STROUD, A SKETCH OF THE LAWS RELATING TO SLAVERY IN THE SEVERAL STATES OF THE UNITED STATES OF AMERICA v–vi (1827) (Preface: "Having been under the necessity of bringing together the laws of so large a number of independent states, it must be obvious that considerable difficulty existed in assigning to each part its proper place and giving to each its due effect, and, at the same time, preserving the appearance of symmetry in the whole." . . . "Of the *actual* condition of slaves this sketch does not profess to treat. In representative republics, however, like the United States, where the popular voice so greatly influences all political concerns, – where the members of the legislative departments are dependent for their places upon *annual* elections, – the laws may be safely regarded as constituting a faithful exposition of the sentiments of the people, and as furnishing, therefor, strong evidence of the practical enjoyments and privations of those whom they are designed to govern.") (2d ed., 1858).

[139] *E.g.*, JACOB D. WHEELER, A PRACTICAL TREATISE ON THE LAW OF SLAVERY. BEING A COMPILATION OF ALL THE DECISIONS MADE ON THAT SUBJECT, IN THE SEVERAL COURTS OF THE UNITED STATES, AND STATE COURTS. WITH COPIOUS NOTES AND REFERENCES TO THE STATUTES AND OTHER AUTHORITIES, SYSTEMATICALLY ARRANGED (1837).

- roads and highways,[140]
- railroads,[141] and,
- as is noted below, the Centennial Guards that provided security at the Centennial exposition.[142]

At their best, they instruct the user in how to carry out the tasks with which they are charged. They find their forerunners in manuals for justices of the peace of the first half-century of the Republic.[143] Well-conceived and executed

---

[140] *E.g.*, William Duane, A View of the Law of Roads, Highways, Bridges and Ferries in Pennsylvania (1848) (professional manual with procedures extracting statutes); A Counselor at Law, Plank Road Manual, Including the General Law of Plank Roads and Turnpikes of the State of New York, with the References to the Revised Statutes, Also an Appendix, Containing a Short Essay on the Construction of Plank Roads, and All the Necessary Forms and Precedents to Be Used under the Acts (1848).

[141] *E.g.*, Moses M. Strong (Attorney of the Company), A Compilation of the Several Acts of the Legislature of Wisconsin Affecting the La Crosse & Milwaukee R.R. Company: Together with the By-Laws of the Company: Also, Some General Laws of the State in Relation to Rail Road (1856); Bonney, Charles Carroll. Rules of Law for the Carriage and Delivery of Persons and Property by Railway: with the Leading Railway Statutes and Decisions of Illinois, Indiana, Michigan, Ohio, Pennsylvania, New York and the United States: Prepared for Railway Companies and the Legal Profession (1864) ("This book is designed for the guidance of railway companies, their agents, employes [sic] and patrons, in the receipt, transportation and delivery of persons and property; and for the convenience of the profession in advising thereof. ... In other words, I have endeavored to make a book in which the rights, duties and liabilities of passengers, consignors, engineers, consignees and other persons concerned in or affected by the usual course of railway business, may readily be found distinctly presented, and plainly expressed. The statutes are rarely found complete, outside of the State in which they belong; and the decisions condensed and reported, are scattered through so large a number of volumes, as to be unavailable for every-day use"; i) "I cannot resist the conviction, that a familiarity with the subject-matter of this treatise, by the non-professional persons for whose use it is, in part, designed, would prevent many of the losses and accidents which now occur"; ii) Edmund F. Webb (compiler), The Railroad Laws of Maine: Containing All Public and Private Acts and Resolves, Relating to Railroads in Said State, with References to Decisions of Supreme Judicial Court: Also a Digest of the Decisions of the Courts of Said State, on the Subject of Railroads: and Copies of All Mortgages, Deeds of Trust, Leases, and Contracts, Made by Said Railroads (1875) ("The object of this volume is to present the entire body of the railroad law of this State in a convenient and accessible form. ... Railroad laws have so multiplied as to embarrass those having occasion to trace them through so many volumes. It is hoped this compilation may abridge their labors." Unnumbered Preface.).

[142] *See* text at Chapter 6, note 1, *infra*.

[143] *See*, *e.g.*, Eliphalet Ladd (ed.), Burn's Abridgment, or the American Justice; Containing the Whole Practice, Authority and Duty of Justices of the Peace; With Correct Forms of Precedents Relating Thereto, and Adapted to the Present Situation of the United States vii–viii (2d ed., 1792) ("As an American I cannot but love and revere the laws and constitution of my country .... A constitution, – at which the breasts of philosophers have burned with rapture! Laws – which gladden the heart of the peasant in his cottage, knowing himself not beneath their protection. ... Those laws, and that constitution ... have contributed ... to erect a system of LEGAL LIBERTY, as well for the instruction and benefit of mankind, as the delight, wonder, and blessing, of AMERICANS.")

such books give the statutes that they support true effectiveness. People really can carry out the laws themselves.

Occupational literature has requirements that limit distribution: it needs to be authoritative. That means any one book is practically confined to one jurisdiction, or to a group of closely related jurisdictions where it is possible to spell out variations. Useful occupational literature depends on the user being able to rely on the book. That means the law the book reports needs to be comprehensible and stable and not undermined by frequent changes in law.

F. SYSTEMATIZING LAWS FOR THE PEOPLE

"Government of the people, by the people, for the people" Abraham Lincoln, *Gettysburg Address* (1863). Source: Brady's National Photographic Portrait Galleries, President Abraham Lincoln, three-quarter length portrait, seated, May 16, 1861, Library of Congress, LC-DIG-ds-00121, available at http://www.loc.gov/pictures/item/2009630687/ (accessed Feb. 24, 2017).

In 1788, a dozen years after the beginning of the Republic's first century, James Madison foretold in *Federalist No. 62*: "It will be of little avail *to the people*, that the laws are made by men of their own choice, if the laws be so voluminous that they cannot be read, or so incoherent that they cannot be understood."[144]

---

[144] [James Madison], *The Senate, Federalist No. 62*, INDEPENDENT JOURNAL, Feb. 27, 1788. [Emphasis added.]

In 1861, fifteen years before the end of the Republic's first century, President Abraham Lincoln sought the same. In his first state of the Union message, "in the midst of unprecedented political troubles," this is what he said:

> It seems to me very important that the statute laws should be made plain and intelligent as possible, and be reduced to as small a compass as may consist with the fullness and prescience of the will of the Legislature and the perspicuity of its language; these, well done, would, I think, greatly facilitate the labors of those whose duty it is to assist in the administration of the laws, and would be a lasting benefit to the people by placing before them, in a more accessible and intelligible form, the laws which so deeply concern their interests and their duties.[145]

A dozen years later, on the eve of the Centennial Congress adopted the *Revised Statutes of the United States.*

The Centennial Writers were asked to write about progress in American law. Progress meant systematizing. For the first century of the Republic and for another decade thereafter, Americans systematized their laws. Today, that Americans have laws not much systematized beyond compilation is not due to lack of popular desire for systematized laws, but to failures of the political system to carry out their wishes and to deliver a government of laws. The American people have never voted for common law.

1. *Necessity and Difficulty of Systematizing*

Systematizing was – and is – necessary to a well-functioning modern state; in importance it may be second only to the written constitution itself.[146] For rules

---

[145] Abraham Lincoln, *Annual Message to Congress, December 3, 1861, in* 5 THE COLLECTED WORKS OF ABRAHAM LINCOLN 35 (1953). [Emphasis added.]

    Already in 1848 the Judiciary Committee of the House of Representatives (Joseph R. Ingersoll) reported a bill to revise federal statutes, noting "Among the States, occasional revisions of the laws are resorted to. The time has arrived when a similar proceeding has become eminently proper on the part of the general-government." U.S. House, Committee on the Judiciary, *Revision of the Laws of the United States* (to accompany H.R. 671), H.R. REP. NO. 30–671 (1848).

    In August 1860 an English journal, in an article reprinted in Canada, reported a movement to revise federal statutes and that the U.S. Senate had agreed to a resolution "for the appointment of a commissioner to revise the public statutes; to simplify their language; to correct their incongruities; to supply their deficiencies; to arrange them in order; to reduce them to one connected text; and to report them thus improved to Congress for its final action, to the end that the public statutes, which all are presumed to know, may be in such form as to be more within the apprehension of all." *Codification of Law in America*, 4 SOLICITORS' J. AND REP. 833 (1860), *reprinted in* 6 UPPER CANADA L.J. (OLD SERIES) 222 (1860). Lincoln the systematizer has recently been hailed as the codifier of the laws of war. *See* WITT, *supra* note 124.

[146] *See, e.g., Revision of the Laws in Massachusetts*, 13 AM. JURIST AND LAW MAG. 344, 378 (1835) ("The formation of a code is a magnificent enterprise, worthy of a State; success in which is

to guide, they and their contents must be accessible. When one has only a few laws, one can skim through them all to find the rules that one needs. When one has more than a few laws, one organizes the laws to enable finding what one needs. Systematizing is a normal development of written laws. Even such a short set of laws as the biblical Ten Commandments is systematized: the commandments begin with affirmative duties to God, continue with affirmative duties to parents, and conclude with prohibitions of acts harmful to one's fellow men. Systematizing is necessary to a government of laws. In a government of laws, law must be accessible to people. Without system, laws become unknowable, inconsistent and incoherent. Tyrants, not laws, govern. In the 19th century proponents of systemization likened its absence to the reign of the Roman Emperor Caligula, who "published" laws in such ways that no one could read them.[147]

one of the most glorious events in the annals of any community. . . . If well accomplished, it is, next to the formation of a frame of government, pre-eminently the most important and social achievement."). *Cf.* George P. Fletcher, *Three Nearly Sacred Books in Western Law*, 54 ARK. L. REV. 1 (2001) (comparing the French and German Civil Codes with the United States Constitution).

[147] *See, e.g.,* J. Louis Tellkampf, *On Codification, or the Systematizing of the Law*, 26 AM. JURIST & L. MAG. 113 (1841), 283, 288 (1842), *reprinted in* J.L. TELLKAMPF, ESSAYS ON LAW REFORM, ETC. 3, 44 (1st ed., London, 1859) (2d ed., Berlin, 1875) ("To hang up the laws on a high pillar, as . . . the tyrant did, so that no citizen could read them; or, which amounts to the same thing, to bury them under all the materials of learned books, customs, scattered statutes, and collections of decisions or conflicting judgments and opinions, so that a knowledge of jurisprudence can be attained by only a few of the people; such a state of things can in no wise be justified."). *See also, On the Promulgation of the Laws*, 6 AM. L.J. 152k, 152m [sic] (1817); John Adair, *Legislature of Kentucky* [Governor's Message, Oct. 16, 1821], 21 NILES' WEEKLY REG. 185, 189–190 Nov. 17, 1821) ("In free states where the people either make the laws, or choose those who do, the principle of the government is corrupted whenever the people cease to understand those laws."); Joseph Desha, *[Governor's Message]*, JOURNAL OF THE HOUSE OF THE GENERAL ASSEMBLY OF THE COMMONWEALTH OF KENTUCKY 14, 15 ("Unintelligible laws are no better than unpublished laws, known only to the tyrant who makes them.") (Dec. 26, 1827); BENJAMIN JAMES, A DIGEST OF THE LAWS OF SOUTH-CAROLINA, ...; A COMPENDIOUS SYSTEM OF THE GENERAL PRINCIPLES AND DOCTRINES OF THE COMMON LAW, ... THE WHOLE BEING DESIGNED, CHIEFLY, FOR THE INSTRUCTION AND USE OF THE PRIVATE CITIZEN AND INFERIOR MAGISTRATE x (1822); James Brown Ray, *[Governor's Address, December 4, 1827]*, JOURNAL OF THE SENATE OF THE STATE OF INDIANA: BEING THE TWELFTH SESSION OF THE GENERAL ASSEMBLY; BEGUN AND HELD ... ON MONDAY THE THIRD DAY OF DECEMBER, 1827, 9, 26 (1827); Maynard Davis Richardson, *Codification, in* THE REMAINS OF MAYNARD DAVIS RICHARDSON 93, 96 (1833); WILLIAM SCHLEY, A DIGEST OF THE ENGLISH STATUTES OF FORCE IN THE STATE OF GEORGIA; ... xvii–xviii (1826) ("hence the ignorance of many in regard to this branch of our laws, which was as much out the reach of the people, as were the laws of Caligula."); Leland Stanford, *Annual Message of the Governor, January 7th, 1863*, JOURNAL OF THE SENATE OF THE STATE OF CALIFORNIA DURING THE FOURTEENTH SESSION OF THE LEGISLATURE OF THE STATE OF CALIFORNIA: 1863, 27, 44–45 [page 52 of the JOURNAL OF THE ASSEMBLY] ("no person, not versed in law, can with any certainty of correctness, turn to the

Three reasons for systematizing stand out: *governing* rationally through knowable laws, *unifying* laws in governed areas and *reforming* laws. The relative importance of each of these reasons has varied from place-to-place and time-to-time. In many instances, perhaps most and contrary to intuition, law reform is not the major reason for systematizing, but is only incidental to rationalization or unification.[148]

Principal arguments made for systematizing have been similar over time and place.[149] Systematized law is law knowable by the people and law they can abide by. Where a legal answer cannot be known beforehand, systematized law can give transparency to how decisions will be made. Systematized law can control and direct those who govern. Systematized law, as unified law, brings together people in one legal order. Systematized law, as reformed law, as consistent law, promotes equal justice under law.

Principal arguments made against systematizing laws, likewise, have remained steady. Systematized laws, it is said, are inflexible and adjust less well to changes in society over time. Because written law focuses on language and system, if it is the exclusive source of law, it is said to tie the hands of decision makers in individual cases and to make it harder for them to reach just or pragmatic solutions.[150] Systematized law, as unified law, denies legal diversity.

pages of our statute book to ascertain what the law is"); E.W. [presumably Emory Washburn], *We Need a Criminal Code*, 7 AM. L. REV. 264, 266 (1872).

The metaphor originates in SUETONIUS, THE LIVES OF THE TWELVE CAESARS, paragraph 41 (A.D. 121), and was used in England and Germany as well. *See, e.g., On the Promulgation of the Laws*, 1 J. JURISPRUDENCE 241, 242 (1821). Tellkampf, followed Hegel closely and, like Hegel, referred (incorrectly) to the tyrant Dionysius instead of Caligula. *See* T.M. KNOX, HEGEL'S PHILOSOPHY OF RIGHT TRANSLATED WITH NOTES 358 n. 64 (1952). *See also* [James Madison], *The Senate, Federalist No. 62*, INDEPENDENT JOURNAL, FEB. 27, 1788 ("Law is defined to be a rule of action; but how can that be a rule, which is little known, and less fixed? Another effect of public instability is the unreasonable advantage it gives to the sagacious, the enterprising, and the moneyed few over the industrious and uniformed mass of the people.")

[148] E.g., *Report of the Committee*, THE CODE OF THE STATE OF GEORGIA PREPARED BY R.H. CLARK, T.R.R. COBB AND D. IRWIN v, viii (1861).

[149] *See, e.g.,* in reverse chronological order, HUGH COLLINS, WHY EUROPE NEEDS A CIVIL CODE 2–3 (2013); DAVID DUDLEY FIELD, *Codification*, 20 AM. L. REV. 1 (1886) *reprinted in* 3 SPEECHES, ARGUMENTS, AND MISCELLANEOUS PAPERS OF DAVID DUDLEY FIELD 238 (Titus Munson Coan, ed., 1890); DAVID DUDLEY FIELD, *Reasons for the Adoption of the Codes, Substance of an Address before the Judiciary Committee of the Lower House of the Legislature, at Albany, on the 19th of February, 1873, on the Codes, in* 1 SPEECHES, ARGUMENTS, AND MISCELLANEOUS PAPERS OF DAVID DUDLEY FIELD 361 (A.P. Sprague, ed., 1884); [Joseph Story et al.], *[Appendix] Law, Legislation, Codes*, 7 ENCYCLOPÆDIA AMERICANA 576, 581, 586–592 (1834).

[150] Field asserted that "Every argument against a code is, in my judgment, full of sophistry. The only one I shall stop to consider, is that the judges should be left to make the law as they go along." DAVID DUDLEY FIELD, LAW REFORM IN THE UNITED STATES AND ITS INFLUENCE

Arguments against systematizing often go beyond theory to focus on practicalities. Systematizing costs too much. It is too difficult. Its benefits are too few. Some arguments are political: lack of trust in the systematizers or in the systematization or disapproval of changes in law systematized. The practical response of proponents of systematizing is to point to experiences of places that have systematized: who has ever had codes and reverted to no codes?

The persistence of these arguments in the United States is remarkable. Today they are recited with the same conviction of truth as they were two hundred years ago. Yet, in the meantime, the world has developed modern legal methods.[151] The world has seen the successes of French and German code-based methods and has imitated them. It has seen the failures of American contemporary common-law methods. Yet the United States remains without codes.[152] Is there another staple of modern society that the world has which the United States lacks?

The enormity of the work of systematizing well done is hard to appreciate even for legislators, lawyers and judges, not to speak of laymen, historians or law teachers.[153] Legislators when they commission a code seem to expect to get it back by "by return mail."[154] Lawyers in practice work with one case at a time. In counseling they advise how they see the law in one or a handful of fact situations. In litigating they argue for one view that they see as benefiting their client. Judges focus on one set of facts and the laws that might apply to it. Law teachers in America assume the role of lawyers.

Good lawmakers, on the other hand, provide for all possible cases, even though they well know that they cannot anticipate all possible cases. Good lawmakers capture in a few understandable words what they want people to do, even when they themselves may not know what they want people to do in some cases. Good lawmakers make their laws consistent internally and with

ABROAD, REPRINTED FROM THE AMERICAN LAW REVIEW OF AUGUST, 1891, WITH SOME CHANGES AND NOTES 20 (1891).
[151] *See* James R. Maxeiner, *Scalia & Garner's Reading Law: A Civil Law for the Age of Statutes?*, 6 J. CIVIL L. STUDIES 1 (2013).
[152] *See* James R. Maxeiner, *The Cost of No Codes*, 31 MISSISSIPPI COLLEGE L. REV. 363 (2013), *also in* THE SCOPE AND STRUCTURE OF CIVIL CODES (J. César Rivera, ed., IUS GENTIUM Vol. 32, 2014). *See generally* WOLFGANG FIKENTSCHER, DIE METHODEN DES RECHTS IN VERGLEICHENDER DARSTELLUNG (5 vols., 1975–1977).
[153] *Cf.*, *Revised Code of Pennsylvania* 19 AM. Q. REV. [Robert Walsh], 399, 403, 409 (1836) ("The amount and complexity of their labours in this respect are not to be judged by the bulk of their production. Not a trace of two-thirds of the actual expense of time and study, which are necessary to the rejection of what maybe supposed to be redundancies, as to the adoption of new provisions, appears upon the face of the reported bills.")
[154] JOHN WORTH EDMONDS, AN ADDRESS ON THE CONSTITUTION AND CODE OF PROCEDURE AND THE MODIFICATIONS OF THE LAW EFFECTED THEREBY 46 (1848).

other laws. Positivist legal philosopher John Austin famously said that this "the technical part of legislation, is incomparably more difficult than what may be styled the ethical."[155]

Modern Skeptics of Historical Systematization

American professors of common-law myth denigrate systematizing as part of a chimerical quest for what they see as unattainable legal certainty.[156] Some American legal historians discount benefits of systematizing for the legal system as a whole, for public policy, for justice and for law-abiding. For example, Professor Lawrence Friedman writes: "it is hard to see how society can be changed by reforms which only rearrange law on paper."[157] Professor Kermit Hall saw codifiers as "unconcerned about the effects of codification on the poorer classes, stressing instead the lack of uniformity and certainty in U.S. law, especially in matters affecting commercial relations."[158] Hall and others trivialize codifying. If they note it at all, they dismiss it as "a critical response to the judicial creation of an American common law."[159]

Critical legal studies Professor Robert W. Gordon suggests that the idea that the "unruly mess" of the mid 19th century could through rule reform be remedied was "a kind of collectively maintained fantasy of what society would like if everyone played by the rules." According to Gordon, this "fantasy" explains why the proponents of codes in the 1870s and 1880s "should have invested most of their public energy in what may seem to us a relatively sterile and peripheral activity: the improvement of legal science."[160] So today the

---

[155] John Austin, *Codification and Law Reform*, in 2 John Austin, Lectures on Jurisprudence or the Philosophy of Positive Law 1092, 1099 (5th ed., Robert Campbell, ed., 1885).

[156] *See* James R. Maxeiner, *Legal Indeterminacy Made in America: U.S. Legal Methods and the Rule of Law*, 41 Valparaiso L. Rev. 517 (2006). *But see*, James R. Maxeiner, *Legal Certainty and Legal Methods: A European Alternative to American Legal Indeterminacy?*, 15 Tulane J. Int'l & Comp. L. 541 (2007).

[157] Lawrence M. Friedman, A History of American Law 354 (1973) ("Behind the work of the law reformers was a sort of theory: that the legal system is best, and works best, and does the most for society, which conforms to the ideal of legal rationality – the system which is most clearly, orderly, systematic (in its formal parts), which has the most structural beauty, which most appeals to the modern, well-educated jurist. The theory was rarely made explicit, and of course never tested. It was in all probability false . . . .") The third edition, 2004, at 304–305, is similar.

[158] Kermit L. Hall The Magic Mirror: Law in American History 126 (1989).

[159] Kermit L. Hall & Peter Karsten, The Magic Mirror: Law in American History 139 (2d ed., 2009) (giving codifying one page out of 465). *See also* G. Edward White, American Legal History: A Very Short Introduction (2014) (not even a footnote in 149 pages).

[160] Robert W. Gordon, *"The Ideal and the Actual in the Law": Fantasies and Practices of New York City Lawyers, 1870–1910*, in The New High Priests: Lawyers in Post–Civil War America 51, 53–55 (Gerard W. Gawalt, ed., 1984).

United States remains a land without a science of law (in the sense of what in Germany is called *Rechtswissenschaft*).

Such thinking explains the practical disappearance of statutes and their systematizing from American legal consciousness. That which the Centennial Writers saw as the way "to the direct and practical amelioration of mankind,"[161] lawyers on the eve of the sesquicentennial in 1926 suppressed as an un-American attempt "to supplant the parent Common Law" and "to forsake our English heritage and follow the lead of Imperial Rome."[162] Bicentennial writers – in the middle of what Americans were about to call the "Age of Statutes" – celebrated *Common Faith and Common Law* and took no note of statutes or codes.[163] Millennial American and English writers jointly celebrated *Common Law, Common Values, Common Rights*, with no mention of statutes of the century just past, such as the American Civil Rights Act of 1964 or the U.K. Human Rights Act 1998.[164]

The Centennial Writers were right; the code opponents were wrong. Comparison of the century-and-a-half of America's common law failures and civil law success proves it.

2. *Forms of Systematizing: Compilations, Revised Statutes, Codes*

Systematizing requires an ordered inventory (*e.g.*, alphabetical or chronological) of applicable laws that are available for consultation. In American usage laws passed individually over years by legislatures are "compiled." Compiling is a first step in systematizing laws but not the last.[165] Laws exist to govern daily life. When compiling statutes, inconsistencies become apparent. It becomes obvious, moreover, that some statutes have become obsolete. A government of laws deals with inconsistencies and obsolescence. No man

---

[161] *Law in America: 1776–1876*, 122 N. AM. REV. at 174.

[162] J. Carroll Hayes, *The Visit to England of the American Bar Association, in* THE AMERICAN BAR ASSOCIATION LONDON MEETING 1924: IMPRESSIONS OF ITS SOCIAL, OFFICIAL, PROFESSIONAL AND JURIDICAL ASPECTS AS RELATED BY PARTICIPANTS IN CONTEST FOR MOST ENLIGHTENING REVIEW OF TRIP (1925) 9, 15 (reporting the consensus of the bar at the meeting).

[163] POLITICAL SEPARATION AND LEGAL COMMUNITY: COMMON FAITH AND COMMON LAW (Harry W. Jones, ed., 1976).

[164] COMMON LAW, COMMON VALUES, COMMON RIGHTS, ESSAYS ON OUR COMMON HERITAGE BY DISTINGUISHED BRITISH AND AMERICAN AUTHORS (2000). British indifference to statutes is especially remarkable; the Regulations and Directives of the European Union go unnoted.

[165] In 1838 the *American Jurist* explained that even a compilation is a "great good": "The first step is thus taken towards the formation of a written code of laws, in which the whole body of common and statute law shall be amalgamated into one homogenous mass." *Revised Statutes of North Carolina* [Review], 19 AM. JURIST & L. MAG. 484, 485 (1838).

can follow contrary commands. No man should be required to follow laws that have lost their reason for being. In American usage systematizing to make laws consistent and current is to "revise" laws.

Revised laws do not fulfill fully the promise of systematization. To apply law well, one should be able to find and interpret easily the particular laws that govern. One should need to consult as few laws as is commensurate with the complexity of the matter at hand. Historically a common way to make law accessible in this sense has been through "codifying" laws into a limited number of codes. Codes in this sense are systematic statements of particular areas of law. They thus can state laws in ways that facilitate the learning and the applying of the legal rules that they contain. Codifying, more than revising, changes existing law, in form or substance or both.

In American usage "code" is often used in a different sense that does not include systematizing, at least systematizing beyond compiling. "Code" may refer only to a mere compilation. Similarly, "code" may be a shorthand for the complete body of a state's standing laws.

At other times, "codes" in American usage *are* systematized bodies of laws aspiring to, if not reaching the systematization of French or German codes. "Revised laws" may be functionally equivalent to codes in this sense.[166] What sets these American codes apart from their Continental counterparts is not so much the lesser level of systematization as it is the different treatment by the courts. Continental courts start legal reasoning from codes and give codes priority over other sources of law. American courts may ignore codes and defer to other sources of law.[167]

---

[166] For discussions of the distinctions, *see* The First Century of the Republic at 451; Erwin C. Surrency, A History of American Law Publishing 85 (1990). The former draws a sharp line between codes and revised statutes.

[167] Consider already the more Continental style treatment Justice Story and his Commission had in mind for one of those areas of the law to be codified:

IV. The Commissioners are, in the next place, of opinion, that the law of evidence, as applicable both to civil and criminal proceedings, should be reduced to a Code.

And, in order to guard against any objections founded upon a misconception of the nature, objects, and effects of such a codification as the Commissioners propose to insert in such a Code, the following fundamental rules for its interpretation-and application.

I. The Code is to be interpreted and be applied to future cases, as a Code of the common law of Massachusetts, and not as a Code of mere positive or statute law. It is to be deemed an affirmance of what the common law now is, and not as containing provisions in derogation of that law, and therefore subject to a strict construction.

II. Consequently, it is to furnish the rules for decisions in courts of justice, not only in cases directly (*ex directo*) within its terms, but indirectly, and by analogy, in cases where, as a part of the common law, it would and ought to be applied by courts of justice, in like manner.

III. In all cases not provided for by the Code, or governed by the analogies therein contained, the common law of Massachusetts, as now existing, is to furnish the rules for

The Centennial Writers expected that systematizing would advance beyond compiling. The *North American Review* wrote "The practical administration of law depends . . . upon its simplicity . . . No nation, in modern times, can afford to go on accumulating vast masses of authoritative decisions and statutes, without occasionally stopping to digest decisions and to revise written laws."[168] "[Practical administration] can only be attained . . . by resorting to the expedient of codification."[169] Harper's *First Century of the Republic* reported that by 1876 nearly every one of the by then 37 states – including rebelling states – had revised or codified its laws since 1860.[170] It was, as one contemporary wrote, "a necessity, and from the earliest dawnings of law has been so considered."[171]

Revising and codifying are more challenging than compiling. One systematizer can speak for many. In 1835 Mississippi's reviser in reporting to the legislature on his progress in preparing a Revised Code, explained his delay: "The consolidation of numerous statutes into one uniform law, embracing the whole subject of them, requires great care and deliberation. The foundations of the law are to be examined, prior legislation is to be revised and weighted, and the legitimate consequences of the principles embodied, logically deduced. However easy all this may appear to a cursory observer, yet certain I am, that whoever shall attempt the labor, will find an ample field for mental exertion."[172] He fulfilled his commission, but the legislature did not adopt his work.[173]

---

decision, unless so far as it is repugnant to the common law affirmed in the Code, or to the statute law of the State.

Such is the basis of the Code proposed by the Commissioners, and such the principles, by which they propose, that those who shall be called upon to perform the duty of codification, should be guided."
REPORT OF THE COMMISSIONERS APPOINTED TO CONSIDER AND REPORT UPON THE PRACTICABILITY AND EXPEDIENCY OF REDUCING TO A WRITTEN AND SYSTEMATIC CODE THE COMMON LAW OF MASSACHUSETTS, OR ANY PART THEREOF. MADE TO HIS EXCELLENCY THE GOVERNOR, JAN., 1837, at 24–25 (1873).

[168] *Law in America: 1776–1876*, 122 N. AM. REV. at 179.   [169] *Id.*

[170] THE FIRST CENTURY OF THE REPUBLIC at 451 (excluding possibly Pennsylvania and Tennessee). *See also Chapter XXXV. Revised Statutes, in* WILLIAM B. WEDGWOOD, THE GOVERNMENT AND LAWS OF THE UNITED STATES: A COMPLETE AND COMPREHENSIVE VIEW OF THE RISE, PROGRESS, AND PRESENT ORGANIZATION OF THE STATE AND NATIONAL GOVERNMENT 112 (1866) (stating that every state by 1866 had published "Revised Statutes of the State").

[171] P.N. Bowman, *Interstate Revision and Codification*, 3 SO. L. REV. (New Series) 573, 575 (1877).

[172] Letter of P. Rutilius R. Pray, dated January 15th, 1835, to the Honorable P. Briscoe, President of the Senate, *in* JOURNAL OF THE SENATE OF THE STATE OF MISSISSIPPI AT A CALLED SESSION THEREOF, HELD IN THE TOWN OF JACKSON [commencing Jan. 19, 1835] 84, 85 (1835).

[173] A. HUTCHINSON, CODE OF MISSISSIPPI; BEING AN ANALYTICAL COMPILATION OF THE PUBLIC AND GENERAL STATUTES OF THE TERRITORY AND STATE, ... FROM 1798 TO 1848 .... at 67. *See* R. RUTILIUS R. PRAY, NOTES TO THE REVISED STATUTES OF THE STATE OF MISSISSIPPI (1836).

Compilations were non-controversial. Revisions and codifications, on the other hand, were controversial and, at best, partly successful. The records of compilations are fat bound volumes. Records of revisions and codifications often are ephemeral: draft laws, committee reports, legislative debates public discourses, pamphlets, journals and newspapers. But they exist in quantity: a *Bibliography of Codification and Statutory Revision*[174] from 1901 is fifty-seven pages long, lists over a thousand entries drawn from only six libraries in New York State. Hard to find in libraries, today most of these entries are on digital desktops.

G. UBIQUITY OF SYSTEMATIZING

In the first century of the Republic all American states and the federal government systematized their laws. All compiled their laws; all did so before they published official reports of the decisions of their courts. All published some form of revision or codification. There is no room for the idea that statutes and their systematization were ever foreign to America or for the thought that case law, that is, common law, was the one and only true law.

It is unhelpful to characterize systematization as a social, political or religious movement. It has no particular proponents and no particular beneficiaries. It has no particular place in time. It is, as the Centennial Writers and their contemporaries saw, more a natural phenomenon of modern government, such as democracy. If it is to be counted a movement, then it is a movement like public education. Public education is an apt analogy: proponents of the one were often proponents of the other.[175] Their shared goal was and is an educated public.

In the Republic's first century work toward revising and codifying was nearly everywhere – at least at some time, – and nearly every moment – at least somewhere. More often than not, leaders in revising and codifying were leaders in the legal system generally. The amount of energy they and the public put into compiling, revising and codifying was enormous. It is unrecognized today.

---

[174] It is appended to a seventy-five page report on *Statute Law in New York, From 1609 to 1901* which itself is a *Supplement* to [New York (State) Legislature], REPORT OF THE JOINT COMMITTEE OF THE LEGISLATURE OF 1900 ON STATUTORY REVISION COMMISSION BILLS, which itself is available on Google Books as an attachment to the REPORT OF THE SPECIAL COMMITTEE OF THE ASSEMBLY OF THE LEGISLATURE OF 1901 ON STATUTORY REVISION COMMISSION BILLS 1901.

[175] Examples are Thomas Jefferson in Virginia and Horace Mann and Joseph Story in Massachusetts.

1. *Steady Systematizing: The Original Thirteen States*

As noted above the first century of the Republic began with Jefferson rushing home to Virginia to initiate his Revisal of Virginia laws. Throughout the original thirteen states jurists compiled their states' laws. Virginia was the leader in revising. Bill-by-bill its legislature considered Jefferson's handwork.[176] Jefferson credited Madison for overcoming the opposition of "endless quibbles, chicaneries, perversions, vexations of lawyers and demi-lawyers."[177] When Madison went off to the Constitutional Convention in Philadelphia, others in Virginia picked up where he left off.[178] As for the importance of the work for the people, one publisher of the Virginia laws as revised opined: "it is plain that every family in the commonwealth, should, if possible, possess a copy of it."[179] But Virginia was not alone in taking up revision; it was just the first and most successful. South Carolina,[180] North Carolina (with later Associate Justice Iredell) and Pennsylvania (with Associate Justice Wilson) also made starts in the 18th century.

Americans can congratulate themselves on the alacrity with which they undertook – against substantial difficulties – the seemingly mundane task of compiling. Jefferson, before he could focus on reform of substantive law, collected physical copies of the statutes the legislature had adopted. James Wilson, who had the same task, explained to the Pennsylvania Assembly, "How can I make a digest of the laws, without having all the laws upon each head in my view?"[181]

---

[176] See JULIAN P. BOYD (ED.), PAPERS OF THOMAS JEFFERSON, vols. 1 to 3 (1950) (giving bill-by-bill descriptions).

[177] THE AUTOBIOGRAPHY OF THOMAS JEFFERSON, 1743–1790, TOGETHER WITH A SUMMARY OF THE CHIEF EVENTS IN JEFFERSON'S LIFE 71 (Paul Leicester Ford, ed., 1914; New Introduction by Michael Zuckerman, 2005).

[178] ERWIN C. SURRENCY, A HISTORY OF AMERICAN LAW PUBLISHING 80 (1990). The successor *Revised Code of 1792* was characterized by another author as "merely a compilation." Henry E. Ross, *History of Virginia Codification,* 11 VA. L. REG. 91 (1905).

[179] *Preface,* A COLLECTION OF ALL SUCH ACTS OF THE GENERAL ASSEMBLY OF VIRGINIA, OF A PUBLIC AND PERMANENT NATURE, AS ARE NOW IN FORCE v (Samuel Pleasants, Jun. & Henry Pace, 1803). This preface gives particular attention to practical conditions of cost and portability: "In riding ten, or fifteen miles to a county court-house, a gentleman does not always think it worth while to take a portmanteau along with him." *Id.* at ii–iii.

[180] 1 JOSEPH BREVARD, AN ALPHABETICAL DIGEST OF THE PUBLIC STATUTE LAW OF SOUTH-CAROLINA xvii (1814).

[181] 1 THE WORKS OF HONORABLE JAMES WILSON, L.L.D. Preface (Bird Wilson, ed., 1804), *reprinted in* 1 COLLECTED WORKS OF JAMES WILSON 418 (Kermit L. Hall and Mark David Hall, eds., 2007).

In the early Republic, even the task of compiling required a Herculean effort.[182] In the 1790s James Wilson in Pennsylvania and Thomas F. Grimké in South Carolina each reported dealing with over 1700 statutes in their respective states.[183] They had no clerical staffs and no means of reproduction of laws other than manual copying.[184] Communications were slow and mail services lacking. Finding all laws to be compiled could be practically impossible. Had Jefferson not been the avid book collector that he was, had he not had access to his own personal library and the personal libraries of others, he could not well have drafted his revisal.

Nevertheless, by 1800 all of the original thirteen states and the federal government had compiled their laws: Connecticut (1784); Delaware (1797); federal government (1797); Georgia (1800); Maryland (1799); Massachusetts (1788); New Hampshire (1789); New Jersey (1800); New York (1789); North Carolina (1791); Pennsylvania (1793–1797); Rhode Island (1798); South Carolina (1790); and Virginia (1794).[185]

In 1837, at the fiftieth anniversary of the United States Constitution, the *American Jurist and Law Magazine* presented a twenty-five-page detailed list with critical notices of the most recently published revisions, digests and collections of the then twenty-five states and the Federal government. This it did, not to satisfy academic interests, but to facilitate lawyers answering legal questions: "the labor of the inquirer is greatly diminished, by having recourse,

---

[182] The task was no less in England. *See* RICHARD WHALLEY BRIDGMAN, REFLECTIONS ON THE STUDY OF THE LAW 43 (1804) ("the code of statute laws has swollen to a mass so burthensome as to become insupportable even by an *Atlas* or *Hercules*, and to call for the aid of a second *Justinian* to digest, simplify, and reduce them." [emphasis in original]).

[183] THOMAS FAUCHERAND GRIMKÉ, *Preface*, THE PUBLIC LAWS OF THE STATE OF SOUTH-CAROLINA, FROM ITS FIRST ESTABLISHMENT AS A BRITISH PROVINCE DOWN TO THE YEAR 1790, INCLUSIVE .... (1790).

[184] Difficulties of copying dealt a body blow to Edward Livingston's proposed penal code. It was destroyed in a fire the night before he was to deliver it to the printer. JOHN D. BESSLER, THE BIRTH OF AMERICAN LAW: AN ITALIAN PHILOSOPHER AND THE AMERICAN REVOLUTION 335 (2014). The sheer technical demands of handwriting continued until the invention of the typewriter introduced to America at the Philadelphia Centennial Exposition. *Cf.*, REPORT OF THE CODE COMMISSIONERS OF THE STATE OF CALIFORNIA, NOV. 15TH, 1873, at 3 ("The work of copying four Codes, consisting of fourteen thousand one hundred and sixty-five sections, or about twenty thousand one hundred and seventy-six folios, required much time and occupied two Secretaries constantly nine months.") I could not locate a digitized copy of this Report.

[185] CHECK-LIST OF STATUTES OF STATES OF THE UNITED STATES OF AMERICA, INCLUDING REVISIONS, COMPILATIONS, DIGESTS, CODES AND INDEXES (Grace E. Macdonald, compiler, 1937). *See also* STATE LIBRARY OF MASSACHUSETTS, HAND-LIST OF LEGISLATIVE SESSIONS AND SESSION LAWS, STATUTORY REVISIONS, COMPILATIONS, CODES, ETC., AND CONSTITUTIONAL CONVENTIONS (1912).

in the first instance, to some general collection, behind which it is unnecessary to extend his examination."[186] It found "worthy of remark" that nearly fifty years of Congressional legislation had never been revised under the authority of the government.[187] It criticized some works, for example, Delaware (without "systematic arrangement")[188] and Maryland ("not revised or digested, but merely arranged and published in the order of their enactment"),[189] and praised others, for example, Georgia ("carefully and skillfully made")[190] and Louisiana ("the theory of obligations, ... comprising, in a condensed form, one of the most satisfactory digests of the general principles on that subject").[191]

2. *Systematizing Spreads with the People Over the Continent*

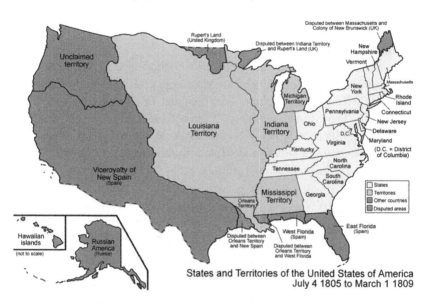

States and Territories of the United States of America
July 4 1805 to March 1 1809

Systematizing spread across the North American continent with the people who settled it. In every state some measure of systematizing occurred. Systematizing was part of the law. Systematizing was something leaders in law did. Systematizing was something the people expected.

---

[186] *A Notice of the Most Recent Revisions, Digests, and Collections of the Statute Laws of the United States and of the Several States*, 18 Am. Jurist & L. Mag. 227 (1837) (emphasis in original).

[187] *Id.* at 228. [188] *Id.* at 232. [189] *Id.* at 241. [190] *Id.* at 233. [191] *Id.* at 235.

By the Centennial in 1876 there were nearly three times as many states as in 1776: thirty-seven. New states, as they joined the Union (and some even before as territories), adopted, compiled, revised and codified laws. New states did not write on blank slates. They, too, faced challenges in compiling. Where original states sometimes could not find the laws that they had passed, new states sometimes could not tell which laws were their laws and where they applied. In the first century of the Republic, America's internal political boundaries changed dozens of times. New states had legal inheritances of laws from as many as a half dozen or more different states, territories and even countries.[192]

To merely say that it was everywhere – in the face of a century of denial – is not enough to challenge contemporary common-law myth. I beg readers' patience to show some of the many manifestations of systematization in America before the Civil War.[193]

Toulmin's Southwest Digests 1802–1823

The influence of Virginia and of Jefferson extended to Kentucky, the new state formed out of Virginia, and to Mississippi and Alabama to the south. Jefferson helped Harry Toulmin, an immigrant Englishman, become President of the Transylvania Seminary.[194] From there Toulmin become second Secretary of State of Kentucky (1796–1804). While Secretary of State he compiled Kentucky's laws[195] and wrote a multi-volume treatise on criminal law intended to be prefatory to a criminal code.[196] In 1804 Jefferson appointed

---

[192] Cf., e.g., George H. Hand, *Preface*, THE REVISED CODES OF THE TERRITORY OF DAKOTA A.D. 1877 iii (1877) ("During their existence as territories, the boundaries and extent of these divisions have been subject to frequent and marked changes, and new names have appeared and old ones have disappeared or become permanent in statues formed out of a part, rendering, until recently, the political geography of the territories more like the figures in the kaleidoscope.")

[193] See Nuno Garoupa & Andrew P. Morriss, *The Fable of the Codes: The Efficiency of the Common Law, Legal Origins, and Codification Movements*, 2012 U. ILL. L. REV. 1442 (2012) (which likewise, for somewhat other purposes, demonstrates wide-spread use of statutes).

[194] On Toulmin, see Paul M. Pruitt Jr., *Harry Toulmin: A Frontier Justinian*, in PAUL M. PRUITT, JR. TAMING ALABAMA: LAWYERS AND REFORMERS, 1804–1929 (2010).

[195] HARRY TOULMIN, SECRETARY TO THE COMMONWEALTH OF KENTUCKY, COLLECTION OF ALL THE PUBLIC AND PERMANENT ACTS OF THE GENERAL ASSEMBLY OF KENTUCKY WHICH ARE NOW IN FORCE, ARRANGED AND DIGESTED ACCORDING TO THEIR SUBJECT; TOGETHER WITH ACTS OF VIRGINIA xv (1802) ("The very confused and undigested state in which the acts of the Legislature of Kentucky have hitherto remained, rendered an arranged collection of them highly necessary both to professional gentlemen and to the public at large."). Toulmin included *A Summary of the Criminal Law of Kentucky as Applicable to Freeman*, at xxviii.

[196] HARRY TOULMIN & JAMES BLAIR, A REVIEW OF THE CRIMINAL LAW OF KENTUCKY (2 vols., 1804).

Toulmin federal judge for the Territory of Mississippi (1804–1819). While Territorial Judge Toulmin compiled the Territory's laws.[197] When the State of Alabama was created in the old Mississippi territory, Toulmin compiled its laws.[198]

Purchases of Civil Louisiana and Civil Florida

In 1803 the United States doubled its size when it purchased the Louisiana territory that had been variously under the civil law systems of France and Spain. The Territory of Orleans, the later state of Louisiana, was separated from the rest already in 1804. In 1808 that territory adopted the civil law-based *Digest of the Civil Laws in Force in the Territory of Orleans*. In 1812 the Constitution of the new state of Louisiana included an anti-reception clause designed to prevent the kind of adoption by reference of English law that some other states had allowed.[199] Notwithstanding popular perceptions, Louisiana was never under the Code Napoleon.[200] Louisiana has, however drawn on French codes in adopting its own laws and has defended its civil law inheritance against common-law intrusions.[201] Louisiana law has introduced French law to Americans.[202]

On the frontier, the object of legislation was clearer than the means. In 1822 at the first meeting of the Legislative Council of the Territory of Florida, the newly chosen President apologized for his lack of "practical experience of the forms of legislation." The Governor told the Council: "The uncertainty as to the laws actually in force in Florida, renders it your duty to give to the

---

[197] THE STATUTES OF THE MISSISSIPPI TERRITORY, REVISED AND DIGESTED BY THE AUTHORITY OF THE GENERAL ASSEMBLY (Harry Toulmin, compiler, 1807).

[198] DIGEST OF THE LAWS OF THE STATE OF ALABAMA: CONTAINING THE STATUTES AND RESOLUTIONS IN FORCE AT THE END OF THE GENERAL ASSEMBLY IN JAN., 1823 (Harry Toulmin, compiler, 1823).

[199] LA. CONST. 1812 art. IV, sect. 11 ("the legislature shall never adopt any system or code of laws, by general reference to the said system or code, but in all cases, shall specify the several provisions of the laws it may enact.").

[200] The territory was transferred four months before the French Code Civil came into force. In any event, however, Louisiana was transferred back to France from Spain for only a few weeks in 1803. It had for decades prior been under Spanish rule and laws.

[201] *See, e.g.,* SHAEL HERMAN, THE LOUISIANA CIVIL CODE: A EUROPEAN LEGACY FOR THE UNITED STATES (1993) (with a bibliography of relevant materials); RICHARD HOLCOMBE KILBOURNE, JR., A HISTORY OF THE LOUISIANA CIVIL CODE: THE FORMATIVE YEARS, 1803–1839 (1987) (discussing, *inter alia,* the debate over sources for the 1808 digest); Augustín Parise, *Private Law in Louisiana: An Account of Civil Codes, Heritage, and Law Reform, in* THE SCOPE AND STRUCTURE OF CIVIL CODES (Julio César Rivers, ed., IUS GENTIUM: COMPARATIVE PERSPECTIVES ON LAW AND JUSTICE, Vol. 32) 429 (2013).

[202] *See* E. Evariste Moise, *Two Answers to Mr. Carter's Pamphlet,* 29 ALB. L.J. 267 (1884); *Jurisprudence of Louisiana,* 4 AM. QUARTERLY REV. 53 (Robert Walsh, ed., 1828).

territory the basis of such a code, as can be clearly and certainly understood by
the great body of the people." The Governor was none too clear about where
that would come from. Notwithstanding "serious objections to the common
law," he advised that "common law be adopted as the basis of our code." His
more general counsel: "combine whatever is excellent in both systems, and
avoid whatever is objectionable in either, as a distinct code."[203] Clear from
that message is, whether substantive rules be common law or civil law origin,
they should be rules of written law.

Livingston's Laws 1824–1833

Through Edward Livingston, a New Yorker and younger brother of Robert
Livingston, is the way most Americans in the first Century of the Republic
learned of Louisiana law. Louisiana engaged Livingston (with others) to revise
the 1808 digest as a civil code, to draft a code of procedure and to prepare a
criminal code.[204] Livingston is known outside Louisiana more for his criminal
law work, which was not adopted, than for his civil law work, which was.[205]
His criminal law proposals were reprinted beginning already in 1824 in England, France, Germany and Quebec.

In 1828 Congress printed Livingston's proposed *System of Penal Law* for
the House of Representatives as Livingston had revised it as Congressman
for the United States.[206] In 1832 a Congressional committee included Livingston's proposal as the criminal law component of a complete code for the
District of Columbia.[207] Livingston's work gave encouragement to later

[203] *Florida*, 23 NILES' WEEKLY REGISTER 23–24 (Sept. 14, 1822) (including the July 22,
1822 message of Governor William P. Duval).
[204] LOUISIANA LEGAL ARCHIVES, [two volumes in one] VOLUME 1, A REPUBLICATION OF THE
PROJET OF THE CIVIL CODE OF LOUISIANA OF 1825, VOLUME 2, A REPUBLICATION OF
THE *PROJET* OF THE CODE OF PRACTICE OF LOUISIANA 1825 (1937); EDWARD LIVINGSTON,
SYSTEM OF PENAL LAW, PREPARED FOR THE STATE OF LOUISIANA; COMPRISING CODES OF
OFFENCES AND PUNISHMENTS, OF PROCEDURE, OF PRISON DISCIPLINE AND EVIDENCE
APPLICABLE AS WELL TO CIVIL AS TO CRIMINAL CASES. AND A BOOK, CONTAINING
DEFINITIONS OF ALL THE TECHNICAL WORDS USED IN THIS SYSTEM (1824).
[205] *See, e.g., The Livingston Code*, in JOHN D. BESSLER, THE BIRTH OF AMERICAN LAW: AN
ITALIAN PHILOSOPHER AND THE AMERICAN REVOLUTION 332 (2014). From the first century of
the Republic, see, *e.g., Edward Livingston and His Code*, 9 U.S. MAG. & DEMOCRATIC REV. 3,
211 (2 parts, 1841); CHARLES HAVENS HUNT, LIFE OF EDWARD LIVINGSTON WITH AN
INTRODUCTION BY GEORGE BANCROFT (1864).
[206] EDWARD LIVINGSTON, A SYSTEM OF PENAL LAW FOR THE UNITED STATE OF AMERICA,
CONSISTING OF A CODE OF CRIMES AND PUNISHMENTS; A CODE OF PROCEDURE IN CRIMINAL
CASES; A CODE OF PRISON DISCIPLINE; AND A BOOK OF DEFINITIONS, PRINTED BY ORDER OF
THE HOUSE OF REPRESENTATIVES (1828).
[207] Edward Livingston, *System of Penal Law for the District of Columbia, in* A SYSTEM OF CIVIL
AND CRIMINAL LAW FOR THE DISTRICT OF COLUMBIA AND FOR THE ORGANIZATION OF THE

codifiers.[208] In 1856 Henry Maine called him "the first legal genius of modern times" and said that it was his "code, and not the Common law of England, which the newest American States are taking for the substratum of their laws."[209]

Digitization promises to disclose influences not previously known. One colorful example that I found was in Indiana. In 1827 the new state's young (age 33) governor, James Brown Ray, proposed that he would write a code based on the "Napoleon or Livingston codes" so as "to enable the people generally to form a tolerable correct idea of that system which controls their actions." It would help in "shaking off this disreputable stigma" of control by British laws. He implored the bar not to suppose "that this attempt to promulgate the laws of the land, will be aimed at their useful profession, or condemn its practicality, until they see the book."[210] One wonders how serious he was when one learns what became of his proposal.

Three years later, in 1830, when the Senate had not received the promised code from the Governor and itself was considering revision, it formally inquired how far he "had progressed in the codification of the laws of the State."[211] The Governor responded that he had been doing it on his own time and that it could not form any part of the revision the Senate was contemplating.[212] There then followed a two month long dispute between the

COURTS THEREIN, REPORTED BY THE JOINT COMMITTEE APPOINTED FOR THE PURPOSE IN OBEDIENCE TO A RESOLUTION OF THE FIRST SESSION OF THE TWENTY-SECOND CONGRESS, DOCUMENT NO. 85, *in* VOLUME II. CONTAINING DOCUMENT NO. 85, of PUBLIC DOCUMENTS PRINTED BY ORDER OF THE SENATE OF THE UNITED STATES, SECOND SESSION OF THE TWENTY-SECOND CONGRESS ... BEGUN DECEMBER 3, 1832 ... IN TWO VOLUMES, at pp. 291–685 (1833).

[208] E.g., *The Statute Laws of Tennessee*, 8 AM. JURIST 298, 314 (1832) ("It must be gratifying to Mr. Livingston to see ... his labors have been duly appreciated, and have been signally useful in softening the rigor of the criminal law in one, at least, of the neighbor states, and in improving the style of their composition.")

[209] H.J.S. Maine, *Roman Law and Legal Education*, 1856 CAMBRIDGE ESSAYS 1, 17 (1856), *reprinted in* HENRY SUMNER MAINE, VILLAGE-COMMUNITIES IN THE EAST AND WEST 330, 360 (3d and enlarged ed., 1880). For a contemporary account of Livingston's life, *see* CHARLES HAWES HUNT, LIFE OF LIVINGSTON WITH AN INTRODUCTION BY GEORGE BANCROFT (1864).

[210] James Brown Ray, [*Governor's Address, Dec. 4, 1827*], JOURNAL OF THE SENATE OF THE STATE OF INDIANA: BEING THE TWELFTH SESSION OF THE GENERAL ASSEMBLY; BEGUN AND HELD ... ON MONDAY THE THIRD DAY OF DECEMBER, 1827, 9, 25–26 (1827), also in MESSAGE AND PAPERS RELATING TO THE ADMINISTRATION OF JAMES BROWN RAY: GOVERNOR OF INDIANA 1825–1831 (Dorothy Riker & Gayle Thornbrough, eds., 1954).

[211] JOURNAL OF THE SENATE OF THE STATE OF INDIANA: BEING THE FIFTEENTH SESSION OF THE GENERAL ASSEMBLY; BEGUN AND HELD ... ON MONDAY THE SIXTH OF DECEMBER, 1830, 61 (1830 [sic]).

[212] Letter of Dec. 10, 1830, *id.* at 63–64.

Governor and the Senate over ownership and possession of what was apparently the only copy of the Louisiana Civil Code in the State of Indiana. Also involved were the Secretary of State, the State Auditor, the State Treasurer, the State Librarian and the State Librarian's predecessor in office. The heart of the dispute the Governor identified as "an evident determination to wrest it from my hands, on the part of those who cannot endure the idea of having a code of laws for Indiana."[213] The book ended up in the State Library and Indiana ended up without a Livingston-like code.[214]

Napoleon's Five Codes as Models

In the first decade of the 19th century France systematized its laws: it adopted Napoleon's five codes, i.e., the *Code Civil* (the "Napoleonic Code," the most famous of the five, first in 1804), as well as codes of Commerce, Civil Procedure, Criminal Procedure and Criminal Law. Americans took note. In 1814, notwithstanding negative perceptions of France under Napoleon, and "the powerful coalition ... arrayed against her," New York attorney John Rodman, in his translation of the Commercial Code, reported that it was "generally admitted that the new system of jurisprudence adopted in France was entitled to the highest commendation, as a production of wisdom and learning."[215] He offered the Commercial Code as an aid to "throw off the shackles of antiquated [common law] rules and precedents, unfounded in reason and truth, and diligently endeavor to ingraff into our system of jurisprudence those pure principles of equity and justice ... ."[216] Throughout the

---

[213] Letter of Jan. 10, 1830, *id.* at 500.
[214] The story is told in the pages of the JOURNAL, *supra* note 212, at 49–50, 63–64, 169, 249–250, 277–278, 500–509, 518–519, 546–553, Appendix (d).
[215] JOHN RODMAN, THE COMMERCIAL CODE OF FRANCE, WITH THE MOTIVES, OR DISCOURSES OF THE COUNSELLORS OF STATE, DELIVERED BEFORE THE LEGISLATIVE BODY, ILLUSTRATIVE OF THE PRINCIPLES AND PROVISIONS OF THE CODE iii–iv (1814). Rodman's was the *second* American translation of the French Commercial Code of 1807. Robert Walsh had already included in the second volume of his journal, *The American Review of History and Politics*, translations of both the Commercial and the Criminal Codes. *Commercial Code of the French Empire. Translated for the American Review, with Explanatory Notes*, 2 AM. REV. HIST. & POLITICS – APPENDIX 91 (Oct. 1811); *Penal Code of the French Empire*, 2 AM. REV. HIST. & POLITICS – APPENDIX 1 (July 1811). Rodman, to increase the reform value of his translation, added what we call today in American English, the legislative history, *i.e.*, the *Motives*. He lamented that he had been unable to get enough subscribers to support publication of his translation of the larger Code Civil. RODMAN, *supra* at iv–v.
[216] *Id.* at xiii.

19th century Americans pointed to Napoleon's codes as examples of the success of written law. Digitization facilitates new examinations of the influence of French codes in America. In England, they inspired Jeremy Bentham the most famous publicist of codes ever.

Bentham: Legislator of the World[217]

Bentham never visited America, but he made his influence felt in the new world. In 1811 he wrote to President Madison, himself famous for drafting the U.S. Constitution, and offered his services to codify American law. He made the same offer to other leaders, including to the Czar of Russia. Madison let the letter sit for five years – the two countries were at war – before he respectfully declined. Bentham then wrote to the governors of states and received modest interest. Bentham's influence was with leaders rather than with the public, and even there it was uneven, for Benthamism was as much about utilitarianism as about codifying. He is said to have had the greatest influence on Edward Livingston,[218] but he also befriended a wide range of notables including John Quincy Adams and influenced other code proponents including David Dudley Field.[219] At the end of the Republic's first century *The Nation* wrote that "The various attempts made, with more or less success, in this country no less than in England, to codify the law are also distinct results of the teachings of Bentham and Austin."[220] Today digitization permits plumbing the depth of Benthamism in American law systematization.

---

[217] *See generally* JEREMY BENTHAM, "LEGISLATOR OF THE WORLD": WRITINGS ON CODIFICATION, LAW, AND EDUCATION (Philip Schofield & Jonathan Harris, eds., 1998); JEREMY BENTHAM, PAPERS RELATIVE TO CODIFICATION AND PUBLIC INSTRUCTION: INCLUDING CORRESPONDENCE WITH THE RUSSIAN EMPEROR, AND DIVERS CONSTITUTE AUTHORITIES IN THE AMERICAN UNITED STATES (1817).

[218] C.W. Everett, *Bentham in the United States of America*, *in* JEREMY BENTHAM AND THE LAW: A SYMPOSIUM (George W. Keeton & Georg Schwarzenberger, eds.) 185, 193 (1948).

[219] PETER J. KING, UTILITARIAN JURISPRUDENCE IN AMERICA: THE INFLUENCE OF BENTHAM AND AUSTIN ON AMERICAN LEGAL THOUGHT IN THE NINETEENTH CENTURY (PhD. diss., Dept. of History, University of Illinois, Champaign, 1961, published Garland, 1986). King devotes one chapter to three befriended politicians (Aaron Burr, John Quincy Adams, and Albert Gallatin), another to three intellectuals (Thomas Cooper, David Hoffman, and Richard Hildreth), and a third to three code proponents (Livingston, David Dudley Field and Richard Vale).

[220] *Modern English Law* [Review], 22 THE NATION 273, 274 (1876), *reprinted in* 3 CENTRAL L.J. 728 (1876). The same review commented on English attempts to codify: "Other causes, no doubt, have contributed to the failure of English reformers to produce a code, but the nature of the House of Commons is the most obvious cause of their want of success." *Id.* at 274.

Grimké & Cooper: South Carolina Codes 1827–1836

In an 1828 article on *Codification in the United States of America*, an English journal, after reporting on Bentham's communications, turned to report on the then ongoing work to codify law in South Carolina. Governor Wilson had proposed appointment of special committee to take up the matter and the legislature unanimously approved. At first limited to statute law, the legislature amended the resolution to include common law. To confine the measure to consolidation of statutes, according to one criticism that the English journal reported, "might benefit the bar, but would leave the citizens in their present state of ignorance of 'the HYDRA, the COMMON LAW,' nurtured by the profession ..."[221] Noted jurist Thomas S. Grimké (later his sisters became famous abolitionists)[222] led a drive for a code and chaired the committee.[223] One supporter of the project following its demise identified the "serious difficulties" the "friends of codification encounter[ed]": "indifference to action, a dread of consequences, the prejudices of education, all are against them. The laws of Carolina, inconsistent and unintelligible as they are, were the laws of our forefathers."[224] That no code came of the effort has been attributed in a modern study to lawyer opponents who feared that codification "might destroy the stability of law and threaten the very existence and fabric of society."[225]

Systematizing was not, however, at an end in South Carolina. Thomas Cooper, a Jefferson protégé whom the third president described as "one of the ablest men in America and that in several branches of science," after resigning as President of what became the University of South Carolina, took up the legislature's commission,[226] as he described it, "to make a

---

[221] *Codification of the Laws of the United States of America*, 2 JURIST Q.J. JURIS. & LEGIS. 47, 50 (1828).

[222] *See* MARK PERRY, LIFT UP THY VOICE: THE GRIMKÉ FAMILY'S JOURNEY FROM SLAVEHOLDERS TO CIVIL RIGHTS LEADERS (2001).

[223] *See* THOMAS S. GRIMKÉ, ORATION, ON THE PRACTICABILITY AND EXPEDIENCY OF REDUCING THE WHOLE BODY OF THE LAW TO THE SIMPLICITY AND ORDER OF A CODE, DELIVERED IN THE CITY-HALL BEFORE THE SOUTH-CAROLINA BAR ASSOCIATION (1827); Thomas S. Grimké], REPORT. SOUTH CAROLINA [of the Committee appointed 20th of December last, to report on the practicability and expediency of a Code of the Statute and Common Law of this State by Thomas S. Grimké) (1827).

[224] W.W. STARKE, SPEECH ... ON CODIFYING THE LAWS DELIVERED IN THE HOUSE OF REPRESENTATIVES IN DEC. 1828 at 5 (1830).

[225] DONALD JOSEPH SENESE, LEGAL THOUGHT IN SOUTH CAROLINA, 1800–1860 at 412 (PhD. diss., Dept. of History, University of South Carolina, 1970).

[226] DUMAS MALONE, THE PUBLIC LIFE OF THOMAS COOPER 1783–1839, at 198, 371–373 (2d ed., 1961).

collection of our laws that shall form the basis of any future revision, condensation, or digest."[227] It was a fitting memento in retirement for a man who decades before published the first American edition of the *Institutes of Justinian.*[228]

Sampson's 1823 New York Discourse[229]

The same 1828 English article on *Codification in the United States of America*, after addressing South Carolina, passed on to consider William Sampson, an Irish-American lawyer. In 1823 Sampson, challenged common law in an address in New York. The journal reported Sampson's "considerable influence" in moving Americans away from common law and toward codification.[230] His influence was later called "electrifying" and seen as leading to the *New York Revised Statutes* of 1829.[231] That legislation catapulted New York into a leadership among all states that it held so long as systematizing remained a live issue.

---

[227] 1 THOMAS COOPER, THE STATUTES AT LARGE OF SOUTH CAROLINA; EDITED, UNDER AUTHORITY OF THE LEGISLATURE (in five volumes) iii (1836) (according to MALONE, *supra* note 228, at 407, it was the "final work of Cooper's life and the chief monument to his legal learning.").

[228] THOMAS COOPER, INSTITUTES OF JUSTINIAN WITH NOTES (1812) (2d ed., 1841) (3d ed., 1852).

[229] SAMPSON'S DISCOURSE, AND CORRESPONDENCE WITH VARIOUS LEARNED JURISTS, UPON THE HISTORY OF THE LAW, WITH THE ADDITION OF SEVERAL ESSAYS, TRACTS, AND DOCUMENTS, RELATING TO THE SUBJECT. COMPLIED AND PUBLISHED BY PISHEY THOMPSON (1826). This is a collection of many comments on Sampson's discourse and gives an idea that he did get attention for his ideas.

[230] *Codification of the Laws of the United States of America*, 2 JURIST Q.J. JURIS. & LEGIS. 47, 54 (1828) (reporting his writings "have had considerable influence in the United States, and have been greatly instrumental in drawing the attention of the profession, and the public of that country, to the necessity and practicability of amending the law by a mature and decided revision of its principles and present state, especially the common law.");

[231] CHARLES P. DALY, THE COMMON LAW: ITS ORIGIN, SOURCES, NATURE, AND DEVELOPMENT AND WHAT THE STATE OF NEW YORK HAS DONE TO IMPROVE UPON IT 54 (1894) ("it electrified the public mind. ... and led within a decade thereafter to the enactment of the [New York] Revised Statutes. What it urged was felt to be necessary, – a thorough revision and reconstruction of the entire system then existing in this State"). *Accord*, James Dunwoody Brownson De Bow, *Louisiana*, 1 COMMERCIAL REV. 386, 417 note † (1846), *reprinted* 1 J.D.B. DE BOW, THE INDUSTRIAL RESOURCES, ETC., OF THE SOUTHERN AND SOUTHWESTERN STATES 417, 433 note † (1846). Just before Sampson gave his address, Henry Sedgwick published THE ENGLISH PRACTICE: A STATEMENT SHOWING SOME OF THE EVILS AND ABSURDITIES OF THE PRACTICE OF THE ENGLISH COMMON LAW, AS ADOPTED IN SEVERAL OF THE UNITED STATES, AND PARTICULARLY IN THE STATE OF NEW YORK ... BY A LOVER OF IMPROVEMENT (New York: 1822). Three years later David Dudley Field joined Sedgwick's firm, first as clerk and then as associate.

New York's Revised Statutes of 1829

EXCELSIOR. 1829: *Revised Statutes of the State of New-York*[232]

New York may have been destined to become the nation's leader in revising and codifying. It was, and is, after all, the Empire State. New York City was, and is, the nation's commercial capital; it was first political capital under the Constitution. For the first century of the Republic, with very little let-up, even in war, statutes were a topic of discussion and development. If there had been no other activity in the United States that in New York would disprove contemporary common-law myth that statutes were not relevant.

New York began dealing with statutes already in the colonial era.[233] It was quicker to compile laws after the Revolution than most states, and sooner to regularize the practice. Already in 1792, 1801 and 1813 it published compilations. A fourth, initiated in 1825, led to the *Revised Statutes of 1829* that provided the legal framework for New York through to the end of the 19th century.

The *New York Revised Statutes* of 1829 were a code in the modest American sense in all but name. The 1825 Act that authorized them appointed three eminent jurists, Chancellor James Kent, Erastus Root and Benjamin F. Butler, to do the work. When Kent declined to serve the governor appointed another prominent jurist, John Duer. Butler and Duer set out to do more than compile statutes: they proposed a complete revision of New York laws. Unexpectedly, the legislature agreed.[234] The result four years later was the *New York Revised Statutes* of 1829.

---

[232] This rendition is printed on the title pages of the *Revised Statutes of the State of New-York* (1829) and second edition (1836).

[233] The British government is reported to have encouraged the colonies to create collections of their statutes for use by the public and government officials. *See* Erwin C. Surrency, *Revision of Colonial Laws*, 9 AM. J. LEGAL HIST. 189 (1965).

[234] Root, who wanted to follow the old approach, was replaced by Henry Wheaton, Supreme Court Reporter, who himself was later replaced by John C. Spencer. Spencer was later

The New York Revised Statutes find no place in contemporary common-law myth. Although ignored in the academy, their history is told in contemporary reports and in secondary works.[235] They were a product of a rational give-and-take between drafters and legislators.[236] Their authorization followed according to the proposal debated in 1825. In 1826 the revisers reported on their progress. In 1827 the revisers delivered six volumes of printed reports of their proposals published.[237] After months of consideration in legislative session, the legislature adopted the *Revised Statutes* in 1828 and they were published in 1829 in three large volumes.

The New York Revised Statutes were seen abroad "as a practical specimen of the procedure and principles of American codification."[238] At home, they served as inspiration and model in other states. For example, nearly thirty years later, Thomas Cooley compiled Michigan laws "after the manner of the Revised Statutes of New York."[239] Closer to home in distance and in time were their apparent influences on Pennsylvania and Massachusetts in the 1830s and 1840s.

Revised Code of Pennsylvania of 1836

In 1830 the Pennsylvania legislature provided for appointment of a commission to "render the statute laws of Pennsylvania more simple, plain and perfect." The Commissioners worked six years to general approval. The legislature spent almost an entire session on just thirteen of the bills the

---

Secretary of War and sponsor of the first American translation of Alexis de Tocqueville's *Democracy in America*.

[235] *See* ERNEST HENRY BREUER, THE NEW YORK REVISED STATUTES – 1829. ITS SEVERAL EDITIONS, REPORTS OF THE REVISERS, COMMENTARIES AND RELATED PUBLICATIONS UP TO THE CONSOLIDATED LAWS OF 1909 (Typescript, University of the State of New York, New York State Law Library, 1961); Robert Ludlow Fowler, *Observations on the Particular Jurisprudence of New York, 1821–1846*, 25 ALBANY L.J. 166 (1882); John W. Edmonds, *Introduction, Extracts from the Original Reports of the Revisers* [of 1827], in 5 STATUTES AT LARGE OF THE STATE OF NEW YORK, COMPRISING THE REVISED STATUTES, AS THEY EXISTED ON THE 1ST DAY OF JULY 1862, at 235–249 (1863).

[236] For a sharp contemporary criticism of the proposal, see *Review "Revision of the Laws,"* 2 ATLANTIC MAGAZINE 458–466 (1825).

[237] Although published in print runs of 750, complete sets of these volumes are "very scarce." Breuer, *supra* note 237, at 5–6, reports only two sets. The only digitization of which I am aware is *Extracts from the Original Reports of the Revisers*, in 5 STATUTES AT LARGE OF THE STATE OF NEW YORK, COMPRISING THE REVISED STATUTES, AS THEY EXISTED ON THE 1ST DAY OF JULY, 1862, 251–435 (John W. Edmonds, ed., 1863). I own a copy of volume 4 from the library of T. Sedgwick & D.D. Field, which includes the reports of the first six chapters of Part III. I also own a bound collection that predates the six volumes and includes reports as well as a bound collection of the reports to the first six chapters of Part I.

[238] *Codification of the Laws of the United States of America*, 2 JURIST Q.J. JURIS. & LEGIS. 47, 59 (1828).

[239] 1 THE COMPILED LAWS OF THE STATE OF MICHIGAN, COMPILED AND ARRANGED BY THOMAS M. COOLEY iv (1857).

"Commissioners to revise the Civil Code" presented.[240] Lamented was that
the work was not complete and was limited to statute law.[241] Still, Harvard's
Professor Charles Warren early in the 20th century wrote that what was done,
was done "so thoroughly as practically to construct a Civil Code."[242]

Massachusetts Revised Statutes of 1836

If New York was leader, Massachusetts was a close follower for nearly thirty
years – and sometimes itself leader.[243] February 24, 1832 the Massachusetts
legislature authorized the governor to appoint three Commissioners "to revise,
collate and arrange ... all general statutes of the Commonwealth."[244] The
Commissioners started from the example of the *New York Revised Statutes* and
hoped to effect "a general conformity among the codes of the different States
of the Union."[245] Although styled "Revised Statutes," the *American Jurist and
Law Magazine* considered the revision to be a code. The journal in discussing
the project addressed what a good code would look like. It noted that the issue
of codification no longer had the "direful import" it once had, since the two
sides had come considerably closer. By 1835 the "advocates of each form of the
law, admit[ed] that there must be some of both forms; they only disagree[d] as
to the proportional amount."[246] The *American Jurist* applauded the Commissioners' suggestion that their final report should be "*sent to all town officers,
that the public judgment upon its merits might be early matured*, and such
errors as might be detected be set right."[247] A little over a year later, the
American Jurist returned to consider an adopted and published *Revised Statutes of the Commonwealth of Massachusetts* to pronounce the close of "this

---

[240] *Advertisement* in 2 BENJAMIN PARK & OVID F. JOHNSON, A DIGEST OF THE REVISED CODE AND
ACTS, FORMING WITH PURDON'S DIGEST OF 1830, A COMPLETE DIGEST OF THE LAWS OF
PENNSYLVANIA TO THE PRESENT TIME, TWO VOLUMES IN ONE (1837).

[241] GEORGE SHARSWOOD, LECTURES INTRODUCTORY TO THE STUDY OF THE LAW 260–261 (1870).
For positive and extensive contemporary accounts, see *Revised Code of Pennsylvania*, 13 AM.
Q. REV. 30 (Robert Walsh, ed., 1833), and *Revised Code of Pennsylvania*, 19 AM. Q. REV. 399
(Robert Walsh, ed., 1836).

[242] 2 CHARLES WARREN, HISTORY OF THE HARVARD LAW SCHOOL AND OF EARLY LEGAL
CONDITIONS IN AMERICA 259 (1908).

[243] The July 1859 issue of the *American Law Register* illustrates the competition nicely. First, it
gives three pages to note publication of the 1389 page STATE OF MASSACHUSETTS-REPORT OF
THE COMMISSIONERS ON THE REVISION OF THE STATUTES ("We are seldom called upon to pass
upon labors of greater magnitude than those now before us.") and follows those pages
immediately with three pages noting publication of STATE OF NEW YORK – FIRST REPORT OF
THE COMMISSIONERS OF THE CODE (designed "to reduce into a systematic code such of the
laws of that State as were not comprised in the codes of civil and procedure already
completed"). *Notices of New Books*, 7 AM. L. REG. 568, 571 (1859) (respectively).

[244] *Revision of the Laws in Massachusetts*, 13 AM. JURIST AND LAW MAG. 344, 347 (1835).

[245] *Id.* at 351, 355–356.   [246] *Id.* at 341.   [247] *Id.* at 352 [emphasis in original].

great and important undertaking" and "the improved state to which, by means
of it, our statutory law has been advanced."[248] The *Revised Statutes of Massachusetts* were noted abroad – as was the "extraordinary amount of labor" given
to them: three years to prepare the final report, fifty-one days of a special joint
committee and special session of the whole legislature.[249]

Justice Story's Code Commission Report of 1837

HOUSE......   ......No. 8.

REPORT

ON

C O D I F I C A T I O N

OF THE

COMMON LAW.

All which is most respectfully submitted.

JOSEPH STORY,
THERON METCALF,
SIMON GREENLEAF,
CHARLES E. FORBES,
LUTHER S. CUSHING.

Commissioners.

REPORT

OF THE

COMMISSIONERS

APPOINTED TO CONSIDER AND REPORT UPON THE

PRACTICABILITY AND EXPEDIENCY

OF REDUCING TO A

WRITTEN AND SYSTEMATIC CODE

THE

Common Law of Massachusetts,

OR ANY PART THEREOF.

MADE TO HIS EXCELLENCY THE GOVERNOR,

JANUARY, 1837.

Boston:
DUTTON AND WENTWORTH, STATE PRINTERS.
1837.

Massachusetts did not stop its systematizing with its own *Revised Statutes*. In the
very year of their publication – 1836 – the governor proposed, the legislature

---

[248] *Revised Statutes of Massachusetts*, 15 AM. JURIST AND LAW MAG. 294, 294–295 (1836). The
journal added an endorsement for legislation: "How far the changes introduced are judicious,
is a question to be settled, in the main, by time and experience; and the felicity of legislation is
so great, that a statutory evil can be remedied, the moment the pressure is felt." *Id.* at 318.

[249] *Law Commission, Report of the Commissioners for Revising and Consolidating the Laws, in*
JOURNAL OF THE LEGISLATIVE COUNCIL OF THE PROVINCE OF NEW BRUNSWICK, FROM 7TH
JAN. TO 7TH APR. 1852 at 356, 359 (1852) and *in* 1 THE REVISED STATUTES OF NEW BRUNSWICK
vii, xiii (1854). The Report noted that Maine paralleled Massachusetts in systematizing its
statutes.

authorized, a blue-ribbon panel headed by Justice Joseph Story was appointed, and the panel reported upon the "practicablity and expediency of reducing to a written and systematic code the Common Law of Massachusetts or any part thereof."[250] The Commissioners reported favorably: much, but not all common law, they counseled, was suitable for codification. Proponents of codification took Story's Report as an endorsement of codification and at least twice reprinted it years later.[251]

Story was a lifelong practitioner of systematization.[252] In an oft-reprinted address to the Suffolk County Bar Association, he alerted the bar to "the fearful calamity which threatens us of being buried alive ... in the labyrinths of the law," for which he knew "of but one adequate remedy, and that is, by a gradual Digest, under legislative authority," through which "we may pave the way to a general code, which will present in its authoritative text the most material rules to guide the lawyer, the statesman, and the private citizen." He held up the "modern code of France" as "perhaps the most finished and methodical treatise of law that the world ever saw." He called on "the future jurists of our country and England, to accomplish for the common law what has been so successfully demonstrated ... in the jurisprudence of other nations."[253]

---

[250] REPORT OF THE COMMISSIONERS APPOINTED TO CONSIDER AND REPORT ON THE PRACTICABILITY AND EXPEDIENCY OF REDUCING TO A WRITTEN AND SYSTEMATIC CODE THE COMMON LAW OF MASSACHUSETTS OR ANY PART THEREOF (1837).

[251] LAW REFORM TRACTS NO. 3. CODIFICATION OF THE COMMON LAW. REPORT OF THE COMMISSIONERS APPOINTED TO CONSIDER AND REPORT UPON THE PRACTICABILITY AND EXPEDIENCY OF REDUCING TO A WRITTEN AND SYSTEMATIC CODE, THE COMMON LAW OF MASSACHUSETTS, PUBLISHED UNDER THE SUPERINTENDENCE OF A LAW-REFORM ASSOCIATION (1852); CODIFICATION OF THE COMMON LAW, LETTER OF JEREMY BENTHAM, AND REPORT OF JUDGES STORY, METCALF AND OTHERS (David Dudley Field, ed., 1882).

[252] When still a relative youth, he published the first collection of precedents of pleadings (an important part of applying law in common-law pleading). As a junior legislator, he oversaw printing of one of the first compilations of Massachusetts laws. THE LAWS OF THE COMMONWEALTH OF MASSACHUSETTS FROM NOV. 28, 1780 TO FEB. 28, 1807, 3 VOLS IN 1 at [unnumbered vi] (1807). As youngest Supreme Court Justice he oversaw the most frequently cited collection of federal laws (so SURRENCY, *supra* note 122, at 105), THE PUBLIC AND GENERAL STATUTES PASSED BY THE CONGRESS OF THE UNITED STATES OF AMERICA FROM 1789 TO 1827 INCLUSIVE ... PUBLISHED UNDER THE INSPECTION OF JOSEPH STORY . . ., (3 vols., 1828). He began his treatise publishing career with American editions of English law treatises, and ended up in the 1830s publishing the first editions of his systematic commentaries on various branches of law.

[253] It was first printed as the first article in the first volume of the *American Jurist and Law Magazine*. An Address delivered before the Members of the Suffolk Bar, at their anniversary, on the fourth of September, 1821, at Boston, 1 AM. JUR. AND LAW MAG. 1, 31–32 (1829). It was reprinted, not only in several editions of Story's collected works, but also abroad, in Scotland, as A DISCOURSE ON THE PAST HISTORY, PRESENT STATE, AND FUTURE PROSPECTS OF THE LAW (1835) as LAW SERIES NO. II: THE CABINET LIBRARY OF SCARCE AND CELEBRATED TRACTS, and

Story was a "codifier."[254] Yet, while promoting codifying, he affirmed a role for "the forming hand of the judiciary."[255] It is suggestive of the strength of contemporary common-law myth that some of the most careful of American scholars of legal history might turn 'Story the codifier' into 'Story the common law champion'[256] who accepted codification only with "serious reservations"[257] and sometimes was even "hostile" to it.[258] Why should it be so important to call into question Story's advocacy of codifying? Professors of common-law myth may think that code-based systems leave no room for judicial innovation, but code-system jurists do not. There is room for both civil and common-law methods in one system.

Perhaps hostility to codifying is somewhere in Story's works, but I have not seen it. Shouldn't digitization show it, not just in his writings, but in how his contemporaries understood him? Moral philosopher Jasper Adams resided at Harvard nearly contemporaneously with Story's writing of the Massachusetts Code Commission Report. Adams included in his moral philosophy chapters supporting codification, with no hostility evident. In his preface he thanked Justice Story for consulting with him "as often as it suited me" and acknowledged that "several of my chapters have derived the greatest advantages from the consultations which were thus encouraged."[259] Story's own son, William Wetmore Story, considering the Code Commission, wrote: "The Report goes on to state the objections which have been urged against codification and triumphantly answers them."[260] Out in the old West, Timothy Walker, one of Story's best students, Story's "worthy Son in Law," took up the cause of codifying.

in England in an article titled *Improvement and Study of the American Laws*, 11 Legal Observer or J. Jurisprudence 510 (Supplement for Apr., 1836).

[254] Hall, *supra* note 54, at 126 (1989).

[255] Story, *supra* note 254, 1 Am. Jurist & Law Mag. at 31.

[256] *See* James R. Stoner, Jr., Common Law Liberty: Rethinking American Constitutionalism 14 (2003).

[257] R. Kent Newmyer, Supreme Court Justice Joseph Story: Statesman of the Old Republic 274 (1986).

[258] G. Edward White, History of the Supreme Court of the United States, Oliver Wendell Holmes Devise History, Vols. III–IV, The Marshall Court and Cultural Change, 1815–1835, at 150–151 (1988). *Cf.*, Arthur Rolston, *An Uncommon Common Law: Codification and the Development of California Law, 1849–1874*, 2 Cal. Legal Hist. 143, 146–147 (2007) (reading the report to conclude that codifying the common law was "neither possible nor expedient" in general but allowing for limited codification).

[259] Jasper Adams, Elements of Moral Philosophy xii (1837).

[260] 2 William W. Story, Life and Letters of Joseph Story, Edited by His Son, William W. Story 247 (1851). The paragraph continued: "It then proceeds to recount its advantages with great clearness and force, and recommends that the labors of codification should be specially devoted to these three branches of law." *Id.*

The Old West: Ohio's Timothy Walker & Salmon P. Chase

Timothy Walker, perhaps more than any other student of Story's, was the Justice's "worthy Son in Law";[261] Walker was also the leading advocate of codification in the old West in the antebellum era.[262] He left for Ohio already in his first year at Harvard in 1830. There he became friends and collaborated with later Supreme Court Chief Justice Salmon P. Chase. In 1833 and 1834 Chase published a multi-volume innovative compilation of the laws of Ohio. Chase designed it with professional practice in mind, to deal with the "perplexity" caused by "the huge mass of law which the legislation of forty-three years had accumulated."[263] In 1835 Walker addressed the Cincinnati Legislative Club on codification.[264] In 1837 he published the first edition of his pro-codification and highly successful, *Introduction to American Law* discussed below in the next section.[265] Walker's codifying work was cut short when he was run down by a drunken driver and died of his injuries.[266]

---

[261] WALTER THEODORE HITCHCOCK, TIMOTHY WALKER, ANTEBELLUM LAWYER, Introduction (1990).

[262] Hall speaks of the two together as the leaders of a second block of codifiers. HALL, *supra* note 54.

[263] 1 THE STATUTES OF OHIO EDITED BY SALMON P. CHASE 5 (1833). Charles Warren described Chase's work as "exceptionally able." HISTORY OF THE HARVARD LAW SCHOOL AND OF EARLY LEGAL CONDITIONS IN AMERICA 259 (1908).

[264] Timothy Walker, *Codification – Its Practicability and Expediency – Being a Report Made to the Cincinnati Legislative Club, in 1835,* WESTERN L.J. 433 (1844).

[265] A recent review of legal literature in Ohio can be taken as a marker of the power of contemporary common law myth. Notwithstanding Walker's national renown, a two volume work on Ohio legal history gives Walker's work few words and then largely reports his work's deprecation by others and demise after more than 75 years. John F. Winkler, *The Legal Literature of Ohio, in* 2 THE HISTORY OF OHIO LAW 501, 510–512, 522 (M.L. Benedict and J.F. Winkler, eds., 2004). This history of Ohio law gives case reporters more notice. Digitization – not available in 2004 – shows alternative views were in Ohio. One critic in 1855, in an unlikely place, a report on schools in Cincinnati, urged readers to follow the path plotted by Walker: "The slow progress of our Universities and Colleges, has been averted to, but the perfection – not of human reason, but of the power to stand still in this go-ahead age, is to be found in our adherence to the common law. ... The codification of laws has always been spoken of as a desideratum, but no steps have ever been taken by those who have adopted the English common-law system, to accomplish this object, notwithstanding the universal acknowledgment of its expediency." JOHN P. FOOTE, THE SCHOOLS OF CINCINNATI AND ITS VICINITY 23–24 (1855). Foote's criticism of American law is unvarnished. He had particular scorn for law administered to the Indian natives. "We have invented one kind of law, which is peculiar to our nation . . . . It is neither based on the law of nations, the law of God, or the law of humanity. ... It is not even Lynch law." *Id.* at 25.

[266] Gordon A. Christenson, *A Tale of Two Lawyers in Antebellum Cincinnati: Timothy Walker's Last Conversation with Salmon P. Chase,* 71 U. CINCINNATI L. REV. 457 (2002).

Massachusetts General Statutes of 1860

As result of Story's Code Commission Report Massachusetts appointed a commission to codify criminal law. It completed work in 1841; finally, in 1844 the legislature rejected the project.[267] Despite that rejection, ten years later the legislature returned to systematizing. In 1854 it resolved that the governor should appoint three Commissioners, "on the basis, plan and general form and method of the Revised Statutes," for "consolidating and arranging the general statutes of the commonwealth." The Commissioners completed their "revision" in fall 1858 and presented it in print form in 1859, when the legislature considered in about eighty days of hearings of a joint special committee during the recess of the legislature, and then in a special session of the legislature in the last four months of the year.[268]

Systematizing in the *American Jurist and Law Magazine*

J.L Tellkampf, by Valentin Schertle[269]

---

[267] The governor initially proposed a Commission to codify the common law. The legislative committee concurred, but the whole legislature demurred, and authorized instead, a Commission to consider the issue. The story is told in CHARLES M. COOK, THE AMERICAN CODIFICATION MOVEMENT: A STUDY OF ANTEBELLUM LEGAL REFORM 173–181 (1981).

[268] *Preface, in* THE GENERAL STATUTES OF THE COMMONWEALTH OF MASSACHUSETTS: REVISED BY COMMISSIONERS APPOINTED UNDER A RESOLVE OF FEBRUARY 16, 1855, AMENDED BY THE LEGISLATURE, AND PASSED DEC. 29, 1859, iii, iv (1860).

[269] VALENTIN SCHERTLE, PORTRAIT OF J.L. TELLKAMPF, Lithograph (1848). Original in possession of the author. Not known to be digitized.

Legal and general journals of the day took note of revising and systematizing of statutes. Among these was America's foremost legal journal, the *American Jurist and Law Magazine* (1829–1846). For a time, it was America's only law journal. In 1841–1842 it took the unusual step of publishing a lengthy two-part article *On Codifying and Systematizing of the Law* by J.L. Tellkampf, then a professor at Union College in Schenectady New York. An intriguing, yet unanswered question, is how much influence Tellkampf, either through his article, or personally may have had on David Dudley Field.[270] Tellkampf's article is good instruction for the United States even today.

Constitutional Commitments to Codes

In 1846 New York held a constitutional convention to draft a new constitution for the state. Proponents of codification secured inclusion in the constitution of a mandate that the legislature appoint two commissions to codify the substantive and procedural laws. One, the "Code Commission," was "to reduce into a written and systematic code the whole body of the law of the state."[271] The other, the "Practice Commission," was to "revise, reform, simplify and abridge the rules of pleadings, forms and proceedings of the courts of record of this State."[272] David Dudley Field eventually led both commissions. A Belgian contemporary saw the move as a way to overcome historic "Anglo-Saxon" opposition to codification and written law.[273] The Committee on Law Reform at the 1847 Constitutional Convention for Illinois

---

[270] Tellkampf came to the United States in 1838 with the backing of the Prussian government and of Alexander von Humboldt to study American penology. With the help of Justice Story and Henry W. Longfellow, he placed the article while teaching at Union College. He went on to teach at Columbia College in New York City. There are many hints of a personal connection to Field, but no contacts that I have been able to confirm. Field must have known the article. Tellkampf returned to Germany to play a role in the 1848 Frankfurt Parliament. He republished the article in London in 1858 and in Berlin in 1875. *See generally* James R. Maxeiner, *The First Humboldtian Research Trip into the Polis: J.L. Tellkampf in the United States 1838–1847, in* RECHTSSTAATLICHES STRAFEN: FESTSCHRIFT FÜR PROF. DR. DR. H.C. MULT. KEIICHI YAMANAKA ZUM 70. GEBURTSTAG AM 16. MÄRZ 2017 at 771 (2017); James R. Maxeiner, *J.L. Tellkampf: German Legal Scientist in the U.S. (1838–1847) in an Age of Reform,* 50 YEARBOOK FOR GERMAN-AMERICAN STUDIES 1 (2016).

[271] N.Y. CONST. of 1846, art. 1, sect. 17.   [272] N.Y. CONST. of 1846, art. 6, sect. 24.

[273] LUCIEN JOTTRAND, LA NOUVELLE CONSTITUTION DE NEW-YORK POUR 1847. AVEC UN COMMENTAIRE 7 (1847). *Cf.,* ROBERT BAIRD, THE CHRISTIAN RETROSPECT AND REGISTER: A SUMMARY OF THE SCIENTIFIC, MORAL AND RELIGIOUS PROGRESS OF THE FIRST HALF OF THE XIXTH CENTURY 176–177 (1851).

proposed a similar provision that would, in today's talk, sunset common law and English statutes after 1870.[274] The Convention did not adopt it.

The New York Constitution of 1846 was not the first state constitution to mandate systematizing. Already the Indiana Constitution of 1816 mandated a complete codification of part of the law, *i.e.*, criminal law: "It shall be the duty of the General Assembly, as soon as circumstances will permit, to form a penal code, founded on principles of reformation, and not of vindictive justice."[275] The Alabama Constitution of 1819 copied the Indiana language exactly.[276] In another separate section the Alabama Constitution directed that within five years, and every ten years thereafter "the body of our laws, civil and criminal, shall be revised, digested, and arranged under proper heads, and promulgated."[277] The Missouri Constitution of 1820 included similar language limited, however to "all the statute laws."[278]

The New York Constitution of 1846 was also not the last state constitution to mandate systematizing. The Kentucky Constitution of 1850, the Maryland Constitution of 1851, the Indiana Constitution of 1851 and the short-lived Reconstruction Arkansas Constitution of 1868 all had provisions substantively similar to those of the New York Constitution.[279] The Ohio Constitution of 1851 had a similar provision limited to civil process.[280] The author of notes to the Maryland Constitution described the seventeenth section as embracing "some of the most useful provisions that are to be found in the whole Constitution."[281] The debates in Kentucky show the influence of other states and of popular opinion. "This is the day of reform. Our sister states have set us a glorious example of legal reform: our constituents expect it, they demand it, at

---

[274] JOURNAL OF THE CONVENTION, ASSEMBLED AT SPRINGFIELD, JUNE 7, 1847 ... FOR THE PURPOSE OF ALTERING, AMENDING, OR REVISING THE CONSTITUTION OF THE STATE OF ILLINOIS 309 (1847).

[275] IND. CONST. of 1816, art. IX, sect. 4.   [276] ALA. CONST. of 1819, art. 6, sect. 19.

[277] ALA. CONST. of 1819, art. 6, sect. 20.

[278] MO. CONST. of 1820, art. III, sect. 35. Maine, which entered with Missouri as part of the Missouri Compromise, inherited the Perpetual Statutes of Massachusetts.

[279] KY. CONST. of 1850, art. VIII, sect. 22; MD. CONST. of 1851, III, sect. 17; IND. CONST. of 1851, art. VII, sect. 20; ARK CONST. of 1868, art. XV, Sect. Eleven

[280] OHIO CONST. of 1851, art. XIV.

[281] EDWARD OTIS HINKLEY, THE CONSTITUTION OF THE STATE OF MARYLAND ... WITH MARGINAL NOTES AND AN APPENDIX 78 (1851) ("This State has long been suffering for want of a proper Codification of its laws."). William Price had five years before agitated in the state for codification as the only solution: "What other remedy can be suggested for the hugeness and discordance of the mass of materials from which the most ordinary rule of Law must be drawn and which existing in an hundred different phases, can only be applied into one, but which one is to govern his case, no man can tell." [WILLIAM PRICE], PARAGRAPHS ON THE SUBJECT OF JUDICIAL REFORM IN MARYLAND: SHEWING THE EVILS OF THE PRESENT SYSTEM, AND POINTING OUT THE ONLY REMEDY FOR THEIR CURE 66 (1846). Price hoped for a code that "in all its general features, should be the same over the entire Union .... " *Id.*

our hand."[282] Opponents focused, not on principle, but on practicality. One conceded that most members of the body "agree that the object aimed at is desirable, provided it can be attained without too much expense and labor."[283] Other opponents argued that they did not believe the legislature was technically competent to codify.[284]

Criminal Codes

Constitutional mandates specific to criminal law are reminders that already in the first century of the Republic the American penchant for codifying seen by the Centennial Writers manifested itself, not only in system-wide revisions, but in specific areas of law.[285] In my readings, no area of substantive law appeared as often as criminal law. The reason for focus on criminal law is obvious: two basic principles of criminal law are "no crime without statute" (*nullum crimen sine lege*) and "no punishment without statute" (*nulla poena sine lege*). Nowhere is the need for written law to guide and control the governors, as well as to guide and protect the governed more firmly felt than in criminal law.[286]

Digitization gives access to the many specifically criminal law codification projects of the first century of the Republic.[287] Although not all systematization projects were successful, statutory rather than common-law crimes have

---

[282] REPORT OF THE DEBATES AND PROCEEDINGS OF THE CONVENTION FOR THE REVISION OF THE CONSTITUTION OF THE STATE OF KENTUCKY 905 (1849) (remarks of Mr. Gholson). Referenced in the debates were, *inter alia*, Justinian, Bacon and Brougham in England, Livingston and Louisiana, and New York.

[283] *Id.* at 903 (remarks of Mr. Triplett).

[284] 1 DEBATES AND PROCEEDINGS OF THE MARYLAND REFORM CONVENTION TO REVISE THE STATE CONSTITUTION 319–320, 32 (1851) 1 (remarks, respectively of Mr. Merrick and Mr. Harbine).

[285] Such a sectorial approach is the approach of contemporary systemization proponents such as the Uniform Laws Commission and of the American Law Institute.

[286] Success has been elusive. *See, e.g.,* ELIZABETH DALE, CRIMINAL JUSTICE IN THE UNITED STATES, 1789–1939, at 5 (2011) ("Ultimately, the picture that emerges from this study is that of a criminal justice system that was far more a government of men than one of laws in the first 150 years after ratification of the Constitution.") For a study of the principle in American law, see STANISŁAW POMORSKI AMERICAN COMMON LAW AND THE PRINCIPLE *NULLUM CRIMEN SINE LEGE* (2d, revised and enlarged ed. [first in English], 1975).

[287] To name only a few examples through the decades of the first century of the Republic: HARRY TOULMIN & JAMES BLAIR, A REVIEW OF THE CRIMINAL LAW OF KENTUCKY (2 vols., 1804); REPORT, MADE BY JARED INGERSOLL, ESQ., ATTORNEY GENERAL OF PENNSYLVANIA, IN COMPLIANCE WITH A RESOLUTIONS OF THE LEGISLATURE, PASSED THE THIRD OF MARCH, 1812, RELATIVE TO THE PENAL CODE 5 (1813) (endeavoring "to systematize and arrange all the acts for the punishment of crimes that are to be found in the statute book"); CODE OF CRIMINAL LAW PREPARED FOR THE LEGISLATURE OF NEW JERSEY, BY VIRTUE OF A RESOLUTION OF THE COUNCIL AND GENERAL ASSEMBLY ADOPTED FEB. 27, 1833 [Lucius Q.C. Elmer], iii (1834) ("an effort has been made to present a systematic digest of the criminal law, and to introduce some improvements") [this is a personal copy; I have not located a digitized version]; PRELIMINARY REPORT OF THE COMMISSIONERS OF CRIMINAL LAW [Willard Phillips, Preliminary Report of the Commissioners for reducing so much of the Common Law as relates to crimes and punishments, and the incidents thereof, to a written and systematic code], MASS. SENATE

been the American norm since the 19th century. Already in 1812 the United States Supreme Court rejected a federal common law of crimes.[288] In 1834 one Ohioan proudly wrote: The leading characteristic of our *criminal law*, is, that it is all of statutory provision. . . . We acknowledge no part of the common law in regard to crimes. Our criminal code is probably the most humane and the most simple, that has been tried in modern times."[289]

One would expect that a statutory criminal law is an explicit rejection of contemporary common-law myth. Yet some professors of that myth today teach, and their students may believe, that criminal law is a common-law subject.[290]

Field's Codes 1848–1894

David Dudley Field, by Alexander Hay Ritchie[291]

No. 21 (Feb. 1839); PLAN OF A PENAL STATUTE, PROPOSED FOR ADOPTION TO THE LEGISLATURE OF KENTUCKY [S.S. Nicholas] vii (1850) ("How are our citizens [to know what the law has forbidden, and what it has enjoined] unless the legislature affords them the means for its acquisition? . . . It is a mere mockery to refer us to the unwritten law of England."); H.S. SANFORD, THE DIFFERENT SYSTEMS OF PENAL CODES IN EUROPE; ALSO, A REPORT OF THE ADMINISTRATIVE CHANGES IN FRANCE, SINCE THE REVOLUTION OF 1848, 33D CONGRESS, 1ST SESS., SENATE, EX. DOC. NO. 68 (1854); E.W. [presumably Emory Washburn], *We Need a Criminal Code*, 7 AM. L. REV. 264 (1872).

[288] United States v. Hudson & Goodwin, 11 U.S. (7 Cranch) 32 (Feb. 13, 1812). The Court held that "Although this question is brought up now for the first time to be decided by his Court, we consider it as having been long since settled in public opinion." Although cast in jurisdictional terms, it can reasonably be understood, in part, as a manifestation of the popular demand for written law that stood behind constitutional mandates of criminal law codification. *See generally*, Robert C. Palmer, *The Federal Common Law of Crime*, 4 LAW & HIST. REV. 267 (1968).

[289] *Ohio Legislation*, 11 AM. JURIST & L. MAG. 91, 93 (1834) [emphasis in original].

[290] *See* Kevin C. McMunigal, *A Statutory Approach to Criminal Law*, 48 ST. LOUIS U.L.J. 1285 (2004) (relating the survival of that belief).

[291] ALEXANDER HAY RITCHIE (1822–1895), DAVID DUDLEY FIELD. (Not known to be digitized; original in possession of the author.)

If the first century of the Republic were bereft of all systematizing except Jefferson's Revisal at the beginning of the century and Field's codes at the end, contemporary common-law myth would still be untenable. Jefferson and Field wrote new laws as did no other Americans. Both legislated for what was in their respective times the most populous state in the Union. Both overturned common law and substituted modern statutory law. Both had stature outside the United States. Field was *the* American codifier.[292] With first-hand youthful exposure to European legal systems behind him, in the 1830s he began his fifty-year long campaign to rationalize and systematize American law in all its branches. To relate even ten percent of his work would consume this entire book. On his death in 1894 he was praised as "the most conspicuous legal figure of the world for the last half century."[293]

Field's first major success in law reform came in 1842 when the Committee on the Judiciary of the New York State Assembly reported his bill: "An Act To improve the administration of justice." Field was not a member of the legislature, so he accompanied his proposal with a fifty-page (printed) letter on law reform.[294] Field supported adoption of the provisions of the Constitution mandating process and substantive law codification and creation, respectively, of Process and Code Commissions.

Although not originally appointed to either commission, he succeeded to a vacancy on the Process Commission and soon became its leader. The Commission reported a Code of Civil Procedure (first reported 1848,[295] reported complete 1850) and a Code of Criminal Procedure (first reported 1849,[296] reported complete 1850). The former the legislature passed immediately; the latter it did not adopt until three decades later. In 1857, after both Commissions expired without the Code

---

[292] ARTHUR T. VANDERBILT, MEN AND MEASURES IN THE LAW 86 (1949) ("Field almost became the American Justinian.")

[293] Irving Browne, *David Dudley Field*, 6 GREEN BAG 245 (1894). For a brief biography, *see* James R. Maxeiner, *Field, David Dudley, Jr.* [biography] in 7 AMERICAN NATIONAL BIOGRAPHY 878 (1999).

[294] *A Letter from D.D. Field Esq. of New-York, on Law Reform, in Appendix, To the Report of the Committee on the Judiciary, in Relation to the More Simple and Speedy Administration of Justice, in an Act To Improve the Administration of Justice, in* State of New-York, Doc. No. 81, *In Assembly, March 2, 1842, Report in Part of the Committee on the Judiciary, in Relation to the Administration of Justice, in* 5 DOCUMENTS OF THE ASSEMBLY OF THE STATE OF NEW-YORK, SIXTY-FOURTH SESSION [*sic*, 65th] at 19 (1842). Professor John Head states concisely Field's problem through five decades: "his enthusiasm far outstripped his authority." John Head, *Codes, Cultures, Chaos, and Champions: Common Features of Legal Codification Experiences in China, Europe, and North America*, 13 DUKE J. COMP. & INT'L L. 1, 86 (2003).

[295] *Sub nomine* FIRST REPORT OF THE COMMISSIONERS ON PRACTICE AND PLEADING: CODE OF PROCEDURE (1848).

[296] *Sub nomine* FOURTH REPORT OF THE COMMISSIONERS ON PRACTICE AND PLEADING: CODE OF CRIMINAL PROCEDURE (1849).

Commission ever having taken action, Field secured that commission's reestablish-
ment and his appointment to it. He self-funded its work. Between 1858 and 1865
Field's Code Commission drafted three codes, a Political Code (reported complete
1860), a Civil Code (first reported 1862, reported complete 1865), a Penal Code (first
reported 1864, reported complete, 1865). The legislature did not take them up at the
time, but turned to them more than a dozen years later after the Centennial.

After the Civil War Field began working independently on a Code of
International Law. He floated the idea already in 1867.[297] He published "draft
outlines" in 1872,[298] in an enlarged edition in 1876,[299] and in French in
1881.[300] From 1873 to 1875 he spent two years in Europe as first President of
the Association for the Reform and Codification of the Law of Nations, which
he had helped found. Except for those two years, in the decade after the Civil
War, Field was active in high profile disputes, constitutional litigation,[301] the
1876 election controversy,[302] and commercial litigation.[303] Those high-profile
disputes later, it seems, cost him support in seeking adoption of his codes.

For Field codification was a matter of course. "[W]hether a code is desirable,"
he wrote, "is simply a question between written and unwritten law." That that
question ever could have been debatable was "one of the most remarkable facts in
the history of jurisprudence." Of course rules are written. "If the law is a thing to
obeyed, it is a thing to be known; and, if it is to be known, there can be no better,
not to say no other, method of making it known than of writing and publishing it."
Written laws are on a plane with written constitutions. "If a written constitution is
desirable, so are written laws."[304] Codification chooses the legislature over the
judiciary as the principal source of law: "the true function of the legislature is to
make the law, the true function of the judges is to expound it."[305]

---

[297] DAVID DUDLEY FIELD, AN INTERNATIONAL CODE, ADDRESS ON THIS SUBJECT, BEFORE THE
SOCIAL SCIENCE ASSOCIATION, AT MANCHESTER, OCT. 5, 1866. In this address he did not
discuss the wartime codification of Lincoln and Lieber of the laws of war. *See* note 123 *supra*.

[298] DAVID DUDLEY FIELD, DRAFT: OUTLINES OF AN INTERNATIONAL CODE (1872).

[299] DAVID DUDLEY FIELD, OUTLINES OF AN INTERNATIONAL CODE (1876).

[300] DAVID DUDLEY FIELD, PROJET D'UN CODE INTERNATIONAL (Alberic Rolin, trans., 1881).

[301] *Ex parte* Milligan, 71 U.S. 2 (1866); Cummings v. Missouri, 71 U.S. 277 (1867); and *Ex parte*
McCardle, 74 U.S. 506 (1869). He returned to the Court in the Centennial year to argue
United States v. Cruikshank, 92 U.S. 542 (1876).

[302] DAVID DUDLEY FIELD, THE VOTE THAT MADE THE PRESIDENT (1877).

[303] On behalf of the reviled railroad magnates Jay Gould and James Fisk in the Erie railroad and
the infamous "Boss" Tweed of the infamous Tammany Hall machine *See* MICHAEL JOSEPH
HOBOR, THE FORM OF THE LAW AND THE CODIFICATION MOVEMENT IN NEW YORK,
1839–1888, at 318–95; Renée Lettow Lerner, *Thomas Nast's Crusading Cartoons*, 2011 GREEN
BAG ALMANAC 59, 66–77.

[304] FINAL REPORT OF THE CODE COMMISSION, FEB. 13, 1865, *reprinted in* 1 SPEECHES, ARGUMENTS
AND MISCELLANEOUS PAPERS OF DAVID DUDLEY FIELD 317, 321 (A.P. Sprague, ed., 1884).

[305] REPORT OF THE SPECIAL COMMITTEE APPOINTED TO CONSIDER AND REPORT WHETHER THE
PRESENT DELAY AND UNCERTAINTY IN JUDICIAL ADMINISTRATION CAN BE LESSENED, AND IF

Field's five codes for New York paralleled Napoleon's five codes for France: each had codes of civil law and civil procedure and of criminal law and criminal procedure. They differed in only one of the five codes: Field had a political code where Napoleon had a code of commerce. Not only did Field follow the division into four fields of the French prototype, in style he followed it too. Lawrence Friedman describes Field's code of civil procedure of 1848 as "a colossal affront to the common-law tradition." It was, Friedman observes, "couched in brief, gnomic, Napoleonic sections, tightly worded and skeletal; there was no trace of the elaborate redundancy, the voluptuous heaping on of synonyms, so characteristic of Anglo-American statutes. In short it constituted a code in the French sense, not a statute. It was a lattice of reasoned principles, scientifically arranged, not a thick thumb stuck into the dikes of common law."[306]

The code that is known as the "Field Code" was Field's Code of Civil Procedure. It was the most successful of them all.[307] Already before the Civil War eight states and territories, all in the West, had adopted it.[308] In 1873 Field boasted that by then 23 states and territories (plus the consular courts in Japan!) had introduced some or all of it.[309] In 1884 the New York *Mail* took pride that the "State of New York has given laws to the world to an extent and degree unknown since the Roman Codes followed Roman conquests." It reported that as of 1884 twenty-three other states and territories as well as four provinces in India (!) had adopted the Code of Civil Procedure; seventeen other states (and India) had adopted the Code of Criminal Procedure (adopted by New York only in 1881); two other states or territories had adopted the criminal code (adopted by New York), two states or territories had adopted the Civil Code (still not enacted in New York although twice passed the legislature), and one state the Political Code (still not considered by New York). By the end of the 19th century most states had modeled their civil procedure laws on Field's Code. Four states had adopted his other codes: California, Montana and the Dakota Territory. New York never did adopt his Civil Code and disfigured his Code of Civil Procedure beyond recognition.

California Adopts Field's Procedure Codes in 1851
In 1848 the United States annexed California. As a consequence of discovery of gold, in just two years American immigrants flooded California. In 1849, still under military government, the unorganized territory held a constitutional

---

So, and by What Means? (1885) *reprinted in* Annual Report of the 8th Annual Meeting of the American Bar Association 323, 348 (1885).

[306] Lawrence M. Friedman, A History of American Law 293 (3d ed., 2007).

[307] It was reviewed at length abroad in 12 L. Rev. & Quarterly J. of Brit. & Foreign Juris. 366–398 (1850).

[308] *Id.* at 295.   [309] Field, *Reasons for the Adoption of the Codes, supra* note 151, at 365.

convention in the summer and adopted by popular vote the proposed Constitution in the fall. California became a state September 9, 1850.

The Constitutional Convention considered what California's future laws would be.[310] The Convention considered but decided against mandating code commissions along the lines of the New York Constitution of 1846. When the legislature met for the first time in January 1850, eighty lawyers petitioned it to adopt American common law; seventeen lawyers submitted a counter-petition calling for the legislature to retain civil law in California and to adopt a code based on Louisiana law. In February the legislature's Judiciary Committee reported in favor of common law.[311] The legislature that year adopted a reception statute. It also, however, adopted laws governing civil and criminal procedure largely based on Field's original drafts of his codes.

Meanwhile, Field's younger brother, former law firm partner and later U.S. Supreme Court Associate Justice, Stephen J. Field in late December 1849, arrived in California seeking his fortune. In November 1850 the younger Field was elected to the state legislature. He reworked his brother's codes as reported complete in New York in 1851 and brought about their adoption in California that year. After the Civil War he was instrumental in California's adoption of his brother's civil, criminal and political codes.[312]

H. LEGAL EDUCATION AND SYSTEMATIZING LAWS

Seal of Columbia College: (1876) [Law schools] give the student a general and systematic outline of legal principles; Columbia Law School (1876)[313]

---

[310] *See* text at note 27–39, *supra*.

[311] *Report on Civil and Common Law* (Feb. 27, 1850), *printed at* 1 CAL. 588 (1850).

[312] *See* Ralph N. Kleps, *The Revision and Codification of California Statutes 1849–1953*, 42 CAL. L. REV. 766 (1954).

[313] T.W. Dwight (Warden), *School of Law – Columbia College, in* HISTORICAL SKETCH OF COLUMBIA COLLEGE IN THE CITY OF NEW YORK, 1754–1876, 81, 92 (1876).

If common-law methods had the hold on America that contemporary common-law myth imagines, American lawyers today would study law in law offices: their learning would, in today's language, be wholly experiential. In 1776 there was no teaching of law in classrooms. Aspiring lawyers taught themselves law, usually while working as copy clerks in law offices.[314]

Formal legal education in classrooms and outside of law offices got off to a rocky start in the New Republic. It took three different tacks: chairs of law within colleges, proprietary law schools and law schools affiliated with colleges. The first two, created in the first years of the Republic, largely disappeared by about 1835. The latter, the university professional schools of today, were created only as the former disappeared, did not achieve stability until the 1850s, and did not achieve their present dominance until the second century of the Republic. In 1876 most lawyers were still law office trained.

By the Centennial year, however, university law schools had established themselves. In the decade after the Civil War more university law schools were founded (about thirty) than were founded in the eight decades before. Something monumental had happened. Before the Civil War law school studies were seen as "ornamental appendages to the office instruction," but by 1876 they were becoming indispensable.[315] Legal education was moving from the law office into the law school classroom. Still in the future was the peculiar American development of classroom study displacing law office study altogether. The fundamental issue of legal education at the Centennial was how legal education should be divided between law schools and law offices.[316]

In the first century of the Republic, legal education established itself by working to provide that which the profession could not provide: systematization of law. Teachers of law in the first century were few in number, but most were leaders in systematizing. It is an irony of American legal history that in the second century of the Republic, when the bar no longer had use for copy clerks and gave up its role in professional instruction, the academy assumed

---

[314] Lest there be any misunderstanding in this day of office printers, copy clerks copied legal documents longhand. Among the first office "type-writers" were those displayed at the 1876 Philadelphia Exposition. *See* Robert Messenger, *The World of Typewriters* 1714–2014, http://oztypewriter.blogspot.com/2012/11/on-this-day-in-typewriter-history10.html.

[315] WM. G. HAMMOND, AMERICAN LAW SCHOOLS IN THE PAST AND IN THE FUTURE, at 9 and 4 respectively (1881).

[316] *See* THEODORE W. DWIGHT, EDUCATION IN LAW SCHOOLS IN THE CITY OF NEW YORK COMPARED WITH THAT OBTAINED IN LAW OFFICES. A LECTURE DELIVERED TO THE STUDENTS OF COLUMBIA COLLEGE LAW SCHOOL, ON MONDAY EVENING FEB. 7, 1875 (1876).

that instructional role and largely abandoned its scientific role in systematization.[317]

No matter which venue – college, proprietary law school or professional law school – the leading teachers of American law in the first century of the Republic systematized. They taught rules for law applying and not skills for law synthesizing. They taught law as a science: not as a natural science (as Harvard's Langdell later would claim), but as a systematizing science. The great advantage of law school learning was systematic study. Legal educators understood that systematic law is more easily learned than the alternative of unsystematic law.[318] They characterized law office study as drudgework that interfered with real learning.[319]

1. College Chairs

A statute started classroom legal education in America. Jefferson's Revisal authorized a professorship of law at the College of William & Mary. As governor of Virginia Jefferson saw the chair into being and the appointment to it of his Revisal's co-author, George Wythe.[320]

Although Wythe and his successor, St. George Tucker, enjoyed some success at William & Mary in attracting students, similar attempts at other colleges failed. In some, Harvard and Yale, plans were discussed, but did not come to fruition until much later. In others, Pennsylvania College, Columbia, and Maryland, professors were named and began work – James Wilson at Pennsylvania, James Kent twice at Columbia, David Hoffman at Maryland – only to suspend lectures for want of students.

In the 1840s America's colleges were just beginning to aspire to become universities. Columbia "College" through the 1840s resolutely remained an institution of teachers, pupils and a set curriculum and resisted becoming a

---

[317] *See* JAMES R. MAXEINER, EDUCATING LAWYERS NOW AND THEN: AN ESSAY COMPARING THE 2007 AND 1914 CARNEGIE FOUNDATION REPORTS ON LEGAL EDUCATION AND A REPRINT OF THE 1914 REPORT THE COMMON LAW AND THE CASE METHOD IN AMERICAN UNIVERSITY LAW SCHOOLS BY JOSEF REDLICH (2007).

[318] *See, e.g.,* JAMES GOULD, A TREATISE ON THE PRINCIPLES OF PLEADING IN CIVIL ACTIONS vi, viii (1832) ("was originally made for instruction of *Students at Law*" ... "to render the doctrines of Pleading *more intelligible and more easy of attainment*" [emphases in original]).

[319] *See, e.g.,* JOSIAH QUINCY, PRESIDENT, AN ADDRESS DELIVERED AT THE DEDICATION OF DANE LAW COLLEGE IN HARVARD UNIVERSITY, OCT. 23, 1832 (1832).

[320] ALFRED ZANTZINGER REED, TRAINING FOR THE PUBLIC PROFESSION OF THE LAW: HISTORICAL DEVELOPMENT AND PRINCIPAL CONTEMPORARY PROBLEMS OF LEGAL EDUCATION IN THE UNITED STATES WITH SOME ACCOUNT OF CONDITIONS IN ENGLAND AND CANADA 116 (CARNEGIE FOUNDATION FOR THE ADVANCEMENT OF TEACHING BULLETIN No. 15, 1921).

university of professors, students and research. It hired the German jurist, J.L. Tellkampf, away from Union College in Schenectady, where he had been teaching courses in law and history, only to refuse to allow him to teach anything but German language and literature.[321]

What the colleges' professors left behind were important works of systemization. For Wythe, it was Jefferson's Revisal. For the others, the legacies were systematizing texts: Wilson's _Lectures on Law_, Kent's _Commentaries on American Law_, Tucker's edition of _Blackstone's Commentaries_, Hoffman's _Course of Legal Studies_, and Tellkampf's _On Codification, or Systematizing of the Law_.

2. _Proprietary Law Schools_

Contemporaneous with the college appointments, practitioners established independent proprietary law schools to conduct law training more closely tied to practice. Where college teaching anticipated supplemental law office study, proprietary law schools did not. One, the school in Litchfield Connecticut (1780–1833), was a great success. Most others failed; some eked out an existence with a small number of students. They were creatures of the lawyers who created and conducted them. When the lawyers died or retired their schools closed.[322] One might suppose that the proprietors of these law schools would have focused on practice skills and have ignored systematizing.[323] Yet that does not seem to have generally been the case. Many proprietors practiced systematizing:

Zephaniah Swift

Zephaniah Swift, proprietor of the law school in Windham Connecticut, prepared the first compilation of federal laws (The Folwell edition of 1797), wrote the first all-encompassing treatise of an American state's law, _A System of the Laws of the State of Connecticut_ (6 vols. 1795) as well as the first American treatise on the law of evidence.[324]

---

[321] _See_ sources cited in note 274 _supra_.

[322] _See_ Craig Evan Klafter, Reason over Precedents: Origins of American Legal Thought 133–177 (1993) (listing proprietary schools and giving statistics).

[323] One short-lived proprietary school did rely principally on moot courts. Creed Taylor, Journal of the Law-School and of the Moot-Court Attached to It: At Needham, in Virginia v (1822) ("The _law-school_ was established, not with a view to lectures by the patron, but for the purpose of aiding and assisting the student in the art and science of pleading.").

[324] Zephaniah Swift, A Digest of the Law of Evidence in Civil and Criminal Cases and a Treatise on Bills of Exchange and Promissory Notes (1810).

Henry St. George Tucker

Henry St. George Tucker, proprietor of the Winchester Law School in Virginia, wrote a Blackstone-based students' text for his state, *Commentaries on the Laws of Virginia* (1831).

Theron Metcalf

Theron Metcalf, after conducting the short-lived law school at Dedham Massachusetts (1828–1829), became co-reviser with famous educator Horace Mann of the Massachusetts Revised Statutes. In 1837 he was one of five Commissioners of the Massachusetts Code Commission of 1837 chaired by Justice Story.[325]

Peter van Schaak

Peter van Schaak was one of the revisers of the colonial laws of New York[326] before conducting a long-lived law school at Kinderhook New York.

Tapping Reeve & James Gould, Litchfield Law School

Tapping Reeve and James Gould, proprietors of the highly successful Litchfield Law School, published three texts intended to organize the law of husband and wife, descents and pleading.[327] Although they taught the common law, Klafter concludes, that they did so critically with a view to replacing it through statutes.[328] The *American Quarterly Journal* in a survey of American education institutions reported that Litchfield's proprietors taught rules and the principles on which they rested.[329] Reeves, in his *Treatise on the*

---

[325] Report of the Commissioners Appointed to Consider and Report upon the Practicability and Expedience of Reducing to a Written and Systematic Code the Common Law of Massachusetts or Any Part Thereof, Made to His Excellency the Governor, Jan., 1837, at 48 (House No. 8, 1837).

[326] Peter van Schaack (ed.), Laws of New-York, from the Year 1691 to 1773, Inclusive: Published According to an Act of the General Assembly (2 vols., 1774).

[327] Tapping Reeve, The Law of Baron and Femme, of Parent and Child, of Guardian and Ward, of Masters and Servant Preface (1816) ("to bring into one connected view" ... "beneficial to the learner") (3d ed., 1867); Tapping Reeve, A Treatise on the Law of Descents in the Several United States of America (1826); James Gould, A Treatise on the Principles of Pleading in Civil Actions vi, viii (1832).

[328] Klafter, *supra* note 324. *See also,* Ellen Holmes Pearson, Remaking Custom: Law and Identity in the Early American Republic 175–176 (2011).

[329] *See Education and Literary Institutions,* 5 [American] Quarterly Register 273 (1833). "The lectures, which are delivered every day, and which usually occupy an hour and a half, embrace every principle and rule falling under the several divisions of the different titles. The examinations, which are held every Saturday, upon the lectures of the preceding week, consist

Law of Descents in the Several United States of America (1825), set out the statutory law of all of the then fifteen states.[330]

3. College Professional Law Schools

College affiliated professional law schools grew out of the older models. In 1816 Harvard finally appointed a professor of law, Isaac Parker. In 1824 Yale took over a proprietary school. The risk of failure was high. In 1831, there were nine "law schools," counting all three types of approach, which by a partial count showed six faculty and 127 students.[331] It wasn't much in international comparison. Alone the law faculty of Tellkampf's home university, Göttingen, in then English-ruled Hannover, had more faculty and more students than all American law schools combined.[332]

Among notable failures were those of New York University in 1838 and of the College of New Jersey (the later Princeton) in the 1840s. Harvard and Yale had both to be "re-founded." Not until the 1850s did university law schools begin to achieve stability. In 1863 there were eighteen law schools; some were attached to colleges and others were independent.[333] The most important of legal educators of the 1830s to the early 1850s were Justice Story at Harvard (died 1845)[334] and his student (his "worthy Son in Law"), Timothy Walker at Cincinnati (died 1856). Both were renowned as supporters of systematizing.[335] They were succeeded in the late 1850s by Theodore Dwight at Columbia.

---

of a thorough investigation of the principles of each rule, and not merely of such questions as can be answered from memory without any exercise of judgment."

[330] REEVE, *supra* note 329, at ii. He lamented that "When we became a nation, we found ourselves divided into a number of distinct sovereignties; each possessing the power to enact laws affecting the property within its own jurisdiction, with the federal government, binding all the states together with political bands, had not the remotest concern. . . . Thus what has probably fallen to the lot of no other civilized country, this nation may be justly said to have no general law of descents."

[331] *United States, Professional Schools* 18 THE EDINBURGH ENCYCLOPÆDIA, … CONDUCTED BY DAVID BREWSTER … THE FIRST AMERICAN EDITION, CORRECTED AND IMPROVED BY THE ADDITION OF NUMEROUS ARTICLES RELATIVE TO THE INSTITUTIONS OF THE AMERICAN CONTINENT 229, 860 (1832) ("They are all of recent origin, and are here presented rather to give a ground to conjecture what will in future be the method of conducting legal studies than to show what is the course now pursued.")

[332] Maxeiner, *Tellkampf, First Humboldtian*, *supra* note 272, at 777.

[333] George -A. Matile, *Les Écoles de Droit aux États-Unis*, 9 Revue HISTORIQUE DE DROIT FRANÇAIS ET ÉTRANGER 539, 543–544 (1863), *translated in* 1 SHEPPARD 319, 321 (Steve Sheppard, ed., 1999).

[334] *See* DANIEL R. COQUILLETTE & BRICE A. KIMBALL, ON THE BATTLEFIELD OF MERIT: HARVARD LAW SCHOOL, THE FIRST CENTURY 157–188 (2015).

[335] *See* note 41 and text at notes 255–264, *supra*.

In the 1850s Theodore W. Dwight, first at Hamilton College and then, from 1858 at Columbia Law School, invigorated law schools with the "Dwight" method of instruction. Dwight departed from a straight lecture format and used an interactive lecture or recitation format. Dwight later in the second century opposed codifying. (I am not sure why.) In 1870 Christopher C. Langdell introduced the case method of instruction. It did not reach beyond Harvard until the 1890s.

I. SUMMARY OF SYSTEMATIZING 1776–1876

It seems that the Centennial Writers were right: "The *great* fact in the progress of American jurisprudence which deserves special notice and reflection is its tendency towards *organic statute law* and towards the *systematizing of law*; in other words, towards *written constitutions* and *codification*."[336] Legal methods were not assumed in the first century of the Republic, but were under construction.

The Centennial Writers did not claim success for systematizing.[337] They hoped for future success. *The First Century of the Republic* begged for understanding: "These achievements of Jurisprudence, when compared with the works of her sisters in other fields of labor, appear moderate, plain and plodding, rather than rapid, brilliant or extensive. But then, for many, many centuries, Jurisprudence has had no gift of new powers. . . . All we can say for her in the century now closing is that, with her antique tools, 'she had done what she could.'"[338]

Systematizing in the first century of the Republic was a story of high hopes and disappointing delivery. Everywhere people worked on systematizing. Complete success was nowhere, while disappointment was just about everywhere. Sometimes work was rejected out-of-hand. More often, what was done was less than what the systematizers had hoped would be done. Systematizers had to settle: not all laws, but only some laws; not a codification of statutes and common law, but only a revision of statutes. Usually, what they did do was greeted with appreciation, but not always.[339]

---

[336] *Law in America, 1776–1876*, 122 N. Am. Rev. at 174 [emphasis in original].

[337] For a critical comparative view of American skills with legislation at the time, see *German Legislation*, 10 Am. L. Rev. 270 (1875).

[338] The First Century of the Republic at 452, 453. The quotation is from Mark 14:8. The Centennial writer, Abbott was such a disappointed systematizer. The Revised Statutes of the United States on which he had worked he called "a simple consolidation." *Id.* at 451.

[339] The 1831 revision in Tennessee, apparently, was one such failure. The preface acknowledged the criticism and appealed for understanding. James Whiteside, *Preface*, in 1 STATUTE LAWS OF

Perhaps reasons for lack of success of systematizing may be found in what was not much discussed in the first century of the Republic: nationalizing and institutionalizing systematizing. Both topics came to the top of discussion in the years just after the Centennial. As far as nationalizing goes, the assumption was that codes in one state would be copied in another. To an extent this occurred, but less often than expected. As far as institutionalizing goes, the most substantial manifestation had been constitutional mandates to revise laws on a continuing basis.

THE STATE OF TENNESSEE OF A PUBLIC AND GENERAL NATURE; REVISED AND DIGESTED BY JOHN HAYWOOD AND ROBERT L. COBBS (1831) ("The fault is the materials out of which the work is made; and indeed, nothing short of an entire remodeling of the Statute Law of the State, will divest any work of the kind from the same objections, to which the present one may be considered obnoxious.") One reviewer gave it no sympathy. *The Statute Laws of Tennessee*, 8 AM. JURIST 298, 305 (1832). ("As matters lie, at present, our legislators are in the condition of an ignoramus to whom the management of an apothecary's shop with mislabeled bottles has been committed. Confusion, terror, and death are scattered all about." *Id.* at 305. "The digesters ... were to touch the confused statute book with the wand of harmony, and out of a chaos they were to produce order. Instead of which confusion has been worsened." *Id.* at 315.) On systematizing in Tennessee, *see* Samuel E. Williams, A *History of Codification in Tennessee (two parts)*, 10 TENN. L. REV. 61, 165 (1932).

6

The Rise and Fall of Codes Fin de Siècle

When Americans celebrated the Centennial of national independence in 1876 they expected that the United States would one day have a government of laws. By 1889 when they celebrated the Centennial of the inauguration of the federal government, the expectation of a government of laws was fading. When David Dudley Field died on Friday the 13th day of April 1894, it had largely disappeared.

A. THE CENTENNIAL MOMENT AT HOME AND ABROAD

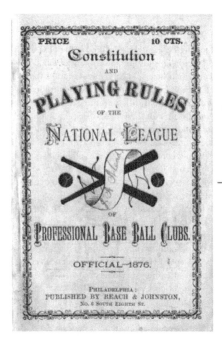

Three Systems of Rules at the Centennial[1]

---

[1] The Centennial Celebration itself had its own rules. Although it had no law exhibit, it did have its own "Bureau of Protection" complete with police force (the "Centennial Guard," at first, of over 1000 officers) and its own magistrate's court. For a picture, see FRANK LESLIE'S HISTORICAL REGISTER OF THE UNITED STATES CENTENNIAL EXPOSITION, 1876 at 296 (1877).

The Centennial Writers had good reasons to look forward to codes in a second century of the Republic. They had just witnessed fifteen years of codification at home and abroad. At home, President Abraham Lincoln's proposed revision of Federal laws of 1861 came to fruition with the publication in 1874 of the first edition of the *Revised Statutes of the United States*. Benjamin Vaughan Abbott, Harper's Centennial Writer, had helped Field with his work and had been one of the Commissioners of *the Revised Statutes*.

In 1862 Field's New York Commission published the first draft of a New York Civil Code. In Georgia, the pre-war Code of *all laws of every type* went into effect.[2] In 1864 the New York Commission published the first draft of a Penal Code, and in 1865 the final draft. In the latter's forward, Field thanked Abbott for his help. Also in 1865 the Commission published the final draft of the New York Civil Code. In 1867 the Dakota Territory adopted all five Field codes.[3] In 1872, California followed.[4] In the 1870s, New York – not to Field's

---

The Director-General didn't wait for his court to develop precedents to govern the Guard but promulgated rules. He reported: "The rules and regulations for the government of the Centennial Guard were issued in a manual of convenient size, and each member was supplied with a copy, and required to familiarize himself with its contents before he was permitted to enter on his duties. The manual contained information and instructions in detail, and specifically on the following subjects, viz.: the organization of the Guard, discipline, duties of officers and patrolmen, rank and command, promotions, punishments, resignations and discharges, reports, arrests, laws of arrest, prisoners, fires, pay, property, responsibility for uniforms and accouterments, drill, roll-call, orders and communications, lost children and lost property, tobacco, liquor, etc." *Department of Protection* [Report] in 2 UNITED STATES CENTENNIAL COMMISSION, INTERNATIONAL EXHIBITION, 1876, REPORT OF THE DIRECTOR-GENERAL, INCLUDING THE REPORTS OF BUREAUS OF ADMINISTRATION 679, 680 (1879).

[2] THE CODE OF THE STATE OF GEORGIA PREPARED BY R.H. CLARK, T.R.R. COBB & D. IRWIN vi (1861) ("The mingling together in condensed and intelligible form the common and statute Laws, Constitutional provisions and Court Decisions, and thus to place the whole body of all the Law within the reach of the people was in the opinion of your Committee the great end aimed at by the Legislature, and this end has been kept in view, and to every practicable and attainable extent ably and efficiently accomplished by the Commissioners.").

[3] *See* William B. Fisch, *The Dakota Civil Code: Notes for an Uncelebrated Centennial*, 43 N.D.L. REV. 485 (1967) & 45 N.D.L. REV. 9 (1968). Another Western state, Montana, on admission, followed. *See* Andrew P. Morriss *et al.*, *Montana Field Code Debate*, 61 MONT. L. REV. 370 (2000); Andrew P. Morriss, *Decius S. Wade's* The Common Law, 59 MONT. L. REV. 225 (1998).

[4] On codifying in California there is recent scholarship. *See* Rolston, *Uncommon Common Law: Codification and the Development of California Law, 1849–1874*, 2 CAL. LEGAL HIST. 143 (2007); Lewis Grossman, *Codification and the California Mentality*, 45 HASTINGS L.J. 617 (1994). Field's brother, Stephen J. Field, led the effort there. Another Western state, Montana, on admission in 1889, did the same. *See* Andrew P. Morriss *et al.*, *Montana Field Code Debate*, 61 MONT. L. REV. 370 (2000); Andrew P. Morriss, *Decius S. Wade's* The Common Law, 59 MONT. L. REV. 225 (1998).

pleasure – revised much of his 1848 Civil Procedure Code into a Code of Remedies.[5] Most other states, as the Centennial Writers noted, revised or codified laws in the fifteen years before the Centennial. Iowa, under the leadership of legal educator William Gardiner Hammond, was in the forefront. Important for future legal metaphors, the National League of Professional Baseball Clubs adopted a Constitution and Playing Rules.[6]

Abroad in both "civil" and "common" law countries there was enthusiasm for codes. In Germany and in Italy, civil wars in the 1860s were followed by adoption of unifying national codes.[7] In Latin America, the four largest countries, Mexico, Argentina, Brazil and Columbia, all adopted codes. Even in the British Empire codifying was in the air. Beginning in the 1830s Britain imposed codes on India.[8] In 1857 the Legislative Assembly of the Province of Canada, commissioned a codification in English of the civil law of Lower Canada, i.e., New York's next-door neighbor Québec, which was duly made and took effect in 1866.[9]

Great Britain itself debated not whether, but what and when to codify. In 1863 the Lord Chancellor called for revision of the laws to get "a harmonious whole, instead of having, as at present, a chaos of inconsistent and contradictory enactments."[10] The code proponents were "unwilling that the work of codification should be postponed."[11] One writer in an English law review in 1869, noting conditions in New York, commented: "At the present day, the subject of Codification has passed out of the domain of theory and has

---

[5] *See* MONTGOMERY H. THROOP, THE CODE OF REMEDIAL JUSTICE; SHALL IT BE REPEALED OR COMPLETED? A COMMUNICATION TO THE JUDICIARY COMMITTEES OF THE LEGISLATURE OF THE STATE OF NEW YORK BY … ONE OF THE COMMISSIONERS TO REVISE THE STATUTES 4–5 (1877) (discussion of revision work undertaken 1870 to 1876).

[6] CONSTITUTION AND PLAYING RULES OF THE NATIONAL LEAGUE OF PROFESSIONAL BASE BALL CLUBS (1876). *See* HEARING ON THE NOMINATION OF JOHN ROBERTS TO BE CHIEF JUSTICE OF THE SUPREME COURT BEFORE THE SENATE JUDICIARY COMMITTEE, 109TH CONG., 1ST SESS. 56 (Sept. 12, 2005) (testimony of John Roberts: "I will remember that it's my job to call balls and strikes and not to pitch or bat.")

[7] Franz von Holtzendorff, *Imperial Federalism in Germany*, 5 INT'L REV. 82, 88 (1878).

[8] For a recent recounting, *see* ELIZABETH KOLSKY, COLONIAL JUSTICE IN BRITISH INDIA Chapter 2 (2010).

[9] *See* THE CIVIL CODE OF LOWER CANADA … BY THOMAS McCORD, ADVOCATE, SECRETARY TO THE CODIFICATION COMMISSION v–x (1867), *reviewed in* 2 AM L. REV. 331 (1868); BRIAN J. YOUNG, THE POLITICS OF CODIFICATION: THE LOWER CANADA CIVIL CODE OF 1866 (1994). At the same time, a code of civil procedure was adopted.

[10] *The State of English Law: Codification* [reviewing Speech of the Lord Chancellor on the Revision of the Law], 83 WESTMINSTER REV. – AM. ED. 210, 219 (1865) (excerpting the speech at pp. 23–27).

[11] *Id.*

become a practical question."[12] In 1873 the *London Quarterly Review*, in reviewing Sheldon Amos' 1873 book, *An English Code*, commented: "Codification has engaged the attention of the minds of great statesmen in every civilised country." The review catalogued more than a dozen places, including "several states of the North American Union," that had made "laudable, if not perfectly successful, attempts." In reviewing Amos' book on "difficulties" of an English code, and "modes of overcoming them," it found "every reason to believe that ere long" England would join other civilized nations and accomplish something systematic in the way of codifying its law.[13]

The community of nations began work on a code of the law of nations. Field brought public international law into his portfolio of Codes.[14] Soon he was working on creating an international body to promote codifying of international law. In June 1873 invitations were sent out from America and in October the founding meeting of the Association for the Reform and Codification of the Law of Nations was held in Brussels.[15] In the Centennial Year James B. Angell, President of the University of Michigan, in an address in Detroit in May 1876, observed that: "The question of framing a code of international law is one which is now earnestly engaging the attention of many distinguished publicists. . . . Most of the arguments *pro* and *contra* are as applicable to the codification of international as of municipal law."[16] Field, nearly on the day of the Centennial, published a second edition of his *Draft Outlines of a Code of International Law*. In September, the international organization held a meeting in the Centennial Celebration's main conference hall; Field himself addressed the meeting.[17]

---

[12] T.L. Murray, *The Codes of New York*, 27 Law. Mag. And Law Rev. 312 (1869). On proposals to codify English law see, *inter alia*, Sheldon Amos, An English Code; Its Difficulties, and the Mode of Overcoming Them (1873) (positive for codification, but Chapter V views New York codes as a negative example).

[13] *Review: An English Code; Its Difficulties, and the Mode of Overcoming Them, by Sheldon Amos*, 40 The London Quarterly Rev. 499 (1873). *See* Nuno Garoupa & Andrew P. Morriss, *The Fable of the Codes: The Efficiency of the Common Law, Legal Origins, and Codification Movements*, 2012 U. Ill. L. Rev. 1443, 1448–1450.

[14] That there might be a similar code for resolving conflicts of laws in private transactions was seen as of no less importance. *A Code of Private International Law*, 2 Am. L. Rev. 599 (1868).

[15] James B. Miles, Association for the Reform and Codification of the Law of Nations: A Brief Sketch of its Formation, by [its] General Secretary, Boston, U.S.A., Prepared for the Conference at the Hague, Sept. 1st, 1875, at 11 (1875).

[16] The Progress of International Law Read at Detroit, May 13, 1876, at 8 (1876).

[17] *International Law. A General Court of Nations. The International Code Committee as Philadelphia – Papers by Elihu Burritt, Ex-Gov. Washburn, A.P. Sprague, and David Dudley Field – Careful Discussion of Important Matters*, N.Y. Times (Sept. 30, 1876).

B. CODE COMBAT IN UPSTATE NEW YORK

GRAPHIC STATUES, NO. 11.—"MY FIELD IS THE WORLD."

Thomas Nast, *My Field in the World* from THE DAILY GRAPHIC, Apr. 25, 1873[18]

[18] *Graphic Statue No. 11*, 1 [New York] THE DAILY GRAPHIC (No. 46, Apr. 25, 1873) at 1.

At the Centennial of Independence there was little of Blackstone's common law left in the United States.[19] America's legislators by statute had overturned the bulk of it: property law, civil procedure, and criminal law and procedure.[20] Ironically, contract law and tort law, which had had lesser basis in Blackstone's common law,[21] had become (and remain) the bastions of substantive judge-made law. In 1876, not just the Centennial Writers, many Americans expected that codes would soon displace judge-made law altogether.[22]

They were disappointed. According to Professor Lawrence M. Friedman, codification was crushed in one of "the set pieces of American legal history." That set piece, according to Friedman, "has its hero, Field; its villain is James C. Carter of New York ... Codification was wrong, Carter felt, because it removed the center of gravity from the courts [to] the legislature – the code enacting body ... ."[23] For Friedman, the defeat of codification was a personal "snub" to Field and not of importance for the legal system. "One child labor act or one homestead act can have more potential impact than volumes of codes."[24] He is wrong. A glance beyond America's borders shows otherwise. Part III shows that.

1. NY City Bar Kills Civil Code in NY Capital Albany – Twenty-Three Times

So what does this set piece look like? It's hyperbole, but if it's a set piece, let's make it dramatic. Much as the Declaration of Independence marked the

---

[19] 1 WILLIAM BLACKSTONE, COMMENTARIES ON THE LAWS OF ENGLAND 68 (1765).

[20] *Accord,* John F. Dillon, *A Century of American Law,* in PROCEEDINGS OF THE TENTH ANNUAL MEETING OF THE ALABAMA STATE BAR ASSOCIATION ... DEC. 14TH AND 15TH, 1887 (1888), *reprinted in* PROCEEDINGS OF THE NEW YORK STATE BAR ASSOCIATION, THIRTEENTH ANNUAL MEETING, ... ALSO, REPORTS FOR THE YEAR 1889, at 249 (1890).

[21] Joseph H. Beale, Jr., *The Development of Jurisprudence During the Past Century, Address Delivered before the Congress of Arts and Science at St. Louis, September 20, 1904, in the Division of Jurisprudence,* 18 HARV. L. REV. 271, 272 (1905). *See* WILLIAM M. WIECEK, THE LOST WORLD OF CLASSICAL LEGAL THOUGHT, LAW AND IDEOLOGY IN AMERICA, 1886–1937, 46 (tort law), 102–103 (contract law) (1998).

[22] E.g., the *Albany Law Journal* wrote: "It would be sheer blindness not to perceive the fact that the jurisprudence of the whole world is rapidly and irresistibly tending toward codification." *Book Notices,* 13 ALBANY L.J. 151 (Feb. 28, 1876). Codification was, Professor Mathias Reimann notes, "on the verge of success." Mathias Reimann, *Transatlantic Models: Influence between German and American Law,* 41 SEOUL L.J. 229, 242–243 (2000).

[23] LAWRENCE M. FRIEDMAN, A HISTORY OF AMERICAN LAW 302 (3d ed., 2004), 351 (1st ed., 1973). An excellent discussion of the code debate of the 1880s is Andrew P. Morriss, *Codification and Right Answers,* 74 CHI. KENT. L. REV. 355 (1999). Dean Morriss analyzes the arguments on both sides from a legal system point of view and draws on a range of sources not much considered in the pre-digitalization era.

[24] *Id.* at 305 (3d ed.), at 354 (1st ed.).

beginning of a thirteen-year struggle for an American Constitution – a framework for democratic government of laws and not men – the Centennial of the Declaration marked the beginning of a thirteen-year struggle for the laws of that government. Only in the later struggle the lawyers in New York City won and the American people lost.

In the 1870s and 1880s Field and his friends repeatedly took three of his four unadopted codes (the Civil Code, the Penal Code, and the Code of Criminal Procedure) to the New York Legislature. Over and over again the people's representatives approved them; over and over again the lawyers of the Association of the Bar of the City of New York (City Bar) overruled the people's representatives. In 1879, the legislature approved all three codes. The governor vetoed them. In 1880, the legislature again approved the Code of Criminal Procedure. The governor again vetoed it. In 1881, however, it began to look as if all three codes were on their way to becoming law. The legislature again approved the Penal Code and the Code of Criminal Procedure. Only this time, the governor did not veto them.

Alarmed by developments, March 15, 1881 the City Bar established a Special Committee "To Urge the Rejection of the Proposed Civil Code." Before the special committee could "perfect its organization" the Assembly, i.e., the lower house of the legislature, passed the Civil Code by an overwhelming vote of eighty-three to three. The Special Committee sprang into action and arranged for an April 21 hearing before the Senate committee considering the bill. The Civil Code was not reported out of committee: the legislature adjourned in July without action.[25]

So the struggle continued like that for nearly a decade. Field's supporters took the Civil Code to the legislature and the City Bar opposed it by every means at hand. The Special Committee was reappointed and delivered its annual report. Ten annual reports there were in all. In 1882 the City Bar had to rely again on a gubernatorial veto to stop the Civil Code.[26] James C. Carter, joined the Special Committee that year to take the role of lead advocate;

---

[25] ASSOCIATION OF THE BAR OF THE CITY OF NEW YORK, REPORT OF THE SPECIAL COMMITTEE "TO URGE THE REJECTION OF THE PROPOSED CIVIL CODE"; APPOINTED MAR. 15TH, 1881. PRESENTED OCT. 21ST, 1881, at 5–7 (1881). The special committee reported that "the proposed Code is intended to exterminate the Common Law as a system of jurisprudence." *Id.* at 8.

[26] The Special Committee printed the governor's veto message in its report. ASSOCIATION OF THE BAR OF THE CITY OF NEW YORK, REPORT OF THE SPECIAL COMMITTEE "TO URGE THE REJECTION OF THE PROPOSED CIVIL CODE;" REAPPOINTED NOV. 1, 1881. PRESENTED OCT. 10TH, 1882, at 8–9 (1882). The reappointed special committee increased in size from six to sixteen and added two of the principal antagonists: James C. Carter and Theodore W. Dwight.

Theodore W. Dwight joined then and in 1883 became chair.[27] Each side let loose plagues of pamphlets as each year the Code made its appearance in legislative committee and sometimes on the floor.[28] The two sides battled for victory. For the City Bar Special Committee that meant no civil code at all; never did it propose a better code.

2. *The Battle of Saratoga Springs and Other Bar Brawls*

After the governor vetoed the Civil Code in 1882, Field took the fight for codes national: to the newly founded American Bar Association (ABA, founded 1878), to other newly founded state bar associations and to newly important law schools. For a time, it looked like Field might triumph nationally. In 1886 the ABA adopted Field's resolution that "The law itself should be reduced, so far as its substantive principles are settled, to the form of a statute."[29]

All across the country lawyers took up the subject of codification. In 1887 the President of the Tennessee Bar Association reported that thanks to the "very careful consideration" that the ABA had given codification at its annual meetings, the topic had been subject to "very numerous" discussions around the country and that legal literature was "replete" with the discussion. He told of his personal experience with this "perplexing" topic: "it is a matter that will not down at our bidding. It is a question that has been learnedly discussed in able and eloquent addresses at every State Bar Association to which I have had access. We are all familiar with the careful consideration it has received at the hands of the American Bar Association at its annual meetings at Saratoga."[30] Just about every state bar association took it up.

---

[27] It was an interesting pairing. Dwight was then Dean of Columbia Law School. Carter had secured Langdell's appointment as Dean at Harvard and was a principal benefactor of that school. Langdell's case method disciples would at decade's end bring about the ouster of Dwight from Columbia.

[28] The special committee was authorized to print its reports in substantial numbers (e.g., 2,500 copies). The Reports now are scarce; I have never seen one offered for sale. But most have been digitized.

[29] REPORT OF THE NINTH ANNUAL MEETING OF THE AMERICAN BAR ASSOCIATION 72, 74 (1886).

[30] W.C. Folkes, *President's Address*, PROCEEDINGS OF THE FIFTH ANNUAL MEETING OF THE BAR ASSOCIATION OF TENNESSEE, HELD AT MEMPHIS, THURSDAY, JULY 1, AND FRIDAY, JULY 2, 1887, at 83, 93. One early 20th century retrospect remarked: "It may seem difficult to imagine any phase of codification that has not been discussed and exhausted at the meetings of our bar associations and kindred learned bodies since David Dudley Field joined issue with James Coolidge Carter." Nathan Isaacs, *The Aftermath of Codification*, REPORT OF THE FORTY-THIRD ANNUAL MEETING OF THE AMERICAN BAR ASSOCIATION HELD AT ST. LOUIS, MISSOURI, AUG. 25, 26, 27, 1920, 524 (1920).

Field, as he had before the Civil War, took the campaign to the academy. He personally addressed the Law Academy of Philadelphia in April 1886;[31] a supporter gave the Yale Law School commencement address in June 1884.[32] Field probably counted as sympathizers two contemporary leaders in legal education, Baldwin, Dean at Yale, and William Gardiner Hammond, Dean at Washington University in St. Louis. But the Deans at Harvard, Columbia and Hastings in California seem to have lined up against him. Field's number one opponent, James C. Carter, who spearheaded the City Bar's opposition, was closely tied to Harvard Law School and its Dean Christopher Columbus Langdell.[33] Theodore Dwight, Dean at Columbia and no friend of Langdell's new teaching method, was himself Chairman of the City Bar's opposition committee. In the far West, John Norton Pomeroy, at Hastings College of Law, who had been an early supporter of Field's Codes in California, was so widely cited in posthumous opposition, that his earlier support is forgotten.[34]

For a moment in the fall of 1886, it looked like codes might triumph so well as to exclude common law. A scant six weeks after the ABA approved Field's Resolution, one of the Centennial Writers, Bispham, came to the defense of common law. He made the "progressive capacity of the unwritten law," the theme of his introductory lecture at the Law Department of the University of Pennsylvania. He worried that statute law might practically displace judge-made law altogether.[35]

---

[31] David Dudley Field, Codification: An Address Delivered before the Law Academy of Philadelphia ... April 15, 1886 (1886).

[32] George Hoadly, Codification in the United States: An Address Delivered before the Graduating Classes at the Sixtieth Anniversary of the Yale Law School, on June 24th, 1884 (1884).

[33] Carter had been instrumental in the selection in 1870 of Langdell as Dean, was a founder and the first President of the Harvard Law Alumni Association and endowed a chair at the Harvard Law School.

[34] Lewis Grossman, *supra* note 4. *Compare* John Norton Pomeroy, The Hastings Law Department of the University of California, Inaugural Address, Aug. 8, 1878 (1878) with John Norton Pomeroy, The "Civil Code" in California ... Reprinted from the West Coast Reporter (1885). Joel Bishop, a prolific treatise writer whom one might have supposed would have been neutral or inclined toward codes, came out in defense of common law methods. Joel Prentiss Bishop, Common Law and Codification; or, The Common Law as a System of Reasoning, – How and Why Essential to Good Government; What Its Perils, and How Averted. An Address Delivered before the Sour Carolina Bar Association, at Columbia, Dec. 8, 1887.

[35] of Unwritten Law. An Introductory Address Delivered before the Law Department of the University of Pennsylvania, Oct. 1st, 1886, 7–8 (1886). For emphasis in his talk Bispham reported the original version: "all law should be reduced as far as possible, to the form of the statute."

3. *Field's Last Hurrahs*

Victories with bar associations did not translate into adoption of the Civil Code in New York or in other major states. In 1887 the Assembly again passed the Civil Code. This time the governor had committed to sign the Code, but it never reached his desk. Carter testified before the Senate Judiciary Committee and there, as in 1881, the Code again died. In testifying against the Civil Code, Carter made a personal attack on Field. Little noted then or now, in his testimony Carter conceded that his arguments did not apply to codes of public law. He claimed a common law advantage only for private law.[36]

In 1888 the Senate passed the Civil Code, but that year the Assembly voted it down.[37] The *New York Times* reported that this was the twenty-third time that the Civil Code had failed of adoption. The article commented:

> it remains for some other legislature to give to the people of the State the benefit of a codification of the common law of the State. The lawyers had their say for and against the code to-day, and few laymen were presumptious [*sic*] enough to discuss the question. Most of them voted as their lawyer leaders indicated, without any conception of the code, and few of them seemed to even know what a code is.[38]

Professor Friedman says of Field's Code: "New York would have none of it."[39] It was not New York that would have none it: it was the City Bar that would have none of it. Years later City Bar crowed about its great accomplishment "in saving the people of the State."[40]

In 1888 Field was elected President of the ABA. In 1889 he presided over the ABA's first annual meeting held away from Saratoga Springs. In a centennial year of the Constitution, he closed his address as President calling on his colleagues one last time: "you must ... give speedy justice to your fellow-citizens, more

---

[36] James C. Carter, Argument of James C. Carter in Opposition to the Bill to Establish a Civil Code: Before the Senate Judiciary Committee, Albany, Mar. 23, 1887, at 26. But a Louisiana lawyer noted it already in Carter's earlier writings. E. Evariste Moise, *Two Answers to Mr. Carter's Pamphlet*, 29 Alb. L.J. 267 (1884).

[37] Association of the Bar of the City of New York, Eighth Annual Report of the Special Committee "To Urge the Rejection of the Proposed Civil Code;" Reappointed Dec. 11th, 1888. Adopted Dec. 11th, 1888, at 7 (1889).

[38] *Politics in the Senate ... The Field Code Defeated*, N.Y. Times, May 2, 1888, at 5.

[39] Friedman, *supra* note 23.

[40] Edward W. Sheldon, The Association of the Bar of the City of New York, Historical Sketch 1870–1920, Prepared for the Semi-Centennial Celebration, Feb. 17th, 1920, at 49. See Morriss, *Codification and Right Answers*, *supra* note 23 (identifying popular support and City Bar opposition).

speedy than you have yet given, and you must give them a chance to know their laws."[41] It was a swan song and not a call to action. Two years later in August 1891, nearing the end of his long life, he published a retrospect on *Law Reform in the United States and Its Influence Abroad.*[42]

Although reaching the end of his life, Field continued to promote an international code. In 1890 President Benjamin Harrison presented a draft international code to Congress that had been proposed at an international congress.[43]

Field died Friday the 13th of April 1894.[44] That was the end of America's campaigns for codes. Never again would America seriously contemplate a civil code such as France in 1894 already had had for ninety years, or such as Japan and Germany would adopt only two years later. Like the gravestones of Adams and Jefferson, Field's gravestone remembers his life's work for written law.

DAVID DUDLEY FIELD
BORN IN HADDAM CONN FEB 13, 1805
DIED IN NEW YORK CITY, APRIL 13, 1894

HE DEVOTED HIS LIFE TO REFORM THE LAW
TO CODIFY THE COMMON LAW
TO SIMPLIFY LEGAL PROCEDURE
TO SUBSTITUTE ARBITRATION FOR WAR
TO BRING JUSTICE WITHIN THE REACH OF ALL MEN.

---

[41] *Address of David Dudley Field, of New York, President of the Association*, REPORT OF THE TWELTH ANNUAL MEETING OF THE AMERICAN BAR ASSOCIATION HELD AT CHICAGO, ILLINOIS, AUG. 28, 29, AND 30, 1889 149, 234 (1889).

[42] DAVID DUDLEY FIELD, LAW REFORM IN THE UNITED STATES AND ITS INFLUENCE ABROAD REPRINTED FROM THE AMERICAN LAW REVIEW OF AUG., 1891, WITH SOME CHANGES AND NOTES (1891).

[43] *See, e.g.*, MESSAGE FROM THE PRESIDENT OF THE UNITED STATES, TRANSMITTING A REPORT OF THE INTERNATIONAL CONFERENCE TOUCHING A UNIFORM CODE OF INTERNATIONAL LAW, 51ST CONG., 1ST SESS., SENATE, EX. DOC. NO. 283 (1890); PAPERS ON THE REASONABLENESS OF INTERNATIONAL ARBITRATION, ITS RECENT PROGRESS, AND THE CODIFICATION OF THE LAW OF NATIONS (Henry Richard, ed., London, 1887).

[44] He was buried in Stockbridge, Massachusetts. Coincidentally, the day before, William Gardiner Hammond, a like-minded voice in law schools, died.

7

Historical Epilogue

From Past to Present

Codification has an ugly sound to most American lawyers. We have been trained to believe that no code can be expressed with sufficient exactness, or can be sufficiently elastic to fulfill adequately the functions of our common law. The iridescent legal utopia proposed by Bentham and his followers, in which every one should readily know the law, or be able quickly to find it by turning to a code, and in which the professional lawyer would be abolished, has been proved a dream.

Samuel Williston (1914)[1]

Following the death of David Dudley Field in 1894, contemporary observers saw his campaign for codification as going dormant.[2] In fact, the code ideal died and was forgotten.

The ideal motivating Field's codes, an ideal that seems so natural to laymen the world over – that law consists of rules known to the people to be applied by them to facts – became suspect among the then newly solidifying legal professions. Legal professionals put aside the ideal of a system of statutes in which their role was to help build and implement the best cosmos possible. They chose instead to deal transactionally with chaos and find for themselves and their clients within that chaos the best possible solutions.

---

[1] SAMUEL WILLISTON, THE UNIFORM PARTNERSHIP ACT WITH SOME OTHER REMARKS ON OTHER UNIFORM COMMERCIAL LAWS, AN ADDRESS BEFORE THE LAW ASSOCIATION OF PHILADELPHIA DEC. 18, 1914, 1 (1915) *reprinted in* 63 U. PA. L. REV. 196, 196–197 (1915). Willston acknowledged that this was not true abroad: "It must not be forgotten, however, in any criticism of codification, that practically the whole civilized world, except English speaking countries, is governed by codes; that these codes have been adopted chiefly during the past century after trial of systems of unwritten or customary law; and that foreign expert opinion seems practically unanimous in favor of codification.") *Id.*

[2] *See, e.g.,* RICHARD FLOYD CLARKE, THE SCIENCE OF LAW AND LAWMAKING: BEING AN INTRODUCTION TO LAW, A GENERAL VIEW OF ITS FORM AND SUBSTANCE AND A DISCUSSION OF THE QUESTION OF CODIFICATION (1898).

The foregoing is my hypothesis.[3] Here I cannot explore it or defend it. Here I only show facts that lead me to suggest it in order to connect the past ideals discussed in Chapters 4 to 6 to the present reality discussed in Chapters 9 to 13. Many of these changes were well underway by 1914; most were completed by 1938.

A.   FROM LAWS FOR PEOPLE TO PRECEDENTS FOR PROFESSIONALS

In 1876, Americans wanted systematized laws that they could read and apply; a half-century later, legal professionals told them that codification is un-American and that lawyers inform the people of the law. In 1876, Americans looked to legislatures to make laws; a half-century later legal professionals told them that judges make laws. In 1876, most laws were state laws; a half-century later legal professionals told them that most important laws were national. In 1876, the United States Supreme Court hesitated to put statutes out of force; a half-century later it had made declaring statutes unconstitutional its moniker. In 1876, judges at all levels thought they followed statutes; a half-century later, they made statutes do their bidding.

1. *From Systematizing Statutes to Restating Cases*

With the final defeat of Field's Civil Code in 1888 America's legal professionals gave up on stating laws in systematic codes. They organized statutes in alphabetical collections much as laymen had done in Massachusetts in 1648. In making statutes consistent they lagged Jefferson's Revisal, the New York Revised Statutes of 1829 and even the less successful United States Revised Statutes of 1874. The tormented release of the disappointing,

---

[3]   For similar conclusions from the 1880s codification debate for today, *see* Andrew P. Morriss, *Codification and Right Answers*, 74 CHI. KENT L. REV. 355, 389 (1999) (first, "in the courtroom, judges and lawyers alike seem to view the common law only as an endlessly expanding catalogue of causes of action rather than a system of internally consistent rules containing limits as well. All too often public policy argument, and usually not very good ones at that, dominate legal analysis in both briefs and opinions." And second, "modern statutes rarely exhibit any of the codifiers' concerns with systematization of the law. Instead of creating a coherent framework for resolving similar issues, statutes today employ ad hoc approaches, treating each problem as distinct.")

New York Proposal 1904.[4]

Used with permission of Thomson-Reuters.

non-binding and ill-named United States Code in 1926 is proof enough of that failure.[5] I discuss it in Chapter 9.

Survivors on both sides of the code combats of the 1880s came together in the early 20th century to promote the idea of nonstatutory alternatives to codes: systematic orderings of case law. Digests and encyclopedias of laws had been around for a long time, but the idea of them as an alternative to codes in the era of codes gained credibility with the emergence of the modern law book industry in the last quarter of the 19th century.

An 1873 Report of the then-newly organized Association of the Bar of the City of New York had found "radical changes" necessary in case reporting.[6]

---

[4] REPORT OF THE SPECIAL COMMITTEE OF THE ASSEMBLY OF THE LEGISLATURE OF 1900 ON STATUTORY REVISION COMMISSION BILLS 1901 COMMITTEE (Adolph J. Rodenbeck, James T. Rogers and James E. Smith): PLAN FOR COLLATING THE STATUTES PREPARATORY TO THE WORK OF CONSOLIDATION AND REVISION: CONTAINING THE REPORT OF THE CHAIRMAN ON A GENERAL PLAN FOR THE CONSOLIDATION AND CLASSIFICATION OF THE STATUTES AND A DETAILED PLAN FOR MAKING A CARD RECORD OF THE HISTORY AND SUBSTANCE OF THE STATUTES OF THE STATE: PREPARED UNDER THE DIRECTION OF THE BOARD OF STATUTORY CONSOLIDATION OF THE STATE OF NEW YORK: CREATED BY CHAPTER 664 OF THE LAWS OF 1904: PASSED MAY 9, 1904.

[5] *See* Chapter 9, Section B, *infra.*

[6] REPORT OF THE COMMITTEE ON LAW REPORTING OF THE ASSOCIATION OF THE CITY OF NEW YORK 5 (1873). For a contemporary account of similar issues in England, *see* W.T.S. DANIEL,

Case reports of that day were not reliable in frequency or accuracy of publication, were not readily available and were not easily used. West Publishing Company, founded in 1876, changed all that. When a decade later the American Bar Association (ABA) met in Saratoga Springs, New York, to debate codification of case law, West of St. Paul Minnesota had its *National Reporter System* in operation. West built its digests (e.g., the *American Digest*[7]) and its *Key Number System* on its regular publication of case reports. It offered a much-improved way of finding precedents. At least for a while many legal professionals accepted the idea that cases could substitute for statutes.

Soon after the defeat of codes there were attempts to classify cases in ways intended to provide systematizing benefits of codes.[8] Two major projects of the first quarter of the 20th century survive into the 21st century as moss-covered monuments to the quest for case law alternatives to codes: the *Corpus Juris* encyclopedia and the Restatements of the Law of the American Law Institute (ALI). Both works are similar. Both were intended to systematize laws, like codes, but were (are) private publications not dependent on legislative adoption. *Corpus Juris* was intended to be a "'tacit codification' – that is 'expository codification' as distinguished from 'legislative codification.'"[9] The restatements were to be "critical," that is, "more than an improved encyclopedia of the existing law."[10] *Corpus Juris* is all-encompassing; the Restatements are field-specific (e.g., contracts, property, torts).

Both works were directed to the legal professions and not to the people. *Corpus Juris* was intended to satisfy "The imperative demand by the profession." It *"would be the vade mecum of every lawyer and every Judge. It would be the one indispensable tool of his art."*[11] The Restatements are directed to judges

THE HISTORY AND ORIGIN OF THE LAW REPORTS TOGETHER WITH A COMPILATION OF VARIOUS DOCUMENTS SHOWING THE PROGRESS AND RESULT OF PROCEEDINGS TAKEN FOR THEIR ESTABLISHMENT (1884).

[7] The "father of the American digest" was Benjamin V. Abbott, the Centennial writer for *The First Century of the Republic*. ERWIN C. SURRENCY, A HISTORY OF AMERICAN LAW PUBLISHING 119 (1990).

[8] What appears to be the first scholarly examination of these efforts is the valuable article by Professor Richard A. Danner, *James DeWitt Andrews: Classifying the Law in the Early Twentieth Century* (June 19, 2017). Duke Law School Public Law & Legal Theory Series No. 2017-44. Available at SSRN: https://ssrn.com/abstract=2989081. *See* James DeWitt Andrews, *Classification and Restatement of the Law*, 14 ILL. L. REV. 465 (1920). The ALI, on the other hand, has received much scholarly attention.

[9] Lucien Hugh Alexander with George W. Kirchwey & James DeWitt Andrews, *Memorandum in re Corpus Juris*, 22 THE GREEN BAG 59, 65 (1910).

[10] REPORT OF THE COMMITTEE ON THE ESTABLISHMENT OF A PERMANENT ORGANIZATION FOR IMPROVEMENT OF THE LAW PROPOSING THE ESTABLISHMENT OF AN AMERICAN LAW INSTITUTE 14 (1923).

[11] Alexander, *supra* note 9 [emphasis in original].

deciding cases and are intended to be suggestive of solutions to problems. Legal luminaries of the day endorsed both projects.[12]

The very factors that made *Corpus Juris* and ALI Restatements possible – routine case publishing and no need for legislative adoption – limited their utility for practice, for the people, or for law reform. On the one hand, neither is binding: not even on judges. They do not guide the people. On the other hand, the cases they restate soon become old precedents when in contemporary common law new precedents are more authoritative than old ones. For more than one hundred years, West has been publishing "Law Books by the Million."[13] In the end, neither *Corpus Juris* nor the restatements bring their users the most basic element of a government of law: authoritative texts.[14]

Both continue to exist. *Corpus Juris Secundum*, i.e., the second edition of *Corpus Juris*, however, is not an "indispensible tool," but is a mere "finder of case law."[15] The ALI Restatements have done better. They have authority of their own among judges. But users cannot rely on them to state the law in any given jurisdiction without consulting cases.

2. Half-Hearted Institutionalizing of Lawmaking

In the decade after the Centennial, American jurists began discussing institutionalizing lawmaking. Looking to foreign models, some suggested establishing permanent lawmaking institutions to be charged with maintaining the quality of legislation.[16] These discussions foreshadowed the development,

---

[12] The stunning array of founding endorsers of the ALI is well known still today, but the founding endorsers of the Corpus Juris were no less impressive and more international. *See Opinions upon the American* Corpus Juris *Project by Leaders of Bench and Bar,* 22 THE GREEN BAG 90 (1910).

[13] WEST PUBLISHING COMPANY, LAW BOOKS BY THE MILLION: AN ACCOUNT OF THE LARGEST LAW-BOOK HOUSE IN THE WORLD – THE HOME ESTABLISHMENT OF THE NATIONAL REPORTER SYSTEM AND THE AMERICAN DIGEST SYSTEM 1901, *reprinted in* 14 GREEN BAG 2D 311 (2011).

[14] Justice Cardozo, one of the principal proponents of the ALI emphasized that the role of the restatements was not to be an authoritative text but a guide to judicial decision. Benjamin N. Cardozo, *To Rescue "Our Lady of the Common Law," The Dragon of Uncertainty Which Has So Long Baffled and Harried the Profession, and Which Has Threatened with Death or Dishonor "Our Lady of the Common Law," Should Be Tracked to Its Lair and Destroyed by the Work of the American Law Institute,"* 10 ABA J. 347 (1924) ("the work of judicial decision . . . is a technique that is founded upon the experience of judges and not a technique that is founded upon the interpretation of authoritative texts.").

[15] KENDELL F. SVENGALIS, LEGAL INFORMATION BUYER'S GUIDE & REFERENCE MANUAL § 17 Legal Encyclopedias (2016 ed.).

[16] *See* ASSOCIATION OF THE BAR OF THE CITY OF NEW YORK, REPORT ON A PLAN FOR IMPROVING THE METHODS OF LEGISLATION OF THIS STATE, BY A COMMITTEE OF THE ASSOCIATION OF THE BAR OF THE CITY OF NEW YORK (1885). The committee consisted of Simon Sterne, Chairman, James M. Varnum, Theron G. Strong, and George H. Yeaman. Id. at 19. *See also* Simeon E. Baldwin, *Byrce on American Legislation,* 14 NEW ENGLANDER AND YALE REV. 39 (1889);

beginning in the early 20th century, of the legislative research bureaus and the offices of legislative counsel of today. I discuss in Chapter 10 how they have failed to systematize statutes as their founders must have hoped.

3. *From State Law to Would-Be National Law*[17]

A national economy needs national law. That became acutely evident in the last quarter of the 19th century. Truly national law applies throughout the country without conflicting state laws; there is no need to consult individual state law on matters covered by national law. Federal law that admits of contradictions with state law, does not provide the same benefits as truly national law.

National laws in federations take two principal forms: (1) federal laws that are applicable throughout the land and (2) uniform state laws. Both approaches to national law enjoyed a boom in the United States at the end of the 19th century. Beginning in the 1880s the federal government began making robust use of its authority under the commerce clause of the Constitution to govern commerce among the states. Beginning in the 1890s, representatives of the states began drafting uniform laws for states to adopt.

Both approaches failed to provide consistently authoritative laws that people can rely on. Americans have today what Professor Abbe R. Gluck calls "our [national] federalism." She writes: "It is a 'law' problem. When it comes to legal doctrines to deal with this new world of federalism, ours is a sorry state of affairs."[18]

People cannot rely on federal laws as national law because federal laws do not displace state laws. They are not truly national laws. Federal law is supreme, but it is not generally exclusive, that is, what lawyers call preemptive

CHARLES REEMELIN, TREATISE ON POLITICS AS A SCIENCE 55 (1875); HENRY WADE ROGERS, THE LAW-MAKING POWER. A PAPER READ BEFORE THE KANSAS BAR ASSOCIATION, JAN. 24, 1894 (1894), *reprinted in* 3 NORTHWESTERN L. REV. 39 (1894); SIMON STERNE, OUR METHODS OF LEGISLATION AND THEIR DEFECTS. A PAPER READ BEFORE THE NEW YORK MUNICIPAL SOCIETY ON THE EVENING OF JAN. 6, 1879 (1879); Simon Sterne, *The English Methods of Legislation Compared with the American, Read before the Penn Monthly Association, March 13th, 1879,* 10 PENN MONTHLY 336 (May 1879); Simon Sterne, *The Prevention of Defective and Slipshod Legislation,* REPORTS OF THE SEVENTH ANNUAL MEETING OF THE AMERICAN BAR ASSOCIATION, HELD AT SARATOGA SPRINGS, NEW YORK, AUG. 20, 21 AND 22, 1884 275 (1884); Simon Sterne, *Defective and Corrupt Legislation: The Cause and the Remedy* in the popular (*Questions of the Day,* volume no. XXII, 1885); FRANCIS WAYLAND, ON CERTAIN DEFECTS IN OUR METHODS OF MAKING LAWS, OPENING ADDRESS [OF THE PRESIDENT] BEFORE THE AMERICAN SOCIAL SCIENCE ASSOCIATION, AT ITS ANNUAL MEETING, SARATOGA SPRINGS, SEPT. 5TH, 1881 (1881). J.L. Tellkampf was among the first to propose the idea in his habilitation in Göttingen in 1835. *See* J.L. TELLKAMPF, UEBER VERBESSERUNG DES RECHTSZUSTANDES IN DEN DEUTSCHEN STAATEN (1835). He repeated the suggestion in his 1842 article in the *American Jurist* which article he reprinted England in 1859 and in Germany in 1875.

[17] *See* Chapter 11, *infra.*
[18] Abbe R. Gluck, *Our [National] Federalism,* 123 YALE L.J. 1996, 1997 (2014).

of states' laws. Although the Constitution in a few areas (e.g., immigration, bankruptcy, patents, copyrights) makes federal law exclusive, in most areas, the Constitution allows federal and state laws to exist side-by-side without demarking limits to either. To know the law, people need to consult two laws within one state or fifty-one laws within the whole country.

The Supreme Court has tried to demark lines between federal and state authority ("preemption" doctrines). Its success is necessarily limited. The people should be spared having to comply with two conflicting laws. But Supreme Court allocations come only after – and not before – conflicting laws are in place. Statutes are needed to state beforehand whether they are pre-emptive. But where powers are concurrent, only a Constitution can well determine when federal or state laws preempt the other.

Nor have uniform state laws provided the national uniformity promised. The foremost reason is that few have been adopted by all states, or even by a majority of states: perhaps no more than twenty. Unlike the "directives" of the European Union – the EU's uniform state laws – there is no obligation of state adoption. Another reason for disappointment is piecemeal coverage. The Uniform Commercial Code, for example, does not cover all contracts or all commercial dealings, but only some transactions. And even here, it relies on "common law and equity . . . to supplement its provisions in many important ways."[19] And if all that were not debilitating enough, for this, one of the most successful and important uniform laws, a decade's worth of amendments to the Uniform Commercial Code have failed to deal with the digital age.

4. From Supreme Court to Constitutional Court

The central role that the Supreme Court holds today in the American legal system was only nascent in the first century of the Republic. The Founders did not seem to have intended it. The Constitution allowed, but did not mandate, lower federal courts. The Constitution made no provision for constitutional review. The Supreme Court was thought "the least dangerous branch." It was to interpret and apply laws. And that it is what it mostly, if not exclusively, did in the first century of the Republic. Admiralty cases made up a large portion of its docket.

Today, every legal professional and most laymen know of the remarkable – practically suffocating – influence of today's Supreme Court on the American legal system. Appointing its judges has become one of the most contentious of political decisions in the nation. Its dominating position in the American legal system is rooted in constitutional review. Much of law applying in America takes place in the shadow of the Supreme Court's decisions.

---

[19] Uniform Commercial Code § 1–103 Official Comment 2.

The Constitution does not bestow the authority of constitutional review on the Supreme Court. The Supreme Court assumed the power in its 1803 decision of *Marbury v. Madison.*[20] Having assumed the power, the Court for decades made sparing use of it. Its most noted use before the Civil War, *Dred Scott v. Sandford,*[21] helped pave the way to the Civil War and is widely regarded as its worst decision ever.

That the Supreme Court greatly expanded use of constitutional review after the Civil War is well known. It is taught in high schools, colleges and law schools across the land: often in disapproving terms. One of the most taught examples is the Court's 1906 decision in *Lochner v. New York.*[22] Likewise taught is the Court's backing off decisions invalidating New Deal legislation in the 1930s ("the switch in time that saved nine"). Although the Court backed off using the power, it did not renounce it. Indeed, it has since claimed still greater power: judicial supremacy in constitutional interpretation. Judicial supremacy claims the Court's interpretation in constitutional law is final even when not putting statutes out of force.[23]

Little known are seemingly technical aspects of how the Supreme Court operates in general and how it conducts constitutional review in particular. Many of today's practices were first set in motion at the end of the 19th century. Important changes from the time include control over its own docket (i.e., it gets to choose which cases it decides) and the creation and expansion of intermediate appellate courts.

In the economic expansion in the years after the Civil War, the Supreme Court, as well other high courts fell behind in deciding cases on their dockets. The newly organizing bar associations took these delays on as issues of their own. The genesis of the 1886 ABA code debate in Saratoga was not a desire to simplify laws for the people, but the bar's dissatisfaction with delays in the courts in general. The 1885 ABA Report that spawned the code debate addressed foremost court delays. It set in motion the idea that in the Supreme Court "appeals should be so limited as not to exceed the court to hear and decide them as they arrive."[24]

[20] 1 Cranch (5 U.S.) 137 (1803).   [21] 60 U.S. 393 (1857).
[22] 198 U.S. 45 (declaring limits on working time unconstitutional).
[23] *See* MICHAEL STOKES PAULSEN & LUKE PAULSEN, THE CONSTITUTION: AN INTRODUCTION (2015).
[24] REPORT OF THE SPECIAL COMMITTEE APPOINTED TO CONSIDER AND REPORT WHETHER THE PRESENT DELAY AND UNCERTAINTY IN JUDICIAL ADMINISTRATION CAN BE LESSENED, AND IF SO, BY WHAT MEANS, *reprinted in* ANNUAL REPORT OF THE EIGHTH ANNUAL MEETING OF THE AMERICAN BAR ASSOCIATION, HELD AT SARATOGA SPRINGS, NEW YORK, AUG. 19TH, 20TH AND 21ST, 1885 323, 361 (1885). The Justices were hardly lazy. The Committee reported that in the immediate past term the Court had heard oral arguments in 196 cases and delivered 272 opinions, in other words, more than double the production of the current Court.

Six years later in 1891 Congress overhauled the federal courts in response to the crisis.[25] It remains the most significant reconfiguration of the federal judicial system ever. Congress eliminated the burdensome "circuit riding" duties that had required justices of the Supreme Court to visit far corners of the land to act as lower court judges. It created the Circuit Courts of Appeal, which thereafter took over appeals as of right (mandatory appeals) from federal trial courts and relieved the Supreme Court of this burden. With those two measures Congress gave the justices the most precious of commodities: time.[26] They used the time for constitutional review.

In subsequent years, Congress continued to reduce the mandatory jurisdiction of the Supreme Court. Today, the Supreme Court has almost complete control over which cases to hear on appeal.[27] It chooses to decide fewer than one hundred cases a year. Most of these involve constitutional review.

Congress created the circuit courts of appeals to relieve the burden of business on the Supreme Court. At about the same time, many state legislatures introduced intermediate appellate courts to relieve their highest courts.[28] Today, most states have intermediate appellate courts; only a few do without.

For the judges of the highest courts, this was a great relief. For litigants, it was a mixed blessing. If a case ended with the first appeal, they got justice faster than otherwise. If, however, the case went to a second appeal, relief was delayed and more expensive.

For the people, intermediate appellate courts were (and are) a disaster. In state systems, intermediate appellate courts delay final decisions by yet another layer of judges. In the federal system, where the chance of an appeal to the Supreme Court is negligible, they don't delay decisions, but they fragment the law. Federal intermediate appellate courts, although not required to, apply the principle of *stare decisis* by circuit. They require lower courts to follow the precedents of the Court of Appeals for that circuit. Conflicting precedents are common. Lawyers speak of law for each circuit. Only belatedly, if at all, does the Supreme Court resolve these conflicts.

Congress did try to deal with the delay due to the extra layer of appeals in important cases getting to the Supreme Court. In the first decade of the 20th

[25] Act of March 3, 1891, ch. 517, 26 Stat. 826 ("Evarts Act").

[26] *See* Martha J. Dragich, *Once A Century: Time for a Structural Overhaul of the Federal Courts*, 1996 Wis. L. Rev. 11, 18–21. Already in his first State of the Union message of 1861 Lincoln had proposed relieving the justices of circuit riding duties and building out the lower federal courts. In another way Congress in 1886 gave the justices time: it authorized payment of a law clerk for each justice. John Bilyeu Oakley & Robert S. Thompson: Law Clerks and the Judicial Process 15 (1980). The justices now are allowed four clerks each.

[27] David Fontana, *Docket Control and the Success of Constitutional Courts, in* Comparative Constitutional Law (Tom Ginsburg & Rosalind Dixon, eds., 2011).

[28] *See* Roscoe Pound, Organization of Courts 225–241 (Judicial Administration Series, 1940).

century it provided for three-judge district courts that would consider certain types of action, such as to invalidate federal action or state laws, from which appeals would lie directly to the Supreme Court. The expedited system did not work as hoped. According to one critic, the Supreme Court made the process "complex and unworkable."[29] It may just have been that it annoyed Supreme Court Justices since it limited their control of their docket. Today, a three-judge court is available only in a small number of cases.

5. From Judges that Apply Law to Judges that Make Law

Today's judges assume supremacy in interpreting the Constitution and statutes. They make law. Their reading of laws governs absent legislative amendment. With respect to the Constitution, the dominance of this doctrine is generally dated to the late 19th century.[30] With respect to statutes, the issue has hardly been explored (or even noted), but in date seems to parallel the constitutional claim.[31] In 1912 Congressman Robert Lafollette, practical leader of the Progressive movement, charged that by "presuming to read their own views into statutes without regard to the plain intention of the legislators, [judges] have become in reality the supreme law-making and law-giving institution of our government."[32] Judicial supremacy takes concrete form in the doctrine of "statutory *stare decisis*," also known as "statutory precedent." I discuss it in Chapter 13.

Between the Centennial in 1876 and the Sesquicentennial in 1926, changes were palpable. Judges stopped asserting that they only found law and accepted that they did make it. In 1876, legislatures revised statutes; case reporting was erratic. In 1926, legislatures gave up on revising statutes; legal

[29] *The Three-Judge Court Act of 1910: Purpose, Procedure and Alternatives*, 62 J. CRIM. L., CRIMINOLOGY & POLICE SCIENCE 205 (1971).
[30] *See*, Lawrence M. Friedman, *Introduction*, in COMMON LAW, COMMON VALUES, at 11, 15; CHRISTIAN WOLFE, THE RISE OF MODERN JUDICIAL REVIEW: FROM CONSTITUTIONAL INTERPRETATION TO JUDGE-MADE LAW (1986).
[31] FRED A. CAHILL, JR., JUDICIAL LEGISLATION. A STUDY IN AMERICAN LEGAL THEORY 20 (1952). Much as Bispham, having promoted written law was concerned about keeping unwritten law, Eugene Wambaugh, having promoted case law, worried about keeping written law. EUGENE WAMBAUGH, THE PRESENT SCOPE OF GOVERNMENT (1897).
[32] Robert M. Lafollette, *Introduction*, GILBERT EMSTEIN ROE, OUR JUDICIAL OLIGARCHY v (1912). Lafollette continued: "They have taken to themselves a power it was never intended they should exercise; a power greater than that entrusted to the courts of any other enlightened nation." *Id. See* Horace A. Lurton, *A Government of Law or a Government of Men?*, 193 N. AM. REV 3, 23 (1911) ("In this indisputable function of interpreting and construing applicable constitutional or statutory law to the case in hand there lurks, however, an immeasurable power, which is all the more dangerous to the public welfare because under its cover it is possible of a bad or ignorant judge to defeat the legislative purpose.")

publishers provided regular reports of nearly all appellate cases. In 1876, there were few intermediate appellate courts to make law; in 1926, there were many.

Changes at all levels of court procedure begun in the 19th century promoted judge-made law. With the demise of common-law pleading and its single-issue focus, trial judges instructed jurors in the law more often and with greater complexity. Judges were discouraged from commenting on evidence, could use their statements of the law to shape the law and guide jurors to outcomes they prefered. The first major book of jury instructions was published in 1881.[33]

In the 1880s and 1890s many states and the federal government created and enhanced intermediate appellate courts. These intermediate courts follow the model of high courts and not of the trial courts. They do not find facts; they correct legal error (e.g., bad jury instructions). If they do not like the result in the trial court, they cannot reevaluate facts or find new ones. They can only remand the case to the trial court, for a new trial, or change the law. Adding intermediate appellate courts increased the number of precedents geometrically and the possibilities for conflicts among precedents.

B. TODAY'S LEGAL PROFESSIONS

1. *Bar Associations: From Councils of Citizens to Trade Associations*

Today's bar associations are trade associations. They principally look after their members' professional interests and those of their members' clients. Their interests in law reform and legislation are incidental to that work.

State and national bar associations date from the last quarter of the 19th century. They were founded in an earlier tradition of public service rather than in professional interest.[34] Law reform and legislation were central and not incidental to their missions. At its founding, the ABA gave the uniformity of legislation as a reason for its being.[35] Soon more practice-minded lawyers

---

[33] FREDERICK SACKETT, INSTRUCTIONS AND REQUESTS FOR INSTRUCTIONS, FROM THE COURT TO THE JURY IN JURY TRIALS (1881). This expansion of judge-made law through procedural decisions is reminiscent of the start of law reporting in the United States: Connecticut's statute of 1795 that required judges to write out their decisions of law and led to the first volume of reports in the United States by Kirby. *See* Chapter 4 at note 69.

[34] *See generally*, Simeon E. Baldwin, *The Founding of the American Bar Association*, 3 A.B.A.J. 658 (1917).

[35] Article I of its Constitution of 1878 provided that one of the ABA's three objects was to promote "the uniformity of legislation throughout the Union AMERICAN BAR ASSOCIATION, CALL FOR A CONFERENCE, PROCEEDINGS OF CONFERENCE, FIRST MEETING OF THE ASSOCIATION; OFFICERS, MEMBERS, ETC. (1878) at 16 (as proposed), at 30 (as adopted). Article III required

challenged the early reform-mindedness and changed the associations' direction.[36] In 1892, the President of the Mississippi Bar Association in his annual
address, saw the change coming and objected: "It has been said that lawyers
should only deal with the administration of the laws, and that as a class
we have no concern with making them. But to this doctrine I cannot sub-
scribe."[37] By 1918, however the transformation seems to have been complete.
Ernst Freund, then America's premier proponent of legislation, lamented the
lack of interest in legislative problems: "The business of the legal profession is
litigation and not legislation."[38]

2. *Law Professors: From Systematizers to Synthesizers to Simulators*

Today's law professors teach "thinking like a lawyer." That means they teach
how to argue to a trial or an appellate court what the law is. They do not teach
statutes or how to write statutes or how to apply statutes to cases. Today's law
professors still use Harvard Dean Christopher Columbus Langdell's 1870 "case
method" or "case dialogue method" to teach their charges.[39] They engage
students in the close reading of precedents and in the synthesis of rules from
those precedents as rules to resolve disputes in in litigation.

The mission of American law professors is professional: advancement of
their students' careers. Their mission is not legislation or system building or
law reform or education in law. Legal education is not a combination of
academic learning and of practical training. It is not a partnership of scholars
and practitioners. It is a monopoly of law professors. Law professors are not
practitioners but neither are they scholars. They are not trained to systematize
knowledge in a doctoral dissertation and then teach it in the classroom; they
are taught how common law judges make law in particular cases and they
convey that skill to students.

Today's law school world is not distant from the world of 1914 and the
Carnegie Foundation's first study of legal education but is quite unlike the

---

that the President open each annual meeting with an address on the "most noteworthy changes
in statute law ... during the preceding year." *Id.* at 18, 32. The former was diluted in the new
1919 Constitution; the latter was dropped already in 1913.

[36] *See* Adolph Augustus Berle, *Modern Legal Profession, Legal Profession and Legal Education*, 9
ENCYCLOPEDIA OF THE SOCIAL SCIENCES 340, 344, 345 (1933).

[37] Hon. L. Brame, *President's Address*, in PROCEEDINGS OF THE MISSISSIPPI BAR ASSOCIATION AT
ITS SEVENTH ANNUAL MEETING HELD JAN. 7TH, 1892, 7, 9 (1892)

[38] Ernst Freund, *Prolegomena to a Science of Legislation*, 13 ILL. L. REV. 264, 272 (1918).

[39] CARNEGIE FOUNDATION FOR THE ADVANCEMENT OF TEACHING, EDUCATING LAWYERS:
PREPARATION FOR THE PROFESSION OF LAW (2007).

world of the 1876 Centennial or even of 1892 and the first major study of American legal education.

Until the Civil War, legal education meant predominantly law office study. Law schools were exceptional and mostly unsuccessful. Only after the Civil War did law school education gain a firm footing as a supplement to law office study. Only at the end of the 19th century did law school education supplant law office study.

In the pre–Civil War era, law schools predominantly used lecture methods of presentation of rules of law to students. After the Civil War, progressive professors taught students "to regard the law as a *system of principles*, and not as a mere aggregation or collection of cases decided by the courts."[40] In what was known as the "Dwight method," students started from texts setting out principles. They read precedents as illustrations of applying those principles to decide cases.[41]

Newly named Harvard Law School Dean Langdell introduced the now celebrated and dominant case method of instruction at Harvard in 1870. Until 1890 use elsewhere was rare. By 1914, however, it was dominant among elite schools, but still not pervasive as it is today among all schools.[42] The case method starts students from cases, the "original sources" and from cases has students synthesize rules. Students make law for each case rather than apply law to particular cases.[43] Statutes have no role in the classic case method of instruction.

Just as lawyers debated the role of statutes in American law in the 1880s, so too did law professors debate the role of statutes and of systematizing in legal education. In June 1886 the trustees of Cornell University in Upstate New York, founded a law school because they thought the nation needed lawyers who could deal with statutes. They stated: "Ours is not a government of precedent, so much as a government of statute." They asserted that the "influence of lawyers in the mere framing of laws is not likely to be overestimated."[44]

---

[40] George Chase, *The "Dwight Method" of Legal Instruction*, 1 CORNELL L.J. 74, 75 (1894).

[41] Id., at 81 [emphasis in original].

[42] Harvard's crusade is told in detail in Bruce A. Kimball, *The Proliferation of Case Method Teaching in American Law Schools: Mr. Langdell's Emblematic "Abomination," 1890–1915*, 46 HIST. ED. Q. 192 (2006). *See* Appendix.

[43] Cf. ANTONIN SCALIA & BRYAN A. GARNER, READING LAW: THE INTERPRETATION OF LEGAL TEXTS 7 (2012) (deploring the continuing devotion of American legal education to training common law lawyers and common law judges).

[44] CORNELL UNIVERSITY, REPORT OF A SPECIAL COMMITTEE ON THE ESTABLISHMENT OF A DEPARTMENT OF LAW 6 (1886). They also noted that judges were making law: "what may be called the law-making powers of the bench has come to be universally recognized as a matter of

In the 1880s the curricula of law schools began with subjects that lawyers practice (e.g., contracts and torts). In the early 1890s the ABA's Committee on Legal Education under the chairmanship of William Gardiner Hammond, dean of Washington University School of Law in St. Louis, proposed a change: "the abandonment of the present method of teaching law mainly by distinct topics, at least during the first year of the course, and the substitution for it of a careful and systematic study of the system as a whole after the European method."[45] It didn't happen. Hammond died April 12, 1894, one day before Field.

Harvard's case method and course curriculum had triumphed.[46] The subject of law study was cases and cases only. In 1900, famed English jurist and friend of Harvard, Albert Venn Dicey explained Harvard's victory: "*The Harvard Law School is a professional school.*"[47] The professors were "educating their students for a definite professional purpose – namely, success as lawyers."[48] Harvard's course of instruction prized professional practice over education in abstract or speculative subjects.[49]

The triumph of Harvard Law School's case method sealed the fate of teaching a government of laws in America's law schools. The case method makes excerpts of reported court cases the exclusive basis of classroom instruction and the arguing of law the principal purpose of legal education. Harvard's professors fostered prejudice against written law's goals of legal certainty and system.[50] They focused on resolution of private law disputes to the near exclusion of application of public law. They pretended that there was a national common law and thus avoided having to deal the chaos of competing

---

the first importance." *Id.* It was followed by REPORT OF THE EXECUTIVE COMMITTEE ON THE PROPER ORGANIZATION OF THE LAW DEPARTMENT OF CORNELL UNIVERSITY (1886).

[45] *Report of the Committee on Legal Education*, REPORT OF THE FIFTEENTH ANNUAL MEETING OF THE AMERICAN BAR ASSOCIATION HELD AT SARATOGA SPRINGS, NEW YORK, AUG. 24, 25 AND 26, 1892 317, 360 (1892).

[46] *See* DANIEL R. COQUILLETTE & BRUCE A. KIMBALL, ON THE BATTLEFIELD OF MERIT: HARVARD LAW SCHOOL, THE FIRST CENTURY 557 (2015); JAMES R. MAXEINER, EDUCATING LAWYERS NOW AND THEN: AN ESSAY COMPARING THE 2007 AND 1914 CARNEGIE FOUNDATION REPORTS ON LEGAL EDUCATION 7 (2007).

[47] A.V. Dicey, *The Teaching of English Law at Harvard*, 13 HARV. L. REV. 422 (1900). Four times, twice in italics as a header, Dicey says that. *Id.* at 424 (twice), 426, 437.

[48] *Id.* at 429.   [49] *Id.* at 437, 429 respectively. *See* Appendix.

[50] *E.g.*, SAMUEL WILLISTON. THE UNIFORM PARTNERSHIP ACT WITH SOME OTHER REMARKS ON OTHER UNIFORM COMMERCIAL LAWS, AN ADDRESS BEFORE THE LAW ASSOCIATION OF PHILADELPHIA DEC. 18, 1914, at 1–2 (1915), *reprinted in* 63 U. PA. L. REV. 196 (1915). *See* Max Radin, *Modern Legal Education, Legal Profession and Legal Education*, 9 ENCYCLOPEDIA OF THE SOCIAL SCIENCES 334, 338 (1933).

statutes and cases that was and is the reality of American law.[51] With the triumph of the case method came the creation of books in "finding law" and courses in "legal research."

In 20th century America there was no law school but Harvard, and Langdell was its prophet. In 21st century America, judges, lawyers and law professors have joined together to question and to revise Langdell.[52] Langdell, critics say, was wrong to focus on redacted appellate cases as the key to legal education. Langdell's focus on learning the law through cases taught by academics without practice experience belittled learning important practical skills lawyers need.

Judges and lawyers who challenge Langdell and contemporary legal education demand law school graduates who are "practice ready." Law professors find common cause with the accreditation authority, the ABA, by adding to the curriculum "experiential" courses, i.e., simulations and clinical work. If truth be told, the experientialists would bring American legal education full circle: back into the law offices. They offer no replacement for the Langdellian case law order.[53]

3. Bar Leaders: From Code Cosmopolitans to Common Law Anglophiles

When in the early 1890s the ABA's Committee on Legal Education considered the past, present and future of legal education, in the cosmopolitan spirit of the day, it looked at legal education the world over. In its 1893 *Report on Legal Education*,[54] it dedicated two of its three chapters, 117 pages of its 187 substantive pages, to legal education *outside* the United States. And that was predominantly to legal education *outside* common law countries. Subsequent American reports on legal education in America pay legal education

---

[51] According to an English admirer of the time, graduates "who are going to settle outside New England and New York, would have first to master the practice and statute law of the State in which they intend to establish themselves." GEORGE BIRKBECK HILL, HARVARD COLLEGE BY AN OXONIAN 254 (1894).

[52] *See* Symposium: *Revisiting Langdell: Legal Education Reform and the Lawyer's Craft*, 51 WAKE FOREST L. REV. 231–420 (2016).

[53] For a critical discussion of these developments, *see* James R. Maxeiner, EDUCATING LAWYERS NOW AND THEN: AN ESSAY COMPARING THE 2007 AND 1914 CARNEGIE FOUNDATION REPORTS ON LEGAL EDUCATION AND A REPRINT OF THE 1914 REPORT THE COMMON LAW AND THE CASE METHOD IN AMERICAN UNIVERSITY LAW SCHOOLS BY JOSEF REDLICH (2007).

[54] COMMITTEE OF THE AMERICAN BAR ASSOCIATION AND THE U.S. BUREAU OF EDUCATION, REPORT ON LEGAL EDUCATION (1893; Advance Sheets from the REPORT OF THE COMMISSIONER OF EDUCATION FOR 1890–1891).

outside of common law countries no mind and give little attention even to legal education in England, Canada or Australia.

The ABA Annual Meeting, held September 26 to 28, 1904 in conjunction with the St. Louis World's Fair was sandwiched between the International Congress of Arts and Science held the week of September 19, which included sections on Jurisprudence and on History and Law, and the Universal Congress of Lawyers and Jurists, held September 28 to 30 under the joint sponsorship of the Exposition and of the ABA.[55] Such cosmopolitanism in American law soon followed codifying into oblivion.[56] When the ABA met in London in 1924, on the eve of the nation's sesquicentennial, the consensus was that to adopt a code was an un-American attempt "to supplant the parent Common Law" and "to forsake our English heritage and follow the lead of Imperial Rome."[57]

Dicey's observations in the decade of the 1890s put Harvard at the epicenter of America's common law myth. "The Harvard Law School," he wrote, "is a professional school for the practical teaching of English law...."[58] Harvard students wanted "to learn English law."[59] Harvard's teachers had "intense enthusiasm for the Common Law of England, or rather of the English people." They were "apostles of English law." "Their whole aim is to elucidate the principles of English law."[60] Rule Britannia.

Dicey acknowledged, unintentionally, the weakness of the claim that the case method was the scientific superior to the Dwight method when he wrote that the leaders of Harvard Law School had a "special attachment . . . to the concrete law of the English people, because it specially qualifies them to maintain their peculiar form of teaching which is at once scientific and professional."[61] Ten years later in 1910, Roscoe Pound confirmed that when he wrote that American legal scholarship began and ended in Anglo-American case law.[62]

---

[55] Official Report of the Universal Congress of Lawyers and Jurists Held at St. Louis, Missouri, U.S.A. Sept. 28, 29, and 30, 1904 (1905)

[56] See Richard A. Cosgrove, Our Lady the Common Law: An Anglo-American Legal Community, 1870–1930, 14 (1987) ("Given this background of minimal interaction between the American and English legal systems, the emphasis after 1870 on the similarity, if not identity, of the American legal system to its English predecessor, which blossomed into an article of faith on both sides of the Atlantic, becomes a remarkable phenomenon.")

[57] J. Carroll Hayes, *The Visit to England of the American Bar Association, in* The American Bar Association London Meeting 1924: Impressions of Its Social, Official, Professional and Juridical Aspects as Related by Participants in Contest for Most Enlightening Review of Trip (1925) 9, at 15.

[58] Dicey, *supra* note 47, at 424   [59] *Id.* at 425.   [60] *Id.* at 429.   [61] *Id.* at 431.

[62] Roscoe Pound, *Law in Books and Law in Action*, 44 Am. L. Rev. 12, 25 (1910).

Dicey's observations are not to be dismissed as the enthusiastic comments of a foreign visitor taking pleasure at finding something from home abroad. There is plenty of praise of English common law from the American side of the Atlantic.[63] There is no shortage of detritus of English common law in America's law schools even today. The most apparent are 19th and 20th century English precedents found in most first year casebooks such as *Hadley v. Baxendale, Carlill v. Carbolic Smoke Ball Co., Donoghue v. Stevens* (snail in drink), and many others. American law reviews celebrate old English cases with symposia issues.

Important for this book is the bequest that Dicey left America. It was Dicey who in 1885 coined the term "rule of law."[64] Dicey's English-based "rule of law" has largely displaced Adam's government of laws." In content the terms are similar but they have a not so subtle difference: "Rule of law" suggests lawyers and judicial process; "government of laws" suggests statutes and governing. By 1928 Justice Cardozo described the founding of a new law school as the opening "of a new shrine to be devoted to the cult" of "Our Lady of the Common Law." That cult was all about process tied to "our English brethren in their home across the seas." The new school's first graduates he told, "will find that law itself is in reality unkown," but you will find that "the main thing is to dare." Quoting Aristotle, "it is not the finest and strongest men who are crowned, but they who enter the lists for out of these, the prizemen are selected."[65]

---

[63] *See* RICHARD A. COSGROVE, OUR LADY THE COMMON LAW: AN ANGLO-AMERICAN LEGAL COMMUNITY, 1870–1930 (1987).

[64] Chapter 4 "Rule of Law," in Albert Venn Dicey, *Introduction to the Study of the Law of the Constitution* (1885).

[65] Benjamin N. Cardozo, *Our Lady of the Common Law*, Address to the first graduating class of St. John's Law School (1928), 18 CATHOLIC LAWYER 276, 282, 283 (1972).

PART III

Comparative Part

Ways to a Government of Laws

LEARNING FROM OTHERS

It is by comparison of our rules and practices with those of foreigners, that we become fully sensible of what is defective or excellent, and therefore of what is to be cherished and upheld, or to be disapproved and abolished in our institutions. Nothing more inevitably checks improvement than a jealous or contemptuous rejection of foreign, and an overweening admiration of domestic habits, customs and principles.

Caleb Cushing (1820)

The only people who ever stop trying to learn from the experience of others are those who think that they have attained perfection. And in their circle, surely, we do not wish to be included.

Rudolf B. Schlesinger (1976)

8

Inviting Comparison
A Gift Horse in Two Lands

In his last words as President of the American Bar Association (ABA) David Dudley Field, at age 84, begged his colleagues to give to their fellow citizens "a chance to know the law." As chair of an ABA Committee four years before he told a parable that revealed how they might do that:

> We can imagine a primitive society, in which a king and his judges were the only magistrates. They had made no laws. The judges decided each controversy as it arose, and by degrees what had been once decided came to be followed, and so there grew up a system of precedents, by the aid of which succeeding cases were decided. Hence came judge-made law. But could any sane man suppose that this was a scheme of government to be kept up when legislatures came in?[1]

Field died without seeing his vision fulfilled. But whatever doubts one might have had then about the efficacy of case-law methods versus statutory systems they are conclusively resolved by the more than 120 years that have passed since. Philip K. Howard reminds us of the magnitude of our failure to follow Field's advice: "If people cannot know hundreds or thousands of rules, neither can they comply with them. Even companies with large legal departments can't keep it all straight. ..."[2] Systematized written laws are the norm worldwide.[3] They are best practices. Systematizing is not unusual or peculiar: it is normal and bland, albeit difficult.

---

[1] REPORT OF THE SPECIAL COMMITTEE APPOINTED TO CONSIDER AND REPORT WHETHER THE PRESENT DELAY AND UNCERTAINTY IN JUDICIAL ADMINISTRATION CAN BE LESSENED, AND IF SO, AND BY WHAT MEANS? (1885) *reprinted in* REPORT OF THE EIGHTH ANNUAL MEETING OF THE AMERICAN BAR ASSOCIATION, HELD AT SARATOGA SPRINGS, NEW YORK, AUG. 19TH, 20TH, AND 21ST, 323, 348 (1885). The principal other committee member was John Dillon.

[2] PHILIP K. HOWARD, THE RULE OF NOBODY: SAVING AMERICA FROM DEAD LAWS AND BROKEN GOVERNMENT 36 (2014).

[3] *See, e.g.,* THE SCOPE AND STRUCTURE OF CIVIL CODES [Selected Papers from the 2nd International Academy of Comparative Law Thematic Conference] (J. César Rivera, ed., Ius

Part III shows how contemporary methods of American lawmaking fail to realize a government of laws while statutory methods succeed abroad. I show in this introductory chapter how hard it can be for Americans to know the rules that govern them. In the five chapters that follow, I demonstrate how Americans might achieve a government of laws through methods Germans long have used and some of which Americans once saw as their own. In summary, a government of laws has a system of laws (Chapter 9), that are made in legislative procedures that consult those affected and help create laws serving common good and justice (Chapter 10), that are coordinated with laws of other lawgivers (Chapter 11), that are constitutionally valid (Chapter 12) and that are routinely applied as written (Chapter 13).

A. GOVERNING GIFT HORSES

Katherine lives in Westchester County, New York. It is a suburban New York City community (of nearly 1 million people) where it is easier to find a public stable for horses than a public pool for swimming. Katherine grew up occasionally riding horses. She loves them.

Katherine's mother is from Montana. Her mother's sister, Aunt Turan, like many women in Montana, is a horsewoman. Aunt Turan has a horse named Bijou that she has decided to give to Katherine. Katherine will have to come to Montana, however, to get Bijou. That will give her a chance to ride Bijou for a few days. Aunt Turan will provide an old horse trailer to take Bijou to New York. It's a long drive (nearly 3000 miles), but a straight-shot via Interstate 90 staying on the New York Thruway (when I-90 branches off to Massachusetts) to Westchester.

Katherine is delighted. She would love to have a horse. Moreover, she has always wanted to show her high school friend, Cassandra, the mountains of Montana. They decide to fly out to Montana together and drive Bijou back to Westchester.

Katherine is a responsible citizen. She decides to read the laws that she needs to know for her trip, and the laws she needs to know eventually for when she has Bijou home. She writes down six questions that come to her mind.

(1) How will people know that Bijou is mine? Are horses titled like automobiles?
(2) May I ride Bijou on state highways and into town?
(3) May Cassandra and I drive Bijou in a horse trailer to New York from Montana?
(4) Are there laws that protect Bijou?

Joseph Keppler, *Always Look a Gift-Horse in the Mouth*, from PUCK, Dec. 22, 1909

(5) Are there laws that govern my liability for Bijou?

(6) Are there laws that govern my sale of Bijou?

Section B identifies the American laws that would govern. Section C then considers the same for Germany where Bavaria stands for Montana and suburban Schleswig-Holstein near Hamburg for Westchester, New York.

I could have chosen any area of law for an example of the difficulty of knowing American rules. I have three reasons for choosing horse law: (1) It's an area that today is both somewhat exotic, yet somewhat familiar. (2) Historically, horse law has been used as an area to parody the common law rule of let the buyer beware (*caveat emptor*).[4] Finally, (3) "horse law" is used to refer to the phenomenon of making a field of law out of what are business-specific applications of different general rules.[5] Such "horse law" may not be a good way of professional development of law, but responds to how laymen look for information specific to their lives.

B. AMERICA'S HORSE LAWS ARE FOR PEDESTRIANS

In the United States, knowing horse law is likened to learning a mystery that requires one to go back, not just to the "dawn of time," but to "the darkness before Time dawned." A "very basic guide," *Maryland Equine Law* cautions that one should "never forget that equine law is governed by multiple sources. One needs to know the law at the federal, state, county and municipal levels as well as any rules that may apply through membership in any equine related association."[6]

Maryland Equine Law explains first, as its Chapter 1, "The Sources of Equine Law." It's a mini-lesson in legal methods that parallels this book. Concisely and accurately the book sets out the five sovereignties (of seven types) that horse owners in just one state, Maryland, must concern themselves

---

4   *See, e.g.,* J.K. PAULDING, *The Perfection of Reason, in* THE MERRY TALES OF THE THREE WISE MEN FROM GOTHAM 145, 157 *et seq.* (1826); CAVEAT EMPTOR [George Stephen], THE ADVENTURES OF A GENTLEMAN IN SEARCH OF A HORSE (1835, first Am. ed. 1836).

5   *See* Frank H. Easterbrook, *Cyberspace and the Law of the Horse*, 1996 U. CHICAGO L. FORUM 207; Lawrence Lessig, *The Law of the Horse: What Cyberlaw Might Teach*, 113 HARV. L. REV. 501 (1999).

6   KATHLEEN J.P. TABOR & JAN I. BERLAGE, MARYLAND EQUINE LAW: A LEGAL GUIDE TO HORSE OWNERSHIP AND ACTIVITIES v, 13 (2011) (the "darkness before Time dawned" refers to the resurrection of Aslan in C.S. Lewis's *The Lion, the Witch and the Wardrobe*).

with: (1) Federal, (2) State, (3) County (in Maryland of three types); (4) Municipal Governments; and (5) Horse Governing Associations. From these five sovereigns, the book explains, come four types of laws: (1) statutes, (2) regulations, (3) common law and (4) municipal ordinances. To explain common law requires setting out two court systems for Maryland: (a) the Federal court system (with three levels of courts) and (b) the Maryland state court system (with five levels of courts).[7]

Oh, but that is just for Maryland. What about other states? As the book explains, "Transactions across state lines can present complicated questions as to where a case should be tried (venue and jurisdiction) as well as what law should apply (choice of law)." The subdivision on choice of law implicates not only (a) contract and (b) tort, which laymen may have heard of, but a mysterious third concept, Federal Courts Sitting in Diversity Jurisdiction.[8]

Most readers get the message: get a lawyer!

Only a few years ago, if Katherine were thinking about rules in other states and municipalities that she might visit or travel through on her way to Westchester, she could not have possibly found them herself. She would have had to go to a law school library or find someone willing to let her use a private subscription to a commercial database, e.g., Lexis or WestLaw to know laws in Montana and the states that she would cross coming home. And none of those databases would have the ordinances for all the municipalities through which she would drive.

Katherine might have looked for books on horse law.[9] The problem their authors and users face in our day is even more acute than in the 19th century: too much variation from state-to-state, too many differences from municipality-to-municipality and too frequent changes to be up-to-date to be reliable guides to the laws that govern.

Today the Internet gives the public free and direct access to the laws. In theory, "anyone can find, read and interpret the law for himself or herself

---

[7] *Id.*, 15–18. The book explains that Maryland "is notable among U.S. states for having a relatively small number of local governments." Its twenty-three counties are unusual because they are not "weak administrative divisions" but have "substantial authority" (presumably lawmaking authority). These twenty-three counties alone, not counting other local governments, are of three different varieties (four if one counts an independent city separately).

[8] *Id.*

[9] There are others. *See, e.g.*, ROBERT J. ALLEN, THE BUSINESS AND LAW OF HORSES: A GUIDE FOR THE SMALL HORSE OWNER AND BREEDER (2012); MILTON C. TOBY, THE COMPLETE EQUINE LEGAL AND BUSINESS HANDBOOK: LEGAL INSIGHTS AND PRACTICAL TIPS FOR A SUCCESSFUL HORSE BUSINESS (2007); GARY KATZ, EQUINE LEGAL HANDBOOK, Revised Ed. (2001).

without a lawyer."[10] I qualify the quotation by saying "in theory," because the Internet lays open to the public what the profession has long known: American law is a jumble of uncoordinated statutes and precedents.

Thanks to the Internet, it is theoretically possible, or soon will be, to collect all laws about horses. But that is only theory; it remains humanly impracticable. For on the Internet there are hundreds or thousands of such laws for the United States.[11]

Federal, fifty state and countless local governments have horse laws. On top of these laws, courts have piled precedents. Horse laws are, like American laws generally, mostly state and not federal laws. Katherine will not be much affected by federal laws, because federal horse laws mostly address commercial activities. Katherine might, however, wish that federal laws *were* important and preempted state laws. Businesses sometimes lobby for one single federal law to avoid having to deal with fifty different state laws.

State laws governing horses are unique to each state. While similar in goals, they are all different. Even those with similar substance usually use different language. But many laws are not similar in substance. Many do not have counterparts in other states.

Compiling the laws is only the first step in trying to make sense of them and in figuring out how they fit together to answer Katherine's questions.

1. *How Will People Know that Bijou Is Mine? Are Horses Titled Like Automobiles?*

Horses are not titled like automobiles. Nor, are they, in the United States (it's different in Europe), identified with a horse equivalent of a vehicle identification number. In Texas, and perhaps in other states (I can't track them all down), it seems Katherine would need a written transfer from Aunt Turan and, if she did not have it, would be in legal jeopardy. On trial of her property right to Bijou, "possession of the animal without the written transfer is presumed to be illegal."[12] In some states, horses are branded, like cattle, to show ownership.

---

[10] Amy E. Sloan, *The 95 Theses: Legal Research in the Internet Age*, 20 J. Legal Writing Institute 45, 46 (2015).

[11] To get an idea of the challenge, readers might consult the American Bar Association's National Inventory of the Collateral Consequences of Conviction, http://www.abacollateralconsequences .org/. It lists more than 47,000 state and federal statutes. that impose collateral consequences (e.g., occupational restrictions) for criminal convictions. It does not list local laws.

[12] Tex. Agric. Code § 146.001

2. May I Ride Bijou on Highways and into Town?

Where Katherine can ride is a state law issue and the states are all over the place. In Louisiana it is illegal to ride horses on *paved* state highways.[13] In other states, such as California[14] and New York, equestrians have rights and duties of drivers generally.[15] California even requires other drivers give special care to equestrians.[16] New York, however, bans riding at night.[17] Montana defines "vehicle" to exclude "devices moved by animal power" and thus leaves equestrians outside the Montana Vehicle Code.[18] Even a fifty-state survey would not yield all possible variations through local laws. In Indiana, for example, whether one may drive an all-terrain vehicle (ATV) on county roads varies from county to county![19]

3. May Cassandra and I Drive Bijou in a Horse Trailer from Montana to New York?

Driving a trailer from state-to-state is a multistate question. If Katherine and Cassandra drive Interstate 90 all the way, they will start out in Montana, drive through Wyoming, South Dakota, Minnesota, Wisconsin, Illinois, Indiana, Ohio, Pennsylvania before they finally reach New York, i.e., ten states in all. For each of these states they have to consider how to comply with, if there is one, among other applicable laws, (a) different brand laws, (b) different veterinarian inspection laws, (c) different vehicle laws and (d) different driver laws. They also should check (e) federal laws.

   (a) Montana's brand law requires that before Bijou can be removed from the county (let alone the state) that she have been inspected for brands by a Montana stock inspector and that a certificate of inspection is issued locally.[20] Failure to comply is a misdemeanor subject of up to a fine of $500 and up to six months imprisonment.[21] Sometimes people are tempted to regard the requirement as a formality not enforced, but the *in terrorem* effect is substantial. It is all the more so in Wyoming, through which Katherine is to drive, where failure to get an inspection is prima facie evidence of intent to avoid inspection and "to steal, take and carry away the animals," i.e., felony-larceny

---

[13] LA. REV. STAT. TITLE 3 AGRIC. & FORESTRY § 2851.   [14] CAL. MOTOR VEH. CODE § 21050.
[15] N.Y. VEH. & TRAF. LAW § 1261.   [16] CAL. MOTOR VEH. CODE § 21759.
[17] N.Y. VEH. & TRAF. LAW § 1264.   [18] MONT. CODE § 61-1-101(90)(a).
[19] *See* Indiana Dept. of Natural Resources, *Off Roading in Indiana: Legality of Riding ATVs on County Roads*, http://www.in.gov/dnr/outdoor/4431.htm (map showing four variations by county) (last visited Jan. 2, 2016).
[20] MONT. CODE § 81-3-211.   [21] MONT. CODE § 81-3-231.

punishable with up to a $10,000 fine and ten years in jail.[22] To be sure, Wyoming law exempts interstate transshipment by "common carrier or contract carrier,"[23] but Katherine might prefer to drive around Wyoming rather than take the chance that she and Cassandra would not fall under this exemption.

(b) By comparison, state statutes on veterinary inspections look tame. Many require something along the lines of New York's law that no horse shall be imported into the state without a veterinarian-issued certificate of health finding no equine infectious anemia.[24] Although these requirements are all probably similar, Katherine being the compulsive law abider that she is, will want to check to make sure that *her* certificate satisfies the requirements of all ten states.

(c) Assuming that everything is OK with Bijou, what about the trailer that Bijou will be riding in? Regulations in New York prescribe in detail construction requirements, e.g., "if slatted partitions are used, there shall be gaps of no more than two inches between the slats." Fortunately, for Katherine, these rules apply only to trailers that hold six or more horses.[25] I set these out in the margin because they demonstrate the American style of detailed prescriptions in regulations, and I will compare them later to the more flexible Continental style of regulations.

I don't know whether any of the other nine states have similar requirements. Katherine will want to check. Those that don't may have laws against cruelty to animals that limit horse trailers.

---

[22] Wyo. Stat. §§ 11–20-203(b), 6-3-402.   [23] Wyo. Stat. §§ 11–20-209.
[24] N.Y. Agric. & Mkts. Law § 95-c(3); N.Y. Codes, Rules & Regs tit. 1, §§ 64.1 *et seq.*
[25] (b) Every vehicle utilized for the transportation of more than six horses shall meet the following specifications:

> (1) Doorways used by horses shall be wide enough to allow each horse to enter and exit without touching the sides of the doorway. The top of each doorway shall be at least 12 inches above the withers of the largest horse, while that horse is in a natural standing position, transported in the vehicle.
> (2) All structures above each horse shall be at least 12 inches above the withers of that horse while it is in a natural standing position.
> (3) There shall be sufficient space for each horse carried in the vehicle to allow each horse to be transported in a humane manner and without the infliction of pain, suffering, injury or death.
> (4) The top of all partitions shall be at least five feet from the floor. If there is a space between the floor and the bottom of the partition, it shall be 12 inches. If slatted partitions are used, there shall be gaps of no more than two inches between the slats.

N.Y. Codes, Rules & Regs tit. 1, §§ 64.10(b)(4) *et seq.*

(d) Katherine and Cassandra have ordinary and not commercial driver licenses. They will want to check whether the combination of trailer and truck or car can be driven with their licenses. Each state has its own requirements.

(e) It does not look like there are federal requirements that will limit the trip. Their trailer combination might exceed 10,000 pounds and be subject to Department of Transportation rules, but since Katherine and Cassandra do not seem to have any commercial purpose, they would be excused from those requirements. For over a century, the federal government has had a twenty-eight-hour rule requiring that after twenty-eight hours of consecutive travel livestock be unloaded for feeding, water and rest. Although it applies only to common carriers, it might inform application of any general laws against cruelty to animals.[26]

Katherine's Other Questions

By now readers probably get the point: there are a lot of laws and they don't fit together well. That's even more true of laws that govern keeping Bijou than those of transporting her.

4. *Are There Laws that Protect Bijou?*

The National Agricultural Research Center advises of states' animal cruelty statutes that "while there are many similar characteristics, the actual codified provisions vary drastically from state to state. [Yet] familiarity with these statutes is essential to anyone who interacts with animals . . . ."[27] This variation among state laws continues into variations among county ordinances. For example, more than ten counties (of sixty-two) in New York, including Westchester County, have animal abuse registry laws similar to those for sex offenders![28] These laws are similar, but are not uniform. Although most animal protection laws are local, there is one federal law that protects horses against one particular practice: "soring," that is irritating a horse's legs to achieve a particular gait.[29]

---

[26] 49 U.S.C. § 80502(a).

[27] Elizabeth R. Rumley, State's Animal Cruelty Statutes, http://nationalaglawcenter.org/state-compilations/animal-cruelty/ (accessed Dec. 30, 2015).

[28] WESTCHESTER CO. N.Y. CODE OF ORDINANCES ch. 680, §§ 680.01–680.11 Animal Abuser Registry Law (last visited Jan. 2, 2016).

[29] 15 U.S.C. §§ 1821–1831.

Katherine's first four questions all involved matters that are principally public law issues. The last two, liability and contract, are private law issues. That means that they have produced much litigation and, therefore, many thousands of precedents.

5. Are There Laws That Govern My Liability for Bijou?

Liability cases typically are tort cases based on common law. Common-law litigation tends to turn factual issues into legal ones,[30] so precedents get extra attention. Horse law is also one place where long ago tort-reformers from industry fought back with statutes. In many states – but not all, and varying from state-to-state – industry has achieved laws that limit liability for ordinary risks. Parsing those statutes becomes an important aspect of litigation.

6. Should I Decide to Sell Bijou, Are There Laws that Govern that?

Contract law is the flip side of the coin. Here, states have made strides with statutes. The sale of Bijou within the United States is governed by Article 2 (Sales) of the Uniform Commercial Code. Although calling it commercial confuses law students as well as laymen, it is a law that is largely uniform across the United States. That means that the sale of Bijou, whether in Montana or in New York, is governed by the same law. That uniformity, however, has been undermined, somewhat, by different treatment of the law in different states. Although all the states but Louisiana have adopted the law with few variations, they have made some changes, and those are in an area particularly important for horse sales, i.e., the "warranty" or "guaranty" that comes with sale. Moreover, states and local governments have adopted consumer protections law that may override provisions of the sales law. Finally, as is discussed in Chapter 11, the Uniform Commercial Code is subject to interpretation by courts. Since the Uniform Commercial Code is state law, interpretations sometimes vary from state-to-state. All of this, coupled with the love of lawyers and judges for precedent, create uncertainty in the law. It is the same story of many decisions turned into legal precedents. Here are all the horse stories of *caveat emptor*, hidden defects and the like.

---

[30] *See* Pierre Lepaulle, *Administration of Justice in the United States*, 4 WEST PUB. CO. DOCKET 3192, 3194 (No. 4, 1928).

C. GERMANY'S HORSE LAWS ARE FOR EQUESTRIANS

Even before the Internet, Katherine would have had a good chance to find the laws that govern her conduct in Germany. Most important German laws are federal laws, which means that they are uniform across Germany. In some areas, for example zoning and education, state laws are important. But in all areas, whether federal or state laws, they are coordinated with one another. As discussed in Chapter 11 , only one law – state or federal – governs.

Even before the Internet, German laypersons could access the laws themselves. Although the total number of laws is great, Germans can usually buy inexpensive editions of the laws that govern matters of personal concern. Popular introductory texts guide readers in applying those laws to themselves.

As is discussed in Chapter 9, Internet availability makes already accessible laws even more accessible. In particular, Internet availability makes it less likely that one will overlook a particular law. Although most matters of daily life are governed by a handful of principal laws, e.g., the Civil Code, there are other laws that address particular topics.

1. *How Will People Know that Bijou Is Mine? Are Horses Titled Like Automobiles?*

In Germany horses are not titled like automobiles. Proof of ownership usually depends on possession of a bill of sale. In that respect Germany is like the United States. But in Germany, and throughout the European Union, all horses are required to have a unique identifying number. Depending upon how one views one's horse, one can analogize the number to a person's social security number or to an automobile's vehicle identification number. Perhaps it is more like the latter, because the most common way to connect the number to the horse is surgical implantation of a microchip.

Katherine would easily find this law – in force since 2009 – through an Internet discussion of horse laws or through a direct search of applicable laws on the Internet. A search of "horse" in the official database of federal statutes and regulations turns up only fifty-eight hits. One of those is the Livestock-Transport-Regulation (*Viehverkehrsordnung*), a topic of immediate interest to Katherine. That law consists of fifteen chapters divided into forty-eight sections. One chapter is titled "Identification of Equines according to the EU Regulation 504/2008." To read up further on it, she could read the law itself: it is not difficult. In fewer than 700 words – that's the length of a typical newspaper op-ed – the law states what is required to get a "horse passport." The horse passport does not prove ownership, but like a vehicle identification number, it helps to establish ownership.

2. *May I Ride Bijou on Highways and into Town?*

The traffic law is federal law. Its § 28 (of fifty-three sections in all) governs animals. Subsection (1) provides that no animals that endanger traffic are allowed on the streets. That might include a horse ridden by a novice rider. But subsection (2) allows riding generally and provides that riders "are subject as appropriate to the uniform existing rules and regulations for all traffic." It then sets out the specific requirements for illumination.[31]

3. *May Cassandra and I Drive Bijou in a Horse Trailer to Westchester?*

In the German variation of the hypothetical Katherine and Cassandra are driving from the Alpine region of Bavaria to the coast of Schleswig-Holstein, just north of Hamburg. It's pretty much a straight shot on a couple of Autobahns. It's only about 600 miles. One route is Bavaria, through two states in old East Germany, Thuringia and Saxony-Anhalt, then through Lower Saxony and Hamburg to Schleswig-Holstein. That's a lot fewer states than would have been in 1789 or even 1814.

Ten years ago, most of these questions were governed by German federal laws (not state laws). Today, however, they are mostly governed either by European Union (EU) regulations (directly applicable in Germany) or by European Union Directives (implemented by German laws).

   (a) There are no provisions for brand inspection. There is the requirement
       of a horse passport.

---

[31] ("unterliegt sinngemäß den für den gesamten Fahrverkehr einheitlich bestehenden Verkehrsregeln und Anordnungen.") *See* "Straßenverkehrsordnung—nicht für Autos," http://www.pferde-welt.info/reiten-lernen/ausbildung/56-stvo.

(b) There are no general provisions for a certificate of veterinary inspections for transport within Germany.

(c) In 2009 the previously applicable German regulation that governed horse trailers was replaced by European Union Council Regulation (EC) No 1/ 2005 of December 22, 2004 on the protection of animals during transport and related operations and amending Directives 64/432/EEC and 93/119/ EC and Regulation (EC) No 1255/97. Although the German law applied to most trailers, the EU law is concerned only with commercial use. (It is an example of deregulation for small shops.) Annex II details regulations that apply to such horse trailers. These requirements parallel the old superseded German regulations and in style are typical for German and German safety regulations generally. First, they are not limited to horse trailers, but apply to means of animal transport generally. Second, they do not prescribe specific measures, but set out results required of those measures. These are extensive; they are set out in the margin to demonstrate the approach, which uses flexible and indefinite concepts.[32]

[32] 1. Provisions for all means of transport

1.1. Means of transport, containers and their fittings shall be designed, constructed, maintained and operated so as to:
(a) avoid injury and suffering and to ensure the safety of the animals;
(b) protect the animals from inclement weather, extreme temperatures and adverse changes in climatic conditions;
(c) be cleaned and disinfected;
(d) prevent the animals escaping or falling out and be able to withstand the stresses of movements;
(e) ensure that air quality and quantity appropriate to the species transported can be maintained;
(f) provide access to the animals to allow them to be inspected and cared for;
(g) present a flooring surface that is anti-slip;
(h) present a flooring surface that minimises the leakage of urine or faeces;
(i) provide a means of lighting sufficient for inspection and care of the animals during transport.

1.2. Sufficient space shall be provided inside the animals' compartment and at each of its levels to ensure that there is adequate ventilation above the animals when they are in a naturally standing position, without on any account hindering their natural movement.
...

1.4. Partitions shall be strong enough to withstand the weight of animals. Fittings shall be designed for quick and easy operation.

1.5. Piglets of less than 10 kgs, lambs of less than 20 kgs, calves of less than six months and foals of less than four months of age shall be provided with appropriate bedding material or equivalent material which guarantees their comfort appropriate to the species, the number of animals being transported, the journey time, and the weather. This material has to ensure adequate absorption of urine and faeces.

(d) Today there is a single driver's license regime throughout the European
   Union. Since horse trailers exceed 750 kilograms, Katherine and
   Cassandra need either a class BE (auto under 3500 kg + trailer over
   750 kg) or C1E (truck to 7500 kg + trailer over 750 kg, total below 12000
   kg), issued in every Member State. Confusion sets in only when one is
   concerned with driving privileges under old license regimes.[33]

4. Are There Laws that Protect Bijou?

In 2002 the German Constitution was amended to add Article 20a protecting
animals: "Mindful also of its responsibility toward future generations, the state
shall protect the natural foundations of life and animals by legislation and, in
accordance with law and justice, by executive and judicial action, all within
the framework of the constitutional order." Legal protections of animals reach
back into the 19th century.

The federal law that implements this article is the Animal Welfare Act
(*Tierschutzgesetz*). Section 2a of that Act authorizes the Federal Ministry of
Food and Agriculture to issue, with the consent of the Bundesrat (Council of
States), regulations that implement the Act. These include the Animal Protection Transport Regulation mentioned earlier in this section. All the laws are
conveniently collected in popularly priced paperbacks available in many
bookstores[34] as well as in texts with commentaries available at modest prices
in law bookstores.[35] Katherine could buy them or read them in a library, and
they are available on the Internet.

5. Are There Laws that Govern My Liability for Bijou?

The laws governing liability for horses are the ordinary civil and criminal laws.
Principally these are §§ 823–853 of the Civil Code. Their application to
horses is explained in guides to equine law[36] and on various Internet sites.

---

[33] My German class 3 license issued in September 1981 remains valid until January 2033 for
present classes B, B1 and C1E.
[34] E.g., TIERSCHUTZRECHT: TIERHALTUNG, TIERTRANSPORT, SCHLACHTTIERE, VERSUCHSTIERE
(dtv Beck Texte) (3d ed. 2014) (current price € 14.90).
[35] ALBERT LORZ & ERNST LORZ, TIERSCHUTZGESETZ: TIERSCHUTZGESETZ MIT ALLGEMEINER
VERWALTUNGSVORSCHRIFT, RECHTSVERORDNUNGEN UND EUROPÄISCHEN ÜBEREINKOMMEN
SOWIE ERLÄUTERUNGEN DES ART. 20A GG KOMMENTAR (7th ed., 2018) (price €60.00).
[36] E.g., JOST APPELL, PFERDERECHT: KOMPAKT, VERSTÄNDLICH, PRAXISNAH Chapter IV, 137–171
(2015); PETER ROSBACH, PFERDERECHT: EIN HANDBUCH FÜR PFERDEKÄUFER, REITER,
REITVEREINE, REITSTALLBESITZER, HUFSCHMIED UND TIERÄRTZE Chapter 7, 188–236 (2011).

One equine lawyer asserts that his site provides in fewer than ten pages a comprehensive guide to the topic.[37] There are no special laws limiting liability.

6. Should I Sell Bijou? Are There Laws that Govern that?

As with tort liability, ordinary law from the Civil Code governs sales of horses. Books and Internet sites discuss the application of this law to horse sales and report cases as examples (not as precedents).[38] Formerly, there were separate laws for horse sales, but these now are treated as sales generally.

In short, German horse laws are laws made for people. The following chapters show how.

---

[37] Stephan Pahl, *Pferderecht: Haftungsfragen rund ums Pferd*, RECHTS-ANWALT STEPHAN PAHL, http://www.pferde-recht.de/haftungsfragen/ (last visited Jan. 1, 2016).

[38] E.g., JOST APPELL, PFERDERECHT: KOMPAKT, VERSTÄNDLICH, PRAXISNAH Chapter I, 15–83 (2015); PETER ROSBACH, PFERDERECHT: EIN HANDBUCH FÜR PFERDEKÄUFER, REITER, REITVEREINE, REITSTALLBESITZER, HUFSCHMIED UND TIERÄRTZE Chapter 1, 1–76 (2011); Stephan Pahl, *Pferderecht: Gewährleistung beim Pferdekauf*, RECHTSANWALT STEPHAN PAHL, http://www.pferde-recht.de/pferdekauf/index.html (last visited Jan. 1, 2016).

9

Systematizing and Simplifying Statutes

Every citizen in the state, ought to acquire a knowledge of those laws, that govern his daily conduct, and secure the invaluable blessings of life, liberty and property. The best method to diffuse this knowledge thro all ranks, is to simplify, and systematize the laws.

Zephaniah Swift (1795)[1]

A. KNOWING THE LAWS THAT GOVERN

It is an axiom of a government of laws that people have a chance to know which laws govern them and what those laws mean.[2] In order that people may learn the laws, governments systematize and define their laws. The previous chapters show that Americans worked to systematize and simplify their laws in the 18th and 19th centuries until lawyers largely gave up in the early 20th century. The people have never given up.

---

[1] Zephaniah Swift, A SYSTEM OF THE LAWS OF THE STATE OF CONNECTICUT 1 (1795). Cf. JEAN-ÉTIENNE-MARIE PORTALIS, PRELIMINARY ADDRESS ON THE FIRST DRAFT OF THE CIVIL CODE PRESENTED IN THE YEAR IX BY MESSRS. PORTALIS, TRONCHET, BIGOT-PRÉAMENEU AND MALEVILLE, MEMBERS OF THE GOVERNMENT-APPOINTED COMMISSION (1801), translated at http://www.justice.gc.ca/eng/pi/icg-gci/code/index.html. ("Simplifying everything is a process on which there must be agreement. Foreseeing all is a goal impossible to attain. There must be no unnecessary laws. They would weaken the necessary laws; they would compromise the certitude and majesty of legislation.")

[2] See, e.g., Address of David Dudley Field of New York, President of the Association, in REPORT OF THE TWELFTH ANNUAL MEETING OF THE AMERICAN BAR ASSOCIATION HELD AT CHICAGO, ILLINOIS, AUG. 28, 29, AND 30, 1889, 149, 234 (1889). See id. at 231 ("It is the first duty of a government to bring the laws to the knowledge of the people. That the laws of the land should be known beforehand, should seem to be political axioms and self-evident.") More recently retired Supreme Court Justice Sandra Day O'Connor explained that "the principle that ordinary citizens must know – and be able to understand – the law of the land" is a "bedrock feature of the rule of law" that is not controversial. Sandra Day O'Connor, Foreword, Rule of Law Symposium in Honor of John Attanasio, 67 SMU L. REV. 693, 694 (2014).

In a government of laws, knowing which law governs should be easy and unproblematic.[3] Understanding what that law means should likewise be straightforward. Governments can then rightly charge people with knowing the law. Facts may be uncertain and subject to investigation, and application of laws to those facts indefinite,[4] but laws should not be.

When laws are chaotic or complex, when people cannot know the laws, they must act at their peril or they must pay others to interpret those laws for them. When even lawyers do not know the laws, then a government of laws is lost.

In outward form, America's and Germany's legal systems look similar. Constitutions control statutes that control regulations; federal law preempts state law. State law limits municipal law. Reports of decided cases inform law application. In Germany, there is an added twist that European Union (EU) law preempts German law.

Yet under surface similarities lie differences that make knowing the laws that govern difficult in the United States when it is easy in Germany. American laws are poorly systematized and ill-defined. As discussed in Chapter 13, they are subject to being undermined by an unreliable process of application. German laws are mostly well systematized and well defined. They benefit from a reliable process of application.

In this chapter, I address America's failings in making laws known and knowable and contrast them to Germany's successes. I defer consideration of some topics to later chapters, namely Federalism and Localism to Chapter 11, Constitutional Review to Chapter 12, and Applying Law to Chapter 13.

B. AMERICA'S LAWS ARE OUT OF ORDER

1. *America's Laws Summarized*

The principal laws that govern the people of the United States are: (1) the Constitution of the United States; (2) federal statutes; (3) federal regulations; (4) state constitutions; (5) state statutes; (6) state regulations; and

---

[3] See, *e.g.*, already J.L. Tellkampf, *On Codification, or the Systematizing of the Law* [Part II], 26 AM. JURIST & L. MAG. 283, 288–289 (1841) ("A code should contain a system of leading principles, arranged in such order that the right mode for determining any particular case should be visible on the face of it, and be within the grasp of any person of scientific attainments.")

[4] For many of those issues, see JAMES R. MAXEINER WITH GYOOHO LEE AND ARMIN WEBER, FAILURES OF AMERICAN CIVIL JUSTICE IN INTERNATIONAL PERSPECTIVE (2011).

OFF THE SCENT.

Thomas Nast, *Off the Scent* from HARPER'S WEEKLY, Aug. 14, 1875.

(7) local laws.[5] These are all statutory. They are written laws. America lives in an "Age of Statutes." Common law, that is law based only on precedents, is

---

[5]   There are other laws that do not fall in these categories, *e.g.*, international laws.

exceptional. Common law continues to exist principally as an overlay on statutory law (doctrine of statutory *stare decisis*, also known as "statutory precedent" discussed in Chapter 13).

Most American laws are state laws. People looking for the law that governs them usually should look first to state laws. Yet federal law gets, and long has gotten, the lion's share of educators' and scholars' attention. One reason, at least today, is that federal legal methods often serve as models for state laws.[6] Perhaps a more important reason is practicality: one can discuss one federal law and state variations. To discuss fifty different state laws is impractical. Regrettably, I follow the convention.

Federal Laws

Federal laws are first published individually in chronological order as adopted ("session laws") in an official periodic print publication, the *United States Statutes at Large*. They are compiled into what is called the *United States Code ("U.S.C.").*[7] In print, U.S.C. is huge – tens of thousands of pages in dozens of volumes – and is not completely current. Delays in printing the compilation into the United States Code have recently been reduced in an official online version available for free. Until then, an added burden in time and money was determining if the published laws were up-to-date.

The United States Code is maintained by the Office of the Law Revision Counsel of the United States House of Representatives.[8] The Office of the Law Revision Counsel should not be confused with two other different, but similarly named offices, the Office of the Legislative Counsel of the United States House of Representatives and the Office of the Legislative Counsel of the United States Senate. I discuss the latter two in Chapter 10.

Federal regulations are another form of statutory law. Like statutes, they provide rules. These rules implement statutes. Based on statutory authorizations, other actors in the government besides Congress issue regulations. These regulations or rules – the two terms are used largely interchangeably – can direct either the people externally or only the government internally or both. The other actors typically are executive branch departments or independent federal agencies. The Office of Information and Regulatory Affairs (OIRA) of the Office of Management and Budget reviews proposed regulations.

---

[6] E.g., the Federal Rules of Civil Procedure and the United States Code.
[7] For information on laws not in U.S.C., see Will Tress, *Lost Laws: What We Can't Find in the United States Code*, 40 GOLDEN GATE U. L. REV. 129 (2010).
[8] http://uscode.house.gov/.

Federal regulations are first published individually in chronological order as adopted in an official periodic print publication, the *Federal Register*.[9] They are compiled into the *Code of Federal Regulations ("CFR")*. In print, CFR is huge – tens of thousands of pages in dozens of volumes – and not completely current. Delays in printing the compilation into the CFR have recently been reduced in an official online version available for free: eCFR. Until then, an added burden, in time and money, was determining if the published regulations were up-to-date.

Presidential executive orders and proclamations are similar to regulations. As Congress has come to standstill, presidents have come to rely on executive orders not only to implement statutory policy but also to forward presidential initiatives. Like regulations, executive orders are directions to government officials on how to implement laws. Like regulations they are reviewed by the Office of Information and Regulatory Affairs and are published in the *Federal Register* and compiled in the *Code of Federal Regulations* (in Title 3). Unlike regulations, they are not subject to notice, hearing and public comment before release.[10]

The eCFR is not an official legal edition of CFR. It is an editorial compilation of CFR material and *Federal Register* amendments produced by the National Archives and Records Administration's Office of the Federal Register (OFR) and the Government Publishing Office.[11] The Federal Register and the CFR are under the direction of the OFR.[12]

State Laws

Most state laws are printed in fifty state compilations (commonly called codes) that are similar to the United States Code. State regulations vary in access.

State compilations are similar to each other only in overall form. More than a century ago the American Bar Association (ABA) resolved that among the

---

[9] The Federal Register is the official government gazette. It includes more than new regulations, e.g., proposed regulations, announcements, etc. It was not created until 1935. The Code of Federal Regulations followed. *See* THE OFFICE OF THE FEDERAL REGISTER, A BRIEF HISTORY COMMEMORATING THE FIRST ISSUE OF THE FEDERAL REGISTER MAR. 14, 1936 (ca. 2006) available at www.ofr.gov (last visited Jan. 2, 2016); Erwin S. Griswold, *Government in Ignorance of the Law – A Plea for Better Publication of Executive Legislation*, 48 HARV. L. REV. 198, 213 (1934) ("the need for putting order into our administrative material is very great.").

[10] *See* LOUIS FISHER, THE LAW OF THE EXECUTIVE BRANCH: PRESIDENTIAL POWER 101–106 (2013).

[11] Electronic Code of Federal Regulations, http://www.ecfr.gov/cgi-bin/ECFR?page=browse.

[12] The Office of the Federal Register, *about Us*, http://www.ofr.gov/AboutUs.aspx (last visited Jan. 2, 2016).

collections of state statutes "it is desirable that there be substantial uniformity of plan and classification." The sponsor of the resolution explained that it is important "so that any man, layman or lawyer, may be able to know the law of all the states on any given subject."[13] This has not happened. Any man cannot know the laws of all the states on any given subject: fifty-state surveys are unusual and expensive. I showed that in Chapter 8 with respect to horse law. In Chapter 11, I address problems specific to state and local laws and their relations to each other and to federal laws.

Local Laws
Local laws are often, but not always, available from the individual county, town, city, village or other local entity that issues them. In Chapter 11 I discuss how important these have become in the United States in recent years. Tens of thousands of municipal entities can issue laws without supervision. Many of these are now available online.

Accessing Laws
Today, Americans have easier access than ever before to their laws. No longer are laws available only in expensive print copies found only in a handful of law libraries. Now everyone with an Internet connection can access most of these laws and usually for free.[14] Free online availability of laws is overcoming problems that once plagued print distribution: expense of acquisition, locating and consulting the volumes, and keeping results current.[15] Formerly – and still recently – updating statutes, let alone precedents has been a major part of law finding.

Finding and Knowing Governing Laws
Accessing laws should not be confused with knowing which laws govern one's own life. Already Madison, writing in the *Federalist*, saw that access alone is not enough: "It will be of little avail to the people ... if the laws be so voluminous that they cannot be read, or so incoherent that they cannot be

---

[13] Remarks of E.Q. Keasby, REPORT OF THE THIRTY-SEVENTH ANNUAL MEETING OF THE AMERICAN BAR ASSOCIATION HELD AT WASHINGTON, D.C., OCT. 20, 21, AND 22, 1914, 25–28, 527–530 (1914) (Report of the Committee on Law Reporting and Digesting).

[14] *See* Amy E. Sloan, *The 95 Theses: Legal Research in the Internet Age*, 20 J. LEGAL WRITING INSTITUTE 5 (2015).

[15] Peter G. LeFevre, *The United States Code: Its Accuracy, Accessibility, and Currency*, 38 ADMIN. & REG. L. NEWS 10 (2013).

understood."[16] Accessing laws is the beginning of finding and knowing the law that governs a particular point. It is not the end.

Paradoxically, easier access can make knowing law harder. America's laws are poorly systematized. Often they conflict with each other. Often they are poorly written. Easy access sometimes means more of what Americans euphemistically call "legal research" and unearthing more legal issues.[17]

Laymen cannot reasonably be expected to do legal research. Clients do not want to pay for junior lawyers to do legal research.[18] Senior lawyers have better uses for their time.

Knowing which laws govern and what they require should not be hard; applying them might be. Access, if coupled with systematized laws, can realize the goals of the authors' of the 1648 *Lawes and Libertyes of Massachusetts* for laws "wherein (upon every occasion) you might readily see the rule by which you ought to walke by."[19] Looking abroad, Americans see those goals realized, but not at home.[20]

The curricula of American law schools posted online are "Facebook confessions" of America's failure to make laws known to people. Just about every law school requires students to take a course typically and euphemistically called "Legal Research and Writing." Why should it take an entire course to teach students where to find applicable laws? Such courses and textbooks were practically nonexistent in the 19th century, when everyone expected codes and foresaw a Caligula-like crisis in their absence.[21] They owe their origins to the early 20th century as instruction in how "to find" the law. Now in the 21st century, such courses give up on finding and teach instead "arguing," "synthesizing," or "predicting" law.

---

[16] James Madison, *The Senate*, FEDERALIST NO. 62 (1788).

[17] Some place hope in software to deal with these issues. *See* William Lee *et al.*, *Law is Code: A Software Engineering Approach to Analyzing the United States Code*, 10 J. BUS. & TECH. L. 297 (2015).

[18] I have been the client asking the law firm partner not to send an associate out to conduct research. *See* Aliza B. Kaplan & Kathleen Darvil, *Think [and Practice] Like a Lawyer: Legal Research for the New Millennials*, 8 LEGAL COMMUNICATION & RHETORIC: JALWD 153, 159 (2011).

[19] THE BOOK OF THE GENERAL LAWES AND LIBERTYES CONCERNING THE INHABITANTS OF THE MASSACHUSETTS, Reprinted from the copy of the 1648 edition in the Huntington Library preface (Thomas G. Barnes, ed., 1982).

[20] *See, e.g.*, *Report of the Special Committee on Drafting of Legislation*, REPORT OF THE THIRTY-SEVENTH ANNUAL MEETING OF THE AMERICAN BAR ASSOCIATION HELD AT WASHINGTON, D.C., OCT. 20, 21, AND 22, 1914, 629, 640 (1914). *See* text from the Report at Epigraph *supra*.

[21] *See* Chapter 5, text and note at note 148 *supra*.

2. *America's Laws are Confounding*[22]

America's laws are not laws for people. Making laws accessible on line does not change that. America's laws do not form a system of laws or even fifty-one state and federal systems of laws.[23]

America's laws duplicate, overlap and contradict each other. Some are unnecessary. Many are obsolete. Others are unstable. As a result, to "find the law" that governs, one must often examine many laws and fit them together ("synthesize" them, law professors say). A layperson cannot be expected to do that. Even lawyers find it hard and, sometimes, impossible.

United States Code

The United States Code is a throwback to earlier statutory compilations. It was not designed as and is not maintained as a system of laws. It is not a code.[24] It is not a revision. It enacted no new law and repealed no existing law. Adopted in 1925, it was less advanced than the century-older New York Revised Statutes of 1829.[25] It did not: (1) weed out unnecessary or obsolete laws; (2) concentrate

---

[22] Part II demonstrates that systematization is not incompatible with America's legal culture. Suggesting that it is, see PHILIP HAMBURGER, IS ADMINISTRATIVE LAW UNLAWFUL? 451 (2014).

[23] *Contra*, THOMAS LUNDMARK, CHARTING THE DIVIDE BETWEEN COMMON AND CIVIL LAW 268 (2012) (saying that it is wrong to assert that America's law is not systematic).

[24] Its principal compiler, Professor William L. Burdick, emphasized that it "is not a *revision* of the laws of the United States, but merely a *compilation* of the statutes. . . . the work is not, speaking accurately, a 'code.'" William L. Burdick, *The Revision of the Federal Statutes*, 11 ABA J. 178, 181–182 (1925) [emphasis in original].

[25] In the stead of many, consider the Act of April 21, 1825 chap. 324, 1825 LAWS OF THE STATE OF NEW-YORK 446 (1825) by which New York State directed a commission to revise its statutes: "I. . . . are hereby authorised to collate and revise all such public acts of the legislature of this state . . . ; and that in the performance of such duty, they shall carefully collect and reduce into one act the different acts and parts of acts which, from similarity of subject, ought, in their judgment, to be so arranged and consolidated, distributing the same under such titles, divisions and sections, as they shall think proper, and omitting all such acts or parts of acts before passed, as shall have been repealed, or have expired by their own limitation, or be repugnant to the present constitution of this state; and that in every other respect, they shall complete the said revision in such manner as to them shall seem most useful and proper, to render the said acts more plain and easy to be understood; . . .

II. And be it further enacted, That when the said acts shall be so presented to the legislature for re-enactment, the said revisors shall also suggest to the legislature such contradictions, omissions or imperfections, as may appear in the acts so to be revised, and the mode in which the same may be reconciled, supplied or amended; and may also designate such acts or parts of acts, if any, as, in their judgment, ought to be repealed, with their reasons for advising such repeal; and may also recommend the passage of such new acts or parts of acts, as such repeal may, in their judgment, render necessary."

Compare: Section (2)(a) of the enacting clause of the United States Code provided, "nothing in this Act shall be construed as repealing or amending any such law, or as enacting as new law

law so that one matter is governed by only one law; or (3) promote continuity of existing law. Yet these are traits that make laws usable. Today, after almost another century, it is still no better than a compilation.

The United States Code is no more than a compilation because Congressmen, ever protective of their prerogatives, wanted it that way. Congress approved it in 1926 as an official republication in convenient form of the general and permanent laws of the United States. Congress did not adopt it as positive law, as it had the Revised Statutes of 1874, but published it only as prima facia the law. "It is presumed to be the law. The presumption is rebuttable ... ."[26]

The United States Code consists of the session laws passed by Congress of "a general and permanent character" compiled in about fifty subject-based "titles." It excludes temporary laws, such as appropriation acts and special laws, such as laws naming post offices. Appropriation acts can include provisions that modify application of laws in the Codes Most of the Code's titles date from its original 1926 publication. Most titles are printed in alphabetical order from Title 7 Agriculture to Title 50 War and National Defense. Titles are further broken down into chapters.

When the United States enacts a new law, the Office of the Law Revision Counsel determines whether the new law is of a general and permanent nature. If it finds so, it inserts the constituent parts of the session law piecewise into one or more of the Code's fifty-some titles.[27] Law Revision Counsel looks for a logical and appropriate placement, but only after the Congressional bill has become law. Law Revision Counsel cannot question whether the new law is necessary. It cannot review the new law for consistency with old law. It cannot adjust other already existing law. It can only hope that Congress addressed those issues.[28]

---

any matter contained in the Code." The Code of Laws of the United States of America of a General and Permanent Character in Force December 7, 1925 ... Consolidated, Codified, Set Forth, and Published in 1926, in the One Hundred and Fiftieth Year of the Republic ..., 44 Stat. Part 1, at 1 (1926). For today's statement, see 1 U.S.C. § 204(a), which takes over one hundred words to state the current status.

[26] Roy G. Fitzgerald, Chairman of the Committee on the Revision of the Laws of the House of Representatives, *Preface*, Code of Laws, *supra* note 25, at v. It followed a failed attempt from 1897 to 1904 "to codify the great mass of accumulating legislation" that cost over $300,000 [about $ 7.5 million in current dollars]. *Id.*

[27] Office of the Law Revision Counsel, United States Code, about Classification of Laws to the United States Code, http://uscode.house.gov/aboutclassification.xhtml

[28] Before a German law is adopted it is reviewed for its compatibility with higher law, for its conflict-free ordering within existing laws and regulations, and for its internal logic and consistency. Bundesministerium des Innern, Handbuch zur Vorbereitung von Rechts- und Verwaltungsvorschriften 118 (2d ed., 2012). *See* Chapter 10.

Consequently, whatever "system" as the United States Code gives, it is not integral to lawmaking. The Code is a collection of rules rather than a rulebook; it is a "law locator."[29] Its motto might be, "adopt first, systematize afterwards."

Since 1947 the United States has enacted about half of the titles into positive law. Congress itself amends these titles directly. For titles not enacted into positive law, the Office of the Law Revision Counsel treats the amendments as new laws. It attempts to place them into the overall system of the Code. The Code for these titles is only a compilation such as any private person might make. The process of updating is termed "cut and bite" amendment. There is no enacted document that shows the law as amended.[30] And of course, this means Congress probably did not debate the revised law as a whole.

A lawyer formerly with the Office of Legislative Counsel of the House describes the result: "a Frankenstein's monster of session laws." He explains the process: "The Code is made by taking the session laws, hacking them to pieces, rearranging them, and stitching them back together in a way that gives them a false life. .... That is all the code is, and that is all that it is supposed to be."[31]

Officially, the Office of the Law Revision Counsel describes an only slightly less fearsome monster. It warns that "closely related laws that were enacted decades apart may appear in different volumes of the Code."[32] It advises that: "The law contained in the Code is the product of over 200 years of legislating. ... As a result, not all acts have been handled in a consistent manner in the Code over time."[33]

The Deputy Legislative Counsel of the House of Representatives advised judges "finding an authoritative copy of the laws of the United States is a tricky job."[34]

And that does not take note that the United States Code does not incorporate the comparably large body of equally binding regulations.

---

[29] Tobias A. Dorsey, *Some Reflections on Not Reading the Statutes*, 10 GREEN BAG 2D 283, 284 (2007).

[30] For a semiauthoritative description of the peculiar positive law/compilation focus of the United States Code, see M. DOUGLASS BELLIS, DEPUTY LEGISLATIVE COUNSEL, STATUTORY STRUCTURE AND LEGISLATIVE DRAFTING CONVENTIONS: A PRIMER FOR JUDGES by 2–4 (Federal Judicial Center, 2008). This is a concise description of the Code's twilight existence between private and public compilation.

[31] Tobias A. Dorsey, *Some Reflections on Not Reading the Statutes*, 10 GREEN BAG 2D 283, 284 (2007). Dorsey was a lawyer in the Office of the Legislative Counsel of the United States House of Representatives.

[32] Office of the Law Revision Counsel, United States Code, Positive Law Codification, Importance of Positive Law Codification, see Statutory Structure and Legislative Drafting http://uscode.house.gov/codification/legislation.shtml. For example, federal employment discrimination laws are in title 42, Public Welfare, and not title 20, Labor.

[33] Office of the Law Revision Counsel, United States Code, Detailed Guide to the United States Code Content and Features, I. In General, http://uscode.house.gov/detailedguide.xhtml

[34] BELLIS, *supra* note 30, at 7.

Code of Federal Regulations (CFR)

The (CFR) similarly gathers federal regulations that were first published in the *Federal Register* (the government's official gazette) in a single "code" and distributes them into fifty subject-based titles. On paper, it consists of more than 200 volumes. It prints most of the original titles in alphabetical order from Title 4 Accounts to Title 50 Wildlife. These titles do *not* correspond to the titles in the United States Code. For example, there is no CFR title for U.S.C. Title 18 Crimes.

The CFR does not share the limited systematizing aspirations of the United States Code. It breaks down its titles not by chapters determined by subject, but by "Regulatory Entity" that issued the Regulations. It breaks these chapters down into individual parts, sections, and paragraphs.[35] Regulatory entities themselves are responsible for placement, content and organization of their regulations. There is no counterpart to the Office of the Law Revision Counsel to coordinate, or at least place, similar regulations together.

3. *America's Laws Are Confusing*

America's laws are often hard to understand. Too many are ambiguous, incoherent or incomprehensible.

When Americans discuss making laws more understandable, commonly they speak of "plain language laws." These mandate that legislators use language that readers know and can relate to. To my knowledge, none of these laws provides for plain language police to patrol whether drafters' comply. I don't address in this book how to go about drafting statutes. Legislative drafting manuals, once uncommon, are now available in quality works.[36] Here I note a number of other systemic shortcomings.

Lack of Consistency

Systematizing laws not only helps in finding governing laws, it makes understanding laws easier. One assumes that a term in a statute is used consistently within that statute. But how much easier would it be if a term were used consistently throughout a category of laws or even throughout all laws? Terms and concepts learned in one law could safely be assumed to the same when encountered elsewhere. This is not the case in the United States. To the contrary, one cannot assume that terms carryover from one statute to another.

---

[35] Parts are rules on a single program or function, *e.g.*, Title 16 CFR, Part 453 has regulations of "Funeral Industry Practices" issued by the Federal Trade Commission. Sections 453.1 to 453.9 are provisions of that regulation. Sections may be broken down into as many as six levels of paragraphs.

[36] *See, e.g.*, Arthur J. Rynearson, Legislative Drafting Step-by-Step (2013). *See generally*, Grace E. Hart, *State Legislative Drafting Manuals and Statutory Interpretation*, 126 Yale L.J. 438 (2016).

Worse still, even within the same statute, a term may have one meaning in one place and a different meaning in another.

Political Lacunae
Lawmaking in the United States is a political process of making deals as laws are drafted. As parts of these deals, important issues can be deliberately left undetermined to be decided by courts in applying the law. So, until the courts decide, it is anyone's guess what the law means.[37]

Rigidity
But then other laws present the opposite failure: they are intended to resolve every issue beforehand. This happens when legislators fear giving governing officials or courts room for judgment or discretion in how to apply law. And it happens because America's legal methods don't work to grant and control discretion.[38] Legislators don't know how to draft laws that grant measured room for judgment or discretion. Judges and officials don't have methods to find, apply and justify their decisions.

America's laws, in their lack of system and piecemeal approach to legislation, confound future decision-making. They seek to determine every instance and control every action.[39] When they fail to do this well, either a decision less than the best results, or those charged with applying the law, torture it, bend it, twist its rules out-of-shape, or simply abandon rules altogether. When they do that, not only do they render reliance on that law doubtful, they contribute to undermining respect for all laws.

Statutory Precedent
Another impediment to understandable laws is the doctrine of statutory *stare decisis* (statutory precedent) that I discuss in Chapter 13. American legislators since Jefferson and Madison have regarded statutory language as tentative until the language is interpreted by courts, or as the founders presciently put it, "liquidated."[40] Legislators are loath to alter liquidated language, even when

---

[37] *See, e.g.,* Sykes v. United States, 564 U.S. 1, 35 (2011, Scalia, J. dissenting) (referring to "Fuzzy, leave-the-details-to-be-sorted-out-by-the-courts legislation."). *See generally* Chapter 10.

[38] *See* KENNETH CULP DAVIS, DISCRETIONARY JUSTICE: A PRELIMINARY INQUIRY (1969); DISCRETIONARY JUSTICE IN EUROPE AND AMERICA (Kenneth Culp Davis, ed., 1976).

[39] *See* PHILIP K. HOWARD, THE RULE OF NOBODY: SAVING AMERICA FROM DEAD LAWS AND BROKEN GOVERNMENT (2014).

[40] *See, e.g.,* THE FEDERALIST NO. 37 (James Madison) ("All new laws, though penned with the greatest technical skill, and passed on the fullest and most mature deliberation, are considered

they would simplify understanding for readers, because then they would create new language for courts to interpret.

Legal Publishing

The doctrine of statutory precedent has its fall-out on knowing the law. The bar cannot get enough precedents. It howls when the federal courts of appeals fail to publish all of their decisions. Legal publishers oblige. By the end of the 19th century they had down publishing all high-court decisions. Publishers put together massive digests to enable finding precedents and equally massive encyclopedias trying to order them in some fashion. Since 1973 they have made precedents available electronically. Full-text searching displaced earlier thematic systems (for example, Key Numbers).

Publishers have supported the supremacy of precedents over statutes by publishing "annotated" collations of statutes rather than systematic commentaries. These monstrosities print snippets of case-after-case often repeating what one court or another has said in applying a particular statute. A systematic statutory commentary such as is the norm in Germany is almost unheard of.[41]

There is no science of law to make statutes coherent such as in Germany. Long ago leading law professors gave up on producing doctrinal texts. No wonder: doctrinal texts largely collect precedents from all states. Professors spend their time spinning legal theories that judges ignore or deprecate as useless.[42] Students, who once noted court decisions, now follow their professors in creating "theories." They do not support with systematizing dissertations their mentors' systematizing efforts.[43]

---

as more or less obscure and equivocal, until their meaning be liquidated and ascertained by a series of particular discussions and adjudications.")

[41] The commentary for an American statute perhaps closest to a German code commentary is now long out-of-date. *See* THOMAS M. QUINN, QUINN'S UNIFORM COMMERCIAL CODE COMMENTARY AND DIGEST (2d ed., 1992).

[42] *See* Harry T. Edwards, *Another Look at Professor Rodell's* Goodbye to Law Reviews, 100 VA. L. REV. 1483 (2014); Harry T. Edwards, *The Growing Disjunction between Legal Education and the Legal Profession*, 91 MICH L. REV. 34 (1992); Richard A. Posner, DIVERGENT PATHS: THE ACADEMY AND THE JUDICIARY (2016); Diane P. Wood, *Legal Scholarship for Judges*, 124 YALE L.J. 2592 (2015).

[43] Biting European critiques of "legal scholarship" in America include ALAN WATSON, LAW OUT OF CONTEXT 140 *et seq.* (2000); Reinhard Zimmermann, *Law Reviews: A Foray through a Strange World*, 47 EMORY L. J. 659 (1998).

America's Successes

Americans can and do draft systematic, coherent laws. Since 1892 the Uniform Laws Commission has proposed for state adoption legislation that in language is of high quality. Not long after that legislatures began creating offices of legislative counsel to provide drafting assistance. I discuss the former in Chapter 11 and the latter in Chapter 10. They have brought improvement to American statutes, but in each case, their successes have been limited by limitations of their mandates. States do not have to adopt uniform laws; legislators do not have to use offices of legislative counsel.

C. GERMANY'S LAWS ARE A HOUSE IN ORDER[44]

1800 – CENTURY POSTCARD – 1900: Justitia standing on *Civil Code* of 1900, from *The New Century*

[44] Frederick William Maitland, *The Making of the German Civil Code: A Presidential Address delivered to the Social and Political Education League*, INDEPENDENT REVIEW (Aug. 1906), reprinted in 3 THE COLLECTED PAPERS OF FREDERICK WILLIAM MAITLAND 474, 475–476 (H.A.L. Fisher, ed., 1911) ("he has set his legal house in order"). *Compare*, Albert J. Harno, *A Ministry of Justice*, 39 J. AM. JUDICATURE SOC. 35, 36 (1955) ("... ours in a nation governed by law. ... it is the responsibility of the profession to keep our legal house in order.") John D. Randall, *Looking Beyond Tomorrow, The President's Annual Address*, 46 A.B.A.J. 954, 956 (1960) ("The lawyer is in a sense the legal housekeeper of his community.").

1. *Germany's Laws Summarized*

The principal laws that govern the people of Germany are: (1) the treaties of the European Union (EU); (2) the Regulations of the European Union; (3) the Constitution of Germany (*Grundgesetz*, *i.e.*, "Basic Law"); (4) federal statutes; (5) federal regulations; (6) state constitutions; (7) state statutes; (8) state regulations; and (9) ordinances of local governments and quasi-public bodies.[45] Noteworthy also are two types of laws that indirectly affect people, that is, EU Directives and German administrative provisions. The former are European directions to member states to adopt their own laws. Occasionally they can apply directly. Administrative provisions are instructions to government agencies for internal application.

German laws are the international gold standard for legislation. In the late 19th century, Japan adopted the German system of laws wholesale. In 1906, England's iconic legal historian, Frederic William Maitland, praised the then new Civil Code as "rational, coherent, modern, worthy of [the] country and our century."[46] In October 1914 at the outbreak of World War I, the ABA Special Committee on Drafting of Legislation pointed to the strengths of European legislation techniques in general and to the "intelligibility" of German laws in particular.[47] Today Germany's laws often are models for European Union regulations and directives.

Federal Laws and Regulations

The most important laws in Germany are federal laws and federal regulations. Chapter 11 shows how preeminence of federal law does not diminish the importance of federalism in Germany. People looking for the law that governs them look first to federal laws and regulations, unless they know that state laws govern (for example, education). In German federalism, rarely do both state and federal laws govern the same issues.

---

[45] Customary international law governs Germany directly; international law incorporated in treaties has a status not dissimilar to that of European Union Directives, *i.e.*, it applies as incorporated by German statute.

[46] Maitland, *supra* note 44, at 476. The same month Roscoe Pound, later Dean of Harvard Law School, in perhaps the most famous of American law reform addresses, pointed to "the wonderful mechanism of modern German judicial administration." *The Causes of the Popular Dissatisfaction with the Administration of Justice*, REPORT OF THE TWENTY-NINTH ANNUAL MEETING OF THE AMERICAN BAR ASSOCIATION HELD AT ST. PAUL, MINNESOTA, AUGUST 29, 30 AND 31, 1906, 395, 397 (1906).

[47] *Report of the Special Committee on Drafting of Legislation*, *supra* note 13, at 640.

In Germany, regulations (*Rechtsverordnungen*) are written by executive authorities, and are created in processes similar to those used to adopt statutes. Some require Bundesrat (Council of States) approval; all can be revised by the Bundestag (Parliament). The underlying statutes that support regulations ordinarily provide explicitly for implementing regulations. Regulations are usually included in editions of the statutes that authorize them. Professionals and laymen alike read regulations.

Regulations in Germany are not as numerous as in the United States, perhaps because regulations binding on the people are treated separately from administrative provisions (*Verwaltungsvorschriften*) that govern internal operations of government.[48]

Federal laws and regulations are published first in the official gazette (*Bundesgesetzblatt*) individually in chronological order as adopted. There are no printed counterparts to the United States Code and the Code of Federal Regulations that collect statutes or regulations. Now the Federal Ministry of Justice and Consumer Protection publishes federal statutes and federal regulations together in a free online database: http://www.gesetze-im-internet.de/. Although the Ministry cautions that the texts in the official gazette remain the official ones, it makes every effort to assure that the database includes all valid federal laws and regulations. It is searchable by law title or by word. It lists the statutes by the customary acronyms used to identify statutes (e.g., StGB for *Strafgesetzbuch*, i.e., Criminal Code).

People who are unsure of which laws govern can visit the Internet pages of the federal ministries responsible for the matter concerned. The individual ministries are responsible for the official publication of laws adopted in their areas of responsibility. Before a law passed by parliament becomes law, the minister must sign it. Today, ministry Internet sites typically provide texts of

---

[48] Administrative provisions are abstract, general directions to the ministry that issues them to govern the workings of that ministry. Because they have no binding effect outside the ministry that issues them, ordinarily they require no statutory authorization, need not be approved by parliament, and need not be published, although commonly they are. The Ministry of the Interior now publishes some of them on a freely accessible internet site, http://www.verwaltungsvorschriften-im-internet.de/. These and others may be obtained directly from the issuing ministry.

An authoritative guide for creation and application of administrative provisions is Part VI of the Ministry of the Interior's own book, BUNDESMINISTERIUM DES INNERN (ed.), HANDBUCH ZUR VORBEREITUNG VON RECHTS- UND VERWALTUNGSVORSCHRIFTEN 145–160 (2d ed., 2012). Exceptionally statutory authorization or publication may be required. These exceptions are beyond the scope of this book. For a detailed discussion of administrative provisions, see Fritz Ossenbühl, *Autonome Rechtsetzung der Verwaltung* § 104, in 5 HANDBUCH DES STAATSRECHTS DER BUNDESREPUBLIK DEUTSCHLAND 305–352 (3d ed., 2007).

the laws that they supervise. They also include drafts of proposed laws. All laws fall in the competence of a specific government office; federal laws fall within one of fourteen federal ministries.

The Internet has not made a revolution in access to laws in Germany. Laws had already been relatively accessible. Private publishers did and do make Germany's laws available in convenient, up-to-date and inexpensive collections. Helpful in this regard is that when a law is amended, the responsible ministry issues a consolidated text working in the amendments.

For the public there are popularly-priced and popularly-sized thematic collections of important laws and regulations. Some editions include only texts. For students, judges and lawyers who need access to nearly all laws, there are three fat loose-leaf volumes, two for federal laws and one for the state where the user is located.[49] Although the books have complete indices, users are counseled to use the tables of contents and a topic-based approach to finding the laws that apply.[50]

Private publishers also publish texts of statutes and regulations with explanations ranging from short notes to long commentaries. Commentaries to the laws elaborate the meanings of the texts. They rely on logic, policy, other laws, legislative history and selected court decisions. They are analytical and thus differ from annotated codes in America, which are only tools for lawyers to find cases to study. German commentaries are useful to lay people as well as to lawyers. Hardly an important law lacks a commentary long: sometimes a commentary appears before the law goes into force.

There are also many study books designed to guide professionals, students and laymen in learning and applying German laws. These are of greater utility than counterparts in the United States because the preeminence of federal laws allows them to be current and national.

State Laws

Access to state laws parallels access to federal laws. Internet sites make state laws, regulations and administrative provisions available. Particularly in the case of smaller states, thematic secondary collections and study books are not always available in up-to-date editions. For that reason, resort to ministry sites is particularly recommended.

---

[49] Two volumes are red and are named after their original editors from the early 20th century, *Schönfelder* for civil and criminal laws, and *Sartorius* for constitutional and administrative laws. The third volume varies in color from state to state and gives the most important state laws. For Bavaria, the book is *Ziegler/Tremel* and the color is blue.

[50] Otto Lagodny, Gesetzestexte suchen, verstehen und in der Klausur anwenden (2d ed., 2012).

Ordinances
Local ordinances (*Satzungen*) have less importance in Germany than in the
United States. Chapter 11 discusses local laws. Other ordinances are rules issued
by private and quasi-public organizations (e.g., standards bodies). Although the
German Constitution guarantees local self-government, its guarantee is of self-
administration and not of local lawmaking. Local governments have only
limited authority to issue laws applicable to the public generally.

Finding and Knowing Governing Laws
Accessing laws is the beginning of finding and knowing the laws that govern
particular points. That's what people want to know: the laws that govern their
affairs. Knowing laws is not hard in Germany. Access, coupled with systematized laws, produces laws for the people. The laws themselves generally are
understandable.

2. *Germany's Laws are Reliable*

Germany's laws form a system. They fit together. They are not supposed to
overlap or to contradict each other and usually they do not. They have
stability. They are primary to precedents interpreting them. They are reliable.

One law governs one issue. As a result, to find the laws that govern a
particular case, one need consult only one or a handful of laws. A layperson
can usually do that.

In a jointly endorsed brochure, the ministries of justice of France and
Germany reveal their recipe for success: "Continental law is characterized
by statutes and codification. Codification is the systematic collection of rules
of law into official compilations such as civil and commercial codes. Far from
being rigid, this ordered compilation, on the contrary, facilitates modernizing
the law as needed."[51]

Systematization, says the brochure, lets people know the law: "Because of such
codification, continental law is accessible to everyone. It is easy to comprehend:
by reading the codes, any person can learn the rules of law that apply to him. It is
also easy to understand because each rule is formulated in simple and general
terms. The legal certainty that ensues is a major advantage for citizens . . . ."[52]

---

[51] CONTINENTAL LAW – GLOBAL – PREDICTABLE – FLEXIBLE – COST-EFFECTIVE 4 (2012), available
at kontinentalesrecht.de.
[52] The brochure contrasts Anglo-American law: "In common law countries, the search for the
applicable law often requires consulting a long series of court decisions in order to find an
appropriate precedent – if one even exists. Understanding all of these court decisions is often

The brochure's claims are not puffery. They tell a truth that reflects warranted national pride.[53] To be sure, not everyone in France and Germany easily finds and understands all rules. The systems are not perfect; there is overlap. Lawyers are not unemployed.[54] But with the provisos that everyone can get some help and that people need only to understand rules that concern them (i.e., statutes directed to specialist audiences, may use specialist language[55]), the claims are credible. In this section, I explain the basis for the claims in Germany.

According to the German Federal Minister of Justice and Consumer Protection, people in Germany have "swift and straightforward access to the law."[56] It's true. I know from personal experience. In recent years, I have been called upon by American colleagues to inform them about German laws about which I knew nothing in fields where I knew little more of American law. Yet, in short order, I can inform my American friends about the German law. My German friends checked my work and found no errors.[57]

---

difficult for non-lawyers, who therefore must rely on professional legal advisers. The need for such legal assistance greatly increases the costs for those seeking to enforce their rights." *Id.*

[53] *But see* Mathias Siems *Comparative Legal Certainty: Legal Certainty and Forms of Measurement, in* THE SHIFTING MEANING OF LEGAL CERTAINTY IN COMPARATIVE AND TRANSNATIONAL LAW 115, 118 (Mark Fenwick, Mathias Siems & Stefan Wrbka, eds., 2017) (using the brochure as exemplary of the "traditional" argument of the "alleged advantage" of codified law and using it as jumping off point to consider "Challenges to the Traditional View.") *See also* (all articles by me with references to those of others) James R. Maxeiner, *Legal Indeterminacy Made in America: American Legal Methods and the Rule of Law*, 47 VALPARAISO U.L. REV. 517 (2006); *Legal Certainty: A European Alternative to American Legal Indeterminacy*, 15 TULANE J. INT'L & COMP. L. 541 (2007); *Some Realism About Legal Certainty in the Globalization of the Rule of Law*, 31 HOUSTON J. INT'L L. 27 (2008); *Law-Made in Germany: Global Standort or Global Standard?, in* DEUTSCHE BERATUNG BEI RECHTS- UND JUSTIZREFORM IM AUSLAND: 20 JAHRE DEUTSCHE STIFTUNG FÜR INTERNATIONALE RECHTLICHE ZUSAMMENARBEIT (IRZ) 43 (Stefan Hülhörster & Dirk Mirow, eds., 2012).

[54] *Cf.,* EVA STEINER, FRENCH LAW: A COMPARATIVE APPROACH 37 (2010) ("Finding the law can be greatly simplified if, instead of grappling with a mixture of legal texts, users are able to gain access to the whole of the law within a given area by consulting a single document. However, this should not mask the difficulties involved in using a code. Codes are numerous: it is anticipated that in the coming years there will be more than sixty codes in France. Moreover, their areas very often overlap and they do not necessarily contain all the law in a given field. Thus finding the law on a particular issue may still necessitate a certain degree of skill.")

[55] *See, e.g.,* PETER BLUM, WEGE ZU BESSERER GESETZGEBUNG – SACHVERTÄNDIGE BERATUNG, BEGRÜNDUNG, FOLGENABSCHÄTZUNG UND WIRKUNGSKONTROLLE, GUTACHTEN I ZUM 65. DEUTSCHEN JURISTENTAG BONN 2004 at I–11 (2004).

[56] FEDERAL MINISTRY OF JUSTICE AND CONSUMER PROTECTION, LAW – MADE IN GERMANY, GLOBAL, EFFECTIVE, COST EFFICIENT 7 (3d ed., 2014), *available at* lawmadeingermany.de. Recently the Federal Ministry of Justice was given additional responsibilities and renamed the Federal Ministry of Justice and Consumer Protection.

[57] *Cf.* Karl N. Llewellyn, *Bar's Troubles, and Poultices–and Cures, The Unauthorized Practice of Law Controversy*, 5 LAW AND CONTEMPORARY PROBLEMS 114, 118 (1938) ("a puzzled

In Germany finding governing laws is easy and unproblematic. Minutes, not days or hours, are required. The beginning is intuitive and the end defined by finding an authoritative statute or regulation.

Codes do not and are not intended to answer all legal questions. Instead, they structure decision-making.[58] Structuring means identifying which rules govern, what they require, who is to decide what, and what are the consequences. The end of law finding is reached ordinarily when the possible laws and regulations governing or determining application are found.[59] Finding laws is only one part – usually the easiest part – of applying laws.

Germany's laws are interrelated in a system.[60] While that the ideal is not perfectly realized, the goal is a system organized as if a single plan governed. Different laws should mesh with each other – none should command contrary action. Inconsistency among laws should be avoided.[61] New laws should fit in without contradiction with existing laws.[62] New laws should be adopted only when necessary.[63]

In principle, all laws that govern the same subject are combined in one legislative act, ideally in a code (for example, Civil Code), but in any case, in a single act, or a limited number of closely related and consistent acts. This idea is so obvious that Germans rarely mention it. When they do, they speak of the principle of "concentration." [64]

Continental lawyer [can] turn to his little library and then turn out at least a workable understanding of his problem within half an hour").

[58] See J.L. Tellkampf, *On Codification, or the Systematizing of the Law* [Part II], 26 AM. JURIST & L, MAG. 283, 288–289 (1841); REINHOLD ZIPPELIUS, INTRODUCTION TO GERMAN LEGAL METHODS xii (Kirk. W. Junker & P. Matthew Roy, transl., 2008; 11th German ed., 2012); JEAN PORTALIS, PRELIMINARY ADDRESS DELIVERED ON THE OCCASION OF THE PRESENTATION OF THE DRAFT OF THE GOVERNMENT COMMISSION, ON 1 PLUVIÔSE IX (1801), available at the Internet site of the Department of Justice of Canada, www.justice.gc.ca.

[59] Sometimes the end may be that one or more laws apply, but which do cannot be determined without determination of facts.

[60] See generally CLAUS-WILHELM CANARIS, SYSTEMDENKEN UND SYSTEMBEGRIFF IN DER JURISPRUDENZ: ENTWICKELT AM BEISPIEL DES DEUTSCHEN PRIVATRECHTS (2d ed., 1983); KARL ENGISCH, DIE EINHEIT DER RECHTSORDNUNG (1935).

[61] PETER RAISCH, JURISTISCHE METHODEN: VOM ANTIKEN ROM BIS ZUR GEGENWART 148–149 (1995)(referring to avoiding *Normspaltung*).

[62] BUNDESMINISTERIUM DER JUSTIZ, HANDBUCH DER RECHTSFÖRMLICHKEIT 17 (3d ed., 2008), available at http://hdr.bmj.de/impressum.html.

[63] JOINT RULES OF PROCEDURE OF THE FEDERAL MINISTRIES § 43(1)(1) (2011) (for finding details, see Chapter 10, n. 37); BUNDESMINISTERIUM DES INNERN, HANDBUCH ZUR VORBEREITUNG VON RECHTS- UND VERWALTUNGSVORSCHRIFTEN 51 (2d ed., 2012). Already Portalis counseled: "There must be no unnecessary laws. They would weaken the necessary laws; they would compromise the certitude and majesty of legislation." *Supra*, note 58.

[64] See BUNDESMINISTERIUM DER JUSTIZ, HANDBUCH DER RECHTSFÖRMLICHKEIT 147 (3d ed., 2008), available at http://hdr.bmj.de/impressum.html; ORGANISATION FOR ECONOMIC

In Germany, thanks to the principles of concentration and consistency, students and people generally stop looking for laws once they find all possibly applicable laws and the particular governing rule(s) within those laws.[65]

Concentration has a long record. Napoleon had five codes. Today, in France, one speaks of perhaps sixty codes.[66] In Germany, the number of codes or single acts is similar or somewhat higher. Still, the number is manageable. The United States Code itself in its total number of titles is of a similar number: its titles could serve the same function if laws were similarly concentrated.

Concentration makes the starting point of law-finding intuitive. Where else would one look for a criminal law other than in the criminal code? Even when there is no intuitive choice, a quick perusal of the possible choices, together with their tables of contents, directs users to a small number of laws to read. Since the number of laws is manageable, as one moves from everyday to occupational life, one will soon know – and buy for few Euros – the laws that govern one's work.

This "concentration" principle means that a German interested in laws governing a particular endeavor can start and often end the search for the right law with the free Internet site already mentioned or with a pocketbook-sized and popular-priced edition of relevant laws. Germany's leading law book publisher offers just short of one hundred such books that cover pretty much all areas of federal law.[67] In areas such as education, where state law dominates, this and other publishers offer similar books by state. Picking the right book requires little legal acumen. If the title alone doesn't tip the buyer off, for example, Criminal Code covers crimes, a quick look at the table of contents will often direct the buyer's purchase.

German students and legal professionals take a similar but somewhat different approach in finding law that they do not know already. Most important laws are collected in three large volumes that students, judges and lawyers still have on their desks even in these days of Internet access. Two volumes are red and are named after their original editors from the 20th century, *Schönfelder* for civil and criminal laws, and *Sartorius* for

CO-OPERATION AND DEVELOPMENT, BETTER REGULATION IN EUROPE – GERMANY 114 (2010), available at http://www.oecd.org/gov/regulatory-policy/germany.htm.

[65] *See* LAGODNY, *supra* note 50, at 15 (the student looks for the "right" law) and 28 (for a "particular rule" within that law).

[66] EVA STEINER, FRENCH LAW: A COMPARATIVE APPROACH 37 (2010).

[67] The website is http://www.gesetzeim-internet.de/. The series is "Beck-Texte im dtv." I prefer the only somewhat larger and somewhat more expensive yellow-orange handy commentaries of the same publisher. They confirm meanings and integrate several statutes and regulations.

constitutional and administrative laws. The third volume varies in color from state to state and gives the most important state laws. For Bavaria, the book is *Ziegler/Tremel* and the color is blue. All three books give the texts with few notes, but complete tables of contents and extensive indices. When a student or judge looks for a law, he or she will choose the appropriate volume and then follow its structure to get to the right law.[68]

German laws are so much better organized than are their American counterparts that I dare to say that Americans who know no German, but have German-English dictionaries and translating tools, often have better chances of quickly finding *which* laws govern their actions in Germany than they do in the United States. In any case, Germans who speak German have a reasonably good chance, even if they are not lawyers.

Once one has found the governing laws and regulations, rarely is it necessary for an everyday user to seek out other laws or legal materials. In particular, users wishing to follow the law ordinarily need not look for case precedents. Precedents are not binding law. They help to understand how judges apply the law in borderline cases.

Concentration permits people and professionals to concentrate on applying law. They need not waste time trying to synthesize laws to apply in their case.

3. *Germany's Laws Are Understandable*

Most of Germany's laws are understandable. There was a time when readers who did not know German could not easily check my assertion. But another benefit of Internet-available statutes is increased availability of translations. Readers need not rely on Google Translate or similar mechanical translators to get an idea of the quality of German drafting. Around seventy-five major German laws are now available in English translation on the same Internet page of the Ministry of Justice that gives Germans access to their laws.[69] One need only click on the tab marked "Translations" in a page otherwise in German. These translations are not always the best possible and are not always the most current, but they serve well enough to make my point of clarity. I challenge skeptical readers to read these laws in translation and compare their clarity with comparable American laws. It's hard to think of laws as elegant: Germans complain of "bureaucratic German" (*Amtsdeutsch*) much as Americans complain of "legalese."[70] But German laws can be elegant. Many provisions of the original 19th century codes remain as written.

---

[68] *See* LAGODNY, *supra* note 50.   [69] http://www.gesetze-im-internet.de/
[70] *See, e.g.,* RALF HÖCKER, LANGENSCHEIDT ANWALT – DEUTSCH / DEUTSCH – ANWALT (2009).

Consistency

Most individual German laws are well-defined and consistent internally and with other laws. A system helps define individual laws. Laws follow each other in approach. Terms and concepts are understood the same way, not only in one law but throughout many or all laws. Once a concept has been learned, it need not be reconsidered each time it is applied in a different point.

Writing German laws well is as challenging as writing American laws well. Experience helps. It is a specific skill to be learned much as writing well generally is. In both Germany and the United States there are manuals of legislative drafting that help structure laws and make individual provisions understandable. In Germany, their use is mandatory.

Finding the right code or single act still does not get one to the applicable rule. But here, too, systematization helps the law-seeker. German laws have an internal structure that helps lead the law-seeker to the right norm or norms. These structures are not always the same. In Germany, however, the Ministry of Justice seeks to regularize these approaches as much as it reasonably can.

Americans could do the same. Some of the best products of American legislation, whether drafted by the Uniform Laws Commission, the American Law Institute, law revision commissions or offices of legislative counsel, are in the league of German statutes.

The difference in quality between American and German laws is not to be attributed to a lack of good drafters in the United States. It is to be seen in two features of lawmaking that I address in the next chapter: quality control and coordination. Often politics preclude both in the United States.[71]

The system in Germany is enhanced by legal publishing that increases content clarity and application predictability. Every code and most major statutes have systematic, privately written commentaries. These commentaries set out statutory provisions. But unlike the annotated codes of the United States, which merely identify cases for lawyers to read, German code commentaries systematically discuss the statutes, their purposes, and their implications. Commentaries review interpretative questions that have arisen or may arise. They report how courts and scholars have addressed those issues. Some commentaries are written by the drafters of the laws themselves. Some have continued for more than a century and are regularly updated by scholars and

---

[71] *See, e.g,* Tress, *supra* note 7, at 159 (2009) ("Congress-not the Code editors-writes laws, and the haste and disorder of the legislative process cannot be constrained by the editorial requirements of direct amendment.") The history of the abortive attempts to "repeal and replace" the Affordable Care Act has yet to be written, but will dramatically demonstrate this. The last failed attempts were not even disclosed to Senators more than a few hours before the legislative votes.

practitioners in the field. Some enjoy enormous authority and can be readily relied on for their interpretation of the law. Huge, multivolume "large" commentaries treat just about every issue that might arise. Some one-volume "short" commentaries consist of around 3,000 oversized octavo pages. Almost all lawyers own or have ready access to these "short" commentaries.

German laws in individual provisions follow a strict syllogistic format. They define: (1) legal results, (2) the decision maker(s) where formal decisions are required, (3) indefinite legal concepts to allow flexibility in application, and (4) grants of discretion to choose the best possible result in a particular instance.

These characteristics help maintain the authority of law.

German lawmakers recognize that laws cannot anticipate all future events. As much as laws are to limit people and government in the present, they are to authorize decisions in the future. Laws can structure and guide those decisions, even if they cannot determine them. Such law application does not create new law but honors existing law.

Germany is known for being a land of rules that are closely – and sometimes senselessly, it is said – adhered to. The civil law in general is often seen in the United States as trying to predetermine every outcome.

Earlier I suggested that departures from rules in America undercut the authority of law. Sometimes these departures are seen as necessary because American laws try to predetermine every outcome.

In Chapter 13 I discuss approaches to statutory interpretation that explain why rigidity is more a feature of American law than of German law.

In this section, I show how German legal methods work to maintain the integrity of law while allowed the flexibility needed to deal with unpredictable circumstances. Germany has an extensive literature on legal methods and on legislation. This literature sees the structuring of authority as the "backbone" of the legal system. When legislation cannot predetermine the results – as often is the case – it can at least order decision making. Here I address two common approaches to bringing certainty and predictability while maintaining statutory integrity.[72]

---

[72] I have addressed these issues and those of discretion elsewhere and therefore do not repeat here citations to German-language materials given there. *See* (all works by me), Policy and Methods in German and American Antitrust Law: A Comparative Study 41–44, (1986); *Legal Certainty: A European Alternative to American Legal Indeterminacy, supra* note 53, 15 Tulane J. Int'l & Comp. L. at 559–562; *Thinking Like a Lawyer Abroad: Putting Justice into Legal Reasoning*, 11 Wash. U. Global Studies L. Rev. 55, 86–89 (2012); *Scalia & Garner's Reading Law: A Civil Law for the Age of Statutes*, 6 J. Civil L. Studies 1, 26–30 (2013).

Indefinite Legal Concepts

German statutes use indefinite legal concepts in so-called general clauses to take into account the many sides of life that do not lend themselves to definition in clearly defined concepts. By using general clauses, legislation need not be fragmentary, but can be gap free.[73] While indefinite legal concepts threaten legal certainty, different techniques are used to counter that threat. General clauses do not permit judges simply to decide what they think is "fair" or in the "general welfare." Instead, case groups develop in an almost common-law manner. Only where there are no prior decisions do judges have some freedom in reaching new solutions. Sometimes the legislature notes the development of these case groups and enacts them into law or introduces its own groups of cases.

Some indefinite clauses are merely descriptive, that is, they relate to objects and events in the physical world, such as darkness; they are empirical. Other general clauses are normative and require a valuing, such as what constitutes "good faith" or "good morals."

Discretion

Sometimes statutes deliberately do not bind decision makers to one correct decision, but leave decision makers discretion to reach their own decisions based on their own responsibility and independent choice. It is used to permit a purposeful and just decision in the individual case. Discretion in choice of action is appropriate, but not in determination of the prerequisites for action. This distinction marks a difference between indefinite legal concepts and discretion: the former leaves room for judgment in the prerequisites of action, while the latter provides for freedom of action.

While German statutes use both indefinite concepts and grants of discretion to deal with future events that cannot be fully foreseen, they use them differently. While they may freely grant discretion to administrative authorities to make policy decisions, they eschew giving discretion to judges for such decisions. They do assign judges decisions that require them to make value judgments in individual cases. Administrative authorities may make policy-oriented decisions upon their own responsibility; they may choose on the basis

---

[73] See KARL ENGISCH, EINFÜHRUNG IN DAS JURISTISCHE DENKEN 124 (1st ed., 1956; 11th ed. by Thomas Würtenberger & Dirk Otto, 2010), ENGISCH, KARL, EINHEIT DER RECHTSORDNUNG (1935). German indefinite legal concepts are best known in the United States through two general clauses of the German Civil Code, sections 138 and 242, which have become part of American law through adoption in the Uniform Commercial Code (U.C.C. § 1–304 Good Faith; § 2–302 Unconscionability).

of current and local interests among several possibilities. This freedom is acceptable because administrative authorities are politically accountable. Where statutes do not bind administrative authorities, they are nonetheless obligated to exercise their freedom of choice in the public interest.

Relaxation of binding to statute for judicial decisions, on the other hand, is preferably limited to situations where necessary to permit judges to do justice in individual cases. Judges are not politically accountable; they are guaranteed independence to permit them to do justice. The German legal system uses rules in this way to depoliticize certain decisions. It attempts to separate legal questions from political ones. A legal question should be subject to resolution without having to value public interest, because the valuing of public interest is a peculiarly political task.

10

Lawmaking for the Common Good

The peculiar duty of draughting statutes, or examining them after they have been drawn, devolves on nobody. ... Each individual, ... without any official duty or experience, prepares the statute which he desires to submit, and it is passed or rejected without any particular reference to its terms, or correction of its ambiguity.

House of Representatives, Committee on the Judiciary (1848)[1]

A. LAWS ARE MADE BY AND FOR EVERYBODY

Governments of laws and not of men are purposeful. Paradoxically governments need men and women to make laws that govern. Men and women initiate and write laws, men and women consult on laws' goals, men and women integrate laws into systems, and men and women maintain laws as times change. In well functioning systems men and women are responsible for quality control in making and maintaining laws. Men and women assure that all affected people are consulted. No invisible hand does that.[2]

Laws are abstract directions for society. Laws should serve common good now and in the future. They should not serve primarily to decide competing claims from the past and present.

---

[1] U.S. House of Representatives, Committee on the Judiciary (Joseph R. Ingersoll), *Revision of the Laws of the United States* (to accompany H.R. 535), H.R. REP. 30–671 (1848). *See also* JOSEPH STORY, A DISCOURSE PRONOUNCED UPON THE INAUGURATION OF THE AUTHOR, AS DANE PROFESSOR OF LAW IN HARVARD UNIVERSITY 16–17 (1829) ("We are apt to think that men are born legislators; that no qualifications beyond plain sense and common honesty, are necessary for the management of the intricate machine of government.")

[2] *See* Preamble, CONSTITUTION OR FRAME OF GOVERNMENT OF THE COMMONWEALTH OF MASSACHUSETTS (1780) ("the whole people covenants with each citizen, and each citizen with the whole people, that all shall be governed by certain laws for the common good. It is the duty of the people, therefore, in framing a Constitution of Government, to provide for an equitable mode of making laws ....").

Every citizen of a democratic government of laws ought to be able to contribute to the making of laws.[3] People know of laws in the making because someone tells them that laws that may affect them are being made. Laws seek common good, because lawmakers learn and take into account the views of people generally.

From a child's schoolbook view, lawmaking in America and Germany are similar. There are two-lawmaking bodies. Someone in one body introduces a proposed law, i.e., a "bill." It is publicly read, discussed and voted on. If it passes, it goes to the other body. It is publicly read, discussed and voted on. If it passes, it goes to the president. If the president signs it, it becomes law.[4]

Underneath the surface similarity stops. Here I examine three critical differences:

- In the United States no one "owns" a law; in Germany every law has its owner, that is, an identifiable government ministry is responsible for it.
- In the United States laws are written as they are adopted by legislatures. In Germany laws are written before they are presented to legislatures for possible adoption.
- In the United States writers of laws compete. In Germany writers of laws cooperate.

Some readers may see my focus on legislative lawmaking as anachronistic in reference to the United States. They might say that much as American courts provide judge-made law to make up for deficiencies of legislatures, American executives use presidential executive orders and department regulations to furnish rules where legislatures have not.

Insofar as this is true, it is another demonstration of the failure of American lawmaking and another reason to look closely at German lawmaking.

To do justice to a thesis of regulations and executive orders as an alternative to statutes, I would need to address in detail administrative law in the United States and Germany. This would be a worthy task, but it is one beyond the scope of this book.[5]

---

[3] In a democratic state this is a corollary to the axiom that everyone living under a government of laws ought to have a chance to know the laws. *Cf.*, SAMUEL G. GOODRICH, THE YOUNG AMERICAN: OR BOOK OF GOVERNMENT AND LAW; SHOWING THEIR HISTORY, NATURE, AND NECESSITY; FOR THE USE OF SCHOOLS 47 (8th ed., 1847) ("In savage or barbarous countries . . . the people have nothing to do in making the government. All they are required to do is to submit.").

[4] *Id.* 47.

[5] For information on contemporary German administrative law, see MARTINA KÜNNECKE, TRADITION AND CHANGE IN ADMINISTRATIVE LAW: AN ANGLO-GERMAN COMPARISON (2007);

B. AMERICA'S LAWS ARE MADE BY NOBODY FOR SOMEBODY

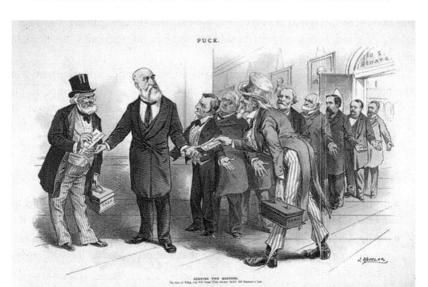

Joseph Keppler, *Serving Two Masters*, from PUCK, June 23, 1886

1. *America's Malady: Laws Without Responsibility*

Americans are fed up with their legislatures. They speak of "the dysfunctional Congress,"[6] of "the broken branch,[7] and of the "most disparaged branch."[8] One critic, briefly a presidential candidate, lamented of a "republic, lost."[9]

MAHENDRA P. SINGH, GERMAN ADMINISTRATIVE LAW IN COMMON LAW PERSPECTIVE, 2d ed., 2001). The German Research Institute for Public Administration (*Deutsches Forschungsinstitut für öffentliche Verwaltung*), located at the German University of Administrative Sciences in Speyer (*Deutsche Universität für Verwaltungswissenschaften Speyer*) has published scores of volumes, some of which are in English. See http://www.foev-speyer.de/de/forschung.php.

6 KENNETH R. MAYER & DAVID T. CANNON, THE DYSFUNCTIONAL CONGRESS? THE INDIVIDUAL ROOTS OF AN INSTITUTIONAL DILEMMA (1999).

7 THOMAS E. MANN & NORMAN J. ORENSTEIN, THE BROKEN BRANCH: HOW CONGRESS IS FAILING AMERICA AND HOW TO GET IT BACK ON TRACK (2006).

8 *Symposium: The Most Disparaged Branch: The Role of Congress in the Twenty-First Century*, 89 BOSTON U.L. REV. 331–870 (2009) (more than 500 pages and more than thirty contributors!).

9 LAWRENCE LESSIG, REPUBLIC, LOST: HOW MONEY CORRUPTS CONGRESS – AND A PLAN TO STOP IT (2011).

America's lawmaking fails because no one is responsible for making, coordinating and maintaining its laws. A century ago one study of legislative practices diagnosed America's malady: "an absence of responsibility for the drafting of measures and an absence of security for the conformity of statutes to general principles and their consistency with each other."[10]

Congress as maker and maintainer of a system of good laws is a practical impossibility. Madison foresaw that in 1788 in *Federalist No. 62*. A popular assembly lacks "due acquaintance with the objects and principles of legislation." Missing is "a knowledge of the means by which that object can be best attained." "Mutability" of popular assemblies leads to "continual change even of good measures" and to "errors in the exercise of their legislative trust."[11]

Madison offered the Senate as solution. It did not work as he had hoped. In 1913 in the 17th amendment the United States scrapped Madison's Senate of representatives chosen by the states and introduced a popularly elected senate, but did not otherwise adjust the role or function of the Senate.

Within today's Congress one might imagine – for a few seconds – that Committee staffs, who often do write laws, could take on the function of maker and maintainer of a system of good laws, or at least of some laws. One need not ruminate on the idea for long, for committees lack the needed continuity, expertise, resources and clear competences to actually do that.

The obvious shepherds of the laws are the institutions charged with carrying them out: the departments and agencies of government. It is their job to know the laws and to know how they are working. For decades individual departments have sometimes sought to play such a role. Congress has not seen fit to give them that role. It has held tightly to its control over lawmaking. It turns to departments and agencies only for technical assistance in statutory drafting.[12]

---

[10] Jacob van der Zee, *The Drafting of Statutes*, in STATUTE LAW-MAKING IN IOWA (Benjamin F. Shambaugh, ed.) 473, 487 (1916).

[11] THE FEDERALIST No. 62, *The Senate* (James Madison).

[12] CHRISTOPHER J. WALKER, FEDERAL AGENCIES IN THE LEGISLATIVE PROCESS: TECHNICAL ASSISTANCE IN STATUTORY DRAFTING. FINAL REPORT TO THE ADMINISTRATIVE CONFERENCE OF THE UNITED STATES 1–4 (2015). *See* Scott Levy *Drafting the Law: Players, Power, and Processes* in PARTY AND PROCEDURE IN THE UNITED STATES CONGRESS (Jacob R. Straus & Matthew E. Glassman, eds., 2d ed., 2017); Jared Shobe, *Agencies as Legislators: An Empirical Study of the Role of Agencies in the Legislative Process*, 86 GEO. WASHINGTON L. REV. 451 (2017). *See also* Reed Dickerson, *The Catholic University Study of Federal Legislative Drafting in the Executive Branch*, Foreword 21 CATH. U.L. REV. 702 (1972).

2. *"Legislative Process" as Game*

America's legal scholars talk about "legislative process" rather than about making laws for governing by law. That lets them focus on procedures rather than on outcomes. They forget that process is conducted with results in mind. Process is not an end in itself. Legislative process should result in laws of general application. But that is not always so in America, where legislative process often is about mollifying private interests. For a lucky few, that means laws that serve their private interests. For others, thousands of introduced but failed bills serve to keep up pretenses that government is doing something for people.

It requires a stretch of imagination to characterize what Congress does as a production process for crafting laws. That statement is not provocative to those in the know. For decades each two-year Congress has "considered" 8,000–13,000 bills and resolutions. In no year has it adopted as many as 15 percent of all bills and resolutions introduced. In the last decade enacted laws have not exceeded 3 percent of all introduced legislative measures.[13] Such a dismal record of completion is characteristic not of a production process, but of desperate treatments of terminal diseases or of lottery selections of winners.

Committee System of Legislative Process

For generations America's school children have learned the classic committee system of legislative process. Since 1975 they have watched the classic production by School House Rock, *I'm Just a Bill*.[14] If you haven't seen it, do. Here is the basic committee system for bills that begin in the United States House of Representatives (it's different, but similar, if they begin in the Senate). Note that this summary assumes the improbable: that the bill makes it up each step. Most do not get past step (2) assignment to committee.

1) A Congressman submits a bill (a proposal for a law).
2) The House parliamentarian or the Speaker of the House refers the bill to a committee or committees of House members.

---

[13] Statistics and Historical Comparison, https://www.govtrack.us/congress/bills/statistics.

[14] DAVE FRISHBERG (Music and Lyrics), SCHOOLHOUSE ROCK LYRICS, I'M JUST A BILL (1975), http://www.schoolhouserock.tv/Bill.html. A video is available at SCHOOLHOUSE ROCK: AMERICA – I'M JUST A BILL MUSIC VIDEO https://youtu.be/FFroMQlKiag. Another classic introduction to the procedure is a scene in the movie MR. SMITH GOES TO WASHINGTON (1939), *How to Propose a Bill According to Jean Arthur*, https://youtu.be/BZFRP67sX8o. A thorough description is THE CENTER ON CONGRESS AT INDIANA UNIVERSITY, THE LEGISLATIVE PROCESS, http://congress.indiana.edu/legislative-process (last visited Dec. 19, 2016).

3) The House committee holds hearings.

4) The House committee "marks up" the bill, i.e., revises it.

5) The House committee reports the bill to the whole House.

6) The whole House debates the bill, may amend it and passes it.

7) The passed bill is introduced into the Senate.

8) The passed bill is referred to a Senate committee.

9) The Senate committee holds hearings.

10) The Senate committee "marks up" the bill, i.e., revises it.

11) The Senate debates the bill, may amend it and passes it.

12) If the Senate has changed the bill, procedures are necessary to reconcile the two versions. If the Senate has not changed the bill, as passed by both the House and the Senate it is presented to the President.

13) The President signs the bill and it becomes a law. If the President vetoes the bill, procedures are necessary to overcome the President's veto.

Those in the know teach newly elected representatives and senators that the legislative process is NOT *School House Rock*.[15] The legislative process works to prevent bad laws as much as to enact good laws. It is all about politics. "Congress is a political institution. ... The process is about "WHO ... GETS ...WHAT! ... At every stage of the legislative process, and in every alliance made during the legislative process, Congress is a political institution deciding who, including the president, gets what."[16]

Those in the know teach students that "the most salient aspect of the modern legislative process is that it is filled with a complex set of hurdles that proponents of a new policy must overcome before their bill becomes law."[17] They classify descriptive theories of how the legislative process actually unfolds: proceduralist, interest group and institutional. Popular among

---

[15] Judy Schneider, Presentation to Plenary Session 4: Procedural Hurdles to Legislation in the U.S. Congress, The 3rd International Conference of Legislative Drafting and Law Reform, July 1, 2015 (author's notes). Ms. Schneider is a Specialist on the Congress at the Congressional Research Center and regularly instructs new representatives and senators on the ins and outs of Congress.

[16] JUDY SCHNEIDER & MICHAEL KOEMPEL, CONGRESSIONAL DESKBOOK: THE PRACTICAL AND COMPREHENSIVE GUIDE TO CONGRESS §§ 1.10, 1.20, pp. 3, 5 (6th ed., 2012; emphasis in original). *Id.* at xxv. ("when Congress acts, it is a complex process that has four indivisible aspects – people, politics, policy, and procedure.") Most of what is stated in this section is supported in the *Deskbook*. *Cf.* Peter L. Strauss, *The Common Law and Statutes*, 70 U. COLO. L. REV. 225, 243 (1998) (pointing out the similarity between American legislation and common-law adjudication and speaking of "common law orientation).

[17] WILLIAM N. ESKRIDGE, JR., PHILIP P. FRICKEY & ELIZABETH GARRETT, LEGISLATION AND STATUTORY INTERPRETATION 70 (2d ed., 2006).

proceduralist theories are "obstacle path" theories. There are many "veto gates" through which proposed legislation must pass.

The "legislative process" is a maze. Through this labyrinth the bill has no shepherd. A Minotaur lurks behind every bend ready to devour the bill. "At each step of the legislative process, proponents must build a new majority to get to the next step. . . . Outside groups – constituents, lobbyists, the president and his administration, and the media – are never far from the fray, and they pressure, pressure, pressure to influence the outcome. . . . At each step of the legislative process, proponents must build their majorities within larger groups. . . . [That means] giving as many members as needed for a majority a stake in the outcome."[18]

Rules of the Game

Apologists for American legislative process don't defend the results. Rather they claim that the results are what the founders intended and that "the rules of procedure and organization that each chamber has developed exist equally for the use of proponents and opponents of any proposition.'[19] In other words: it's a game.[20] So devoid is American discussion of alternatives that opponents are more likely to object that the game is rigged than to question whether there should be a game at all.

The rules of the game are not uniform even as between the two chambers. According to a report of the Congressional Research Service, in at least four areas of parliamentary procedure "more differences than similarities emerge when comparing selected House and Senate rules of procedure . . . ."[21]

Legislative rules exemplify deficiencies of American rules generally discussed in the previous chapter. They are disorganized and scattered. They are confusing. They juxtapose without apparent plan almost unlimited discretion in some cases with straitjacket rules to preclude discretion in others.

The People Are Left Out of the Game

The rules of the game prevent the people from participating. Only Congressmen and Senators are assured roles (and even for them, the rules can be manipulated to cut out their involvement).

---

[18] SCHNEIDER & KOEMPEL, *supra* note 16, at § 1.20.
[19] SCHNEIDER & KOEMPEL, *supra* note 16, § 1.20, at 4.
[20] You can play it. Former Supreme Court Justice Sandra Day O'Connor has created a program called iCivics that offers "Lawcraft." *See* https://www.icivics.org/games/lawcraft.
[21] JUDY SCHNEIDER, CONG. RESEARCH SERV., RL30945, HOUSE AND SENATE RULES OF PROCEDURE: A COMPARISON SUMMARY (2008).

America's laws are not made for the "inattentive public"[22]; they are made "for those who show up."[23] Process is a polite name for what are no more than rules of the game.

If the people (and the states!) are lucky, they will learn about the laws before Congress adopts or rejects them. If they are luckier still, Congress will let them read draft laws before crucial votes are taken and compromise amendments negotiated. And if they are especially lucky, they will learn about these laws without having to look for them.

If the people (and the states) should be so fortunate as to learn that Congress is considering new laws, they will have no easy time entering into the discussion. Unless those with assured roles choose to involve them, the public has no role; the states have no role; government departments and agencies have no roles; and even the President of the United States has no role until after a bill is presented to him or her for approval. States are advised to get lobbyists to represent their interests. The people and the states have to watch – if they are lucky – while others decide for them.

3. *Uncoordinated Lawmakers of Federal Laws*

Who is to make laws?

A century ago Congress took off in the right direction. In 1913, coincident with giving up on Madison's state-appointed, expert Senate, Congress began to look for help in crafting laws.[24] In 1918 it created *two* Offices of Legislative Counsel – one for the House and one for the Senate. It recognized then what today is a truism: "the vast majority of members do not write, read, or even review legislative language."[25]

Since then, Congress has poured resources into legislative drafting (but hardly crafting) assistance. Congress engages thousands of people to help it. In speaking of support available to Congress today besides (1) the two Congressional Offices of Legislative Counsel (one for the House of Representatives and one for the Senate), there are (2) the Congressional Research Service (American Law Division); (3) legislative assistants to individual Senators and

---

[22] "R. Douglas Arnold explains why Congress sometimes responds to the interests of the diffuse public, which he terms the inattentive public, and does not solely spend its time legislating on behalf of the organized and attentive public. ESKRIDGE *et al., supra* note 17, at 91, *citing* R. DOUGLAS ARNOLD, THE LOGIC OF CONGRESSIONAL ACTION 68–71 (1990).

[23] JACK DAVIES, LEGISLATIVE LAW AND PROCESS IN A NUTSHELL xi (3d ed., 2007).

[24] *See* KENNETH KOFMEHL, PROFESSIONAL STAFFS OF CONGRESS, chap. XII, 183–200 (1977)

[25] Scott Levy, *supra* note 12, at 22.

Congressmen; (4) Congressional committee staffs; (5) agency or department Offices of Legislative Counsel and of Legislative Affairs. Looking to other legislative support there are: (6) the Congressional Office of Code Counsel (charged with maintaining the U.S. Code); and (7) Office of Management and Budget's (OMB'S) Office of Information and Regulatory Affairs (OIRA), responsible for reviewing regulations.[26]

There is little direction in how these law writers are to work together. Contemporary reports of their activities suggest there is no consistent practice. Cooperation is pretty much on a case-by-case basis. One veteran of Congressional drafting reports colorfully that lobbyist and Congressional staffs alike see the issue similarly: "the person with the pen wins."[27] So accustomed are Americans to such chaos that the mere suggestion of giving coordinating authority generally to OMB's OIRA or another executive branch agency is summarily dismissed as an example of legal scholarship falling flat "because of sheer impracticability."[28]

The result is patchwork laws with bits and pieces coming from everywhere. So here the Organisation for Economic Co-operation and Development finds the fundamental flaw in lawmaking in America: "the United States has found it extremely difficult to improve legislative quality and coherence. ... bills originate from many sources. The result is that there is less attention to quality of laws than to decisions authorised by those laws . . . ."[29] That is a polite way of saying, American laws often serve private interests rather than creation of a system of laws for common good.

The Offices of Legislative Counsel were not when founded, and still are not today, an ideal solution. They are expected to act as scriveners, not framers and maintainers. If it were to have been otherwise, there would be only one Office of Legislative Counsel and it would be tasked with conducting the

---

[26] State counterparts to the offices of legislative counsel are found in most states and state Law Reform Commissions in many. I discuss below in Chapter 11 on Federalism the Uniform Laws Commission and the American Law Institute. The focus of both organizations is on unifying state law across the country.

[27] Scott Levy, *supra* note 12, at 24, 25.

[28] RICHARD A. POSNER, DIVERGENT PATHS: THE ACADEMY AND THE JUDICIARY 45 (2016). And this is the same Judge Posner who characterizes the legal profession in all three of its major branches – the academy, the judiciary and the bar – as "complacent, self-satisfied" and laments that "critics of established practices typically are ignored." Richard A. Posner, *What is Obviously Wrong with the Federal Judiciary, Yet Eminently Curable, Part I*, 19 GREEN BAG 2D 187, 188, 194 (2016).

[29] ORGANISATION FOR ECONOMIC CO-OPERATION AND DEVELOPMENT, REGULATORY REFORM IN THE UNITED STATES 48 (1999).

passage of bills through Congress. More than a century after Congress first considered their creation, although their roles are much enhanced, the Offices of Legislative Counsel still have only supporting roles occasionally in a legislative process that lacks a leading role.[30]

So far as I am aware, lawmaking in state legislatures is similar. No one has moved framing of laws on a regular basis outside the legislatures. Reforms retain the prerogative of the legislators to frame the laws and thus deficiencies of responsibility-free legislation.

Today's Congressional Offices of Legislative Counsel labor under major disabilities:

(1) Their use is optional.[31]
(2) They lack expert information about how laws are presently working and they have no authority to obtain that information.[32]
(3) They have no authority to coordinate disparate Congressmen.
(4) So long as there are no controls on initiation of legislation and most bills are never seriously considered, they are necessarily overworked and understaffed.

To be sure, there have been strides toward better lawmaking. The last forty years are said by one veteran, Jarrod Shobe, to have seen the development of "modern" drafting. Congress has at its disposal "thousands of experts in various substantive areas whose jobs are to ensure that statutes are fully vetted and clearly drafted."[33] Shobe and others are bringing attention to a long-overlooked field. But less than empirical studies or theory of what has been done, a way must be found to put them to work in the future. It's time to learn from others.

---

[30] Reed Dickerson noted that "Those draftsmen who viewed themselves as part of the policy-making process appeared to be more enthusiastic and more committed than those draftsmen who were used, or who looked upon themselves, as mere 'technicians.'" Dickerson, *supra* note 12, 21 CATH. U.L. REV. at 723.

[31] A system requires that all parts fit together. Would you fly in airplane that you knew had 20 percent untested parts?

[32] *Cf.* Shobe, *Agencies, supra* note 12, at [5] (agencies have much more subject mater expertise than congressional staff, and because of this Congress is unable to draft legislation that is both detailed and effective without significant agency input").

[33] Jarrod Shobe, *Intertemporal Statutory Interpretation and the Evolution of Legislative Drafting,* 114 COLUM. L. REV. 807, 810–811 (2015); Jarrod Shobe, *Agencies as Legislators: An Empirical Study of the Role of Agencies in the Legislative Process,* 85 GEO. WASHINGTON L. REV. 451 (2017).

C. GERMANY'S LAWS ARE MADE BY SOMEBODY FOR EVERYBODY[34]

Bundestag Enacts Well-Crafted Laws[35]

1. *Germany's Fortitude: Ministerial Responsibility*

In Germany's federal system the ministry with competence of the subject matter has responsibility for initiating and maintaining laws in its areas of competence. This is part of what is known in German as the "*Ressortprinzip*," i.e., the principle of departmental responsibility.[36]

---

[34] *See* Armin von BOGANDY, GUBERNATIVE RECHTSETZUNG: EINE NEUBESTIMMUNG DER RECHTSETZUNG UND DAS REGIERUNGSSYSTEMS UNTER DEM GRUNDGESETZ IN DER PERSPEKTIVE GEMEINEUROPÄISCHER DOGMATIK (2000); R. DOUGLAS ARNOLD, THE LOGIC OF CONGRESSIONAL ACTION 68–71 (1990) (using the terms attentive and inattentive public).

[35] With the permission of the Deutscher Bundestag and of the artist, Bernd Kissel. Available at https://www.bundestag.de/leichtesprache/wasmachtderbundestag/gesetzgebung (last visited Dec. 18, 2016) https://www.bundestag.de/image/452040/16x9/570/321/6b3af74f2c010a96f79a9fc6a2de2255/YN/schmiedgross.jpg

[36] Hans-Georg Maaßen, § 8 *Gesetzesinitiativen der Bundesregierung, in* GESETZGEBUNG: RECHTSSETZUNG DURCH PARLAMENTE UND VERWALTUNGEN SOWIE IHRE GERICHTLICHE KONTROLLE 194–196 (Winfried Kluth & Günter Krings, eds., 2014); Meinhard Schroeder *in* 2 HERMANN VON MANGOLDT, FRIEDRICH KLEIN & CHRISTIAN STARCK, GG – KOMMENTAR ZUM GRUNDGESETZ, Art. 65, margin nos. 27–31, 1662–1664 (6th ed., 2010).

The *Common Ministerial Rules of Procedure (Gemeinsame Geschäftsord-nung der Bundesministerien*), hereafter referred to by their German acronym "GGO," set out in a scant 73 pages the fundamentals of the organization of the ministries, of their cooperation with each other and other constitutional organs, their external relations, and of how they are to cooperate in making laws. GGO § 1(2).[37]

The GGO provides a common organizational model for all federal government ministries. The atomic particle out of which ministries are built is the individual section (*Referat*). Sections are the initial decision-making author-ities in all matters assigned to them in their areas of competence. Subject areas define areas of competence among sections so that authority and responsibility are clearly visible. GGO § 7. Sections are small. They consist of a section chief (*Referatsleiter*) and at least four other co-workers (*Mitarbeiter*). GGO § 9.

As I discuss in the next chapter, German federalism assigns exceution of federal laws to state governments. The individual federal ministries and their sections are concerned with monitoring and guiding implementation of federal laws by the states. GGO § 3.

The ministries publish their organization plans each year. From the plans one can determine which ministry and which section is responsible for a particular law. The system reminds me of the maxim "everything in its place and a place for everything."

The GGO directs ministries to cooperate and sets out the basis for that cooperation. Key is the concept of "lead" ministry. More than seventy times, for example, an average of once a page, the GGO uses the term *federführend*, literally "leading pen," or "penholder" to describe which ministry or other entity is in charge of action.

The GGO directs that in matters involving multiple organizations, the lead organization must involve the others "in good time." It defines the lead organization to be "that which has the overall responsibility under the business assignment plan, or which is appointed in the case concerned." The GGO provides that in cases of doubt, the organizational section decides which organization is the leading one. For example, GGO § 15(1).

The GGO implements an idea that runs throughout German law: clarity in who is responsible for decisions.

---

[37] GEMEINSAME GESCHÄFTSORDNUNG DER BUNDESMINISTERIEN (Bundesministerium des Innern ed., 2011), *available at* http://www.bmi.bund.de/DE/Themen/Moderne-Verwaltung/ Verwaltungsorganisation/GGO/ggonode.html, available in English translation at http://ec.europa .eu/smart-regulation/impact/bestpracticesexamples/docs/de/jointrulesproceduresfederalministries .pdf.

2. *Process in Bundestag and Bundesrat*

The Bundestag with participation of the Bundesrat (Council of States) enacts all federal laws. They consult on enacting laws that have been written by others. Members do not themselves write laws.

The justification is practical. Members are not educated in formulating laws and it is not their task: they are political spokesmen and not statute experts. They work on putting political points into draft laws and amendments. "Parliament is the lawgiver, it is not the lawmaker, rather it is the receiver of draft laws."[38]

Authorization to Initiate Laws

Authorized to introduce laws in the Bundestag (the concept is that of *Gesetzesinitiative*) are the Federal Cabinet (*Bundesregierung*), members of the Bundestag (Parliament), and the Bundesrat (Council of States). In the cases of the Federal Cabinet and the Bundesrat, the right to initiate laws pertains to the institutions as such and not to their individual members. In the case of the Bundestag, the rules of the Bundestag require that at least 5 percent of its members, the minimum size of a parliamentary grouping (faction), join in the initiative.[39]

In a typical four-year legislative period, the Bundestag considers about nine hundred to one thousand bills, that is a tiny fraction of the 8,000–13,000 bills that the U.S. Congress receives in its much shorter two-year legislative cycle. Surely the limitations on introductions help keep numbers down. So, too, however, does the lead role that the Federal Cabinet takes in legislation in Germany's parliamentary democracy.

The 2009–2013 election period is typical. In all nine hundred bills were introduced in the Bundestag. Of these the Federal Cabinet accounted for 491, the Bundesrat (the Council of States) 131, and Bundestag members 278. The lead role is seen even more in the numbers of bills adopted. Of 506 adopted, 403 had been introduced by the Federal Cabinet, 14 by the Bundesrat, 77 by members of the Bundestag, and 12 by a combination of these. Moreover, sometimes members of the Bundestag, introduce bills at the behest of the

---

[38] Hans-Georg Maaßen, *supra* note 36, at 194 (Winfried Kluth & Günter Krings, eds., 2014) ("Das Parlament ist Gesetzgeber, es ist nicht der Gesetzesmacher, sondern vielmehr der Gesetzentwurfsabnehmer.")

[39] *See* Grundgesetz (GG) Art. 76(1); 2 Johannes Masing *in* 2 Hermann von Mangoldt, Friedrich Klein & Christian Starck, GG – Kommentar zum Grundgesetz, Art. 76, margin nos. 24–42, 2133–2138 (6th ed., 2010).

governing parties or the Federal Cabinet in parallel. Rarely are pure opposition-introduced bills enacted.[40]

Characteristic of bill enactment proceedings are those for bills introduced by the Federal Cabinet. The Bundestag describes the enactment process for them as follows:

1) Bills are drawn up by the specialised divisions in the relevant ministries, the subject matter of each bill being examined carefully, with information from the federal administration as well as from affected groups and other interested parties being taken into account.

2) Coordination between the individual ministries and in the cabinet helps ensure that bills conform to government policy and are also compatible with the scope and limits of the federal budget.

3) [The Federal Cabinet (*Bundesregierung*) submits the bill to the Bundesrat (Council of States) for comments only.] In the course of the initial deliberations in the *Bundesrat*, the *Länder* [States] can draw on their experience of executing legislation when discussing the bill and can make their interests known.

4) [The Federal Cabinet submits the bill to the Bundestag.] The first reading in the *Bundestag* serves to inform the Members of the German *Bundestag* and the public that a legislative process is underway with regard to a particular subject matter and is to be debated in Parliament.

5) The detailed examination of the bill during the committee stage makes it possible for additional expert opinions and political viewpoints to be taken into account; moreover, it allows the views of the parliamentary groups to be incorporated in the bill and is often an opportunity for Members from different parliamentary groups to compromise and reach agreement on the content of the bill.

6) The hearings held by the committees are an opportunity to gather additional information from experts in the subject area covered by the bill; they increase public awareness of the issues at stake and give members of the public and interested organisations another chance to participate in the discussions.

---

[40] Hans-Georg Maaßen, § 8 *Gesetzesinitiativen der Bundesregierung, in* GESETZGEBUNG: RECHTSETZUNG DURCH PARLAMENTE UND VERWALTUNGEN SOWIE IHRE GERICHTLICHE KONTROLLE 191, 192 (Winfried Kluth & Günter Krings, eds., 2014) (summarizing more detailed information 1990–2013 available *in* DEUTSCHER BUNDESTAG, DATENHANDBUCH, Kapitel 10, http://www.bundestag.de/dokumente/parlamentsarchiv/datenhandbuch/10/kapitel-10/475948 (visited Dec. 21, 2016).

7) During the second and third readings in the plenary of the *Bundestag*, arguments for and against the bill are debated and the opinions and arguments of the various parliamentary groups are put forward. Media coverage of the debate by newspapers, radio and television allows the public to form their own opinions on the bill on the basis of the arguments presented in the *Bundestag*. Finally, the bill is adopted.

8) [The bill is sent to the Bundesrat for consent. There are two different types of consent discussed below.] The *Bundesrat's* renewed involvement after the adoption of the bill by the *Bundestag* serves to underline the federal structure of the Federal Republic and the important role played by the *Länder* in terms of the execution of legislation and the consideration given to regional disparities.

9) Under certain circumstances, the Mediation Committee may be requested to convene. This serves to ensure that the conflicts between the Federal Government and the *Länder*, which are an inherent aspect of the federalist structure, are resolved by way of compromise and that legislation which is binding throughout the Federal Republic can be passed.

10) Finally, it is possible for a law to be referred to the Federal Constitutional Court for judicial review, although this is not a common or compulsory step. This review ensures that each of the previous stages has been carried out in keeping with the law, as otherwise the item of legislation in question might be declared invalid. There are thus legal safeguards in place to ensure that the legislative procedure is conducted in keeping with the rule of law and in accordance with the Basic Law [Constitution].[41]

Two major differences between U.S. legislative process and German enactment procedures stand out in this brief recapitulation: the Federal Cabinet provides draft laws (steps (1) and (2)) and the Bundesrat acts differently than just a second chamber (steps (3) and (8)). I turn to the Bundesrat now. In the following section 3 I consider writing of laws.

Bundesrat (Council of States)

The Bundesrat represents the states directly; each state has from three to six votes (and members) based on population. The members of the Bundesrat are

---

[41] SUSANNE LINN & FRANK SOBOLEWSKI, THE GERMAN BUNDESTAG – FUNCTIONS AND PROCEDURES – ORGANISATION AND WORKING METHODS: THE LEGISLATION OF THE FEDERATION [18TH ELECTORAL TERM] 138–139 (2015) [numbers and translations in brackets added] available in print and electronic forms at https://www.btg-bestellservice.de/ under *Basisinformation* as the English edition of *So Arbeitet der Deutsche Bundestag* [last visited Dec. 20, 2016].

themselves members of their states' governments and can be recalled by them.[42] The states cast their votes as blocs in the Bundesrat.

The Bundesrat participates in adoption of every law by the Bundestag, but unlike the United States Senate, how it participates depends upon the nature of the bill involved.

When the Federal Cabinet introduces a bill, it *must* first send it to the Bundesrat for review, i.e., step (3), before introducing it in the Bundestag. The Bundesrat has a limited number of weeks (three to nine) to take a position. If it does the Cabinet may respond within six weeks. Only then may it introduce the bill into the Bundestag. If the Bundestag adopts the bill, then the adopted bill is referred to the Bundesrat for its review.

Unlike in the United States, where there is only one form of assent – adoption by both Senate and House – the assents required of the Bundesrat are of two types. Which type applies depends on whether the bill substantially affects the interests of the states. If it does, then the Bundesrat must consent, i.e., it is a "consent law" (*Zustimmungsgesetz*). For all other bills the Bundesrat can object and block the bill, but the Bundestag can overrule the objection by an absolute majority vote of all its members, i.e., it is an "objection law" (*Einspruchsgesetz*). An alternative to battling votes is invocation of mediation procedures.

Bundestag Consideration
As just noted, before the Federal Cabinet submits the bill to the Bundestag, it has obtained the views of the states through the *Bundesrat*. It may amend its bill before submitting it to the Bundestag.

When the Federal Cabinet's draft bill lands in the Bundestag it is a well-crafted bill ready for immediate adoption. The Federal Cabinet, i.e., the representatives of the governing parties in the Bundestag, have accepted it as consistent with the governing parties' policies. As is discussed below in the next section, the Federal Ministry of Justice and Consumer Protection, the Federal Ministry of Interior, the National Regulatory Control Council and the Better Regulation Unit of the Federal Chancery, have reviewed the bill and approved it or have had least taken a position on it. The assumption is

---

[42]   Until adoption of the 17th amendment in 1913, the U.S. Constitution provided that state legislatures would choose their states' senators. Madison explained in *Federalist No. 62* the role of the States in the Senate: "It is recommended by the double advantage of favoring a select appointment, and of giving to the State governments such an agency in the formation of the federal government as must secure the authority of the former, and may form a convenient link between the two systems. ... No law or resolution can now be passed without the concurrence, first, of a majority of the people, and then, of a majority of the States."

that the Bundestag will adopt the bill. The bill is not one of thousands of proposed measures; it is one of perhaps one hundred. That's not a tiny number but it small enough to assure sensible consideration.

Once the bill arrives, the rules of the Bundestag (following the German acronym for the rules, GOBT), prescribe an ordinary course for it (with possibilities of exceptions) intended to assure that it is timely considered.[43]

Upon receipt there is a first reading and immediate referral to a committee. Only exceptionally upon request by the so-called Committee of Seniors of the Bundestag or by 5 percent of members present or by a parliamentary group, is the bill debated and then only on basic principles. No substantive motions are allowed. GOBT § 79. Only in special cases is the bill referred to more than one committee and then in that case, a lead committee is designated. Also exceptionally by a vote of two-thirds of members present, the bill may skip the committee referral and go immediately to the second reading. GOBT § 80.

Committees are obliged to attend to matters referred to them without delay. If after ten weeks of Bundestag sessions they have failed to report, 5 percent of members or a parliamentary group can require the committee to report. GOBT § 62.

Committee reports are to include the recommendation of the committee with the reasons therefore, the opinion of the minority, the comments of other committees and the comments of local authorities, and the main points of any hearings held. GOBT § 66.

After the committee report is submitted, the Bundestag proceeds to a second reading. It *may* include a general debate on the bill as a whole. It *must* include a general debate on each separate clause in the bill in the order in which the clause appears and must conclude with a debate on the preamble and title. A separate vote is taken on each clause as debated. GOBT § 81. During the second reading, and only then, votes on amendments to clauses under consideration may be taken. So long as the bill is being read in any clause, a motion to return the bill to committee is in order. GOBT § 82.

Usually, the Bundestag follows the recommendations of the committee because the political makeup of the committee mirrors the legislature itself. On the floor, individual legislators may propose amendments in writing. To

---

[43] RULES OF PROCEDURE OF THE GERMAN BUNDESTAG (2014 edition), available at https://www .btg-bestellservice.de/pdf/80060000.pdf (last visited Dec. 21, 2016, English translation of GESCHÄFTSORDNUNG DES DEUTSCHEN BUNDESTAGES (2014 edition), available at https://www .btg-bestellservice.de/pdf/10080000.pdf (last visited Dec. 21, 2016).

have a reasonable chance of success, they must call for specific changes in words, sentences, paragraphs, or other particulars of the bill.[44]

If no changes are made to the bill, the Bundestag may proceed immediately to the third and final reading. If there are changes, the process is repeated with the changes, the bill is read a third time, and then voted up or down. Amendments proposed at the third reading serve largely to make political points.[45] They are in order only with respect to previously amended clauses. GOBT § 85.

The result of this procedure is that the Bundestag usually makes only a few changes in the text of government drafts.[46] Because government drafts are usually well-crafted, legal certainty is enhanced. Last-minute compromises that produce incomprehensible statutory language in the United States,[47] I suppose, occur infrequently if at all in Germany. The receptivity of the Bundestag to Federal Cabinet bills leads some to wonder how democratic the process is. Defenders of the German approach argue that the mere possibility that the legislature, above all through its committees, will engage in a searching examination of the bill is sufficient to assure high quality and moderate drafting.[48]

3. *Cooperation Among Lawmakers*

In Germany, as in much of the modern world, laws are made by others for presentation to the legislature to review, adjust and adopt or to reject. The legislature, even with assistance, does not itself make laws. Generally, the government, that is what Americans call the executive branch, does.

The German Model of Pre-Parliament Law Crafting
In Germany, ministerial experts familiar with the substance of the laws have responsibility for initiating improvements and updates in substance. On their own initiative, or at the direction of the responsible minister or the Federal

[44] This paragraph is based on HANS SCHNEIDER, EIN LEHR- UND HANDBUCH at 80–89 (3d ed., 2002).
[45] This paragraph is based on *id.*
[46] *Id.* at 93 ("Das Parlament ist Gesetzgeber, aber nicht Gesetzesmacher [i.e., the parliament is the giver of statutes, but not the maker of statutes].").
[47] *Cf.* Peter M. Goodloe, *Simplification – A Federal Legislative Perspective*, 105 DICK. L. REV. 247, 249 (2001).
[48] Thomas Ellwein, *Gesetzgebung, Regierung, Verwaltung, in* HANDBUCH DES VERFASSUNGSRECHTS DER BUNDESREPUBLIK DEUTSCHLAND 1093, 1105 (Ernst Benda *et al.* eds., 1983); SCHNEIDER, *supra* note 45, at 93.

Cabinet, they prepare bills for submission to the Federal Cabinet for its submission to the Bundesrat and the Bundestag for approval and enactment.

The ministerial experts seek out the opinions of other ministries, of state and local governments, of professional associations and of the people likely to affected. They engage the Federal Ministry of Justice and Consumer Protection, the Federal Ministry of Interior, the Federal Chancery and the National Regulatory Control Council to control their work for quality in form and substance. After they have done all that work, the Federal Cabinet considers their proposal and then, if it accepts it, the lead ministry presents the bill and shepherds it through the Bundesrat and the Bundestag for enactment. In the last half-dozen four year legislative cycles, the Federal Cabinet has presented each four-year period from 320 to 537 bills with enactment rates running from about 80 to 90 percent.

America's law drafters with whom I have spoken shy from such a leading role. They fear that it would infringe on separation of powers. Yet the idea is not novel in America. More than a century ago an American Bar Association (ABA) special committee pointed to such methods as the basis for successful lawmaking abroad. It did not find assigning the tasks for making the laws to mean legislatures no longer legislated.

The ABA special committee's report explained that "careful legislation" assigns the "framing" of laws to the executive as an administrative function. Parliament legislates, not by itself drafting the laws, but by "its scrutiny, approval, amendment or rejection... [of] the drafting ... done by officials who are legally or technically trained, who have considerable experience in legislation can be held responsible by their superiors for errors and defects which expose the latter to Parliamentary criticism, censure or defeat."[49]

If at first this sounds strange to American ears, on reflection, it should not. In Part II above I show that in the 19th century American legislatures frequently engaged outside experts, not legislators, to compile, revise and codify existing laws. What is remarkable – perhaps even strange – is that legislatures did not similarly outsource the technical side of day-to-day lawmaking as other countries did. In what other field of legislative power do American legislators personally carry out their legislative powers?

Think about it. Congress has the power "to establish post offices," but no one expects Congressmen to design and build post office buildings – they don't have the skills. Congress has the power to declare war, but no one expects Congressmen to engage the enemy on the battlefield – they don't have

[49] *Report of the Special Committee on Drafting of Legislation*, REPORT OF THE THIRTY-SEVENTH ANNUAL MEETING OF THE AMERICAN BAR ASSOCIATION, HELD AT WASHINGTON, D.C., OCT. 20, 21, AND 22, 1914, 629, 634 (1914).

the knowledge or the strength. Why should Americans expect Congressmen to write laws when they lack the skills, knowledge and strength?

Readers who want to get an idea of how the German system of lawmaking works can do so in thirty minutes. They need only read "Chapter 6 Legislation" and its accompanying annexes of the *Joint Rules of Procedure of the Federal Ministries.*[50] At 26 pages and fewer than 11,000 words it's shorter than most elite law school law review articles and a whole lot more understandable! That America's law professors continue to pontificate about theory and empirical observation when a cure for America's lawmaking maladies is on the their desktops is academic malpractice.

The United States lags the modern world in addressing how to craft good laws. Its political scientists describe politics and process that are without showing processes that work. Lawyers, judges and legal academics take the outcomes of politics and legislative process as givens. Many write about statutory interpretation (Chapter 13), but few write about crafting better laws. Outside the United States scholars have developed a "science of legislation." In modern European English it is called "legisprudence"; in German it is *Gesetzgebungslehre.* For the last two decades the Organisation for Economic Co-operation and Development ("OECD") has given better lawmaking a practical boost with programs on better government.[51]

The German model of pre-parliamentary drafting has two principal stages: from idea to staff draft and from staff draft to cabinet draft. The staff draft presents to the Federal Cabinet, ministries and others a complete draft for discussion with supporting materials. The Federal Cabinet revises the staff draft with the goal of reaching political and text agreement to have a final Here I summarize the two.[52]

From Idea to Staff Draft (*Referentenentwurf*)

No matter where the idea for the law comes from,[53] it is the task of the competent section of the competent ministry and its section chief to prepare

---

[50]   Cited at note 37 *supra.*

[51]   Now under the umbrella of The Regulatory Policy Committee (RPC) and Regulatory Policy Division. *See* http://www.oecd.org/regreform/about-us.htm.

[52]   Unless otherwise noted the following two subsections are based respectively on sections III and IV of similar names (in German) in Maaßen, *supra* note 40, at 196–207 and 207–218. Maaßen notes that the United Kingdom and the European Union go a step further and first circulate a more general document ("Green" or "White" book) that describes the contemplated law in general terms. *Id.* at 201.

[53]   BUNDESMINISTERIUM DES INNERN (ed.), HANDBUCH ZUR VORBEREITUNG VON RECHTS- UND VERWALTUNGSVORSCHRIFTEN 50 (2d ed., 2012) (BMI HANDBOOK). If the section lacks for necessary subject-matter or legal expertise, the section chief is to seek temporary additional

a first draft. There are no special sections for legislation.[54] Two guides, or perhaps better directives since the GGO commands their use, tell section chiefs how to proceed:

- The Federal Ministry of the Interior provides a 187-page guide to the process to take from drafting through promulgation [hereafter BMI Handbook];[55]
- The Federal Ministry of Justice and Consumer production provides a 296 page guide for how to draft laws [hereafter BMJ Handbook].[56]

An early task of the section, perhaps first only after confirming its own jurisdiction, is to determine whether new rules are required and, if so, what form they should take, e.g., statute, regulation, some other government measure or self-regulation. BMI Handbook 51, 58; GGO § 43(1). It may be necessary or simply prudent for the section to get formal opinions from other sections both within and without the section's own ministry. In any case, sections are not to produce politically-motived, superfluous "shop window statutes."[57] On the other hand, where the impulse for a new law is external, the section should consider whether the draft should be expanded to encompass other areas of law.[58] When the ministry decides to pursue a draft, it is to notify the Federal Chancery.

Throughout the crafting of the draft, the section consults with other sections, ministries and offices. Direct and informal contacts at section levels, including in other ministries, to reach consensus are preferred to escalating issues up to higher levels and formal decisions. The former can be time-consuming. Escalation to ministerial or coalition level should be rare. BMI Handbook 71. Consultation at the section level can work well because across the federal government, section chiefs are generally knowledgeable about the laws they supervise and about their implementation.

Early on the drafting section is to establish a timetable for carrying out its work. There are no stated time expectations for preparation of the first draft for internal circulation, although several months or more seems usual. The section may be advised to consult already at this time with others in government outside

---

forces for the section. The section chief is to assign most of the drafting work to subordinates. Maaßen, *supra* note 36, at 200.

[54] BMI Handbook 42.   [55] *Id.*

[56] Bundesministerium der Justiz (Ed.), Handbuch der Rechtsförmlichkeit: Empfehlungen zur Gestaltung von Gesetzen und Rechtsverordnungen (3d ed., 2008).

[57] Maaßen, *supra* note 36, at 197 ("*Schaufenstergesetze*").   [58] *Id.* at 198.

its section. It may convene a committee of outside experts. If the costs are substantial, the section needs approval of the Federal Chancery.

Already in the early stages the section is to consider the "regulatory impacts" such a law might have. These impacts include public and private and on federal, state and local governments. The lead ministry is to collect necessary information. Other ministries provide support in calculating impacts. GGO § 46.

Now the section gets to write a first draft. This is said to be "the most beautiful part of the whole lawmaking process," for the section members can exercise their professional skills to the fullest.[59] Drafts must follow the instructions of the BMJ Handbook as to language. The draft consists of more than the language of a statute. It must include a cover page and an explanatory memorandum, which explains the law, the need for it, its regulatory impact, and effects on existing laws listing other laws necessarily to be amended. These later will have to accompany the draft sent to the Bundesrat and the Bundestag. GGO § 43. These should be well done, for as the BMI Handbook counsels, otherwise later, when time in short, many changes may be necessary. BMI Handbook 62. My mnemonic for this: "well begun is half done" (Mary Poppins).

The section then presents the draft (it is still not a staff draft) to the ministry's leadership for approval. Approval means that the ministry endorses the draft as a staff draft and that everyone in the ministry has been consulted. The ministry notifies the Federal Chancery that it will now circulate the staff draft with the intention of submitting a draft to the Federal Cabinet for adoption within as little as two months.

From Staff Draft to Federal Cabinet Draft

Upon the adoption of the section's draft as a ministry staff draft, matters accelerate. The ministry may now circulate the staff draft throughout the federal government, to Bundestag members, to state and local governments, to trade associations and interest groups and to the public. Now the GGO and the BMI Handbook set out expected times for consideration and review. Section chiefs who in the preparatory stages were more thorough then may be glad for their earlier thoroughness. Now what before was more-or-less an academic exercise in drafting the best law possible, becomes an object of politics. This is when "better lawmaking" is challenged. Those in the know remark wryly "how rational, intelligent and satisfactory work on laws could be, if only the evil actors of

---

[59] *Id.* at 203.

politics and parties, trade associations and interest groups, agencies and courts, and newspaper editors and television producers did not exist."[60]

Appendix 6 to the GGO lists fourteen federal ministries and one federal commission the section is to involve if the staff draft affects matters in their areas of competencies. The section is to obtain consent of ministries consulted, even if that means escalating consent up in the ministry's hierarchy. The draft the lead ministry presents to the Federal Cabinet should not require the Cabinet to decide among ministries. Such decisions can be necessary, particularly when a coalition government is in power, as each ministry is assigned to one party or another.

Although the section potentially has to consult all federal ministries affected in their areas of competency, it *must* consult three: the Federal Ministry of Finance, the Federal Ministry of the Interior and the Federal Ministry of Justice and Consumer Protection. These three ministries serve as quality controls for a government of laws. In some areas of their responsibility they have a legal or practical veto over the staff draft.

The Federal Ministry of Finance has the strongest *de jure* role. Its minister under the Rules of the Federal Cabinet can in matters of financial importance object to any cabinet decision. The objection can be overridden only by a majority vote of the entire cabinet joined by the Federal Chancellor at a meeting where the Finance Minister is present. GOBReg § 26(1).

The Federal Ministry of Interior has close to as strong a position *de facto* in some areas. It is to review the section draft for: (a) whether its norms are constitutional; (b) whether norms of the laws proposed fit without contradiction within the existing legal system; (c) effects on local governments (d) effects on data protection; (e) effects on the civil service; and (f) effects on sports. To carry out the constitutional review, it is authorized to obtain an expert opinion from a constitutional law specialist. GGO Annex 6 § 2.

So too does the Federal Ministry of Justice and Consumer Protection have a practical veto over its review areas, namely, constitutionality and whether the norms of the laws proposed fit without contradiction in the existing legal system. It too can commission an expert opinion on constitutional law. In the constitutional review, the Federal Ministry of the Interior has the leading role with respect to the frame of government and the Federal Ministry of Justice and Consumer Protection with respect to basic rights. BMI Handbook 116.

The GGO specially treats the Federal Ministry of Justice and Consumer Protection's "examination of draft legislation in accordance with systematic

---

[60] *Id.* at 203.

and legal scrutiny." It assures the Ministry "sufficient time to examine and debate" the issues that arise. GGO § 46. The Ministry is organized so that particular sections specialize in the subject matters they review. BMI Handbook 118. The sections review not for substance, but for compliance with the forms for laws set out in the BMJ Handbook. The Ministry also has a Unit for Legal Drafting Support that reviews the staff draft – possibly already earlier – for "linguistic accuracy and comprehensibility." GGO § 42(5).

The individual ministries are allowed four weeks for review or, on application, eight. If issues arise that cannot be conveniently dealt with by written exchanges, the chief of the lead section can conduct formal negotiation meetings among the ministries concerned. These may be individual meetings or group meetings.[61]

The National Regulatory Control Council is to be given an opportunity to review and comment. Its opinion is to be attached to the draft. GGO §§ 42(1), 45(2). The National Regulatory Control Council is an independent review body that examines drafts to reduce bureaucracy, make better laws, and estimate costs.

The section is also to involve the state, national associations of local authorities, and expert communities and associations. GGO § 47. In view of future review by the Bundesrat, this review is quite important. In the case of the other bodies, although formally weak, how great their involvement is depends on how important the theme is to the group concerned and the willingness of the ministry to accept such "*Lobbyarbeit.*"[62]

The lead ministry itself or the Federal Chancery is to determine whether to distribute the staff draft to the public generally. GGO § 48(1).[63] If the staff draft is distributed to anyone outside the Federal Government, then it must be sent to all parliamentary group's offices, to the Bundesrat, and, on request, to members of the Bundestag and to members of the Bundesrat.

This brief exposition of German lawmaking, when coupled with the exposition in Chapter 9, demonstrates only that the German system might work and seems to as applied. An analysis of its components must await further examination. It would be beyond the scope of this book. But this exposition should whet Americans' appetite for such an exploration. That the American system fails miserably is common knowledge.

---

[61] *Id.* 210–212 (giving descriptions and suggestions for conducting such meetings.)

[62] *Id.* 212–213.

[63] A recent survey by *Abegordnetwatch.de* reports that only two ministries, albeit the two that account for the most laws, the Federal Ministry of Justice and Consumer Affairs and the Federal Ministry of Finance, routinely publish staff drafts. The other ministries do so only in individual cases.

11

Federalism and Localism

It is obviously impracticable in the Federal Government of these States to secure all rights of independent sovereignty to each, and yet provide for the interest and safety of all. Individuals entering into society must give up a share of liberty for the interest and safety of all. . . .

In all our deliberations on this subject, we kept steadily in our view that which appears to us the greatest interest of every true American, the consolidation of our Union, in which is involved our prosperity, felicity, safety – perhaps our national existence.

George Washington (1787)[1]

A. LAWS ARE FOR PEOPLE AND NOT FOR SOVEREIGNS

The *people* of the United States of America and the *people* of Germany each founded federal states to better govern themselves, i.e., the *people*. Sovereigns did not create states to rule.[2]

The United States in 1787 was among the world's first modern experiments in federalism. So successful has it been in bringing people together that grammatically in English, United States has become a singular noun instead of a plural one: *E pluribus unum*, the national motto, "out of many one," has

---

[1] George Washington, *Letter of the President of the Federal Convention, Dated Sept. 17, 1787, to the President of Congress, Transmitting the Constitution*, 2 DOCUMENTARY HISTORY OF THE CONSTITUTION OF THE UNITED STATES OF AMERICA 1787–1890, 1, 2 (Dept. of State, 1894).

[2] U.S. CONST. Preamble ("We the People of the United States . . ."); BASIC LAW FOR THE FEDERAL REPUBLIC OF GERMANY Preamble ("the German people, in the exercise of their constituent power . . ."). *See* JOHN ORDRONAUX, CONSTITUTIONAL LEGISLATION IN THE UNITED STATES: ITS ORIGIN, AND APPLICATION TO THE RELATIVE POWERS OF CONGRESS, AND OF STATE LEGISLATURES 116 (1891) ("we find that the idea of government with us has never been identified with the State as an independent institution, but always with the people as the primary source of sovereignty. Government with us, therefore, is a question of agency only. Our conception of it begins with the consent of the people, and not with that of a State already organized.")

transformed the national language.[3] So admired has American federalism been abroad, that many states of the world today, both large and small, are federal states, e.g., Austria, Belgium, Brazil, Canada, Germany, India, Russia.[4]

Similarly, the world has discovered the benefits of local self-government or simply, localism. Known in the European Union (EU) as the principle of subsidiarity, there it is explained as the ideal that "decisions are taken as closely as possible to the citizens . . . ."[5] That fits the United States, too.

Both the United States and Germany pledge allegiance to the principle of a government of laws. This chapter is concerned with a narrow aspect of federalism and localism: how can federalism and localism compromise a government of laws?

In outward form, American and German federalism and American and German localism are similar. Constitutions allocate lawmaking authority between federal government and state governments; some allocations are exclusive and others are concurrent. Federal laws are supreme: they preempt state laws. State laws control self-government by localities. In Germany, there is an added twist: European Union law is supreme to German law.

In the United States federalism and localism undermine the goal of a government of laws.[6] In Germany, they do not. In the United States, citizens confront a cacophony of conflicting laws and commands. In Germany, they do not. Why is there such a difference in fulfilling the goal of a government of laws?

In the United States federalism carries trappings of the 18th century: the idea that component federal states must be sovereigns and that these separate sovereigns must have separate laws. Judges protect legislative autonomy of state governments. They determine how federal and state laws coexist. They permit, indeed promote, conflicting laws. They accept conflicts that confound citizens as necessary to federalism."[7] They extend the federal idea and conflicts by analogy to local self-government.

---

[3]   United States remains plural in other languages, *e.g.*, German, *die Vereinigten Staaten* and French, *les états unis.*

[4]   Whether the European Union is a federal state, a confederation of states, or a union *sui generis* is open to debate, but whichever it is, in lawmaking it raises many of the same issues of coordination that federal states and confederations of states raise.

[5]   Treaty on the Functioning of the European Union (Treaty of Lisbon), Protocol (No. 2) on the Application of the Principles of Subsidiarity and Proportionality.

[6]   Gerhard Casper, *The United States at the End of the "American Century": The Rule of Law or Enlightened Absolutism?*, 4 WASH. U. J.L. & POL'Y 149, 169 (2000) ("We suffer from too many layers of government with concurrent jurisdiction. Preemption is nonexistent in too many areas of law. Where just a single level of government would busily produce a regulatory maze, complex and internally inconsistent enough to employ legions of handholding lawyers, we allow two, three, or four to have their say.").

[7]   See text and notes at note 27 *infra.*

In Germany, federalism is no longer linked to preserving petty princes and the autonomy of their principalities.[8] The Constitution, the federation and the states – rarely judges – determine when federal laws preempt state laws. Preemption is total and not partial. Concurrent lawmaking competencies of federation and state are not permitted to produce conflicting commands. No matter who makes the laws, no matter who carries out the laws, citizens are confronted with only one law and one law applier for a single matter. There is a government of laws.

I show in this chapter how America's federalism undermines a government laws while Germany's federalism does not.

B. THE UNITED STATES OF AMERICA'S FIFTY-ONE-PLUS LAWS FOR FIFTY-ONE-PLUS GOVERNMENTS

E pluribus unum – First Proposal for Great Seal of the United States (1776) Pierre Eugene du Simitiere for Franklin, Adams & Jefferson

1. *Historical Note*

In 1787 both the modern concepts of federalism and of a government of laws were novel. Since each was not yet in place, it would have required Herculean effort to put the two together. In 1787 the rulers of the states in the South wanted

---

[8] *See* ARTHUR B. GUNLICKS, THE *LÄNDER* AND GERMAN FEDERALISM 356 (2003).

to protect their investment in slaves. Long after a bloody Civil War ended slavery debates on federalism remain fixated on "states' rights" and protecting the states (and their rulers) to the detriment of citizens' claims to a government of laws.

With the end of slavery and of the Civil War, the issue of state-to-state law coordination burst on the legal scene with vigor and urgency.[9] For the last quarter of the 19th century the need for uniformity of law was a major issue in legal circles.[10] Hannis Taylor, later President of the Alabama State Bar, succinctly stated the generally felt need for national uniformity in wide areas of law:

> as the country has grown older, the people of the United States as a whole – in their personal relations – have become far more united and harmonious than have the various systems of State law by which their commercial and domestic interests are largely governed. For this reason the constant conflict of law which daily arises in the affairs of our national life, with its consequent uncertainties, is becoming an evil so serious that it must soon pass from the hands of the theorist to those of the practical statesman.[11]

Although there was little open opposition to more uniform law, there was no strong commitment to it either and no consensus on how best to achieve it. Should the federal government impose uniform law?[12] Or should the states voluntarily adopt uniform laws?[13]

---

[9]   See, e.g., *The Proper Limits between State and National Legislation and Jurisdiction*, 15 AM. L. REV. 193 (1867).

[10]   See, e.g., THE AMERICAN BAR ASSOCIATION, CALL FOR A CONFERENCE; PROCEEDINGS OF CONFERENCE, FIRST MEETING OF THE ASSOCIATION; OFFICERS, MEMBERS, ETC. 16 (1878) (Article I of the first American Bar Association Constitution in 1878 made "uniformity of legislation throughout the Union" a first purpose of the Association); *Note*, 17 AM. L. REV. 789, 789 (1883) ("scarcely an anniversary bar meeting takes place without suggestions being put forth in favor of uniformity or unification throughout the whole country in some department of the law").

[11]   HANNIS TAYLOR, AN INTER-STATE CODE COMMISSION (1881), *reprinted in* REPORT OF THE ORGANIZATION OF THE FIRST, SECOND AND THIRD ANNUAL MEETINGS OF THE ALABAMA STATE BAR ASSOCIATION 210 (1882).

[12]   Some argued that the federal government already had sufficient authority. *See, e.g.*, George Merrill, *An American Civil Code*, 14 AM. L. REV. 652 (1880) (contending that if the federal government made full use of existing powers, it could enact laws that states would copy); Nathaniel A. Prentiss, *Unification of the Law*, 16 AM. L. REV. 307, 317 (1882); William Reynolds, *A National Codification of the Law of Evidence*, 16 AM. L. REV. 1, 12–13 (1882); Seymour D. Thompson, *Abuses of Corporate Privileges*, 26 AM. L. REV. 169, 196–197 (1892); *Note*, 17 AM. L. REV. 768, 768 (1883) (arguing that the Constitution should be amended to empower Congress to enact broader legislation); *Note*, 18 AM. L. REV. 868 (1884).

[13]   See, e.g., WILLIAM L. SNYDER, THE GEOGRAPHY OF MARRIAGE OR LEGAL PERPLEXITIES OF WEDLOCK IN THE UNITED STATES chs. xx–xxi (1889) (arguing that ways should be found to encourage the states to adopt uniform legislation and proposing a "prohibitory amendment" to encourage states to adopt uniform laws, *e.g.*, prohibiting state laws from outlawing divorce); Peter Winship, *The National Conference of Commissioners on Uniform State Laws and the International Unification of Private Law*, 13 U. PA. J. INT'L BUS. L. 227, 232 (1993) (citing and quoting 1903 PROCEEDINGS OF THE NATIONAL CONFERENCE OF COMMISSIONERS ON UNIFORM STATE LAWS 29) (remarks of Amasa M. Eaton).

2. America's Federalism: Many Sovereigns – Many Laws

The Constitution of the United States of America was path-breaking. It creates a federal government of limited powers and sets out what those powers are. It prescribes that where the federal government has legislative power, federal law is supreme.[14] It provides that powers not delegated to the federal government are reserved to the states.[15] In a few instances, it prohibits states from certain conduct.[16] But beyond these terse clauses, it says little about how state and federal governments are to coordinate laws and administration.

Here lies, said Supreme Court Justice Antonin Scalia, "one of the most troublesome complexities of a federal system." It is "the necessity of deciding upon the separate competencies – and resolving conflict between the separate competencies – of the federal government and the separate component states."[17]

Early in the history of the United States the Supreme Court stepped into the void left by the laconic Constitution. Through the mechanism of constitutional review the Court sought to distinguish legislative powers that are exclusive to the federal government from those that are concurrent with the states. It tried to craft a method for coordinating state and federal legislation. Its chosen method of constitutional review measures both state and federal legislation for compliance with the Constitution's allocation of legislative powers.[18] Federal legislation must be based on a power enumerated in the Constitution; state legislation must not be preempted by federal legislation or by an unexercised grant of legislative power of the federal government.

The Supreme Court through constitutional review has tried to demark exclusive and concurrent competencies of federal and state governments. The task of drawing clear lines has proven impossible to achieve. In the very case where the Supreme Court first attempted to measure state statutes against federal legislative power, *Gibbons v. Ogden*, Justice William Johnson presciently warned that the competing powers "meet and blend so as scarcely to admit of separation."[19] Some scholars believe that workable judicial rules of decision have not and cannot be attained.[20] The Court's decisions suffer from a lack of political legitimacy: how

---

[14] U.S. CONST. art. VI.   [15] U.S. CONST. amend. X.   [16] U.S. CONST. art I, § 10.

[17] Antonin Scalia, *Plenary Speech, in* FEDERALISM IN A CHANGING WORLD – LEARNING FROM EACH OTHER (Raoul Blindenbacher & Arnold Koller, eds.) 539 (2003).

[18] *Cf.* Ernest A. Young, *The Rehnquist Court's Two Federalisms*, 83 TEX. L. REV. 1, 9 (2004) (noting that most "of federalism" is not founded in the "spare text" of the Constitution, but in subsequent judicial development).

[19] 6 U.S. (9 Wheat.) 1, 32 (1824).

[20] *See, e.g,* Grant S. Nelson & Robert J. Pushaw, Jr., *Rethinking the Commerce Clause: Applying First Principles to Uphold Federal Commercial Regulations but Preserve State Control Over Social Issues*, 85 IOWA L. REV. 1, 7 (1999).

legislative competencies should be shared among federal and state governments is quintessentially a political question subject to being revisited over time.

The situation, Justice Scalia concluded, is "not ideal." He counseled against leaving the outcome to be decided by the "speculations of a court regarding constitutional and statutory intent." Better, he advised, is "clarity" in the constitutional provisions pertaining to the separate competences and in legislation in affected areas.[21]

Parallel Governments

American federalism establishes, parallel to state courts and state government offices, separate federal courts and federal government offices.[22]

The Constitution does not require such parallel structures; while it establishes one Supreme Court, it merely authorizes Congress to create lower federal courts.[23] James Madison would have liked the Constitution to mandate lower courts, but had to settle for what is called the "Madisonian compromise."[24] This system of dual competencies complicates coordination and causes "a tremendous waste of judicial and private resources."[25] This waste is accepted, with resignation, as a necessary evil.[26] Justice Felix Frankfurter famously dismissed it as "the price of our federalism.[27]

3. *State-to-State Coordination in America*

Differences in laws among the states are a major source of legal uncertainty in modern America. While the uncertainty is real, the differences in substantive

---

[21] Scalia, *Plenary Speech, supra* note 17, at 547.

[22] Guido Calabresi, *Federal and State Courts: Restoring a Workable Balance*, 78 N.Y.U. L. Rev. 1293, 1294 (2003); Ugo Mattei, *A Theory of Imperial Law: A Study on U.S. Hegemony and the Latin Resistance*, 10 Ind. J. Global Legal Stud. 383, 410 (2003).

[23] U.S. Const. art. III, § 1.

[24] Wythe Holt, *"To Establish Justice": Politics, The Judiciary Act of 1789, and the Invention of the Federal Courts*, 1989 Duke L.J. 1421, 1461 (1989). Madison argued that "Confidence cannot be put in the State Tribunals as guardians of the National authority and interests." *Id. See also* Michael G. Collins, *Article III Cases, State Court Duties, and the Madisonian Compromise*, 1995 Wis. L. Rev. 39 (1995).

[25] Coury v. Prot, 85 F.3d 244, 249 (5th Cir. 1996).

[26] *Id.* at 249; *accord* Noel v. Hall, 341 F.3d 1148, 1159 (9th Cir. 2003). Professor Daniel J. Meador, a comparativist, did not accept it. He raised three possible solutions. One would be "essentially the German structure:" abolish the federal district courts. Another I would call essentially the solution of German legislation: eliminate duplicating jurisdictions. Meador thought neither likely to be adopted owing to vested interests that would block legislation. He proposed a third possibility: merge state and federal courts. Daniel J. Meador, *Transformation of the American Judiciary*, 46 Ala. L. Rev. 763, 776–782 (1995).

[27] Knapp v. Schweitzer, 357 U.S. 371, 380 (1958) (Frankfurter, J.). *See generally* Paul E. Peterson, The Price of Federalism (Brookings Institution 1995).

laws generally are not. Often they are only differences in details. With the abolition of slavery, at the latest, the United States rejected the idea that different states could have fundamentally different social, economic, or political systems. Social hot-button issues, e.g., abortion and gay rights, have not permitted different solutions for different states to endure long.

The importance of differences among state rules as a cause of legal uncertainty, however, grew dramatically with the creation of a national market in the 19th century. When the Constitution was adopted in 1789, coordination of the laws of the several states was not a major issue.[28] Travel in 1789 was difficult;[29] commerce among states was limited.[30] But within a century, all that had changed and merchants carried on trade in every state.[31] The effect of this revolution in commerce on the legal system was a common topic in legal literature.[32]

In the first half of the 19th century the issue of state-to-state rule coordination was nascent. It was overshadowed by the overriding question of slavery.[33] Justice Story worried that the nation legally was "perpetually receding farther and farther from the common standard."[34] He sought coordination through a preeminent role for federal law and through an efficient choice of law system. He authored important court decisions enhancing the status of federal law,[35] commentaries that might form the basis of uniform law,[36] and the first book

[28] Maintaining two separate societies – one slave and one free – was.
[29] Leonard A. Jones, *Uniformity of Laws Through National and Interstate Codification, in* REPORT OF THE SIXTH ANNUAL MEETING OF THE VIRGINIA STATE BAR ASSOCIATION 157, 157–159 (1894), *reprinted in* 28 AM. L. REV. 547, 547–548 (1894) (noting that in 1789 it took nearly a week to travel between Boston and New York, the two leading commercial centers of the day).
[30] Edward A. Moseley, *Interstate Commerce, in* 1 1795–1895: ONE HUNDRED YEARS OF AMERICAN COMMERCE 25, 30 (Chauncey M. DePew ed., 1895).
[31] Jones, *supra* note 29.
[32] *See, e.g.*, Note, 17 AM. L. REV. 789, 789 (1883). "When our constitution was framed, the steamboat, the railway, and the magnetic telegraph were not dreamed of." *Id.*
[33] *Cf. The Proper Limits Between State and National Legislation and Jurisdiction*, 15 AM. L. REV. 193, 194 (1867). Code-oriented law reformers concentrated on laws within a single state rather than on harmonizing laws among several states. They assumed that successful efforts in one state would be copied in other states. *See* GRANT GILMORE, THE AGES OF AMERICAN LAW 26 (1977). Montana, California, and the Dakota Territory adopted the codes that David Dudley Field prepared for New York.
[34] Joseph Story, *Progress of Jurisprudence, An Address Delivered Before the Members of the Suffolk Bar, at Their Anniversary, at Boston (Sept. 4, 1821),* 1 AM. JURIST & LAW MAG. 1 (1829) and *in* THE MISCELLANEOUS WRITINGS OF JOSEPH STORY 198, 213, 224 (William W. Story ed., 1852).
[35] *See, e.g.*, Swift v. Tyson, 41 U.S. 1 (1842) (federal common law to govern diversity cases); DeLovio v. Boit, 7 F. Cas. 418 (C.C.D. Mass. 1815) (No. 3776) (applying admiralty jurisdiction to navigable inland waterways). *See generally* TONY ALLAN FREYER, HARMONY & DISSONANCE: THE SWIFT & ERIE CASES IN AMERICAN FEDERALISM (1981).
[36] GILMORE, *supra* note 33, at 27–28.

ever in English on conflicts of law.[37] He thought it "hopeless to expect that any greater uniformity [would] exist in the future."[38]

At the close of the 19th century, the United States tried both approaches. The federal government adopted the Interstate Commerce Act of 1887 and the Sherman [Antitrust] Act of 1890.[39] Several states in 1892 founded the National Conference of Commissioners for Uniform State Law (recently renamed the Uniform Law Commission) and charged it with drafting laws that they might voluntarily adopt in fields such as divorce law and commercial law. This approach was mixed: preferably, uniform laws by voluntary state action, but where necessary, federal laws without constitutional amendment, if federal powers were sufficient.[40]

The optimism of the founders of the National Conference was palpable; its first report asserted: "It is probably not too much to say that this is the most important juristic work undertaken in the United States since the adoption of the Federal constitution."[41] Thirty years later, the founders of the American Law Institute were no less optimistic. Its founders compared their task to that faced by the lawyers of Justinian's day who "produced the codification and exposition of that law which has been the main foundation of all the law of the civilized world

---

[37] *See generally* JOSEPH STORY, COMMENTARIES ON THE CONFLICT OF LAWS, FOREIGN AND DOMESTIC (1834).

[38] *But see, e.g.*, FREYER, *supra* note 35, at 20 (citing JAMES SULLIVAN, THE HISTORY OF LAND TITLES IN MASSACHUSETTS 353 (1801)); JOHN WILLIAM WALLACE, THE WANT OF UNIFORMITY IN THE COMMERCIAL LAW BETWEEN THE DIFFERENT STATES OF OUR UNION: A DISCOURSE DELIVERED BEFORE THE LAW ACADEMY OF PHILADELPHIA (Nov. 26, 1851) (calling for uniform rules).

[39] Both of these relied on the commerce clause of the U.S. Constitution, art. I, § 8, cl. 3. Already in the first five years after the Civil War, the federal government adopted ill-fated national laws based on specific grants of authority: bankruptcy in 1867 that relied on the bankruptcy clause, art. I, § 8, cl. 4; and trademarks in 1870 that relied on the patent and copyright clause, art. I, § 8, cl. 8. The 1867 bankruptcy act was repealed without replacement in 1878; the 1870 trademark act was held in 1879 to have exceeded constitutional authority and was replaced in 1881 by a more limited law based on the commerce clause.

[40] *See, e.g.*, AMERICAN BAR ASSOCIATION REPORT ON UNIFORM STATE LAWS, *excerpted in* 25 AM. L. REV. 832, 834 (1891); Elbert C. Ferguson, *The Necessity of Uniform Legislation*, 4 AM. LAWYER 492, 493 (1896); Francis B. James, *Commercial Aspect of Uniform State Laws*, 5 MICH. L. REV. 509, 509–511 (1907); F. J. Stimson, *National Unification of Law*, 7 HARV. L. REV. 92, 92 (1894). *See also* W. BROOKE GRAVES, UNIFORM STATE ACTION, A POSSIBLE SUBSTITUTE FOR CENTRALIZATION vii–viii (1934) (discussing the urgent need for uniformity and surveying various forms of uniform state action as a "practical workable alternative" to federal action).

[41] Jones, *supra* note 29, at 169, *reprinted in* 28 AM. L. REV. 547, 557 (1894). Stimson's enthusiasm was common. *See, e.g.*, Alton B. Parker, *Uniform State Laws*, 19 YALE L.J. 401 (1910); Walter George Smith, *The Progress of Uniform Legislation*, 1911–12, 24 GREEN BAG 457, 465 (1912) (President's Address delivered at the 22nd Annual Meeting of Commissioners on Uniform State Laws, Milwaukee, Aug. 21, 1912).

except the law of the English-speaking people."[42] Former Secretary of State Elihu Root, honorary chairman of the organizing committee, hoped that the Institute's work might become "the *prima facie* basis on which judicial action will rest."[43]

Neither Uniform Laws nor Restatements have produced the national legal unity that the founders of the two organizations hoped for.[44] Even if their comparisons to the Constitution and to Justinian are dismissed as wishful thinking, the founders surely would be disappointed by the results. In the first century of its existence, the National Conference proposed approximately 200 uniform acts. Only about ten percent of these acts were adopted by as many as forty states; more than half were adopted by fewer than ten states.[45]

Since Restatements are not proposed for legislative adoption, their adoption necessarily is piecemeal. In practice, they are only sometimes the prima facie basis for judicial analysis that Root sought. Long time member of the ALI Council, Gerhard Casper, then President of Stanford University, at its anniversary meeting told the members: "While in these 75 years the Institute has no doubt brought order and rescue to the common law, as Benjamin Cardozo hoped it would, it has not prevented – to quote the title of a 1994 book – "the death of common sense" in the American legal system. The subtitle of Philip Howard's very successful tract (it sold 500,000 copies)

---

[42] Report of the Forty-Sixth Annual Meeting of the American Bar Association Held at Minneapolis, Minnesota, Aug. 29, 30 and 31, 1923, 90 (1923); William Draper Lewis, *The American Law Institute*, 25 J. Comp. Legis. & Int'l L. 25, 28 (1943). The founding document is Report of the Committee on the Establishment of a Permanent Organization for Improvement of the Law Proposing the Establishment of an American Law Institute (1923).

[43] Arthur L. Corbin, *The Restatement of the Common Law by the American Law Institute*, 15 Iowa L. Rev. 19, 22 (1929); *see also* Herbert F. Goodrich, *The American Law Institute to Date*, 8 Or. L. Rev. 3, 7 (1928).

[44] *See* A. Brooke Overby, *Our New Commercial Law Federalism*, 76 Temp. L. Rev. 297, 299 (2003). The limited success of their work is demonstrated by the less than complete success of their best-received collaborative project, the U.C.C. Notwithstanding adoptions in all states, it has not created uniform law. States have adopted different versions of key provisions; in some instances, the U.C.C. even offers alternative provisions. Amendments have been difficult first to agree upon within the two bodies and then difficult to get approved by state legislatures at consistent paces. Since the U.C.C. is state law, there is no single court that can interpret it authoritatively. Overby notes that people interested in uniform law are likely to turn to the federal government to get uniformity. *Id.* This has proven more successful, but creates its own issues of rule reliability, since federal law may not well coordinate with state law. *Id.*

[45] James J. White, *One Hundred Years of Uniform State Laws: Ex Proprio Vigore*, 89 Mich. L. Rev. 2096, 2103–2105 (1991). For semi-official histories of the Uniform Laws Commission, see Robert A. Stein, Forming a More Perfect Union: A History of the Uniform Law Commission (2013); Walter P. Armstrong, A Century of Service: History of the National Conference of Commissioners of Uniform State Laws (1991).

was : "How law is suffocating America."[46] The ALI, now nearing the 100th anniversary of its existence, has not delivered the oxygen to resuscitate American law.[47]

4. Localism in America: 90,056 Lawmakers

America's localism raises similar issues as federalism, multiplied by one or two thousand (!) while adding a new one: amateurism. Local governments can be tiny. Their laws may be deficient technically or even bizarre. Their laws may be executed strangely or illegally. Both local lawmaking and local law execution are subject to little supervision by state authorities.

According to the 2012 Census of Governments there were then in the United States 90,056 local government broken down as follows:

General Purpose Governments	
County	3,031
Sub-County – Municipal	19,519
Sub-County – Town or Township	16,360
Special Purpose Governments	
Special Districts	38,266
Independent School Districts	12,880
All Local Governments	90,056

---

[46] Gerhard Casper, *Address*, 75TH ANNUAL MEETING A.L.I. ANNUAL MEETING SPEECHES 65, 69–70 (1998). On the early history of the ALI by its first leaders, see William Draper Lewis, *History of the American Law Institute and the First Restatement of the Law, in* RESTATEMENT IN THE COURTS: PERMANENT EDITION 1 (1945); HERBERT F. GOODRICH & PAUL A. WOLKIN, THE STORY OF THE AMERICAN LAW INSTITUTE 1923–1961 (1961).

[47] In the interest of full disclosure, I report that I have been a member of the ALI all that time. On the failures of American federalism in achieving uniform law, see James R. Maxeiner, *United States Federalism: Harmony without Unity, in* FEDERALISM AND LEGAL UNIFICATION: A COMPARATIVE EMPIRICAL INVESTIGATION OF TWENTY SYSTEMS (D. Halberstam & M. Reimann, eds., IUS GENTIUM: Comparative Perspectives on Law and Justice Vol. 28, 2013).

Since the 38,910 governments (counties, municipalities and townships) have and generally do exercise lawmaking authority, the possibilities for conflicting laws and perplexing law-abiding people are substantial.[48]

While the problems of American localism for lawmaking parallel those of the federal-state relationship, their origins are different. The U.S. Constitution anticipates that both federal and state governments have lawmaking authority. But unlike the federal German Constitution,[49] it has nothing to say about local governments. Localities have lawmaking authority only by grace of the states.[50] Originally, the states followed what was called "Dillon's Rule." That rule strictly limited municipal powers to those powers expressly granted by the legislature, necessarily implied from the grant or indispensable to the object and purpose of local government. It resolved all doubts in favor of finding that the local government did not have power.[51]

Beginning in the latter part of the 19th century, states began extending to localities municipal home rule. Often, in addition to authority to administer their own affairs, states granted authority to legislate. In the 20th century most states reversed Dillon's Rule. The United States Supreme Court went so far as to conceptualize local government as a "miniature State within its locality."[52] Today localism is characterized as "the intrastate analogue of federalism in American constitutional law."[53] Most states apply a rule that "all powers are granted until retracted."[54] This includes authority to issue

[48] 2012 CENSUS OF GOVERNMENTS, TABLE 2, *available at* http://factfinder.census.gov/faces/
tableservices/jsf/pages/productview.xhtml?src=bkmk. By way of example, in Bronxville NY
where I live, I pay taxes to seven local governments, three general governments, County of
Westchester, Town of Eastchester and Village of Bronxville (all make laws) and four special
purpose governments Bronx Valley Sewer District, Westchester County Waste District,
Eastchester Fire District, and Bronxville Union Free School District. Other than the
peculiarity that I live in both Westchester (County) and Eastchester (Town) at the same time,
my situation is not unusual. How much special districts make law is not known to me.

[49] *See, e.g.*, ARTHUR B. GUNLICKS, LOCAL GOVERNMENT IN THE GERMAN FEDERAL SYSTEM
(1986) (discussing, *inter alia*, that constitution's guarantee of the right of localities to administer
their own affairs).

[50] Frank J. Goodnow, *Municipal Home Rule*, 10 POL. SCI. Q. 1, 1 (1895).

[51] *Id.* at 2 (quoting 1 JOHN F. DILLON, COMMENTARIES ON THE LAW OF MUNICIPAL
CORPORATIONS 145 (4th ed., 1890)). Dillon was president of the American Bar Association
1891–1892 and co-sponsor of Field's code resolution at the 1886 ABA Annual Meeting.

[52] D.C. v. John R. Thompson Co., 346 U.S. 100, 108 (1953); *see* Richard Briffault, *Our Localism:
Part I – The Structure Of Local Government Law*, 90 COLUM. L. REV. 1, 10 (1990) ("an
imperium in imperio, a state within a state, possessed of the full police power with respect to
municipal affairs and also enjoying a correlative degree of immunity from state legislative
interference"); Wayne A. Logan, *The Shadow Criminal Law of Municipal Governance*, 62
OHIO ST. L.J. 1409, 1421 (2001).

[53] Daniel B. Rodriguez, *Localism and Lawmaking*, 32 RUTGERS L.J. 627, 627 (2001).

[54] Briffault, *Our Localism, supra* note 52, at 10; *see also* CAL. CONST. art. XI, § 7. Under the
California Constitution a "city may make and enforce within its limits all local, police, sanitary,

laws[55] as significant as creating criminal offenses and prohibiting trade practices.[56] But broad lawmaking power in local governments diminishes legal certainty. While it might be possible, if difficult, to keep track of the laws of fifty-one lawmakers, no one, not even a huge corporation, could cost-effectively follow the laws of 38,910 general lawmakers, not to mention 51,406 special governments

Granting local governments free lawmaking authority was not inevitable. Nineteenth-century jurists, such as Professor Frank J. Goodnow, the "father" of American administrative law, pointed the way to an alternative approach based on administrative powers of local governments to carry out state laws and to be subject to state administrative oversight. Such an approach would have enhanced rule determinacy, not only by denying local governments "local legal autonomy," but also by subjecting their actions to state oversight.[57]

States could limit the powers of local governments to administering their own affairs and curtail or eliminate altogether legislative authority. States could circumscribe with particularity what legislation local governments are allowed to adopt, and some do to some extent. Additionally, states could automatically review legislation adopted by local governments. Moreover, states could provide local governments with model laws and qualified draftsmen. While other countries with strong local governments do such things,[58] American states largely do not. Nor have they provided other effective mechanisms to coordinate and control the quality of the municipal rules that they have made possible. The principal device they have used is judicial review similar to that which federal courts apply to potential conflicts between state and federal legislation. State courts examine whether local legislation is consistent with state legislation or if state legislation preempts the field.[59] That review is subject to the same difficulties that federal review has discussed above. There are few opportunities to test local laws before they come into force.[60] Yet today local governments are acting globally and there are those who urge less rather than more control.

---

and other ordinances and regulations not in conflict with general laws." Richard Briffault, *Local Government and the New York State Constitution*, 1 HOFSTRA L. & POL'Y SYMP. 79, 99 (1996); Logan, *supra* note 52, at 1421.

[55] Briffault, *Our Localism*, *supra* note 52, at 15.   [56] *See, e.g.*, Logan, *supra* note 52.

[57] David J. Barron, *Reclaiming Home Rule*, 116 HARV. L. REV. 2255, 2301–2309 (2003). Goodnow's studies of foreign approaches surely must have influenced his proposals); *see, e.g.*, FRANK J. GOODNOW, COMPARATIVE ADMINISTRATIVE LAW (1893) (having much in common with the German approach).

[58] *See, e.g.*, GUNLICKS, *supra* 49, at 382.   [59] Briffault, *Our Localism*, *supra* note 52, at 17–18.

[60] *See, e.g.*, Kenneth A. Stahl, *Local Home Rule in the Time of Globalization*, 2016 BRIGHAM YOUNG U. L. REV. 177.

C. THE FEDERAL REPUBLIC OF GERMANY'S ONE LAW FOR
SEVENTEEN GOVERNMENTS

"Consistent Law" (*Einheitliches Recht*) Former Kaiser Wilhelm Monument in Hamburg (1908)

1. Historical Note

In 1789 as the sun was rising on the American Republic and the French
Revolution, the word "Germany" referred to the anachronistic "Holy Roman
Empire of the German Nation." "Germany" consisted of 1789 mostly mini-
and micro-states (*Kleinstaaten*), a ragbag collection of 314 kingdoms, duchies,
electorates, bishoprics, principalities, duchies, free imperial cities and 1,475
knightly estates.[61] In 1806 Napoleon set the sun on the Holy Roman Empire of
the German Nation. Not until 65 years later did night end and the sun rise on
a federal German nation-state.

---

[61] ARTHUR B. GUNLICKS, THE *LÄNDER* AND GERMAN FEDERALISM 16 (2003).

From 1806 to 1871 Germany consisted of some 39 disconnected and unco-ordinated states. The laws of those states were anything but consistent. In 1844 Hunt's *Merchants' Magazine* reported that a traveller in Germany "with one revolution of the wheels of his post chaise" changed "the government, consti-tution, laws and monarch under whom he lives." The traveler found "no single attribute of sovereignty wanting in the smallest of territories through which he passed. Above all, was he called upon to recognize the existence of the right of independent government, which consists in the offering of constant annoying impediments to the change of place of man and merchandize."[62]

Soon after Germany united in 1871 it turned to codifying its laws on a national basis. In 1873 it amended its constitution to give the federation competence over core areas of law. While it was not until 1896 that it adopted a national civil code, in the meantime it introduced national codes of civil procedure, criminal law, criminal procedure, and commercial law.

German federalism today is not a way to perpetuate principalities. It is a way to allocate governing – lawmaking, executing and judging – in a way that promotes the common good of all the people. It seeks to deal with problems at the most effective level. In so doing, it has preserved local autonomy in a way centralized states do not. Berlin does not dominate Germany the way Paris dwarfs France or London lords over the United Kingdom. German states, such as Bavaria and North Rhine Westphalia, have as independent voices in Germany as Texas and California do in the United States. New York City and Washington rule the United States more than Frankfurt and Berlin rule Germany.

Today's Federal Republic of Germany consists of sixteen states. It has sixteen state governments and one federal government. Neither states nor federal government exist for the sake of their rulers or state sovereignty. States are not possessions of princely houses; the federal government is not a gathering of princes. States and the federal government exist to serve their citizens. The federal government serves all people nationwide, and the state governments the people of their separate states.

2. *German Federalism: Many Governments – One Law*

Article 20 of the German Constitution provides that Germany is a federal state. The same article provides that Germany is a government of laws

---

[62] *Germany and the Commercial Treaty of Berlin*, 11 HUNT'S MERCHANTS' MAGAZINE 491, 492 (1844).

(*Rechtsstaat*).[63] The latter principle is held to require that federal and state laws not contradict each other, that is, the principle of non-contradiction of the legal system (*Widerspruchsfreiheit der Rechtsordnung*).[64] The Constitution is written to avoid conflicts of laws by assuring that only federal or only state law governs any particular matter.

The German Constitution shares power to legislate among the federation and sixteen states. The federation is a government of enumerated powers. Article 70 provides that the states have the right to legislate when the Constitution does not confer legislative power on the federation. Article 71 provides that when federal power is exclusive, states may legislate only if a federal law expressly allows them to do so. Article 72 deals with preemption of state laws when the federation exercises concurrent powers of legislation. Article 73 lists 16 areas of exclusive legislative power of the federation. Article 74 lists thirty areas of legislative powers concurrent between the federation and the states.

As in the United States, in Germany issues of allocation of powers arise more often in areas where the federation has concurrent power than in areas where federal power is exclusive. Unlike the United States Constitution, however, which is silent on how to allocate legislative powers in cases of concurrent competence, and which gap courts have tried to fill once laws are in place, the German Constitution addresses the issue head on. It provides a method that fosters democratic legislative resolutions of allocation issues before laws enter into force and that avoids later judicial determinations. The idea is that concurrent legislative competencies need not cause conflicts of laws.[65]

The rule of allocation in cases of concurrent powers is that of Article 72(1): if the federation uses its power to legislate, that use displaces state law existing and future. The sought-after effect is that citizens need mind only one law: state law where the federation has not acted and federation law where it has.

Germany's federalism sweeps away many of the problems that confound American laws. It provides a government of laws where the people

---

[63] Article 20 does not use the term *Rechtsstaat*, but it is the principle of many provisions that provide for what is universally so termed.

[64] BVerfGE 98, 106, 118f. *See* Helge Sodan, *Das Prinzip der Widerspruchsfreiheit der Rechtsordnung*, 1999 JURISTENZEITUNG 864; Reiner Schmidt & Lars Deiderichsen, *Anmerkung*, 1999 JURISTENZEITUNG 37; ULRICH SMEDDINCK, INTEGRIERTE GESETZESPRODUKTION 125 (2006) (noting criticism); REINHOLD ZIPPELIUS & THOMAS WÜRTENBERGER, DEUTSCHES STAATSRECHT: EIN STUDIENBUCH 113 (32d ed., 2008).

[65] HANS SCHNEIDER, GESETZGEBUNG 119 (3d ed., 2002).

can know the law that governs them. Germany's federalism does not have the "troublesome complexities" that plague America's federalism.[66] It embodies Justice Scalia's dreams of "clarity" of constitutional allocation; it does not rely on "speculations of a court" to allocate powers between federation and states.[67] Conflicting laws rarely arise because the Constitution allocates lawmaking competencies between the federation and the states.[68] Courts are spared political decisions of allocation of powers among federal and state governments. Although in Article 31 the German Constitution has a supremacy clause similar to Article VI of the U.S. Constitution, it is little used, since the allocation rules of Articles 70 to 74 are followed.[69]

Adjustments beyond that allocation are made from time-to-time by constitutional amendment. The most substantial changes made to date in the German Constitution – even more substantial than those made in effecting unification of East and West Germany in 1990 – were those made in 2006 to adjust federal and state relations in the "federalism reform."[70]

Article 72 might seem to permit the federation to displace the states altogether, since in many areas of law the federation has concurrent power to legislate. It has not worked out that way: other provisions of the Constitution preserve a vibrant federal system. These provisions look less to preserving a core of sovereignty for independent state action, and more to sharing responsibility for governing. Three factors stand out: Article 72 limitations, Bundesrat consent and state execution of federal laws.

Article 72 Limitations

The basic rule of paragraph (1) allowing federal legislation is limited by paragraphs (2) and (3). Article 72(2) allows federal regulation only "if and to

---

[66] *See* text at notes 17–21 *supra.*   [67] *Cf.* Scalia, Plenary Address *supra* note 17, at 546–547.

[68] Reinhold Zippelius & Thomas Würtenberger, Deutsches Staatsrecht 114 (32d ed., 2008).

[69] Wolfgang März, Bundesrecht bricht Landesrecht: Eine staatsrechtliche Untersuchung zu Artikel 31 des Grundgesetzes 108–112, 204 (1989).

[70] *See* Hans Meyer, Die Föderalismusreform 2006: Konzeption, Kommentar, Kritik (2008); Ines Härtel, *Die Gesetzgebungskompetenzen des Bundes und der Länder in Lichte des wohlgeordneten Rechts in* 1 Handbuch Föderalismus – Föderalismus als demokratische Rechtsordnung und Rechtskultur in Deutschland, Europa und der Welt 527 (Ines Härtel, ed., 2012). *See also* Katrin Gerstenberg, Zu den Gesetzgebungs- und Verwaltungskompetenzen nach der Föderalismusreform (2009); Marcus Hahn-Lorber, Parallele Gesetzgebungskompetenzen (2012). An encyclopedic treatment of federalism in Germany and in comparative perspective is the four volume *Handbuch Föderalismus,* just cited.

the extent" necessary for maintaining legal or economic unity or establishing equivalent living conditions.[71] Article 72(3) in six specific areas (all but one related to lands) allows states to adopt laws that deviate from federation laws.

Bundesrat (Council of States) Consent

As discussed in the previous chapter, the Bundesrat (Council of States) is a constitutional institution separate from the Bundestag (legislature). It represents the states; its delegates are members of the state governments. It participates in making laws. For laws that have a particular effect on the states, its affirmative consent is required (*Zustimmungsgesetze*). For other laws it has a right of objection (*Wiederspruchsgesetze*) that the Bundestag can overcome. This means that federal laws can displace state laws only if a majority of states agree to the displacement.

State Execution of Federal Laws

Unlike the American Constitution, the German Constitution distinguishes law executing powers from lawmaking powers in allocation of powers between federation and states. Article 83 provides that unless the Constitution otherwise provides, the states (and impliedly, not the federation) "shall execute federal laws in their own right." Article 84(3) provides the "Federal Government shall exercise oversight to ensure that the *Länder* execute federal laws in accordance with the law." Articles 85 and 86 provide two deviations from the general rule of Article 83: the former allows state execution of federal laws on "federal commission;" the latter provides for "federal administration" of federal laws. For purposes of this book, these differences need not be addressed.

State execution of federal laws not only serves to preserve vibrant federalism, it protects the people's interest in a government of laws. Citizens confront only one government, not two.[72]

3. *State-to-State Coordination in Germany*

Although German states can have laws that differ from one other without violating the no contradiction principle, rarely do they. The principal vehicle

---

[71] That determination is subject to control by the Federal Constitutional Court in both respects, i.e., if federal action is needed and to what extent. *Pieroth, in* Hans D. Jarass & Bodo Pieroth, GRUNDGESETZ FÜR DIE BUNDESREPUBLIK DEUTSCHLAND KOMMENTAR Art. 72, p. 816, margin no. 23 (12th ed., 2012).

[72] REINHOLD ZIPPELIUS & THOMAS WÜRTENBERGER, DEUTSCHES STAATSRECHT § 14, V. Bundesrecht und Landesrecht, 152 (32d ed., 2008).

of coordination is adoption of a federal law – of course, with the consent of the states and to be implemented by the states. From the founding years of the 19th century federation, this was the route to uniform law that a previously disunited Germany so longed for. Thus, today in most areas laws are federal but administered by the states.[73] Hence German federalism is sometimes called "unitary federalism." Germans expect from a government of laws and get a single law that they can follow.[74] Germans do not pay "the price of our federalism" that Americans do.[75]

The vision of states as laboratories of innovation, so common in the United States, is met with in Germany. Federalism inspired constitutional revisions in 1994 and 2006 sought to encourage them. Yet experiments in lawmaking (it may be different in administration) remain unusual and are most often projects of larger states.[76]

That states implement federal law has not produced substantial complaints of disparate enforcement. In anticipation of the federalism reform of 2006, a blue ribbon panel composed of members of both houses of parliament, the government, the state legislatures, associations of municipalities, and experts extensively examined the role of federalism in Germany. In the resulting hundreds of pages of commission reports and other submissions, nowhere is there any significant criticism founded on legal uncertainty in allocation of lawmaking and law executing authority.[77]

Double-jurisdiction of both federal and state law, such that they could govern in different ways, is in principle foreign to the German Constitution.[78] The very constitutional article that entrusts states with the responsibility of implementing federation law, Article 84, checks their exercise of it. Its paragraph (2) provides that the "Federal Government, with the consent of the Bundesrat, can issue general administrative rules. Paragraph (3), as already quoted, directs the Federal Government to exercise oversight, and further

---

[73] Jochen Rozek in 2 HERMANN VON MANGOLDT, FRIEDRICH KLEIN & CHRISTIAN STARCK, GG – KOMMENTAR ZUM GRUNDGESETZ, Art. 70, margin no. 3, 1805 (6th ed., 2010).

[74] REINHOLD ZIPPELIUS & THOMAS WÜRTENBERGER, DEUTSCHES STAATSRECHT § 14, V. Bundesrecht und Landesrecht, 152 (32d ed., 2008).

[75] *See* text and note 27 *supra.*

[76] Jürgen Adam and Christoph Möllers, *Unification of Laws in the Federal System of Germany, in* FEDERALISM AND LEGAL UNIFICATION (D. Halberstam & M. Reimann, eds., Ius Gentium, Comparative Perspectives on Law and Justice, Vol. 28, 2014).

[77] *Kommission von Bundestage und Bundesrat zur Modernisierung der bundesstaatlichen Ordnung.*

[78] Jochen Rozek, in 2 HERMANN VON MANGOLDT, FRIEDRICH KLEIN & CHRISTIAN STARCK, KOMMENTAR ZUM GRUNDGESETZ, Art. 70, margin no. 1, p. 1804, margin, no. 11, p. 1812 (6th ed., 2010).

authorizes the Federal Government to send commissioners to the states to realize that oversight. Paragraphs (4) and (5) enable the federal government if dissatisfied with state implementation to call on the Bundesrat to undertake measures to compel compliance and, if dissatisfied with Bundesrat action, to challenge it in the Federal Constitutional Court.

In practice compulsory measures are unnecessary. The ministries of the federal government are involved in day-to-day coordination without compulsion.

The states do continue to exercise powers of their own independent of the federation and there they legislate extensively. Particularly noteworthy are police law, education and government organization.[79]

4. Localism in Germany: 10,092 Local Administrations Execute One Law[80]

There are 10,092 municipalities in Germany. Article 28(2) of the German Constitution provides that "Municipalities must be guaranteed the right to regulate all local affairs on their own responsibility." The Constitution guarantees self-administration (*Selbstverwaltung*), but not self-legislation. Municipalities are authorized to issue ordinances regulating their own affairs, such as the terms of use of municipal facilities, access to public utilities and the like. The states supervise the municipalities and can overturn these modest ordinances.[81]

---

[79] Adam & Möllers, *supra* note 76, at 242.

[80] https://de.statista.com/statistik/daten/studie/1254/umfrage/anzahl-der-gemeinden-in-deutschland-nach-gemeindegroessenklassen/

[81] The rights of municipalities are set out in each state's *Gemeinde Ordnung* (Communities Regulation). *See* Dieter Haschke, *Local Government Administration in Germany*, GERMAN LAW ARCHIVE, http://germanlawarchive.iuscomp.org/?p=380

12

Constitutional Review

We are not final because we are infallible, but we are infallible only because we are final.

Justice Robert H. Jackson (1953)[1]

A. VALIDATING LAWS SEAMLESSLY

A government of laws consists of valid laws, i.e., laws adopted by the people consistent with their constitution. Validating those laws should affirm and not undermine the people's reliance on laws.

As with federalism, so too with constitutional review: the United States was there first. Constitutional review was born February 24, 1803 when the United States Supreme Court decided the case of *Marbury v. Madison*.[2] In that case the Court held that it would determine validity of legislation under the Constitution. The United States Constitution does not establish judicial review of constitutionality: consistent with the Constitution, each branch of government could decide for itself whether its actions comply with the Constitution.

Through the 19th century the United States stood alone among the nations with a robust constitutional review. But in the 20th century most countries adopted some form of independent constitutional review. Constitutional review became recognized as an important buttress of a government of laws. It holds men accountable to laws, when it measures laws against constitutions.

---

[1] Brown v. Allen, 344 U.S. 443, 540 (1953) (Jackson, J. concurring).
[2] 1 Cranch (5 U.S.) 137 (1803). *See* 24. FEBRUAR 1803: DIE ERFINDUNG DER VERFASSUNGSGERICHTSBARKEIT UND IHRE FOLGEN (Werner Kremp, ed., 2003).

The world reveres constitutional review. Over one hundred countries have some form of constitutional review. Americans celebrate constitutional review as one of the country's greatest strengths and finest innovations for the world. They commemorate *Brown v. Board of Education* (1954). Constitutional review kills bad laws.

Of course, Americans know that constitutional review sometimes misfires: it kills good laws and revives bad ones. They condemn *Dred Scott v. Sanford* (1857) and *Plessy v. Ferguson* (1896). They accept a few bad decisions as inevitable: a few misfires are a small price to pay for an otherwise excellent institution that supports a government of laws.

Although the world adopted the American idea of constitutional review, most countries did not adopt the American method of review. In the American plan, ordinary courts review constitutional validity as part of ordinary judicial process of applying law. Any court can put a law out of force. The American plan is termed "diffuse review."

Most countries separate constitutional review from ordinary judicial process.[3] Many have separate constitutional courts independent of ordinary courts. In these countries only constitutional courts can put laws adopted by the legislature out of force. This alternative to the American plan is termed "concentrated" review.

The process of constitutional review should integrate validating laws seamlessly into the legal system. It should support lawmaking without undermining law applying. Constitutional review has features of both lawmaking and law applying.

By tying constitutional review to judicial process diffuse review weakens both constitutional review and judicial process. Concentrated review can strengthen both. In this chapter I show how.

The American people did not choose diffuse review over concentrated review. Their judges chose it for them. Were the people to start from scratch today, they would seriously consider European methods.[4]

---

[3] *See generally* Gustavo Femandes de Andrade, *Essay, Comparative Constitutional Law: Judicial Review,* 3 J. CONST. L. 977 (2001). For a then current enumeration, see ARNE MAVČIČ, REPORT, SOME COMPARATIVE COMMENTS TO THE INTRODUCTION OF CONSTITUTIONAL REVIEW IN THE STATE OF PALESTINE, European Commission for Democracy Through Law (Venice Commission), Council of Europe Document CDL-JU (2008)026 (2008).

[4] *See* LARRY D. KRAMER, THE PEOPLE THEMSELVES: POPULAR CONSTITUTIONALISM AND JUDICIAL REVIEW 251 (2004).

B. THE AMERICAN PLAN: THREE FULL INSTANCES

"Sorry your legislation was ruled
unconstitutional, Ferguson, but it
was fun while it lasted!"

Used under license from Cartoonstock, Inc.

1. *The American Plan of Constitutional Review*

The American plan of constitutional review incorporates constitutional review
into ordinary lawsuits. Unlike continental plans, there are no separate constitutional proceedings or constitutional courts. In any lawsuit in any court any
party can challenge the constitutional basis of another party's claim. The court
treats the constitutional argument as it would any other legal argument.
Constitutional process is part of ordinary legal process and is not distinguish-
able from it.

The court's decision of a state or federal constitutional issue is comparable
to its decision of any other point of law. The judgment of the court of first
instance binds only the parties before it. Usually as a matter of right, parties
may, but need not, appeal that decision on grounds of legal error to a higher
court.[5] An intermediate appellate court reviews the decision of the court of
first instance. Its decision of a point of law, including one of constitutional
validity, binds courts subordinate to it and parties to the case. Usually if
permission is granted, parties may appeal that decision of the court of intermediate appeals on grounds of legal error to the appropriate state or federal
supreme court. The supreme court decides the case as it sees fit. That might,
but need not, resolve the constitutional issue. The supreme court's decision

---

[5] American appeals generally do not extend to issues of fact. *See* JAMES R. MAXEINER, FAILURES
OF AMERICAN CIVIL JUSTICE IN INTERNATIONAL PERSPECTIVE, at Chapter 7 (2011).

binds courts subordinate to it and parties to the case. Decisions in the lawsuit of the intermediate appellate court and of the supreme court formally bind only courts subordinate to the appellate courts and the parties to the lawsuit. They bind other agencies of government and other non-parties only indirectly.

The United States Constitution does not address judicial review. This explains why in the United States ordinary courts in ordinary process conduct constitutional review. Early in the history of the Republic in the case of *Marbury v. Madison* (1803) the United States Supreme Court asserted its authority to review the constitutional validity of laws as an incident to its decision of cases determined in ordinary judicial process.

In *Marbury v. Madison*, Chief Justice John Marshall reasoned, that it is the acknowledged duty of judges in ordinary judicial process to determine what the law is. That means, he continued, "Those who apply the rule to particular cases, must of necessity expound and interpret the rule. If two laws conflict with each other, the courts must decide on the operation of each." Since the United States Constitution is, by its terms, the supreme law of the land, Marshall concluded that the constitution must govern the case, and not the ordinary act.[6]

In *Marbury* the Marshall Court did not consider or seek to establish a separate system of constitutional review. For the most part, American consti-tutional review takes place in ordinary process. When that process has changed (for example, the creation of the federal courts of appeal in 1891), constitutional review has moved with it.

Ordinary judicial process has several important features that impact consti-tutional review including, *inter alia*:

- Decision requires a dispute between parties;
- The law applied is in force;
- A party can raise any relevant issue;
- A court is required to resolve every issue properly raised; and
- Parties control the scope of the decision by their choices in bringing or not bringing appeals.

In the context of ordinary litigation, these consequences are not remarkable. But when applied to constitutional review they raise fundamental issues about the suitability of ordinary process for constitutional review. Ordinary process and constitutional review in most cases have different aims. Ordinary process

---

[6]   1 Cranch (5 U.S.) 137, at 177–178.

is an act of law application; constitutional review in validating laws participates in an act of law creation.

Ordinary process is for the parties before the court. They control the scope of the decision. The public has no right to participate. The decision is usually backward looking. It addresses how existing law applies to determined facts.

Constitutional review is for all the people. All the people are interested in the outcome. All the people, through their legislators, participated in the adoption of the law reviewed. The decision is primarily forward looking. It is concerned with whether law will apply to facts not yet known.

I show in the balance of this section how the American inclusion of constitutional review in ordinary process (2) undermines constitutional review, (3) distorts ordinary process, and (4) embitters choice of judges.

2. *Wizards' Work: Zombies, Doppelgänger, Spells and Riddles*

It is of the essence of a government of laws that the people can know and rely on the law. Constitutional review is intended to assure that. In large measure, it does. But the American plan of constitutional review undercuts those intentions. It imports into constitutional review characteristics of American legal methods that are at odds with a well-functioning system of constitutional review. Here I only identify these problems. I do not seek to evaluate their severity. I address four that I whimsically name zombie laws, doppelgänger decrees, common-law spells, and judicial riddles. They refer respectively to uncertain application of laws while review is pending, local federal courts putting federal laws out of force, the Supreme Court's criteria for review, and the Supreme Court's confusing decisions.

Zombie Laws (Laws that Are "Mostly Dead but not "All Dead")

The American plan of constitutional review creates "zombie" laws: laws that are not dead but are not quite alive either. Ever since the Supreme Court began striking down laws regularly in the mid-19th century, Americans have feared the "evil" that results: "The universal uncertainty inevitably prevailing in the interval between the passage of a law of doubtful constitutionality and the final adjudication upon it . . . ."[7]

What are the people to do with an undead law? Do they follow it, at a possibly great cost that later proves pointless, or do they ignore it and risk prosecution or unpreparedness when it eventually does take effect?

---

[7] Henry Reed, *Some Late Efforts at Constitutional Reform*, 121 N. AM. REV. 1, 20 (1875).

Zombie laws are not a minor problem. The Affordable Care Act ("Obama-care") was a "zombie law" from the day President Obama signed it (March 23, 2010) until at least the day that the Supreme Court upheld most (but not all) of it (June 28, 2012).[8] During those two years and three months businesses, states and people – nearly everyone – made decisions based on their best guesses whether the law would be upheld. No one can know now what the costs of those uncertainties were then, but they must have been in the billions of dollars.[9]

Zombie laws have been with Americans for a long time. Already President Franklin D. Roosevelt saw how his political adversaries could use wholesome constitutional review to turn his New Deal laws into zombies by serving up the American plan's three instances of "judicial review." "It is not difficult," he said, "for the ingenuous to devise novel reasons for attacking the validity of new legislation or its application. . . . [N]o important statute can take effect – against any individual or organization with the means to employ lawyers and engage in wide-flung litigation – until it has passed through the whole hierarchy of the courts."[10]

The risk of zombie laws is present whenever there is a lag in time between a law's adoption and its review. To avoid zombie laws, constitutional review must occur before laws enter into force. Some systems provide for that; others seek to approach it. Although efforts are made to achieve the same result, the American tradition of a case or controversy, when coupled with the full three instances of review, makes zombie laws practically inevitable.

Not only high visibility laws become zombie laws: more mundane statutes do, too. They can retain that status for years because of America's diffuse review. Parties raise constitutional questions in ordinary courts at the lowest level, where the constitutional issues may be avoided. Even when consti-tutional issues are addressed in the lower courts, appeals may end short of the Supreme Court. When that occurs, a law may be upheld in one

---

[8]   National Federation of Independent Business v. Sebelius, 567 U.S. 519 (2012). Soon thereafter it was again made a zombie when an issue of statutory interpretation threatened to kill it. *See* King v. Burwell, 576 U.S. *** (June 25, 2015). When President Trump took office, his Republican Party made it a zombie again, threatening to repeal it and then, maybe replace, maybe repair, no one quite knew which, especially the Party itself.

[9]   For all the costs of that delay, President Obama could not object to following the rules. The American plan is so assumed to be a part of American law – although only created by custom – that it has been practically unassailable for nearly a century. President Franklin D. Roosevelt's personal day of infamy was March 5, 1937: the day he criticized the American plan. For even suggesting a change, Roosevelt was reviled for "court-packing."

[10] Franklin D. Roosevelt, Speech, *Judicial Branch Reorganization Plan*, Feb. 5, 1937, *reprinted in* 1937 THE PUBLIC PAPERS AND ADDRESSES OF FRANKLIN D. ROOSEVELT 51 (1941).

jurisdiction, but struck down in another. Since many judges have authority to invalidate laws, and the Supreme Court decides only a few cases each year, "rogue" judges can "get away" with interpretations that the Supreme Court might not accept.[11] Lately, the threat has become greater as individual judges have taken to deciding not only for their jurisdiction, but for the entire country in what I call doppelgänger decrees.

Doppelgänger Decrees (National Injunctions by Local Federal Judges)

James Madison wanted federal courts separate from state courts because he feared the federal government would be undercut by "improper Verdicts in State tribunals obtained under the biased directions of a dependent Judge, or the local prejudices of an undirected jury."[12] Others in support of him "contended strongly that if there was to be a National Legislature, there ought to be a national Judiciary."[13] The Madisonian Compromise permitted but did not require Congress to establish inferior federal courts around the country. The First Congress did.

Ironically, diffuse review has brought about the result that Madison feared fifty-fold. Madison worried that local state courts would put federal laws out of force *locally* in one state. Today local *federal* judges put federal laws out of force *nationally*. Diffuse review facilitates "forum-shopping." That's the practice where a plaintiff seeks out a court – or even a judge – more likely to find his or her claim sympathetic, i.e., a "rogue" judge. Today litigants shop for federal judges willing to deliver a national wallop.

A single local federal judge can prevent a law from taking effect not only in the state where the judge sits, but nationally. That judge is practically anonymous: a lone lark among hundreds of federal judges. That judge sits locally and is usually chosen at the behest of the local state's senator. Yet that solitary political appointee can block federal programs nationwide. Sometimes the halt is temporary; sometimes it is in practical effect permanent. Local judges have delayed, sometimes for years, or in effect defeated, such important national laws as the Affordable Care Act,[14] President Obama's executive orders for immigration reform and overtime provisions for managers,[15] and President Trump's executive orders on immigration.

---

[11] MARK TUSHNET, TAKING THE CONSTITUTION AWAY FROM THE COURTS 253–254 (1999).
[12] 1 MAX FARRAND, THE RECORDS OF THE FEDERAL CONVENTION OF 1787 at 124 (1911).
[13] *Id.* at 125. [14] United States v. Texas, 579 U.S. *** (June 23, 2016).
[15] *See* Samuel L. Bray, *Multiple Chancellors: Reforming the National Injunction* 131 HARV. L. REV. 16–54 (2017).

Common-Law Spells ("Open Sesame" Review)

One problem with assigning constitutional review to ordinary process is that ordinary process does not encompass all laws where constitutional review might be desirable and yet includes some cases where it is not. Once America's courts began to engage in wholesale constitutional review, they faced the problem.

America's courts adopted constitutional review without statutory direction. They dealt with the inclusiveness problem through judicial doctrines. These include such measures as justiciability, standing, ripeness and political question. These all suffer from problems of common law generally: difficulties in identifying an authoritative text, extracting from the text the binding holding, and discarding dicta. Thanks to diffuse review, application of these rules is not direct, but indirect. The judge making the decision at the bottom of the hierarchy in the court of first instance looks to what the court one level up said.

The Constitution could have provided for constitutional review. It did not. Congress could by statute structure constitutional review. It tried one time, when it prescribed a three-judge district court for constitutional review in some cases.[16] Lacking direction, the person who wants to challenge constitutionality must find the right magic words – the "open sesame" – that will open the door to judicial review at three levels of review, for the appellate court might find otherwise than the court of first instance. Yet justiciability, standing, ripeness and political question are all doctrines that have engendered endless debate.

Judicial Riddles (Understanding the Oracle's Opinions)

Chief Justice Marshall succeeded in getting justices to produce a written opinion of the Supreme Court. Previously justices had given opinions seriatim from the bench orally. In recent years, the Court has practically returned to past practices. Justices do not just dissent. Even those that join together to decide a case often do not agree on their reasoning. This results in a plethora of combinations of possible readings that makes knowing what the Court decided difficult or impossible.[17]

---

[16] In 1910 in the Three Judge Court Act of 1910, which was repealed in 1976. Tamara Hall, *The Hyde Bill: An Attempt to Resurrect the 1910 Three-Judge Court Act*, 38 COURT REV. J. AM JUDGES ASS'N, ISSUE 1, AT 32–33 (Spring 1998).

[17] The Supreme Court's decision upholding the Affordable Care Act, National Federation of Independent Business v. Sebelius, 567 U.S. 519 (2012), is an example. The official report states: "CHIEF JUSTICE ROBERTS announced the judgment of the Court and delivered the opinion of the Court with respect to Parts I, II, and III-C, an opinion with respect to Part IV, in which

It is not uncommon that one cannot know what the Supreme Court decided when upholding or striking down a statute. The decision is opaque. Even when the Court decides unanimously, what is the binding holding and what is non-binding dicta can be, as elsewhere in common-law systems, "the deepest secret of juristic life."[18]

Yet the reader of such an opinion has it comparatively easy. Sometimes a majority of the justices do not join in a decision, but render only a "plurality" opinion, or split their opinions in parts, e.g., Justice A issued the judgment of the Court and an opinion in which Justices B, C, D, and E, join in Parts I and III, and Justices . . . This is common.[19]

3. *Constitutionalizing Ordinary Disputes*[20]

Since the United States lacks a loser pays system of attorneys' fees allocation, plaintiffs can with little risk undertake what Justice Antonin Scalia called "give-it-a-try" dispute resolution.[21] When they are already suing on other grounds, they can introduce constitutional claims at virtually no cost. No one knows how much time and money they, their adversaries and the courts squander on such litigation.

JUSTICE BREYER and JUSTICE KAGAN join, and an opinion with respect to Parts III-A, III-B, and III-D. . . .

JUSTICE GINSBURG, with whom JUSTICE SOTOMAYOR joins, and with whom JUSTICE BREYER and JUSTICE KAGAN join as to Parts I, II, and IV, concurring in part, concurring in the judgment in part, and dissenting in part. . . .

JUSTICE SCALIA, JUSTICE KENNEDY, JUSTICE THOMAS, and JUSTICE ALITO, dissenting. It's not the worst example that I could find!

[18] Julius Stone, *The Ratio of the Ratio Decidendi*, 22 MOD. L. REV. 597, 599 (1959). *See also* Allison Orr Larsen, *Factual Precedents*, 162 U. PA. L. REV. 59, 61 (2013); Judith M. Stinson, *Why Dicta Becomes Holding and Why It Matters*, 76 BROOKLYN L. REV. 219, 245–248 (2010).

[19] *See* Berkolow, *Much Ado About Pluralities: Pride and Precedent amidst the Cacophony of Concurrences and Re-Percolation after Rapano*, 15 VA. J. SOCIAL POLICY & THE LAW 299 (2008); James E. Bloom, *Plurality and Precedence: Judicial Reasoning, Lower Courts, and the Meaning of United States v. Winstar Corp.*, 18 WASHINGTON U.L. REV. 1373 (2008); John P. Neuenkirchen, *Plurality Decisions, Implicit Consensuses, and the Fifth-Vote Rule under Marks v. United States*, 399 WIDENER L. REV. 387 (2013). For an historical perspective, see Adam S. Hochschild, *The Modern Problem of Supreme Court Plurality Decision: Interpretation in Historical Perspective*, 4 [Washington University] J. LAW & POLICY 261 (2000).

[20] *See* Robert A. Kagan & Gregory Elinson, *Constitutional Litigation in the United States*, in CONSTITUTIONAL COURTS IN COMPARISON, THE U.S. SUPREME COURT AND THE FEDERAL CONSTITUTIONAL COURT (Ralf Rogowski & Thomas Gawron, eds.) 25 (2d ed., 2016).

[21] ANTONIN SCALIA & BRYAN A. GARNER, READING LAW. THE INTERPRETATION OF LEGAL TEXTS 6 (2012).

Justice Scalia also complained that free availability of constitutional review leads to "constitutionalizing a new sliver of law" and that "that sliver thenceforth becomes untouchable by the political branches."[22] Legislators give in. Numerous "long-arm" statutes that define personal jurisdiction in constitutional terms are examples. California has an open-ended law rooted in constitutional common law: "A court of this state may exercise jurisdiction on any basis not inconsistent with the Constitution of this state or of the United States.[23]

4. *Selecting the Supreme Court's Oracles*

Constitutional review is unlike judging generally. By its nature, it is political. Judges put democratically adopted laws out of force.

Since ordinary legal procedures govern constitutional review and ordinary courts decide constitutional issues, Americans rarely recognize the different roles of constitutional and ordinary judges involved. Confusion results.

The people cry out for judges that will apply but not make law, while they want judges that will decide their way. Judges in their confirmation hearings pander to the public and pretend that they will not make political decisions. Oft quoted is Chief Justice Roberts testimony: "Judges are like umpires. Umpires don't make the rules, they apply them."[24] Yet lawyers know that political decisions are an inevitable feature of constitutional review. That explains why judicial appointments are hotly contested.

Despite all the vitriol expended in judicial appointments over the past two centuries, there is no statutory regulation of the process. For Supreme Court appointments there is just the cryptic language of the Article II, section 2, paragraph 2 of the Constitution that the president "shall nominate, and by and with the advice of the Senate, shall appoint ... judges of the Supreme Court ... ." It says nothing as to qualifications. As to term Article III, section 1, provides they "shall hold their offices during good behavior," which is taken to mean, for life. The statutes establishing the inferior courts only mimic the Constitutional requirements for Supreme Court judges.[25] Appointments of

---

[22] *Id.* at 4.   [23] CAL. CIV. PROC. § 410.10

[24] CONFIRMATION HEARING ON THE NOMINATION OF JOHN G. ROBERTS, JR. TO BE CHIEF JUSTICE OF THE UNITED STATES, HEARINGS BEFORE THE COMMITTEE ON THE JUDICIARY, UNITED STATES SENATE, 109TH CONGRESS, 55 (2005).

[25] 28 U.S.C. § 44 (judges of circuit courts); 28 U.S.C. §§ 133(a), 134(a) (judges of district courts.) They add requirements of residency in the circuit or district concerned.

judges in the inferior courts have long been patronage allowed to the Senators from the states for the courts concerned.[26]

Appointments to the Supreme Court have been considered "the president's" appointments. Presidents are allowed to pick people that share their views, but that are reasonably well regarded as jurists. In recent decades, almost all appointed have been judges of the courts of appeals who graduated from Harvard Law School or Yale Law School. The one non-judge appointment was Dean of Harvard Law School.

As the political role of judges has become clearer, controls on appointment have fallen by the wayside. People see the path to law revision primarily through changing the composition of the Supreme Court itself.[27] Judges might be umpires of baseball games, but their appointment is a football game without referees where the game cannot even get underway. As a result, many federal courts have gone without allocated judges for years.

The stakes of the game are raised by the life tenure allowed Supreme Court Justices. Fourteen Supreme Court justices have served more than thirty years. Long service is more and more common as life expectancies increase and appointments are made at younger ages. Constitutional courts elsewhere typically limit justices to a single term of nine to fifteen years. Some impose mandatory retirement. In Germany the term is twelve years and retirement mandatory at 68.

The appointment process, if it can be called that, reached a new low when the Republican-controlled Senate refused even to consider President Obama's nominee to replace Justice Scalia following the Justice's death. When President Trump nominated his own candidate, the Republican-controlled Senate used the so-called nuclear option to change Senate Rules to allow confirmation with only a simple majority instead of the previous super-majority of three-fifths.

When the Senate refuses to follow the Constitution to advise and consent on the appointment of government officers, when it threatens to change its rules as needed to ram through a judicial appointment, a government of laws has been replaced by one of men.

---

[26] *See* NANCY SCHERER, SCORING POINTS: POLITICIANS, ACTIVISTS, AND THE LOWER FEDERAL COURT APPOINTMENT PROCESS (2005).

[27] *See* LARRY D. KRAMER, THE PEOPLE THEMSELVES: POPULAR CONSTITUTIONALISM AND JUDICIAL REVIEW 228 (2004).

C. THE CONTINENTAL PLAN: A SOUND START

"Upholder of Constitution" and "Protector of Basic Rights" (Constitutional Court of Korea On the German Plan)[28]

1. *The German Plan*

Just as the United States Supreme Court has set the standard for the substance of constitutional review of laws the world over, Germany's Federal Constitutional

---

[28]   Used with permission of the Constitutional Court of Korea. Cover of CONSTITUTIONAL COURT OF KOREA (2008) (21 page comic book).

Court (*Bundesverfassungsgericht*) has set the standard for how to conduct constitutional review.[29] More countries have modeled constitutional review on the German plan than on the America plan. Why? The answer, I think, is because the German model does a better job of effectuating law as rules.

Constitutional review in Germany is not an organic outgrowth of ordinary court procedure. It is a creation by design.[30] It follows the model of the constitutional court that the Austrian-American legal philosopher Hans Kelsen proposed for Austria immediately after the First World War.

The German Constitution withdraws from regular courts (and from ordinary judges sitting alone or in panels) certain questions of broad societal interest related to two principal functions of constitutional law, that is, the frame of government and individual rights, and assigns them to a separate Constitutional Court (national justices sitting in panels of eight). By withdrawing these questions from the regular courts and concentrating them in a separate constitutional court with national, constitutional justices, the system works to assure that constitutional questions are answered quickly, correctly and uniformly for the country. Concentrating constitutional decisions in a separate court with professional constitutional justices also works to protect regular courts from politicization and to keep them on track in applying law.

Decisions of the Federal Constitutional Court are different from decisions of the ordinary courts. They are not applications of law to facts. They are, by their nature decisions about law and policy. They are political in this sense of policy, but not in the sense of political parties. The Internet page of the Court explains:

> The work of the Federal Constitutional Court also has political effect. This becomes particularly clear when the Court declares a law unconstitutional. But the court is not a political body. Its sole review standard is the Basic Law. Questions of political expediency are not allowed to play any part as far as the Court is concerned. It merely determines the constitutional framework for political decision-making. The delimitation of State power is a feature of the rule of law.[31]

---

[29] *See, e.g.,* Bodo *Pieroth, Deutscher Verfassungsexport: das Bundesverfassungsgericht,* 2010 ANWALTSBLATT 8.

[30] While there were antecedents to constitutional review before the German constitution of 1949 (the "Basic Law") created the Federal Constitutional Court, that creation is what made constitutional review of central importance in Germany. The United States occupation regime expected some form of constitutional review, but so too did Germans of the day. To suggest that the United States bestowed constitutional review on Germany is in error.

[31] Bundesverfassungsgericht, *The Court's Duties,* http://www.bundesverfassungsgericht.de/EN/ Das-Gericht/Aufgaben/aufgaben_node.html (last visited Feb. 5, 2017).

That the Federal Constitutional Court commands the highest respect of the nation is thought essential to its role as the guarantor of a government of laws. It is a lawgiver.

This design of constitutional review helps rather than hinders the integrity of a government of laws. The Federal Constitutional Court reviews laws for consistency with the constitution and puts out of force those that its finds unconstitutional. That is what constitutional review is about. But the German design seeks to make review seamless.

The German design does that in a variety of ways. Three particularly important ways are:

- Pre-review.
- Abstract review.
- Concentrated review.

"Pre-Review"

Most German laws are products of the ministries. Ministerial procedures require review for constitutionality by both the Federal Ministry of Justice and Consumer Protection and the Federal Ministry of the Interior before bills are presented to the Bundestag.[32] The Federal Ministry of Justice and Consumer Protection has three sections of several professionals each responsible, respectively, for governmental structure, constitutional rights review and constitutional procedure.[33] The Federal Ministry of Interior also has three such sections with responsibilities shared only slightly differently.[34]

Abstract Review

If there are doubts about compatibility of federal or state law with the Constitution, the Federal Constitutional Court is to decide the issue upon application of the federal government, of a state government, or of one-fourth of the members of the Bundestag.[35] If the issue relates to the legislative competency of the federal

---

[32] GEMEINSAME GESCHÄFTSORDNUNG DER BUNDESMINISTERIEN §§ 45, 46, Appendix 6 (Bundesministerium des Innern ed., 2011), *available at* http://www.bmi.bund.de/DE/Themen/ Moderne-Verwaltung/Verwaltungsorganisation/GGO/ggonode.html, available in English translation at http://ec.europa.eu/smart-regulation/impact/bestpracticesexamples/docs/de/ jointrulesproceduresfederalministries.pdf

[33] Bundesministerium der Justiz und für Verbraucherschutz, www.bmjv.de, Organisationsplan DE 24012017.pdf (last visited Feb. 5, 2017).

[34] Bundesministerium des Innerns, www.bmi.bund.de, PDF Organigramm BMI.pdf (last visited Feb. 5, 2017).

[35] GG art. 93(1), ¶ 2.

government, the Bundesrat, a state government or a state legislature may make application.[36] There is no case-or-controversy requirement for abstract review such as the United States Supreme Court has imposed. Should issues in a case arise subsequent to the law taking effect, the issue can be raised either as part of ordinary process or in a constitutional complaint. In either case, only the Federal Constitutional Court is competent to put a statute out of force. (*Concentrated review.*)

Concentrated Review
Constitutional review in Germany is *concentrated*, that is, only the Federal Constitutional Court has authority to put a federal law out of force. The regular courts cannot do that. If they believe that a law is unconstitutional, they must refer the question to the Federal Constitutional Court.[37] Should a regular court not make such a referral, the person affected by the judgment may bring a constitutional complaint to the Constitutional Court.

All three of these methods work to support reliability of laws. *Pre-review* means most laws are already reviewed even before adopted. *Abstract review* means that questionable laws are reviewed even before they take effect. *Concentrated review* means that adopted laws are reviewed by only one court composed of experts in constitutional law, and are not delayed by multiple layers of review.

2. *Constitutional Review Is Not Magical*

No Zombie Laws
Zombie laws, i.e., laws that are applicable but are of doubtful validity, although not precluded by pre-review and abstract review, are uncommon and cannot have a long existence owing to concentrated review.

No Doppelgänger Decrees
Since constitutional review is concentrated, there can be no doppelgänger decrees where different courts are at odds with each other on conformity with the constitution.

---

[36] GG art. 93(1), ¶ 3. *But see* Alec Stone Sweet, *Why Europe Rejected American Judicial Review: And Why It May Not Matter,* 101 MICH. L. REV. 2744, 2770 (2003).

[37] The European Union has a similar reference procedure for national court treatment of the question of conformity of national laws with EU law. Some American states specifically allow for references from federal courts to state courts of questions of state law. Yet use of these provisions, or ad hoc references, are said to be unusual: "Erie-guesses, not certification, still remain federal courts' preferred method of ascertaining the meaning of unclear state law." Frank Chang, *Note, You Have Not Because You Ask Not: Why Federal Courts Do Not Certify Questions of State Law to State Courts,* 85 GEO. WASH. L. REV. 251, 256 (2017).

No Spells

As with German law generally, statutes, not confusing or contradictory precedents, set out most standards for access. There are two principal ways[38]:

- *Concrete review.* If a serious issue arises in the course of ordinary litigation, the lower court concerned is to refer the issue to the Federal Constitutional Court.
- *Constitutional complaint.* Another form of concrete review is the constitutional complaint (*Verfassungsbeschwerde*). Should an act of government violate a person's constitutional rights, that person may bring a constitutional complaint. The complaining party must first exhaust all other legal remedies and must apply promptly thereafter. There is no charge for the application. Applications are subject to an admission determination similar to the U.S. certiorari proceedings. There are about 6000 such applications each year of which about 2.5 percent are successful.

No Riddles

Decisions of the Federal Constitutional Court are not mix-and-match affairs. The Court delivers one decision of the Court. Although not allowed at first, today justices may deliver dissenting opinions. They do so in a significant, but still a small number of cases.

A statute authorized by Article 94(2) of the German Constitution determines when and how a decision has the force of statute, that is, when it is binding on others as law. Ordinary German court decisions do not have *stare decisis* effect. They do not bind other courts or authorities. German constitutional review is a limited exception to that rule. That exception is so structured, however, as to avoid problems endemic in American case law.

The constitutional court statute provides that only the official syllabus and not the reasoning is binding law. That should ameliorate if not eliminate the American riddle of figuring out what in an opinion is binding law and what is mere dicta. It identifies and reduces what the people have to read and causes the judges to focus on what they are pronouncing. The statute also provides that the decision is binding on all other institutions of government. That eliminates another source of dispute.

---

[38] The Federal Constitutional Court has other special competencies, *e.g.*, impeachment of the Federal President, prohibition of political parties, election supervision.

3. *Keeping Ordinary Courts Regular: Separating Legal from Policy Decisions*

Separating legal from policy decisions is a recurrent theme of German law.[39] Legal questions should be answered objectively by independent judges responsible only to law and justice. Policy decisions should be answered by politically responsible actors. Abstract review and concentration of decisions makes consideration of issues such as federal preemption in ordinary lawsuits and promotion of legal certainty unnecessary.[40] They make difficult using constitutional arguments to upset ordinary lawsuits.

4. *Selecting Wisemen and Wisewomen*

Constitutional judging is different. Even, or perhaps especially, civilians recognize that. Constitutional review is by its nature political. It is not simply application of determinate law to found facts. Constitutional decisions have an undeniable political effect. They are decisions made for the people at large.

The German Constitution has little to say about qualifications and selection of members of the court, principally that some members will be federal judges already on appointment and that half of the court judges will be elected half by the Bundestag and half by the Bundesrat. It leaves details to statute.

The statute imposes requirements that reflect the policy role of the court. Where German judges have life tenure so long as they remain on good behavior, Constitution Justices do not. They are allowed one single 12-year term, subject to mandatory retirement at age 68. They must be forty years old on appointment, when many German judges are considerably younger than that. Six must be federal judges (roughly comparable to judges of America's federal courts of appeal). Those that are not judges, must have qualified to be judges (a requirement for bar membership). Many are law professors.

---

[39] *See* JAMES MAXEINER, POLICY AND METHODS IN GERMAN AND AMERICAN ANTITRUST LAW: A COMPARATIVE STUDY (1986).

[40] *See* WOLFGANG MÄRZ, BUNDESRECHT BRICHT LANDESRECHT: EINE STAATSRECHTLICHE UNTERSUCHUNG ZU ARTIKEL 31 DES GRUNDGESETZES 108–112, 204 (1989) (noting that Basic Law Article 31 is largely superfluous when the competency rules of Articles 70 *et seq.* are followed); *see also* HANS SCHNEIDER, EIN LEHR- UND HANDBUCH at 118–124 (3d ed. 2002); Council of Europe, Venice Comm'n, *The European Model of Constitutional Review of Legislation*, at Ad C, Doc. No. CDL-JU(2006)016 (Mar. 24, 2006) (*prepared by* Ján Mazák), *available at* http://www.venice.coe.int/docs/2006/CDL-JU(2006)016-e.asp (noting that judicial review provides "the assurance of legal certainty" and "[t]he abstract character of judicial review is also linked to the principle of legal certainty").

The selection process is political. Individual justices typically are identified as the choice of one or more political parties. In the past, parties have informally acceded to assigning appointment in rotation.

But judges are not supposed to judge politically and are selected with that in mind. In both the Bundestag and in the Bundesrat, to be elected, a candidate must receive at least a two-thirds vote of the members. Votes are by secret ballots and without public discussion. Controversy on this point is met with the argument that hearings of nominees and open debate would politicize their later judging.[41] To avoid interfering with the work of the Court, strict and short timelines for consideration apply (three month for filling vacancies at end of term; one month for unscheduled vacancies). The kerfuffle following Justice Scalia's death and the Senate's refusal to consider the nomination of Judge Merrick Garland could hardly happen.

---

[41] Entwurf eines Neunten Gesetzes zur Änderung des Bundesverfassungsgerichtsgesetzes (9. BVerfGGÄndG), Bundestag Drucksache 18/2737, 4 (Oct. 10, 2014).

13

Applying Laws

Gentlemen [the Justices of the new Supreme Court]:

I have always been persuaded that the stability and success of the national Government, and consequently the happiness of the People of the United States, would depend in a considerable degree on the Interpretation and Execution of its Laws.

George Washington (1790)[1]

A. ENABLING A GOVERNMENT OF LAWS

Laws alone cannot secure a government of laws. Laws, as President Washington said, require interpretation and execution.[2] If there is no process for applying laws or if the process of applying laws is unreliable in interpreting or executing laws, a government of laws fails. Good law applying enables good lawmaking to realize a government of laws.

I discuss in this chapter three ways that America's legal process fails to enable a government of laws. First, process often is so unpredictable or so expensive that it is practically useless; a useless process is worse than no process at all, for it gives the illusion that laws are regularly executed. Second, when people do rely on process, they find that judges are led by America's procedures to umpire process contests rather than to decide according to law. The stronger position in process, rather than in right, wins cases. Finally, when

---

[1] George Washington, *Letter to the Chief Justice and the Justices of the Supreme Court of the United States upon Commencement of Their First Circuit, April 3, 1789*, THE WRITINGS OF GEORGE WASHINGTON FROM THE ORIGINAL MANUSCRIPT SOURCES 1745–1799, VOL. 31, JAN. 22, 1790–MAR. 9, 1792, at 31 (John C. Fitzpatrick, ed., 1939).
[2] *Id.* Already the 1648 *Lawes and Libertyes of Massachusetts* noted that "The execution of the law is the life of the law." John Adams, in his 1776 *Thoughts on Government* counted as the best form of government that "which is best contrived to secure the impartial and exact execution of the laws."

judges do purport to apply laws, they assert their supremacy over laws, what is called, judicial supremacy. Judges' interpretations of laws, statutory precedents, are superior to the statutes themselves. People cannot rely on what statutes say; they are unable to apply laws to themselves.

In contrast, Germany's process fortifies statutes and enables a government of laws. First, Germany's process is predictable and inexpensive. Losers pay the costs for both sides. Usually it provides a mechanism to execute laws. Second, Germany's process focuses judges on applying laws to facts. The correctness of decisions made according to laws, and not which side played the process better, is the measure of the outcome. Finally, Germany's judges apply laws. They do not decide against statutes, but defer to choices made by legislatures. Legislative supremacy prevails.

America's process makes it difficult or impossible for Americans to apply laws to themselves.[3] People are not able to fit their conduct within laws that they cannot know or rely on. Legal philosophers Hans Kelsen and H.L.A. Hart spoke up for the law abiding. Kelsen counseled that "individuals who have to *obey* the law by behaving in a way that avoids sanctions, must understand the legal norms and therefore must ascertain their meaning."[4] Hart wrote of the need for "certain rules" that people can apply to themselves without additional official direction.[5]

Applying laws correctly to facts is fundamental to a government of laws.[6] It is practically a truism: "in all justice systems of the world the role of civil justice is to apply the applicable substantive law to the established facts in an impartial manner, and pronounce fair and accurate judgments."[7] If there were no civil lawsuits, private parties might use self-help to realize their rights and to

---

[3] Some academics assert that laws are *not* for the people, but for professionals. *See, e.g.*, LINDA D. JELLUM, MASTERING STATUTORY INTERPRETATION 5–7 (2d ed., 2013) ("many laws are intuitive and conform to societal expectations. . . . Legislators write statutes . . . to explain laws clearly for the outliers and enforcers . . . ."); Richard B. Cappalli, *At the Point of Decision: The Common Law's Advantage over the Civil Law*, 12 TEMPLE INT'L & COMP. L.J. 87, 99 (1998) ("Common law rules achieve the generality which law requires . . . only when legally-trained people restate case facts at higher levels of generality.").

[4] HANS KELSEN, PURE THEORY OF LAW § 45, 348 (Max Knight, transl., 2d ed. 1967).

[5] H.L.A. HART, THE CONCEPT OF LAW 130 (2d ed. 1994); *see* ROBERT S. SUMMERS, FORM AND FUNCTION IN A LEGAL SYSTEM: A GENERAL STUDY 379 (2006) (using the term "self-application").

[6] *See, e.g.*, H.D. Clayton, Chair, *Judicial Administration Committee*, 1 SO. L.J. & REPORTER 98, 99 (1880) ("To know the law is the 'sine qua non' of its administration; and it is equally true that to be able to correctly apply it is absolutely essential.").

[7] Alan Uzelac, *Goals of Civil Justice and Civil Procedure in Contemporary Judicial Systems, in* GOALS OF CIVIL JUSTICE AND CIVIL PROCEDURE IN CONTEMPORARY JUDICIAL SYSTEMS 3 (Alan Uzelac, ed., Ius Gentium: Comparative Perspectives on Law and Justice, Vol. 34, 2013). *See* Paul D. Carrington, *Virtual Civil Litigation: A Visit to John Bunyan's Celestial City*, 98 COLUM. L. REV. 1516, 1522–1523 (1998) ("we . . . expect courts to decide cases by applying law to fact.").

resolve their disputes. The stronger, rather than the righteous, would prevail. To preserve peace and right, modern legal systems prohibit self-help except in limited cases. Instead, they seek correct application of law to facts.

Applying laws to facts is a syllogistic process: a legal rule is the major premise and facts found are the minor premise. Facts are subsumed logically under legal rules to reach correct legal consequences. Each element of the major premise of the norm must be fulfilled by a particular fact of the minor premise. If one fails, application of the norm fails.

Applying laws to facts is more difficult than is generally realized. Determining applicable rules and finding material facts are *interdependent* inquiries: until one knows which rules are applicable, one cannot know which facts are material. But until one knows the rules, one cannot know which facts are material. Settle the applicable rules too soon, and facts may be overlooked which would change results were other rules applied. Fail to settle the applicable rules soon enough, and process may detour to find facts that are not material under rules applied. As I show later in this chapter, America's process fails to overcome this challenge.

As failures of America's legal system to apply law to facts have become clearer, some of America's professors of process have looked for other ways to justify process. Some assert that the process itself, rather than whether process leads to decisions according to laws, is what matters.[8] Others claims that process serves other purposes: making and enforcing public law.[9] Either way, putting process ahead of laws disables a government of laws. It is no wonder that America's jurists speak of a "rule of lawyers" rather than of a "government of laws, not men." Some wags call the rule of law out: it is a "rule of lawyers,"[10] or a "rule of legal rhetoric,"[11] or even, a "rule of nobody."[12]

---

[8]   Already in 1906 Roscoe Pound dubbed the process justification the "sporting theory of justice." In the nation's most famous address on civil justice, he said, where the question should be, "what do substantive law and justice requires," it becomes, "have the rules of the game been carried out strictly?" Roscoe Pound, *The Causes of the Popular Dissatisfaction with the Administration of Justice*, REPORT OF THE TWENTY-NINTH ANNUAL MEETING OF THE AMERICAN BAR ASSOCIATION HELD AT ST. PAUL, MINNESOTA, AUG. 29, 30 AND 31, 1906, 395, 405–406 (1906). *See* James R. Maxeiner, *The Federal Rules at 75: Dispute Resolution, Private Enforcement or Decision According to Law?*, in THE DYNAMISM OF CIVIL PROCEDURE – GLOBAL TRENDS AND DEVELOPMENTS 85, 93–99 (C.B. Picker & G.E. Seidman, eds., Ius Gentium: Comparative Perspectives in Law and Justice, Vol. 48, 2015), *originally published* in 30 GA. ST. L. REV. 983 (2014).

[9]   *See* JAMES R. MAXEINER WITH GYOOHO LEE & ARMIN WEBER, FAILURES OF AMERICAN CIVIL JUSTICE IN INTERNATIONAL PERSPECTIVE 265–268 (2011).

[10] WALTER K. OLSON, THE RULE OF LAWYERS: HOW THE NEW LITIGATION ELITE THREATENS AMERICA'S RULE OF LAW (2003).

[11] Geoffrey C. Hazard, Jr., *Rule of Legal Rhetoric*, 67 SMU L. REV. 801, 802 (2014).

[12] PHILIP K. HOWARD, THE RULE OF NOBODY: SAVING AMERICA FROM DEAD LAWS AND BROKEN GOVERNMENT (2014).

B. AMERICA'S PROCESS CORRODES STATUTES

"When I use a word," Humpty Dumpty said in rather a scornful tone, "it means just what I choose it to mean – neither more nor less."

"The question is," said Alice, "whether you can make words mean so many different things."

"The question is," said Humpty Dumpty, "which is to be master – that's all."

Lewis Carroll (Charles Dodgson) *Through the Looking Glass* (1872)[13]

[13] LEWIS CARROLL (CHARLES DODGSON), THROUGH THE LOOKING GLASS: AND WHAT ALICE FOUND THERE, WITH FIFTY ILLUSTRATIONS BY JOHN TENNIEL 118 (illustration), 124 (text) (1872).

Process in the United States undermines a government of laws. Here's why: (1) process is not a reliable option for law-abiders; (2) process fails to apply laws; and (3) process asserts judicial supremacy over statutes and undermines them. Although I discuss these assertions in the context of civil justice, my points find parallels in criminal and administrative justice.[14]

To argue my points took another book.[15] Here I can only give reasons why I believe they disestablish a government of laws. Just to state these reasons is difficult because they rely on seemingly technical points, assumed by lawyers to be inherent in the American system, and discussed, if at all, more from political than from legal perspectives. These technical points are the cost system, the separation of law from facts in process, and the application of *stare decisis* to statutes.

1. *Process Is Rarely a Good Option*

People who turn to American courts to affirm their self-applying of laws are disappointed. Rarely is litigation a good option. People "go to law" out of desperation because there is no other option.

Sometimes litigation is not a good option because lawmaking itself is a failure. Laws are so poorly made that people cannot tell with reasonable certainty which ones apply or what they mean. Where laws are chaotic, seeking judicial application may compound confusion and raise risks in court when wrangling over governing laws and how they apply to facts to be found.

Other times litigation is not a good option because litigation fails. Lawsuits fail to find facts or fail to apply law correctly to facts. As discussed in the next subsection, litigation offers scant relief. Courts can fashion new laws or put existing laws out-of-force. Recalcitrant parties can exploit procedures to frustrate laws' execution.

Even when litigation seems to work, it may be too expensive to be a practical or a worthwhile option. The "American rule" of costs, i.e., the peculiarly American way of determining and allocating attorneys' fees, often renders process pointless. In the United States attorneys' fees are not regulated; attorneys' fees are not assessed against losers (as they are in most countries). Attorneys' fees are potentially boundless, because lawyers largely control the

---

[14] *See, e.g.,* WILLIAM T. PIZZI, TRIALS WITHOUT TRUTH: WHY OUR SYSTEM OF CRIMINAL TRIALS HAS BECOME AN EXPENSIVE FAILURE AND WHAT WE NEED TO DO TO REBUILD IT (1998); WILLIAM J. STUNTZ, THE COLLAPSE OF AMERICAN CRIMINAL JUSTICE (2011).

[15] MAXEINER, FAILURES OF AMERICAN CIVIL JUSTICE, *supra* note 9.

extent of court activity. Party control without fee regulation and without fee shifting mean that law-abiding claimants can find adversary attorneys arguing all possible points; their iron-clad cases are turned into pyrrhic victories.[16] To sue is to lose.[17] Elsewhere I have detailed failures of American civil justice in general and of its cost system in particular.[18]

2. *Judges Umpire Lawyers' Games*

American process does not routinely apply laws to facts. Only a tiny percentage of all American lawsuits – less than one percent – end with what in most legal systems is the hallmark of applying law to facts: a judge's reasoned opinion of the entire case after hearing the parties about facts and law. The percentage is not much higher even if one adds lawsuits that end in the American system's signature product of a jury verdict, which do not result in reasoned opinions. Trials are vanishing.[19]

The signature American jury trial is inconsistent with a government of laws. The usual "general verdict," that is, proven, not proven, is not a verifiable application of law to facts. Since juries do not deliver reasoned opinions and only exceptionally give reasons ("special verdicts"), there is no way to know whether jurors understood and followed the judge's instructions on law.[20] Trial professionals know that applying law to facts is often beyond the

---

[16] *See* Jef De Mot & Alex Stein, *Talking Points*, 2015 U. ILL. L. REV. 1259, 1285 ("our rules of civil liability systematically malfunction. By pitting several defenses against every single violation, they give defendants an undeserved talking points advantage over plaintiffs.")

[17] Legal professionals know this, but rarely own up to it. Professor Samuel Issacharoff is an exception. He tells law students that litigants "are clear losers as soon as they enter the litigation process. ... By bringing lawyers into the mix and by subjecting themselves to the inevitable costs of litigation the parties consign themselves to being worse off. ... The pie starts getting smaller and smaller." SAMUEL ISSACHAROFF, CIVIL PROCEDURE 199 (3d ed., 2012).

[18] *See* MAXEINER, FAILURES OF AMERICAN CIVIL, *supra* note 9, at 32–37; James R. Maxeiner, *The American Rule: Assuring the Lion His Share*, in COST AND FEE ALLOCATION IN CIVIL PROCEDURE: A COMPARATIVE STUDY 287 (Mathias Reimann, ed., Ius Gentium, Comparative Perspectives on Law and Justice, Vol. 11, 2011).

[19] *See, e.g.*, ROBERT P. BURNS, THE DEATH OF THE AMERICAN TRIAL (2009).

[20] A Chamber of the European Court of Human Rights in the case of *Taxquet v. Belgium* held that jury verdicts, because they do not give reasons, violate the fair trial guarantee of Article 6 § 1 of the European Convention on Human Rights. The full court reversed the Chamber's decision and upheld jury verdicts if presiding judges put "precise, unequivocal questions' to juries. *See* NEIL ANDREWS, THE THREE PATHS OF JUSTICE: COURT PROCEEDINGS, ARBITRATION, AND MEDIATION IN ENGLAND 28–29 (Ius Gentium; Comparative Perspectives in Law and Justice, Vol. 10, 2012).

capabilities of juries.[21] They seek victories through finely honed interpretations of law decided by judges before trial or at trial by presenting a simple
"theory of the case" developed in detailed pretrial discovery that requires little
law applying by jurors.

Judges decide a larger but still small percentage of cases on motions before
trial made mostly on papers without hearings. Sometimes they find pleadings
do not meet procedural or substantive requirements. Other times they grant
"summary judgment" motions, so long as they conclude that there is no
genuine issue of material fact.

Most contested cases, however, parties settle before trial without judges
conducting hearings or trials. Many factors motivate parties to settle. How a
judge or jury is likely to apply law after finding facts at an increasingly unlikely
trial is not high on most litigants' lists. At the top of some lists is fear of
unjustifiable decisions, either exorbitant awards (including the possibility of
punitive damages) or nullification of legitimate claims. Near the top of just
about everyone's list is what America's first academic authority on trial evidence colorfully called "the long train of evils, temporal and spiritual in a Law
suit"[22] that includes the unrecoverable costs in attorneys' fees and parties' time
and energies.

Why does applying laws have such a modest role in American civil justice?
Here I suggest some possible explanations.

Separating Laws from Facts

There is an inherent contradiction in American process. Applying laws brings
laws and facts together: it *relates* the two through the legal syllogism.[23] But
process in America *separates* issues of laws from issues of facts.

Law-abiding laymen going to court think that they know what the laws are
and what the facts are. They assume that judges know the laws. They think
they have only to tell judges the facts ("tell it to the judge)" for judges to apply
the laws. Many are surprised to discover that process in the United States has
something other in store for them than bringing laws and facts together.

---

[21] *See, e.g.*, already, HUGH D[AVY] EVANS, AN ESSAY ON PLEADING WITH A VIEW TO AN
IMPROVED SYSTEM 16 (1827) ("This renders a high degree of simplicity necessary in the
questions posed for their consideration.").

[22] Simon Greenleaf (attributed), *To a Person Engaged in a Lawsuit*, 6 PUBS. AM. TRACT SOC. NO.
168 (1827).

[23] *Cf.* SCALIA & GARNER, MAKING YOUR CASE (2008), at 43 ("Figuring out the contents of
a legal syllogism is a matter of finding a rule that works together with the facts of the
case – really a rule that is invoked by those facts.").

America's legal professionals assume that lawsuits separate laws from facts. That's what they were taught in law school. It's essential – they assume – to American process. Judges decide law; jurors decide facts. Before judges can determine law, lawyers have to find it for them. Before jurors can decide facts, lawyers have to discover it for them. Little room remains for their clients, the people, to tell facts to judges who then apply laws.

Only a few legal professionals have given thought to the peculiarity of separating law from facts. One who did was Hugh Evans, a lawyer who lived in Baltimore two centuries ago. In *An Essay on Pleading with a View to an Improved System*, published in 1827, Evans acknowledged that separating laws from facts is not among "the most obvious wants of a judicial system."[24] He saw it as a "peculiarity," but as a "glorious peculiarity." It permitted introducing into litigation a jury of laymen "unused to debate and unskilled in the principles upon which controversies are decided."[25]

Evans saw what few legal professionals see today: separating laws from facts fundamentally changes litigation. Without separation, Evans opined, "the court with comparative safety, [can] be left to collect the subject of the controversy, from the allegations of the parties, in any manner which it may choose to adopt."[26] With separation, however, litigation takes on a whole new object: "the ascertainment of the character of the dispute, and consequently of the tribunal which is to decide."[27]

Today's civil process is not as different from that in Evans' day as legal professionals might think: it is concerned less with carrying out syllogisms of applying laws to facts and more with giving opportunities to challenge the premises of the syllogisms. The difference is that in Evans' day lawyers had to choose only one issue to dispute, either a single element of the major premise of law or a single element of the minor premise of fact (known as "common-law pleading"). Today parties may state as many separate claims or defenses as they have, regardless of consistency (Federal Rule of Civil Procedure 8) and dispute as many elements as they wish. The result is often that which Supreme

---

[24] HUGH D[AVY] EVANS, AN ESSAY ON PLEADING WITH A VIEW TO AN IMPROVED SYSTEM 288 (1827).

[25] *Id.* at 15–16, Evans contemplated only one form of lay participation: one "tribunal" – a jury – separate from another "tribunal" – a court. That fulfilled the ancient maxim of what was called common-law pleading: "that to questions of fact the jury ought to answer, and to questions of law the court." *Id.* at 290. He did not consider lay participation through mixed panels of laymen and professional judges such as is common around the world today.

[26] *Id.* at 15.   [27] *Id.* at 16.

Court saw already in 1858: "an endless wrangle in writing, perplexing to the court, delaying and impeding the administration of justice."[28]

"Presenting the Case"

In the United States the parties' lawyers have the leading roles in litigation. They present their "clients' cases." Judges are passive; they have supporting roles. Lawyers move cases through the process. They make sure judges know which laws apply. They collect facts. In theory (and in rare practice when the usual settlement does not occur), lawyers present facts to jurors, who are supposed to determine whether the facts proven fulfill the requirements of the laws as stated to them by the judge. The lawyers present their clients' cases sequentially: each, first plaintiff's lawyer, then defendant's lawyer, presents that lawyer's view of the whole case in a single, uninterrupted trial.

If lawyers are to present their clients' cases, they need to know beforehand which facts are material to decision. That means they need to know the laws beforehand. But there in opposition stands the back-and-forth nature of law applying. Issues of law, fact and application of law to facts are in flux as a case is under consideration up until the case is finally decided.

For two centuries America's legal professionals have striven to create a system that separates issues of law from issues of facts and yet somehow brings the two back together to apply law to fact, all the while maintaining decision of issues of law for judges and issues of fact for jurors. They have not found a way.

Standing in the way of a solution is the leading role process assigns to lawyers. When lawyers present cases they have foremost in mind reaching outcomes favorable to their clients. In the famous words of English law reformer Lord Henry Brougham, the lawyer "knows but one person in all the world, and that person is his client."[29] Decision of cases, however, is binary: there is a winner and there is a loser. Lawyers have little interest in applying laws to facts if it results in their clients losing.

Left to their own devices, lawyers have little incentive to agree on which issues to have jurors decide. One side must lose. Each lawyer wants to choose only issues that that lawyer's client is likely to win. Lawyers delay.

Reformers call for greater involvement of judges in litigation. Their attempts founder, however, on the perceived need of keeping judges and jurors apart in their deliberations.[30] They encounter the tenacity of lawyers

---

[28] McFaul v. Ramsey, 61 U.S. 523, 525 (1858).

[29] Lord Henry Brougham, *Her Majesty's Defence*, THE IMPORTANT AND EVENTFUL TRIAL OF QUEENE CAROLINE 417, 419 (1820)

[30] Judges are told not to address jurors on evidence. Jurors are told not to determine law. Judges give jurors instructions so that they decide facts necessary to their verdicts. The instructions are incomprehensible when, as often is the case, issues are anything other than simple.

in exploiting infirmities in law and their determination to preserve their control of presenting cases. Lawyers' tenacity turns American civil justice into a contest of champions, what Roscoe Pound damned as the "sporting theory of justice."[31]

The Federal Rules of Civil Procedure

The celebrated Federal Rules of Civil Procedure of 1938, which serve as model for most states' rules, were intended to eradicate the sporting theory. Their drafters sought to facilitate decisions according to law.[32] Their treatment is a striking example of lawyer domination of civil justice at the expense of law applying for the law abiding.[33]

The 1938 rules introduced new measures intended to help judges and lawyers cooperate in applying laws to facts, including less technical pleadings based on "concise and direct pleas" asserted in "good faith" (Rules 8 and 11) and with "good grounds" (Rule 11), informal pretrial conferences "for formulating the issues" (Rule 16), pretrial "discovery" (Rules 26 to 37) so that attorneys could see where facts were not in dispute, and "summary judgments" to dispatch those issues where there was "no genuine issue as to any material fact," which directed courts to "if practicable ascertain what material facts exist without substantial controversy and what material facts are actually and in good faith controverted" (Rule 56).[34]

The 1938 rules gave new emphasis to old tools that were intended to make outcomes rational and transparent. These included, for example, allowing judges to require jurors to make separate findings on each issue of fact through what are called "special verdicts and interrogatories" (Rule 49). They provided directions where courts act without jurors that required judges "to find facts specially and state separately [their] conclusions of law thereon" (Rule 52).[35]

---

[31] See note 8, *supra*.

[32] *See* James R. Maxeiner, *The United States Federal Rules at 75: Dispute Resolution, Private Enforcement or Decisions According to Law?*, in THE DYNAMISM OF CIVIL PROCEDURE – GLOBAL TRENDS AND DEVELOPMENTS 85, 93–99 (C.B. Picker & G.E. Seidman, eds., IUS GENTIUM: COMPARATIVE PERSPECTIVES IN LAW AND JUSTICE, Vol. 48, 2015), *originally published* in 30 GA. ST. L. REV. 983 (2014).

[33] This is not as surprising as it sounds. The Federal Rules were the product of a 32-year campaign to wrest control of trial court procedures from the legislature and give it formally to the courts and practically to the trial bar. Proponents focused first on Congress authorizing courts to create rules for trial courts and not on the contents of the rules themselves.
The rules govern only a part of civil procedure. As adopted they did not touch appeals or costs.

[34] Rules of Civil Procedure for the District Courts of the United States with Index and Notes, 76th Cong., 1st Sess. S. Doc. No. 101 (1939)

[35] *Id.*

The goals of efficient and just applying of law to facts of the Federal Rules fell victim to neglect and to debilitating practices, interpretations and amendments. Judges neglected opportunities to use pretrial conferences and summary judgments to formulate issues. Lawyers turned opportunities for less rigorous pleading and discovery, intended to promote cooperation and reduce gamesmanship, on their heads. They used the tools not for cooperation, that required two to work together, but for competition, that allowed each to work alone.

Lawmaking Displaces Law Applying
When America's proceduralists get together they don't celebrate the triumphs of the Federal Rules in applying laws to facts.[36] They celebrate their claim that "the role of civil litigation in America is somewhat different perhaps from its role in other countries."[37] Civil litigation "privatized a great deal of our law enforcement."[38] Moreover it is said to be Americans' preferred route to reforming law.[39] I think one reason for this is that law schools focus on teaching what individual lawyers might accomplish themselves. They have given up on lawmaking through legislatures.

America's proceduralists acknowledge that these functions are foreign to the goals of civil justice in other countries including in other common-law countries. They realize that their asserted goals of making and enforcing public norms through private initiative is an innovation of the last half of the 20th century.[40] Nonetheless they proudly assert that it "defines the character of our system."[41] Americans, they say, should accept that there is "relatively small likelihood of a change."[42]

I think another narrative is more accurate. The practicing bar turned the Federal Rules into something different from the mundane vehicle of applying law to facts that their drafters intended. Unable to resist the practicing bar,

---

[36] *See, e.g., Symposium: The Federal Rules at 75, published in* 162. U. PA. L. REV. 1517–1952 (Issue No. 7, June 2014).

[37] STEPHEN N. SUBRIN & MARGARET Y.K. WOO, LITIGATING IN AMERICA: CIVIL PROCEDURE IN CONTEXT 37 (2006).

[38] Paul D. Carrington, *Renovating Discovery*, 49 ALA. L. REV. 51, 54 (1997).

[39] *See* David Marcello, *Legislative Drafting 101, Legislative Drafting Series, Part 1 of 4*, THE AMERICAN LEGISLATIVE AND ISSUE CAMPAIGN EXCHANGE, or ALICE, Nov. 19, 2013, *available at* https://youtu.be/wnZOefjHtUA (last visited Dec. 5, 2016).

[40] Richard Marcus, *'American Exceptionalism' in Goals for Civil Litigation, in* GOALS OF CIVIL JUSTICE AND CIVIL PROCEDURE IN CONTEMPORARY JUDICIAL SYSTEMS 123, 129–133, 139 (Alan Uzelac, ed., IUS GENTIUM: COMPARATIVE PERSPECTIVES ON LAW AND JUSTICE, Vol. 34, 2014).

[41] SUBRIN & WOO, *supra* note 37 at 37.

[42] Marcus, *American Exceptionalism, supra* note 40, at 140

proceduralists cast their lot with them. Like the manufacturers of a drug that failed in its intended application, they have latched on to alternative uses to repackage their product.

Making law and enforcing public law norms are noble goals for government, but they have place in civil justice only after the civil justice system meets the goals expected of it to apply and uphold existing law.[43]

The people have never bought into the repackaging. Nor have all legal professionals. Some remain hopeful that the Federal Rules will one day fulfill the goal stated in the second sentence of Rule 1 that these rules "shall be construed to secure the just, speedy, and inexpensive determination of every action." Failure followed the 1938 formulation. In 1993 it was amended to add "and administered" in order, the Committee Notes explain, "to recognize the affirmative duty of court to exercise [its] authority" to these ends. Failure followed. In 2015 it was amended to add "and employed by the court and the parties," in order, the Committee Notes explain, "to emphasize ... the parties share responsibility to employ the rules in the same way."[44] Hope springs eternal.[45]

Appeals on Rules not Rights

Appeals in America reproduce the deficiencies of the first instance. Often they are not a good option for law-abiding people; often they add useless costs and unpredictable risks. Often they do not apply but do change the law. Often they do not find right, but focus on complying with process rules and on separating law from fact.

When the Federal Rules went into effect in 1938, they left untouched important areas of civil procedure, including attorneys' fees and appeals. Attorneys' fees remain largely untouched today with the ill effects for law-abiders and a government of laws described earlier in this chapter. Thirty years later in 1968 Federal Rules of Appellate Procedure went into effect. By then, the lofty goals of the 1938 rules had largely vanished.[46] Appellate Rule 1 sets no goal for procedure in the courts of appeals. The forty-eight appellate rules

---

[43] *See* MAXEINER, FAILURES OF AMERICAN CIVIL JUSTICE, *supra* note 9, at 267–268.

[44] As in force today, the second sentence reads (with the two amendments in italics) "They should be construed, *administered, and employed by the court and the parties* to secure the just, speedy, and inexpensive determination of every action and proceeding."

[45] *See, e.g.*, Chief Justice John Roberts, 2015 YEAR-END REPORT ON THE FEDERAL JUDICIARY at 9 ("The 2015 civil rules amendments are a major stride toward a better federal court system.")

[46] *See generally* PAUL D. CARRINGTON, DANIEL J. MEADOR & MAURICE ROSENBERG, JUSTICE ON APPEAL (1976).

largely regulate filings![47] They too leave historical appellate procedure in America little changed.[48]

Today the federal courts of appeals are said to be in "crisis."[49] The problem is said to be the "crushing" workload of their judges. Overload has not only led to expected consequences such as cursory review, reduced oral hearings, delay and fatigue, but also less easily expected consequences as substitution of "additional decision makers," i.e., law clerks (recent law school graduates) for judges. The obvious solution to this problem, more judges, is resisted by judges who are said to fear a loss of their prestige and a reduction in quality of future colleagues as well as by others who see new judges as costing $1 million per year each. Given the politicization of federal judicial appointments discussed in the previous chapter, a substantial increase in numbers seems unlikely in the short term.[50]

Ordinarily in theory two levels of review are possible in America: by an intermediate appellate court and by a supreme court. In the federal system, this is mostly theoretical, since the Supreme Court of the United States decides with full proceedings fewer than 100 cases a year. Since there are thirteen different intermediate appellate courts, the Supreme Court can hardly deal expeditiously, if at all, with the conflicts in decisions among these courts. The resulting uncertainty is palpable, especially in circuits which have yet to confront an issue.

Courts at both levels of appeals review whether lower courts followed rules of process and stated laws correctly. Ordinarily neither reviews whether the court below reached the right decision, that is, whether that court applied laws to facts correctly or justly. Neither takes further testimony; both rely on the records below. Since the intermediate appellate courts have tasks hardly different from supreme courts they are redundant. Through most of the 19th century few if any intermediate appellate courts existed. They were created in the last years of the century to overcome the workload of supreme courts.

Temporary relief for supreme courts came at a high price for litigants in general and for law-abiders in particular (at least in state courts). Now they have to defend two appeals! On both appeals, there is no cost-shifting, just as

---

[47] *Cf.*, Martin J. Siegel, *Let's Revamp the Appellate Rules Too*, 42 *Litigation*, No. 3, p. 1 (2016).

[48] For the different sorts of appeals, see ROSCOE POUND, APPELLATE PROCEDURE IN CIVIL CASES (1941).

[49] *See, e.g.*, RICHARD A. POSNER, THE FEDERAL COURTS: CRISIS AND REFORM (1985). *See also*, RICHARD A. POSNER, THE FEDERAL JUDICIARY: STRENGTHS AND WEAKNESSES (2017).

[50] *See* Marin K. Levy, *Judging Justice on Appeal*, 123 YALE L.J. 2386 (2014) *reviewing* WILLIAM M. RICHMAN & WILLIAM L. REYNOLDS, INJUSTICE ON APPEAL: THE UNITED STATES COURTS OF APPEALS IN CRISIS (2012).

in the first instance. Even when there was only one appeal, cagey lawyers inflicted costs of appeal to render victories in the trial court Pyrrhic. On both appeals, parties can argue for new law. What do attorneys tell their clients when they bill them for three "wins" where judges say, the law is what the attorney advised the client in their first meeting. Improbable nightmare that it seems, it happens.[51]

The Seventh Amendment to the Constitution limits possibilities for review of fact findings. It provides that "In suits at common law ... no fact tried by jury shall be otherwise reexamined in any court of the United States than according to the rules of the common law." Although this leaves many areas where appellate courts could review findings of fact below or conduct its own application of law to facts, custom discourages such review. Appellate courts rarely if ever take evidence.

This poses a dilemma for America's appellate judges. They are conscientious human beings who would like to see that they reach the best possible result for each controversy that comes before them. But that is not their duty. Their duty is to correct legal mistakes. Often the only way they can do justice in individual cases is *not* to uphold the law, but to upend it. "Hard cases make bad law" is an old saying critical of judges making law.[52] It exemplifies the fatal flaw of contemporary American legal method identified by its number one expositor, Professor Frederick Schauer: "every one of the dominant characteristics of legal reasoning and legal argument can be seen as a route toward reaching a decision *other than* the best all things considered decision for the matter at hand."[53]

A well-functioning government of laws maximizes legal certainty, justice and practicality. But process in America forces a choice among the three. That choice is, in effect, the focal point of arguments in America about statutory interpretation, to which I now turn. In Germany, where law and facts are not separated, there is no such dilemma.[54]

---

[51] *See, e.g.*, Keltner v. Washington County, 310 Or. 499 (1990) (Oregon Supreme Court affirmed holding of Oregon Court of Appeals affirming holding of trial court that an action for breach of contract may not recover damages for purely mental distress).

[52] For an early criticism of the still older maxim, see "W", *The Stability of Judge-Made Law*, 3 CENTRAL L.J. 49, 50 (1876) ("There is no case so hard as to justify the shaking of public confidence in the stability of law."). *See also Official Comment* 1, U.C.C., § 2–302 Unconscionable Contract of Clause ("In the past such policing has been accomplished by adverse construction of language .. ..").

[53] FREDERICK SCHAUER, THINKING LIKE A LAWYER: A NEW INTRODUCTION TO LEGAL REASONING 7 (2009). It appears over a dozen times. *See, e.g., id.* at 8, 9, 10, 11, 30, 31, 32, 36, 41, 43, 61, 62, 64, and 68.

[54] *See* text at notes 114 to 115, *infra. See also* James R. Maxeiner, *Thinking Like a Lawyer Abroad: Putting Justice into Legal Reasoning*, 11 WASHINGTON U. GLOBAL STUDIES L. REV. 55 (2012).

3. *Judicial Supremacy: Statutory Precedents*

Even before people get to courtrooms, America's judges have left their marks on laws and made law applying unpredictable. Judges put judicial interpretations of texts ahead of the texts themselves; they claim exclusive authority to interpret the texts. That is the essence of the doctrine of judicial supremacy. Sometimes judges have no choice: texts are inconsistent with each other or are incoherent in themselves or both. Sometimes judges overrule texts for the sake of justice in individual cases; other times they do so to improve the law as they see it. People coming to court encounter judges changing law after they arrive in court.[55] Many of America's judges believe that changing law as they apply it is the genius (!) of America's common-law methods.[56] I doubt that many law-abiding people agree.

Judicial supremacy is a creation of constitutional law. Judicial supremacy in constitutional law asserts that the Supreme Court is the exclusive interpreter of the Constitution. It is gospel today. But it is relatively new as accepted doctrine. It is usually dated to a 1958 decision of the United States Supreme Court.[57] Judicial supremacy is *not* the same as constitutional review.[58] Judicial supremacy in interpretation does *not* flow inexorably from constitutional review of consistency with the Constitution. A few courageous critics challenge constitutional supremacy as the "Myth of Marbury."[59]

Judges assert a comparable authority over statutes under a less-well known doctrine called statutory *stare decisis* (or statutory precedent) upon which they

---

[55] Geoffrey C. Hazard, Jr., *Rule of Legal Rhetoric*, 67 SMU L. REV. 801, 803 (2014) ("since American courts are relatively activist in redefining the law, in every case lies the possibility that the law will be changed from what it was when the case began.").

[56] RUGGERO J. ALDISERT, LOGIC FOR LAWYERS: A GUIDE TO CLEAR LEGAL THINKING 8 (3d ed., 1997). *See* P.S. Atiyah & Robert S. Summers, FORM AND SUBSTANCE IN ANGLO-AMERICAN LAW 91 (1987); FREDERICK SCHAUER, PLAYING BY THE RULES (1993).

[57] Cooper v. Aaron, 358 U.S. 1, 18 (1958). *See* LAWRENCE GOLDSTONE, THE ACTIVIST: JOHN MARSHALL, *MARBURY V. MADISON*, AND THE MYTH OF JUDICIAL REVIEW (2008). JOSEPH P. DAILEY, THE LAST DEMOCRATS: HOW AMERICA FOUGHT AND LOST THE WAR AGAINST JUDICIAL SUPREMACY 346–347 (2014); MARK TUSHNET, TAKING THE CONSTITUTION AWAY FROM THE COURTS (1999).

[58] *See* Kenneth Ward, *Legislative Supremacy*, 4 WASHINGTON U. JURISPRUDENCE REV. 327–329 (2012). *See also* Edward O. Correia, *A Legislative Conception of Legislative Supremacy*, 42 CASE WESTERN RESERVE L. REV. 1129 (1992).

[59] Michael Stokes Paulsen, *The Irrepressible Myth of* Marbury, 101 MICH. L. REV. 601 (2004); Keith E. Whittington, POLITICAL FOUNDATIONS OF JUDICIAL SUPREMACY: THE PRESIDENCY, THE SUPREME COURT, AND CONSTITUTIONAL LEADERSHIP IN U.S. HISTORY 9 (2007); *see also* LARRY D. KRAMER, THE PEOPLE THEMSELVES: POPULAR CONSTITUTIONALISM AND JUDICIAL REVIEW 229, 249 (2004).

rely in finding law. Just as judicial supremacy is not essential to constitutional review, judicial supremacy is not essential to applying law. Statutory interpretation often is.

Statutory Interpretation

Statutes cannot – and should not – provide answers for all cases. They should provide ways for people to reach answers. Statutory interpretation is one way to reach answers.

Statutory interpretation is mundane, or it should be.[60] Just about everyone expects judges to clarify the meaning of statutes as they decide whether particular cases fall under them. Especially legislators expect that.[61] Sometimes legislators expect too much. Justice Scalia criticized "legislative free-riding, whereby legal drafters idly assume that judges will save them from their blunders"[62] and complained that "in this job, it's garbage in, garbage out."[63]

Blunders and garbage have enormous public importance. The United States Supreme Court decided the 2000 presidential election by choosing between two inconsistent Florida election statutes.[64] After saving the Affordable Care Act from constitutional challenge, it spared it from a potentially deadly statutory challenge by deft interpretation.[65]

Long a backwater of American legal discourse, statutory interpretation has come to the fore in the last generation. It has become a hotly debated issue. I suspect that it is not coincidental that this has occurred as American proceduralists have described lawmaking as a usual goal for America process.

This is one fight in which each judge seems to have a champion. Unusual for legal theory arguments generally, judges have taken the lead in arguments

---

[60] *Compare* Chisom v. Roemer, 501 U.S. 380, 404 (1991) (Scalia, J., dissenting) ("we ha[ve] adopted a regular method for interpreting the meaning of language in a statute") *with* WILLIAM D. POPKIN, THE JUDICIAL ROLE: STATUTORY INTERPRETATION & THE PRAGMATIC JUDICIAL PARTNER xi (2013) ("We are at an impasse about statutory interpretation" and quoting Justice Scalia's "startling assertion.").

[61] *See, e.g.*, THE FEDERALIST No. 37 (James Madison) ("All new laws, though penned with the greatest technical skill, and passed on the fullest and most mature deliberation, are considered as more or less obscure and equivocal, until their meaning be liquidated and ascertained by a series of particular discussions and adjudications.")

[62] ANTONIN SCALIA & BYRAN A. GARNER, READING LAW: THE INTERPRETATION OF LEGAL TEXTS xxviii (2012). Worse still is legislators' practice of leaving for courts decisions they could not agree on.

[63] *Scalia Dissents*, April 6, 2005, Heritage Foundation, http://www.c-spanvideo.org/program/Scalia, Oct. 8, 2009, 1:49:34.

[64] *See* Bush v. Gore, 531 U.S. 98 (2000).

[65] *See* National Federation of Independent Business v. Sebelius, 567 U.S. 519 (2012)

about statutory interpretation. The argument is all about – at least as they see it – the role of judges in reading statutes.

In one corner Justice Scalia backed what he called "textualism" and its fiercer sibling, "originalism." Basic textualism is not surprising for statutory interpretation: read the text (what else?). Originalism is more surprising: read the text as its authors would (what did James Madison think of nuclear bombs?). Scalia's textualism combats "the tendency of judges to imbue authoritative texts with their own policy preferences."[66]

In the other corner is Judge Richard A. Posner who promotes "pragmatism."[67] His academic ally, Professor William D. Popkin, describes judges as "pragmatic judicial partners" with legislators. Their pragmatism focuses on the policy consequences of individual decisions.[68]

Academics might like to see a binary fight: a "contemporary debate in statutory interpretation [that] offers a choice between either continuity with the common-law tradition (and thus creative statutory interpretation) or formalist [i.e., textualist] interpretation that breaks with that heritage."[69] But this ring has more than two corners: textualists speak of their adversaries as "non-textualists" while pragmatists are aligned against "anti-pragmatists." In one other corner are proponents of what is variously referred to as purposivism, intentionalism or teleology. They may not be able to share the corner, for where one finds purpose may make all the difference in one's allies. Justice Scalia had particular scorn for a long-used interpretive tool in American statutory interpretation: legislative history. He saw it as an attack on a government of laws.[70] The ring may not be a quadrangle but an octagon!

Each champion has his own weapons. For the Scalia team it's an armory of canons of construction, that is, a set of rules that direct judges how to decide. For the Posner team, the weapons are the tools of the law and economics

---

[66]   See, e.g., Geoffrey C. Hazard, Jr., *Rule of Legal Rhetoric*, 67 SMU L. REV. 801, 803 (2014); SCALIA & GARNER, READING LAW, *supra* note 62, at xxviii.

[67]   See, e.g. RICHARD A. POSNER, LAW, PRAGMATISM AND DEMOCRACY 1–2 n.1 (2003) (with references to other of his works); RICHARD A. POSNER, HOW JUDGES THINK (2008).

[68]   WILLIAM D. POPKIN, THE JUDICIAL ROLE: STATUTORY INTERPRETATION & THE PRAGMATIC JUDICIAL PARTNER 4 (2013). *See also* WILLIAM D. POPKIN, STATUTES IN COURT (1999); William N. Eskridge, Jr., DYNAMIC STATUTORY INTERPRETATION (1994).

[69]   Jeffrey A. Pojanowski, *Reading Statutes in the Common Law Tradition*, 101 VA. L. REV. 1357, 1359 (2015).

[70]   SCALIA & GARNER, READING LAW, *supra* note 62, at 29 (In the interpretation of legislation, we aspire to be 'a nation of laws, not of men.' This means (1) giving effect to the text that lawmakers have adopted and that the people are entitled to rely on, and (2) giving *no* effect to lawmakers' unenacted desires."). *See generally* CHRISTIAN E. MAMMEN, USING LEGISLATIVE HISTORY IN AMERICAN STATUTORY INTERPRETATION (2002).

school, that is, economic principles. For the purposive team, it's the wealth of legislative history materials available, from committee reports to floor debates.

Authoritative and Doctrinal Interpretation

Little recognized in legal discourse is that statutory interpretation can be either "authoritative" or "doctrinal." Laymen want to know whether their conduct falls under law. They need to understand what statutes may require of them to plan. Most have no interest in what laws require of others. Just explain how the law applies to me. That's what judges of first instance do in other legal systems. That is doctrinal interpretation.

America's legal professionals see legal decisions as authoritative lawmaking. They don't ordinarily speak about how people *understand* laws. More commonly they talk about how they, the professions, *interpret* statutes. They call that "statutory interpretation." Both understanding and interpreting address statutes' contents but in different ways. To *understand* a statute is to know what a statute requires or allows; to *interpret* a statute is to mandate, that is, to state authoritatively, what the statute demands of everyone.[71] *Understanding*, as I use the word now, speaks to people who wish to comply with laws; *interpreting* speaks to people who impose laws.

Justice Scalia was among the few to see the difference, although he did not use the terms: "good judges dealing with statutes do *not* make law. They do not 'give new content' to the statute, but merely apply the content that has been there all along, awaiting application to myriad factual scenarios."[72]

Why does it make a difference? Doctrinal interpretation is concerned with the law applicable to the facts of a particular case. Its focus is on relating the facts of that case to the law.[73] Unlike authoritative application, it is not concerned with hypothetical facts, but only with the facts in the case before it. At least some versions of pragmatism share this case focus.

America's lawyers clamor for authoritative interpretations not because they want to make law, but because the separation of law and facts pushes them to do

---

[71] So Portalis, the principal drafter of the French Civil Code of 1804, referred to the former as "doctrinal interpretation" and to the latter as "authoritative interpretation." JEAN-ÉTIENNE-MARIE PORTALIS, PRELIMINARY ADDRESS ON THE FIRST DRAFT OF THE CIVIL CODE PRESENTED IN THE YEAR IX BY MESSRS. PORTALIS, TRONCHET, BIGOT-PRÉAMENEU AND MALEVILLE, MEMBERS OF THE GOVERNMENT-APPOINTED COMMISSION (1801), translated at http://www.justice.gc.ca/eng/rp-pr/csj-sjc/ilp-pji/code/index.html

[72] SCALIA & GARNER, READING LAW *supra* note 62, at 5.

[73] *Accord, id.* Scalia spoke of a "retail application." He insisted that: "a court's application of a statute to a 'new situation' can be said to establish *the law applicable to that situation* – that is, to pronounce definitely whether and how the statute applies to that situation. But establishing this retail application is [not] 'creating law,' 'adapt[ing] legal doctrines,' and 'giv[ing] them new content.'" [Emphasis in original.]. *Id.*

so. If they are to argue to jurors that certain facts fit the law, they need to know before arguing which facts they need to show. But by so doing, they force courts to decide issues that might better be left undecided until facts are known.

The Federal Rules are rife with requirements that judges decide legal issues with imperfect knowledge of facts. A clear example is the instructions on law that judges give jurors under Federal Rule of Civil Procedure 51. The rule forces judges to anticipate legal issues that jurors may reach depending on the facts they find. That would be problematic alone, but the Rule allows adversary parties to suggest the law. Why not? The maxim that judges know the law, *jura novit curia*, does not apply in common-law courts.[74] America's judges often adopt parties' requests as the easier course.[75] When they do not, rather than write instructions with the apparent facts in mind, they weave together officially approved pattern jury instructions.

This drive for authoritative interpretation undercuts statutory drafting techniques that use indefinite (or vague) terms to cover cases that cannot practically be spelled out in detail or be foreseen (for example, "so far as necessary," "seasonably," "good faith"). Understanding whether the vague term applies is clarified by context, that is, by arguments that relate the facts to the rule.[76]

To these terms too, America's adversary lawyers have long sought authoritative interpretations that drive desired flexibility out of the law. Nearly a century ago a French observer of the American system lamented that "judges, instead of looking at the facts of the case they have before them, directly – concretely – have to fit them into some pigeon hole of a classification that has become part of the law."[77] Their attempts to fit facts into those pigeon holes means that often times courts decide cases for other than the best possible reasons.[78]

The bar promotes predictability of process by prescribing how judges must go about interpreting statutes. So there are proposals for Federal Rules of Statutory Interpretation and for a Restatement of the same.[79] One critic assails these

---

[74]   *See* F.A. Mann, *Fusion of the Legal Professions*, 93 Law Q. Rev. 367, 369 (1977).

[75]   *See* Dennis Jacobs, *The Secret Life of Judges*, 75 Fordham L. Rev. 2855, 2863 (2007) ("judges should accept that . . . lawyer-driven processes and that lawyer-centered solutions can be unwise, insufficient, and unjust, even if our friends in the legal profession lead us that way."). Jacobs was Chief Judge of the United States Court of Appeals for the Second Circuit from 2006 to 2013.

[76]   Scalia & Garner, Reading Law, *supra* note 62, at 32.

[77]   Jean Lepaulle, *Administration of Justice in the United States*, 4 West Publishing Co's Docket 3192, 3193 (1928).

[78]   *See* text at 50 *supra*.

[79]   *See* Nicholas Quinn Rosenkranz, *Federal Rules of Statutory Interpretation*, 115 Harv. L. Rev. 2085 (2012); Gary E. O'Connor, *Restatement (First) of Statutory Interpretation*, 7 N.Y.U.J. Legis. & Pub. Pol'y 333 (2004). *See also*, Lawrence M. Solan, *Is It Time for a Restatement of Statutory Interpretation?*, 79 Brooklyn L. Rev. 733 (2014).

proposals as "The Dumbing Down of Statutory Interpretation."[80] But other law professors see a "distinct field of scholarly inquiry and judicial practice."[81]

None of these rules intended to direct judges are of utility to people who only want to know the law so that they can apply it to themselves. People might ignore these shenanigans as so much voodoo, but for the doctrine of statutory stare decisis.

Statutory *Stare Decisis*

The doctrine of statutory *stare decisis* holds that once a court has interpreted a statute, that interpretation is binding as a legal precedent. It treats practically every judicial application of a statute as an instance of authoritative interpretation.

Statutory *stare decisis* sounds sensible: give the words in a statute the same meaning every time that one applies them. If the legislature has problems with a court's interpretation, all it need do is to revise the law. Only a few judges candidly recognize, however, that "for a court to say that Congress can fix a statute if it does not like the result is *not* a neutral principle in our separation of powers scheme because it is very difficult for Congress to correct a mistaken statutory decision."[82]

The effect of statutory *stare decisis* is that no one, certainly no layman, can find security in a statute before searching for judicial interpretations of it, even if the search only confirms that there are no judicial interpretations.[83]

Of many failures of American legal methods I cannot think of a one that is as devastating in its consequences for a government of laws, which is so easily remedied and which is so often overlooked as that of statutory *stare decisis*.[84] It is one practice that is hardly ever questioned.[85] Its opposite – non-binding judicial applications of statutes – is thought alien. Only in the area of Supreme

---

[80] Glen Staszewski, *The Dumbing Down of Statutory Interpretation*, 95 BOSTON U.L. REV. 209 (2015).

[81] Lumen N. Mulligan & Glen Staszewski, *Civil Rules Interpretive Theory* (July 25, 2016) Available at SSRN: http://ssrn.com/abstract=2814194 or http://dx.doi.org/10.2139/ssrn.2814194.

[82] Brett M. Kavanaugh, *Fixing Statutory Interpretation* [Review of Robert A. Katzmann, *Judging Statutes*], 129 HARV. L. REV. 2118, 2133–2134 (2016) [emphasis in original].

[83] For a contrary view, see LAWRENCE M. SOLAN, THE LANGUAGE OF STATUTES: LAWS AND THEIR INTERPRETATION 4 (2010) ("Most of the time most people understand their obligations well enough and most of the time law's application is clear.").

[84] See Peter L. Strauss, *The Common Law and Statutes*, 70 COLO. L. REV. 225, 231, 244–245 (1999); James R. Maxeiner, *Thinking Like a Lawyer Abroad: Putting Justice into Legal Reasoning*, 11 WASH. U. GLOBAL STUDIES L. REV. 55, 82–83 (2012).

[85] A major exception was Justice Scalia. SCALIA & GARNER, READING LAW, *supra* note 62 (2012). He was plain and to the point: "*Stare decisis* is not a part of textualism. It is an exception to textualism." Yet he could not bring himself to abandon it. Why? "*Stare decisis* has been a part of our law from time immemorial, and we must bow to it?" *Id.*

Court jurisprudence as *statutory precedent* has it received much scholarly attention.[86] But it applies across the United States in all courts. It applies not just when the Supreme Court with all its majesty decides, but whenever the lowliest of federal or state courts applies a statute.

The doctrine is justified on grounds of judicial modesty, judicial efficiency and as protection of the rule of law. It does none of those things. The justification argues that if courts did not follow their interpretations of statutes, how would anyone know what the statute meant? The obvious and overlooked answer is: read it and think!

Statutory Stare Decisis Is not Democratic

The legal professions assume that common-law methods should apply to statutory enactments.[87] Statutory *stare decisis* takes a common-law malady and infects statutes with it. Judge-made common law is undemocratic, inaccessible, unreliable and unsystematic.[88] It is the same of judge-made statutory precedents.[89]

Statutory *stare decisis* upends the democratic legitimacy of government and interferes with political process. By giving interpretations of statutes the force of law, courts arrogate to themselves determination of what the law is until the legislature acts again.[90] Legislators aren't reading case reports looking for decisions to correct!

Courts do not have the charge of making (or remaking) laws.[91] Their task is applying laws that others have made to decide particular cases. Elected legislatures have the charge of prescribing laws for general application. They have institutional knowledge of the whole legal system. They have time and

---

[86] *See, e.g* William N. Eskridge, Jr., *Overruling Statutory Precedents*, 76 Geo. L.J. 1361 (1988); Anita S. Krishnakumar, *Textualism and Statutory Stare Decisis* (2016), http://ssrn.com/abstract= 2724077; Lawrence M. Solan, *Precedent in Statutory Interpretation*, 94 N. Car. L. Rev. 1165 (2016).

[87] Judith S. Kaye, *State Courts at the Dawn of a New Century: Common Law Courts Reading Statutes and Constitutions*, 70 N.Y.U. L. Rev. 1, 6 (1995) ("Even in today's legal landscape, dominated by statutes, the common-law process remains the core element in state court decisionmaking.").

[88] *See* Chapter 3, *supra*.

[89] *See* Kavanaugh, *supra* note 82, at 2120 ("When courts apply doctrines that allow them to rewrite the laws (in effect), they are encroaching on the legislature's Article I power.").

[90] *See* Strauss, *supra* note 84, at 244. "Often presented as if it were an act of self-abnegation . . . giving interpretations precedential force actually dramatizes judicial power; it makes the courts a political competitor with the legislature in the creation of law." *Id.*

[91] Some American academics disagree and claim for judges the role of "pragmatic judicial partner." *See* William D. Popkin, The Judicial Role: Statutory Interpretation & the Pragmatic Judicial Partner (2013).

resources to examine how their work fits into that the system. All people should be able to participate in their deliberations.

Judges are ill-equipped to rewrite the legislatures' general laws. Of the system of laws and of the law rewritten itself what individual judges know is peculiar to the judges assigned. Their knowledge and skills are serendipitous. Gaining more knowledge is not in the interest of expediting deciding cases.[92] They have no mandate for making policy decisions.[93] Courtrooms are not forums for debating laws. People outside the courtroom, i.e., almost everyone, are uniformed of court proceedings and have only limited rights of participation.

No Authoritative Text

Statutory *stare decisis* is not limited to decisions of the highest courts reached after consideration. It applies to all judicial decisions reached by all courts no matter how hasty. That creates questions of quality and quantity.

Every court issues decisions. While not every court issues statutory precedents for every statute, the doctrine of *stare decisis* binds lower courts to decisions issued by courts to which they are inferior. It encourages them to consider precedents issued by other courts (persuasive or non-binding authority). While a statute is stable – at least it does not change without notice in an official gazette – a new binding precedent could be issued at any moment.[94]

In the world of statutory *stare decisis* finding law can consume more energy than applying it. Requiring that judges follow statutory precedents distracts from their task of applying the law. It adds a new layer of complexity. Judges must find the law before they can apply it.[95]

Lawyers take on the role of makers of the law. The maxim of Roman and German law, the court knows the law, *jura novit curia*, does not apply. They collect decisions applying the law. Where yesterday they paged through mammoth books euphemistically called "annotated statutes," which collect synopses of past cases, now they search whole texts in electronic databases.

---

[92] *Cf.* James Maxeiner, Policy and Methods in German and American Antitrust Law: A Comparative Study (1986).

[93] Kavanaugh, *supra* note 81, at 2120 ("The American rule of law, as I see it, depends on neutral, impartial judges who say what the law is, not what the law should be.")

[94] J. Paul Lomio et al., Legal Research Methods in a Modern World: A Coursebook 182 (3d ed., 2011). ("Of course, tomorrow a new case could come along and completely change an earlier and [relied] upon holding.")

[95] It's reminiscent of the 19th century argument in favor of a written over an unwritten constitution.

Ex uno plures (Out of one, many).
Statutory *stare decisis* undermines the unity of American law. It turns the national motto, *E pluribus unum* – out of many, one – on its head: *Ex uno plures* – out of one, many.

A statute has one authoritative formulation. A federal statute or a uniform state statute (if truly uniform) has one formulation for the entire country. A state statute has one formulation for the entire state.

Statutory *stare decisis* engrafts onto legislative law the law of court organization. There are fifty state legislatures and one federal one. These fifty-one jurisdictions have more than fifty-one courts and each court issues many decisions.

Apply a couple of doses of statutory *stare decisis* to a statute and suddenly, where once there was one law, now there are multiple binding precedents. Apply statutory stare decisis in the multilayered, multicircuit, multistate systems of courts that is the United States of America, where once there was one national or one state law, now there are different national or state laws for different circuits, judicial districts and states. Theoretically the Supreme Court resolves conflicting interpretations among different federal courts, but practically it addresses only the most important of them – at best, a few dozen each year. The reality is interstate discordance.[96]

Legal Illiteracy: Cases Before Laws
The outcome of different laws in different courts is as predictable as it is pernicious: nobody reads statutes. Legal professionals read court decisions applying statutes instead. But what if there are no precedents? As a last resort, and not as a first step, legal professionals read statutes.

To foreign jurists this is bizarre or even barbaric. Yet for America's legal professionals it is a matter of course. The United States Court of Appeals for the Second Circuit found no embarrassment in writing in applying the United Nations Convention on the International Sale of Goods: "Because there is virtually no case law under the Convention, we look to its language and to 'the general principles upon which it is based.'"[97] Only in the United States could "emphasizing the centrality of the words of the statute" be thought to have "brought about a massive and enduring change in . . . law."[98] Until words do matter, will legislators take the trouble to write understandable laws?

---

[96] *See* Paul D. Carrington, *The Function of the Civil Appeal: A Late-Century View*, 38 S.C. L. Rev. 411, 427 (1987). In the 1970s and 1980s, there were proposals for creation of a "National Court of Appeals" or an "Intercircuit Panel" that would have handled these kinds of cases, but no such court was established. *See* Erwin N. Griswold, *The Federal Courts Today and Tomorrow: A Summary and Survey*, 38 S.C. L. Rev. 393, 396–397 (1987).

[97] Delchi Carrier SpA v. Rotorex Corp. 71 F.3d 1024, 1028 (Winter, C.J., 2nd Cir. 1995).

[98] Kavanaugh, *supra* note 81, at 2118.

C. GERMANY'S PROCESS FORTIFIES LAWS

Kid's Information on Domestic Violence, From German Public Service Internet Site[99]

Process in Germany supports a government of laws. Here's why: (1) process is a reliable option for law-abiders; (2) process applies laws; and (3) process defers intelligently to legislative supremacy.

1. *Process Is a Good Option*

Law-abiding people who turn to German courts find a system designed to uphold their reasonable choices in applying laws to themselves. Litigation is a good option.[100]

Litigation is a good option because legislatures enact laws that people can find, read and understand. People don't usually need lawyers to know which law governs and to understand its application. In day-to-day matters it's child's play.[101]

---

[99] *"Kidsinfo häusliche Gewalt,"* Multilingual website for victims of domestic violence provided by Frauen helfen Frauen Dortmund e.V., http://www.kidsinfo-gewalt.de/en/what-does-law-say. Image used with permission.

[100] The Federal Ministry of Justice and Consumer Protection endorses bold claims that process in Germany is effective, cost-efficient, predictable and just. *See Law – Made in Germany* 3, 18–29 (3d ed., ca. 2014), available at http://www.lawmadeingermany.de/ (last visited Dec. 10, 2016). The *Rule of Law Index* published by the American Bar Association sponsored World Justice Project supports the Ministry's claims. Overall it ranks German Civil Justice 2nd of 113 systems reviewed for its 2016 ranking. (It places the United States 28th, just barely ahead of Belarus.) In the subcategory "people can access and afford civil justice" it ranks German Civil Justice 5th. (It places the United States 94th (*sic!*), tied with Bangladesh, among other third world countries.) Available at http://worldjusticeproject.org/rule-of-law-index (last visited Dec. 10, 2016).

[101] Literally; it's the subject of game shown on YouTube ("Schönfelder Roulette"). *See* ULI REISSMÜLLER, SCHÖNFELDER-ROULETTE (Jan. 20, 2012) https://youtu.be/t2N9ZwPmCo0.

Litigation is a good option because people can count on judges to find facts and apply law correctly. Process is rational and transparent. Applying law is verifiable. If first instance judges get decisions wrong, appellate judges can make right decisions. Ordinary courts do not create new law or set aside old law. They defer to decisions of democratically elected legislators.

Litigation is a good option because judges and fee schedules keep expenses in bounds and proportionate to amounts in dispute. Losers pay. Law abiders are not charged with the expenses of executing laws. They get back their full rightful claims.

2. Judges Apply Laws to Facts

German process routinely applies laws to facts. Cases end in verifiable official applications of laws to facts in reasoned judicial opinions of entire cases reached after courts have heard the parties on facts and laws.[102]

A substantial percentage of cases settle without judicial judgments, but they settle for different reasons than do lawsuits in America. In the United States unpredictable dangers of outsized awards and high costs of process drive settlements. How laws might be applied to facts plays a lesser role. Not so in Germany where process costs are calculable and awards predictable.[103]

Relating Laws to Facts

German process is about applying laws to facts. It fulfills the expectations of laymen when they go to court that they will tell judges the facts and judges will apply laws to facts. There is a name for this method of applying laws to facts: the *Relationstechnik*, or *relationship technique*. Professional judges apply laws to facts they find to produce carefully reasoned judgments. German process brings laws and facts together.

The syllogism is the basis of the relationship technique: the legal rule is the major premise, the facts to be found are the minor premise, and the judicial decision is the logical conclusion. The individual elements required by statute to establish a claim are the "spectacles" through which judges review parties'

---

[102] *See* Reinhard Zimmermann, *Characteristic Aspects of German Legal Culture, in* INTRODUCTION TO GERMAN LAW 1, 26–27 (Mathias Reimann & Joachim Zekoll eds., 2005). *See also* MAXEINER, FAILURES OF AMERICAN CIVIL JUSTICE, *supra* note 9, at 226–234; James R. Maxeiner, *Imagining Judges that Apply Law: How They Might Do It*, 114 PENN STATE L. REV. 469 (2009). PETER MURRAY & ROLF STÜRNER, GERMAN CIVIL JUSTICE (2004).
[103] *See* LAW MADE IN GERMANY, *supra* note 100, at 27.

cases. What the judge can see through the spectacles matters; everything else is immaterial.[104]

Judgments of German judges are verifiable. As American Justice Scalia observed: "to put an argument in syllogistic form is to strip it bare for logical inspection. We can then see where its weak points must lie, if it has any."[105] Judges teach the relationship technique to all German law students after they finish law school, whether graduates become judges or lawyers.[106] The relationship technique has proven to work for well more than a century of judicial practice.[107] It permits easy appellate review of lower courts' applying of laws to facts.

Relating laws to facts, instead of separating the two, does not require that laymen be left out of process. German courts often involve laymen in deciding cases without, however, cabining them off in jury boxes as separate tribunals. Laymen decide in Germany as lay judges sitting together with professional judges in multijudge panels in certain kinds of cases. Lay judges are the norm in serious criminal cases and in commercial and labor law cases. Since lay judges never decide alone, there is always a professional judge to write the judgment that applies laws.

"Give Me the Facts – I Will Give You Right."

Judges in Germany steer process. They have leading roles. Lawyers have supporting roles. Lawyers do not present "their clients' cases." Judges examine facts presented to them by lawyers. Judges direct lawyers when and what to produce to the court. The maxims *jura novit curia* (the court knows the law) and *da mihi factum, dabo tibi ius* (give me the facts, I will give you right) apply.

Judges are professionally-trained neutral deciders. What they decide is what process is about. The Code of Civil Procedure provides only a few general directions and a few general principles to guide them in reaching decisions; it but not does provide detailed rules to sanction to enforce compliance. Here

---

[104] Joachim Hruschka, Die Konstitution des Rechtsfalles: Studien zum Verhältnis von Tatsachenfeststellung und Rechtsanwendung 22–24 (1965).

[105] Scalia & Garner, Making Your Case, *supra* note 31, at 41 (quoting F.C.S. Schiller, Formal Logic: A Scientific and Social Problem 222 (1922)).

[106] In an idealized form students learn it already in law school as part of legal methods. A basic text on German legal methods is available in English. *See* Reinhold Zippelius, Introduction to German Legal Methods (10th German ed. transl., K.W. Junker & P.M. Roy, 2008).

[107] *Compare* Hermann Daubenspeck, Referat, Votum und Urtheil (1st ed., 1884) *with* its current version, Winfried Schuschke, Martin Kessen & Björn Höltje, Zivilrechtliche Arbeitstechnik im Assessorexamen: Bericht – Votum – Urteil – Aktenvortrag (35th ed., 2013).

are a few examples that I discuss more fully in my book *Failures of American Civil Procedure in International Perspective* with further citations.

Pleading

Judges *ex officio* review plaintiffs' complaints before serving them. They determine whether complaints on their face meet procedural requirements (*Zulässigkeitsprüfung*)[108] and state plausible claims (*Schlüssigkeitsprüfung*).[109] Plaintiffs in their complaints (and defendants in their answers) must substantiate factual assertions and identify, in general terms, the evidence they plan to rely on to prove their claims.

If judges find complaints deficient, they do not summarily dismiss them, but invite plaintiffs to correct them. Should a plaintiff file in the wrong court, in the interest of process economy, the judge transfers the case to the proper court. That's one example of how German process works toward achieving the goal of a just, speedy and inexpensive determination of every action. It puts reaching substantive decisions, and thus applying laws to facts, ahead of process games.[110]

Case Structuring

Early on judges meet with parties personally and with their attorneys to identify laws under consideration for applying, the elements of those rules, and the evidence necessary to establish them. Judges point out to lawyers weaknesses in their clients' claims and inquire of lawyers how they plan to overcome these weaknesses.

Deferred Decision Making

The relationship technique overcomes the interdependency problem by making determinations of applicable rules and findings of material facts concurrently rather than consecutively. It finds facts "just in time;" German judges defer final decisions of individual aspects of cases until they are prepared to decide the case as a whole.

---

[108] For a catalogue of the procedural perquisites, see BECK'SCHE RICHTER-HANDBUCH 14 (3d ed., 2012).

[109] For a discussion of the *Schlüssigkeitsprüng*, see SCHUSCHKE ET AL., *supra* note 107, at 122–129.

[110] A standard handbook for judges makes the point: "The statutory system has the goal of bringing the dispute quickly and finally to the proper court and to avoid pointless useless strife about jurisdiction in favor of a substantive decision." BECK'SCHE RICHTER-HANDBUCH, *supra* note 108, at 37 (author's translation).

Cooperation and Clarification

Judges conduct meetings with the parties and their lawyers, informal by American standards, to address the elements of claims. Judges, with input from lawyers, determine the course of proceedings. Parties do not present separate cases. Parties are under a duty of cooperating with the court. Judges are under a duty to clarify the matters in issue for the parties. Meetings with parties do not constitute taking evidence.

Focused Evidence Taking

When it comes to taking testimony of witnesses, German civil justice is just-in-time justice. The judge takes evidence only on party request and only after the judge so orders.[111] The judge is to order taking evidence only when necessary to convince the judge of the truth or untruth of a particular fact that is disputed by the parties and that is material to the decision of the case.[112]

The Judgment: The Verifiable Applying of Law

The judgment includes a short statement (*Tatbestand*) of the parties' legal claims and of their assertions of fact. It is *not* a finding of facts and thus is not a perfect analogue to the findings of fact of an American bench decision. The justification (*Begründung*) applies law to facts. It determines the facts and subsumes them under the abstract elements of the applicable law.

The judgment certifies that the procedure has fulfilled constitutional guarantees. These include that every exercise of state power has been justified by and grounded in statute, that the parties were heard and that they received equal treatment under law. The judgment is an act of an impartial and impersonal public authority furnishing the official and objective interpretation and application of law.[113] It helps parties understand why the court decided as it did. Ideally it convinces losing parties that the outcome is legally correct; at a minimum, it demonstrates that the process was rational.

---

[111] John Langbein has written eloquently of *The German Advantage in Civil Procedure*, 52 U. Chi. L. Rev. 824 (1985). His main theme is that "by assigning judges rather than lawyers to investigate the facts, the Germans avoid the most troublesome aspects of our practice." *Id.* at 824.

[112] Judges' control of evidence taking does not, however, prevent parties from insisting on taking evidence that they believe is relevant to deciding material issues in dispute. German judges told me that a sure way to bring about reversal on appeal of a lower court judgment is to reject an application to take evidence without strong justification. Such refusal violates the judges duty of clarification.

[113] *See* Reinhard Zimmermann, *Characteristic Aspects of German Legal Culture, in* Introduction to German Law 1, 26–27 (Mathias Reimann & Joachim Zekoll eds., 2005).

Appeals Decide Substantive Rights[114]

German appeals are good options for law-abiders to confirm their rights. Cost and risks are predictable and are proportionate to amounts in dispute. Losers pay. Courts decide cases according to right.

Ordinarily there are a maximum of two levels of appeal. The intermediate level, called *Berufung*, reviews the case completely: fact findings and applications of law to facts, with the possibility of taking new evidence. The final level, called *Revision*, reviews only issues of law. Until 2002 the intermediate level reviewed cases practically *de novo*, even if it did not exactly rehear the case. In response to Germany's own workload issues, the legislature revamped *Berufung* so as not to require a review *de novo*. But its fundamental goal of a decision in accordance with law and right remains unaltered.

The function of *Berufung* today is "to review the judgment of the first instance for its application of the substantive law as well as the correctness and completeness of the determinations reached and to correct any mistakes."[115] Under the new law, the intermediate appellate court is required to accept factual findings of the first instance court "insofar as there is no clear indication of doubt of the correctness or completeness of the fact determinations material to the decision and therefore indication for a new fact determination."[116] If there is such doubt, however, the court, as before, may take new testimony and find new facts.[117]

Syllogistic German judgments facilitate reviews. There are no verbatim transcripts to read through, but only concise analyses of the arguments made and the judges' grounds for decision.

The intermediate appellate courts cannot just affirm on the basis of the record below as is sometimes practice in America. Intermediate appellate courts have responsibility for the material correctness of their own final judgments of cases. Although it is not for them to search for error by the court below, it is for them to insure that the judgment is correct and, if it is not, to reach the correct judgment itself. Now, however, rather than conduct the proceedings of the case itself, the court is to review the trial court's factual findings for correctness and to apply the law to the facts as found.

---

[114] Daniel J. Meador, *Appellate Subject Matter Organization: The German Design from an American Perspective*, 5 HASTINGS J. INT'L & COMP. L. 27 (1981); Daniel J. Meador, *German appellate judges: career patterns and American-English comparisons*, 67 JUDICATURE 16 (1983).

[115] BTDrucks 14/4722, at 64–65, *reprinted in* ROLF HANNICH ET AL., ZPO-REFORM: EINFÜHRUNG – TEXTE – MATERIALIEN 314 (2002) (author's translation).

[116] ZPO § 529(I), para. 1, translated in MURRAY & STÜRNER, *supra* note 102, at 373.

[117] *See id.* § 529(I), para. 2.

By focusing on how the trial court applied the law, these reforms may enhance legal certainty. In any case, other aspects of the reform seek to enhance legal certainty by helping the winner conclude the case sooner. The court is required to review all appeals when initially filed. It is to dismiss, *ex officio*, any appeal that, according to all the members of the court, appears to have no chance of success, raises no legal issue of fundamental importance, imposes a decision for the sake of the development of the law, or requires a uniform interpretation of the law.[118]

Intermediate appellate judges can do justice without facing the dilemma their counterparts in America do. If decisions below seem unjust, the intermediate appellate judges can explore the cases more fully. They can consider other facts, other laws and other legal interpretations. If they see constitutional issues, they can refer cases to the Constitutional Court; if they see issues of European Union law, they can refer cases to the Court of Justice of the European Union.

German courts of appeal, both intermediate and final, have many more judges than do their counterparts in America. The Federal Supreme Court has more than one hundred judges. The intermediate appellate courts, depending on the size of the state and of the judicial district, have from about twenty to more than one hundred judges. They are more like the largest of the federal courts of appeal, the ninth circuit which is authorized to have twenty-nine judges. None of the other circuit courts of appeal of the United States have as many as twenty judges.

Yet the much larger intermediate courts of appeal in Germany do not experience the same kind of coordination issues their counterparts in America do. Professor Daniel J. Meador, renowned as much as anyone in the last generation for studies of America's courts of appeals, explained that "the key to the ability of German appellate courts to manage huge dockets and numbers of judges while maintaining coherence in the law is the subject matter basis of the internal organization."[119]

Under the division system in Germany, each appellate court has standing divisions of multiple judges (typically four to five in the immediate appellate courts, seven in the Federal Supreme Court in civil and criminal matters). Each division is assigned cases of certain types. Assignments are adjusted annually, but panels themselves and judges assigned do not change dramatically frequently.

---

[118] See ZPO § 529(II).
[119] Meador, *Appellate Subject Matter Organization, supra* note 114, at 44, 57.

Meador reviewed how the divisional arrangement works in practice and showed other ways how appellate courts in Germany work to maintain uniformity in laws. He concluded that the German system provides a model that without major alteration is "worth a try" as possibly "the most promising method of preventing doctrinal chaos in the legal system."[120]

3. *Legislative Supremacy: A Government of Statutes*

Legislative supremacy, and this democratic supremacy, are integral components of the German government of laws. Article 20(3) of the Constitution sets the hierarchy in the separation of powers: "The legislature shall be bound by the constitutional order, the executive and the judiciary by law and justice." It is for the elected legislature through legally binding statutes to seek the ends of the state.[121]

Statutory Interpretation

Statutory interpretation in Germany is not at an impasse. There is a regular method for the interpretation of statutes: it is a combination theory. It pulls together approaches that parallel American methods: textual, systematic, historical and purposive.[122] But where American judges champion one or the other approach, or insist on a strict hierarchy among them, German judges flexibly and pragmatically choose among different approaches that most convincingly decide particular cases.

Judges accept the resulting legal uncertainty.[123] But so, too, it seems to me, do the people. I think it reasonably well comports with how laymen read statutes. German academics suggest that in society it well balances the three goals of law, legal certainty, justice and practicality (common good, policy).[124] Here I add a few suggestions why I think it does not imperil a government of laws.

---

[120] *Id.* at 59. Meador noted that Professor Paul Carrington had proposed such a system in 1969 and that Carrington, he and Professor Maurice Rosenberg had promoted it in 1976. *Id.* at 58–59 n. 71.

[121] Zippelius, German Legal Methods, *supra* note 106, at 33.

[122] Winfried Brugger, *Concretization of Law and Statutory Interpretation*, 11 *Tulane Eur.& Civ. L. Forum* 207, 232 (1996). *See also* Reinhard Zimmermann, Statuta Sunt Stricte Interpretanda? *Statutes and the Common Law: A Continental Perspective*, 56 Cambridge L.J. 315, 320 (1997).

[123] Winfried Brugger, *Legal Interpretation, Schools of Jurisprudence, and Anthropology: Some Remarks From a German Point of View*, 42 Am. J. Comp. L. 395, 402 (1994).

[124] *See generally,* Brugger, *Concretization, supra* note 122.

Limits of the Law's Language (*Wortlautgrenze*)
Interpretation is necessary because the language of a law as applied to a case at hand may not deliver an answer. It may not even direct how to find the answer. But judges under the Constitution's Article 20(2) are bound to law and justice. While they are directed to apply laws to reach just solutions and encouraged to reach practical solutions, they may not decide against the law. The legislature's language is supreme.[125] If justice requires that the law not be enforced, then reference to the Constitutional Court discussed in the preceding chapter is the proper course.[126] The people have security in the words of the laws.[127]

Statutory Interpretation Is Usually Case-Focused
Most instances of statutory interpretation are in courts of first or second instance. In the former it is always and in the latter usually doctrinal rather than authoritative interpretation. Judges are not seeking to state rules authoritatively for future cases, but to decide the cases before them in the best possible way, whether that means most just or most practical.

Interpretation Is Justified and Verifiable
Judges in first instance, after hearing all the facts, must justify their applications with respect to those facts in judgments. Their judgments are reviewable by appellate judges who likewise are bound to decide according to law and justice. Authoritative interpretation is usually the province only of the third instance supreme courts or of the Constitutional Court.

Even Authoritative Interpretations Are Not Binding
German lower courts are not bound to follow higher court interpretations of law. They usually do follow them, but when facts require, they are free to depart and

---

[125] *See generally*, MATHIAS KLETT, MAKING THE LAW EXPLICIT: THE NORMATIVITY OF LEGAL ARGUMENTATION (2008); ZIPPELIUS, GERMAN LEGAL METHODS, *supra* note 106.

[126] That a particular case might cause an irresolvable conflict between law and justice is thought unusual if not extraordinary. The President of the Federal Supreme Court opined that for most judges, it is a once in a career experience. Günter Hirsch, President of the Federal Supreme Court, *Address at the Bucerius Law School, Der Richter im Spannungsverhältnis von Erster und Dritter Gewalt* (Oct. 1, 2003), *in* DIE ZEIT, No. 41, 2003, *available at* http://zeus.zeit.de/text/ reden/bildungundkultur/hirschbls ("Vom Auslegungsverbot zum Auslegungsgebot").

[127] *See* JAMES MAXEINER, POLICY AND METHODS IN GERMAN AND AMERICAN ANTITRUST LAW: A COMPARATIVE STUDY 26–46 (1986); *cf.*, PHILIP K. HOWARD, THE RULE OF NOBODY: SAVING AMERICA FROM DEAD LAWS AND BROKEN GOVERNMENT 37, 61–62 (2014) (using the metaphor of "a giant corral", conduct outside the corral is prohibited, but "within the fences … people are free to pursue their goals in their way."

explain in their judgments why. They are bound to follow, as discussed in the preceding chapter, the syllabus of decisions of the Constitutional Court.

Judges Are Reticent to Make Law

The Federal Constitutional Court has recognized that there are occasions where judge-made law is necessary: the goal of a gap-free legal order is unattainable.[128] Within the existing framework of statutes, judges may and do fill gaps.[129] But case law is limited: "statutes, not men, govern."[130] In refusing to create a case law of plea-bargaining in criminal justice, the Federal Supreme Court signaled its discomfort with extensive judicial legislation.[131]

---

[128] BVerfG Feb. 14, 1973, 34 BVerfGE 269 (287) (F.R.G.) ("Soraya")

[129] *Id.* On judge-made law in Germany generally, see Klett, *supra* note 125; ZIPPELIUS, GERMAN LEGAL METHODS, *supra* note 106.

[130] WALTER LEISNER, KRISE DES GESETZES: DIE AUFLÖSUNG DES NORMENSTAATES 5 (2001).

[131] Bundesgerichtshof, Großer Senat für Strafsachen [BGH Gr. Sen. St.] [Federal Court of Justice en banc panel to resolve conflicts among the Senate for criminal cases] Mar. 3, 2005, 50 ENTSCHEIDUNGEN DES BUNDESGERICHTSHOFES IN STRAFSACHEN [BGHSt] 41, 64.

14

Conclusion

Learning from Others

There is no country on earth, which has more to gain than ours by the thorough study of foreign jurisprudence. . . . Let us not vainly imagine that we have unlocked and exhausted all the stores of juridicial wisdom and policy.

Justice Joseph Story (1821)[1]

Learning from others helps societies improve. In 1833 a young physician named Oliver Wendell Holmes (1809–1894) journeyed across the sea to spend three years in Paris to learn new ways of thinking about disease taught in post-revolutionary France. New thinking challenged old doctrines and practices in America, where blood-letting was a normal treatment and physicians did not always wash their hands as they moved from patient to patient.[2] Three years later, in 1836, a lawyer named David Dudley Field (1805–1894) embarked on a year-long study trip to Europe. There Napoleon's codes governed France, Belgium, Baden and other states. The new codes challenged old methods and procedures, including in America, where laws were discordant, incoherent and unknowable and legal procedures were difficult, deleterious and costly

When Holmes and Field returned home they practiced and preached the new methods they had learned. To the consternation and irritation of their fellow professionals, they blamed customary ways of doing things for bringing about, in Holmes' case, needless deaths, and in Field's case, pointless injustices. Physicians who were supposed to be curing patients, were killing them. Lawyers who were supposed to be righting wrongs, were causing injustices.

---

[1] Joseph Story, *Address Delivered Before the Members of the Suffolk Bar, at their Anniversary, on the 4th September 1821*, 1 AMERICAN JURIST 1, 29 (1829).

[2] *See* WILLIAM C. DOWLING, OLIVER WENDELL HOLMES IN PARIS: MEDICINE, THEOLOGY, AND THE ADVANCE OF THE BREAKFAST TABLE ix–xvii (2006); Amalie M. Kass, *A Private Pestilence: Holmes and Perperal Fever, in* OLIVER WENDELL HOLMES: PHYSICIAN AND MAN OF LETTERS 39 (Scott H. Podolsky & Charles S. Bryan, eds., 2009).

Holmes made his professional mark challenging how physicians treated puerperal fever ("childbed fever"), that is, postpartum infections in women who have just given birth.[3] Widespread in the time, it was compared to the plague. Holmes accused his colleagues of carrying infections from patient to patient. He called on them to disinfect themselves before treating the next patient or be sanctioned.[4] His colleagues criticized him as a "contagionist." They protested: "Did [the physician] carry it on his hands? But a gentleman's hands are clean."[5] Eventually, however, Holmes won out. Time and mortality rates proved him right. Physicians in America and abroad wash their hands and have since the mid-19th century. Puerperal fever deaths are largely unheard of today.[6]

Late in the 19th century, after professional debate physicians abandoned bloodletting as a usual treatment. If I told you that America's physicians today oppose hand washing and promote blood-letting, you would be incredulous and outraged. Today, America's hospitals track sanitizing hands electronically.

Switch professions from Holmes's medicine to Field's law: Field's story is different from Holmes's; it does not have a happy ending.

Field made his professional mark writing the New York Code of Civil Procedure of 1848, still known as the "Field Code." For the rest of his long life, Field challenged common-law thinking embodied in chaotic statutes, confusing precedents, and complex procedures. He called on colleagues to systematize laws and rationalize process. As I showed earlier, he wrote five more codes of procedural, substantive and international law. He saw the legal professions eviscerate his Code of Civil Procedure, oppose his criminal codes and kill his civil code. In his last major public appearance, as President of the American Bar Association, he implored his colleagues: "You must ... give speedy justice to your fellow-citizens ... and you must give them a chance to know their laws."[7] In an irony of history, Holmes's son, Oliver Wendell

---

3 *Id.* at 91–100.
4 OLIVER W. HOLMES, PUERPERAL FEVER AS A PRIVATE PESTILENCE (1855), *reprinting* Oliver Wendell Holmes, *The Contagiousness of Puerperal Fever*, 1 NEW ENGLAND QUARTERLY JOURNAL OF MEDICINE AND SURGERY 503–530 (1842–1843).
5 CHARLES DELUCENA MEIGS, ON THE NATURE, SIGNS, AND TREATMENT OF CHILDBED FEVERS 104 (1854).
6 MARLENE M. CORTON, ET AL., WILLIAMS OBSTETRICS, Chap. 37 Puerperal Complications, 682 (24th ed., 2014). Kass, *supra* note 2, at 40. Holmes became Dean of Harvard Medical School and a major 19th century author. A similar story in Austria did not end happily. Ignác Semmelweis made comparable observations and recommendations. His colleagues sent him to an asylum where he died resisting commitment. *See* SHERWIN B. NULAND, THE DOCTORS' PLAGUE: GERMS, CHILDBED FEVER, AND THE STRANGE STORY OF IGNÁC SEMMELWEIS (2003).
7 David Dudley Field, REPORT OF THE TWELFTH ANNUAL MEETING OF THE AMERICAN BAR ASSOCIATION HELD AT CHICAGO, ILLINOIS, AUG. 28, 29, AND 30, 1889, 149, 234 (1889).

Holmes, Jr. (1841–1935), who did not study abroad, but fought valiantly in the Civil War, contributed to the demise of Field's codes and the rise of contemporary common law.

Americans experience the end of Field's story everyday: everywhere they encounter unnecessary failures in legal, social, political and regulatory systems.[8]

Failed legal methods often cause these failures. Nearly two centuries after Field went abroad, too many of America's lawyers, judges and academics are enthralled by the legal equivalent of bloodletting: common-law methods. Where doctors once said, "'Tis a very hard matter to bleed a patient to death," lawyers today idolatrize common law methods.

The legal professions close eyes and ranks in complacency to their complicity in injustice. They follow established practices without hearing criticism; they retreat into the self-satisfied "nonsense" that "the American legal system [is] the envy of the world."[9]

For more than a century America's law professors have belittled foreign successes in legal methods. In 1914 contracts law icon Samuel Williston related how his teachers had taught him to regard as an impossible dream that "every one should readily know the law, or be able quickly to find it."[10] In 1948 Edward H. Levi, one of America's finest jurists in the 20th century, in his widely used *Introduction to Legal Reasoning*, taught students that "The pretense is that law is a system of known rules applied by a judge."[11] In 2009 legal methods guru Frederick Schauer in his *"New" Introduction to Legal Reasoning* teaches students that "A popular conception imagines law as a collection of rules written down in a master rulebook. In many ways this image is highly misleading . . . ."[12]

In Germany and in other civil countries laws that people can find, know, and rely on is *not* a dream. Law *is* a system of known rules applied by the people themselves and by judges. The popular conception of law as a collection of rules in a rulebook *is* correct.

---

[8]   *See*, Richard A. Posner, The Academy and the Judiciary 75–76 (2016).

[9]   Richard A. Posner, *What is Obviously Wrong with the Federal Judiciary, Yet Eminently Curable, Part I*, 19 Green Bag 187, 188, 194 (2016).

[10] Samuel Williston, The Uniform Partnership Act with Some Other Remarks on Other Uniform Commercial Laws, An Address before the Law Association of Philadelphia Dec. 18, 1914, at 1–2 (1915) *reprinted in* 63 U. Pa. L. Rev. 196–197 (1915).

[11] Edward H. Levi, Introduction to Legal Reasoning 1 (1948).

[12] Frederick Schauer, Thinking Like a Lawyer: A New Introduction to Legal Reasoning 103 (2009).

America's academics are, however, correct when they say that America *has* legal indeterminacy and does not have legal certainty. It does not have a government of laws for the people. But America's academics are wrong, when they say Americans must accept the myth that law is what the courts say it is.[13] There is a cure for common law myth: it is civil law.[14]

LAWS FOR THE PEOPLE IN GERMANY

Citizens' Service App, from City of Vilshofen on the Danube[15]

In Part III I showed that Germany has a system of known rules applied by the people themselves and by judges. There is no magic in the German solution. It is the German version of modern civil law methods; they were known and admired in the United States in the 19th century. Isolationism and

---

[13] *See* James R. Maxeiner, *Legal Indeterminacy Made in America: American Legal Methods and the Rule of Law*, 41 Valparaiso U.L. Rev. 517 (2006); James R. Maxeiner, *Legal Certainty and Legal Methods: A European Alternative to American Legal Indeterminacy?*, 15 Tulane J. Int'l & Comp. L. 541 (2007).

[14] To stand for many, see William Price, Paragraphs on the Subject of Judicial Reform in Maryland, Shewing the Evils of the Present System, and Pointing Out the Only Remedy for Their Cure 65 (1846) ("The great question is, what is to be the remedy? ... The only remedy which can be applied with any prospect of success, is a thorough and fundamental revision of the Laws, and their formation into a *written code*." [Emphasis in original.]). Price was United States Attorney for Maryland 1862–1865 and 1866–1867.

[15] Image used with permission of the City of Vilshofen on the Danube, https://www.vilshofen.de.

exceptionalism borne of nativism and two world wars in the 20th century have kept Americans from learning from foreign successes and making improvements at home.

What are the secrets of success in Germany? They are not mysterious. They are as simple as washing your hands.

1. A government of laws is a system of laws that people can know and can apply themselves: one law governs. (Chapter 9.)
2. A government of laws makes laws in public for everyone to see and not in secret or only for those who show up: laws are made for the common good. (Chapter 10.)
3. A federal government of laws coordinates federal and state laws and does not confront people with inconsistent laws: one law governs. (Chapter 11.)
4. A government of laws validates laws' expeditiously and predictably and does not confront people with uncertainty: one law governs. (Chapter 12.)
5. A government of laws applies laws consistently according to law, justice and policy: one law governs. (Chapter 13.)

Americans can do these things. No natural forces stand in their way: just the supernatural forces of myth, ignorance, self-interest and politics.

The Foreign Law Controversy and the Fate of Civil Law Scholarship in American Law Schools

Civil law methods of systematizing statutes in legislatively adopted codes should play a leading role in reforming America's failing legal system They do not. America's law teachers, lawyers and judges count civil law and its methods as foreign, as un-American and without relevance to common law America. At best they ignore, and at worst they suppress, colleagues who would inform them of its benefits.

Part A addresses the foreign law controversy as a contemporary example of the minimal role of foreign law in today's American legal system. Part B notes how civil law and methods, once mainstream in the 19th century, were separated from the American legal system at the turn of the 20th century when the United States became fixated on case law. Part C reports on foreign law in American law schools. Part D reports the fate of those in American law schools who support foreign law.

A. THE FOREIGN LAW CONTROVERSY

The foreign law controversy is a debate about the Supreme Court of the United States citing foreign law.[1] For the first time in a century,

This Essay was prepared in connection with Concurrent Session C: "Legal Scholarship and Foreign Legal Systems," moderated by the author, for the conference, "The Fate of Scholarship in American Law Schools," March 31, 2016 and April 1, 2016, and is loosely based on the presentation there. Footnotes are therefore limited. It assumes background professional knowledge of readers that the rest of the book does not. This essay is to appear in a book with the conference title.

I thank the other panel members, Professors René Lerner, Fernanda Nicola and Peter Quint for their contributions and participation; Professor C.J. Peters, the conference organizer, for the invitation; and Professor Mortimer Sellers for the acceptance of this essay in the conference volume.

[1]   Cases contributing to the controversy include: *Roper v. Simmons*, 543 U.S. 551 (2005) (invalidating application of the death penalty to offenders who were under eighteen when their

mainstream American legal scholars are discussing the role of foreign law in the American legal system.[2] The controversy does not, however, foretell a reawakening of interest in civil law. Instead, it affirms a century-long aversion to legal ideas of foreign origin.

Opponents are dead set against the Supreme Court citing foreign law. *No Thanks, We Already Have Our Own Laws,* is how Judge Richard A. Posner titled his essay on the topic.[3] Justice Antonin Scalia was more dismissive: "Who cares? We have our laws, they have theirs."[4] Two of the nation's most awesome law professors give an article in a Harvard Law School journal the uncompromising title: *Against Foreign Law.*[5]

Opponents fear that judges in giving authoritative interpretations to American laws will adopt foreign law. Justice Scalia worried about "the basic premise of the Court's argument – that American law should conform to the laws of the rest of the world."[6] Similarly, Judge Posner sees a problem in "treating foreign judicial decisions as authorities in U.S. cases, as if the world were a single legal community."[7]

These fears are overstated. Proponents are not advocating adoption of foreign laws. When justices refer to foreign law, says Justice Breyer, usually they are taking into account foreign features of the cases before them. Judicial references are mundane and noncontroversial. For example, judges refer to foreign law in

crimes were committed); *Lawrence v. Texas,* 539 U.S. 558 (2003) (striking down a state law that criminalized homosexual sodomy); and *Atkins v. Virginia,* 536 U.S. 304 (2002) (invalidating execution of mentally retarded defendants).

[2]   *See, e.g.,* Steven G. Calabresi & Bradley G. Silverman, *Hayek and the Citation of Foreign Law: A Response to Professor Jeremy Waldron,* 2015 MICH. ST. L. REV. 1. 10–12, n. 72 (listing over sixty); BASIL MARKESINIS & JORGE FEDTKE, JUDICIAL RECOURSE TO FOREIGN LAW: A NEW SOURCE OF INSPIRATION? (2006); Jenny S. Martinez, *Who's Afraid of International and Foreign Law?,* 104 CAL. L. REV. 1579 (2016); Mark C. Rahdert, *Exceptionalism Unbound: Appraising American Resistance to Foreign Law,* 65 CATHOLIC U.L.R. 537 (2016); CHRISTOPHER ROBERTS, FOREIGN LAW? CONGRESS V. THE SUPREME COURT (2014); THE USE OF FOREIGN PRECEDENTS BY CONSTITUTIONAL JUDGES (Tania Groppi & Marie-Claire Ponthoreau, eds., 2013).

[3]   Richard Posner, *No Thanks, We Already Have Our Own Laws: The Court Should Never View a Foreign Legal Decision as a Precedent in Any Way,* LEGAL AFFAIRS (July/August 2004), *available at* https://www.legalaffairs.org/issues/July-August-2004/feature_posner_julaug04.msp. *See also* Richard A. Posner, *The Supreme Court 2004 Term, Foreword: A Political Court,* 119 HARV. L. REV. 31, 84–90 (2005).

[4]   Antonin Scalia, Luncheon Address at George Mason University School of Law, May 29, 2015, as quoted in Jimmy Hoover, *Scalia Sears Supreme Court For Foreign Law References,* Law 360, available at https://www.law360.com/articles/661690/scalia-sears-supreme-court-for-foreign-law-references (last visited June 10, 2017).

[5]   Robert J. Delahunty & John Yoo, *Against Foreign Law,* 29 HARV. J.L. & PUBLIC POLICY 291 (2005).

[6]   *Roper v. Simmons,* 543 U.S. 511, 125 S. Ct. 1183, 1226 (2005) (Scalia, J., dissenting).

[7]   Posner, *No Thanks, supra* note 3.

interpreting international treaties or in applying parties' contractual choices of law. Justice Breyer in titling his book suggests this modest role: *The Court and the World: American Law and the New Global Realities.* Only rarely do proponents talk of informing (let alone of conforming) American law with foreign law. Justice Breyer in his book consigns such uses of foreign law to a postscript: "although this argument has seemed to occupy the foreground in political discussions about the role of foreign law, it turns out to prove relevant to only a small part of that role, and one that cannot but recede set against the examples discussed elsewhere discussed in this book."[8]

Ironically, the foreign law controversy is misnamed. Only incidentally is it about foreign law. It is a new manifestation of an old complaint: "we want judges that apply and do not make law." It is as much a controversy about common law methods as it is about foreign law. The objections are the same: (1) it is inaccessible; (2) it is undemocratic; and (3) it is dishonest.

Foreign law, Judge Posner observes, is inaccessible.

> The judicial systems of the rest of the world are immensely varied and most of their decisions inaccessible, as a practical matter, to our monolingual judges and lawyers. If foreign decisions were freely citable, it would mean that any judge wanting a supporting citation had only to troll deeply enough in the world's corpus juris to find it.[9]

That has been a familiar complaint of American litigants ever since American precedents began to be published in numbers in the early 19th century. Numerosity, uncertain applicability and indefiniteness of decisions and statutes make American law inaccessible.

Foreign law, Judge Posner says, is "undemocratic."[10] Chief Justice Roberts objects to giving judges chosen in other countries "a role in shaping the law that binds the people in this country."[11] Justice Scalia doubted "whether anybody would say, 'Yes, we want to be governed by the views of foreigners.'"[12] Exactly. American judges are not chosen to make law. Chief Justice Roberts at his confirmation hearings famously told Americans: "Judges and Justices are

---

[8] STEPHEN BREYER, THE COURT AND THE WORLD: AMERICAN LAW AND THE NEW GLOBAL REALITIES 236 (2015).

[9] Posner, *No Thanks, supra* note 3.   [10] Posner, *No Thanks, supra* note 3.

[11] *Second Day of Hearings on the Nomination of Judge Roberts* (September 13, 2005, as transcribed by CQ Transcriptions), NEW YORK TIMES.

[12] Antonin Scalia *in A Conversation between U.S. Supreme Court Justices: The relevance of foreign legal materials in U.S. constitutional cases: A conversation between Justice Antonin Scalia and Justice Breyer,* 3 INT'L J. CONST. L. 519, 522 (2005).

servants of the law, not the other way round. Judges are like umpires. Umpires don't make the rules, they apply them."[13]

Judge Posner says relying on foreign law is dishonest.[14] According to Chief Justice Roberts, "It allows the judge to incorporate his or her own personal preferences, cloak them with the authority of precedent."[15] For Justice Scalia, "To invoke alien law when it agrees with one's own thinking, and ignore it otherwise, is not reasoned decision-making, but sophistry."[16] So long as which law applies is uncertain, and judges must choose, they will have room to incorporate their own personal preferences.

Americans should welcome foreign law. The methods that Justice Scalia longed for were practically civil law methods.[17] Civil law methods well applied, make law accessible, democratic and honest. An American civilian well explained the difference:

> In the civilian system, the Code is central; judges and case law have a distinctly inferior position, in comparison with common law jurisdictions. The controlling conceptualism of the civil law is contained within these written Code texts, which are authoritative because of their political sanction. The Codes have unity and systematic arrangement; their texts have a logical interdependence and coherence born of careful, conscious legislative formulation.[18]

The foreign law controversy might have a different character were the discussion about legislatures drawing on foreign law in enacting American statutes. Justice Scalia, reminded us that "the Founders used a lot of foreign law. ... It is very useful in devising a constitution."[19] He came close to suggesting that lawmakers in legislating should examine foreign law routinely: "of course you consult foreign sources, see how it's worked, see what they've done, use their examples and so forth."[20] The state of Montana in its Constitution adopted verbatim the premier principle of the German Constitution,

---

[13] CONFIRMATION HEARING ON THE NOMINATION OF JOHN G. ROBERTS, JR. TO BE CHIEF JUSTICE OF THE UNITED STATES, HEARINGS BEFORE THE COMMITTEE ON THE JUDICIARY, UNITED STATES SENATE, 109TH CONGRESS, 55 (2005).

[14] Posner, No Thanks, supra note 3.   [15] Roberts, Hearings, supra note 11.

[16] Roper v. Simmons, 125 S. Ct. 1183, 1226 (2005) (Scalia, J., dissenting).

[17] See James R. Maxeiner, Scalia & Garner's Reading Law: A Civil Law for the Age of Statutes?, 6 J. CIVIL L. STUDIES 1 (2013).

[18] Clarence J. Morrow, Louisiana Blueprint: Civilian Codification and Legal Method for State and Nation, 17 TULANE L. REV. 351 [Part 1], 17 TULANE L. REV. 537 [Part 2], 548 (1943).

[19] A Conversation between U.S. Supreme Court justices: The Relevance of Foreign Legal Materials in U.S. Constitutional Cases: A Conversation between Justice Antonin Scalia and Justice Stephen Breyer, 3 INT'L J. CONST. L. 519, 525 (2005).

[20] Id. at 538

"The dignity of the human being is inviolable."[21] ("Die Würde des Menschen ist unantastbar.") If the principle makes sense for America, its German origin should not count against it.

Few embroiled in the controversy note differences between when judges make case law and when legislators adopt statutes. Few follow Justice Scalia's advice and urge legislators to make studies of foreign law routine parts of the lawmaking process. Instead, some use the controversy to rile legislators up against foreign law, to get senators to extract from Supreme Court nominees pledges not to consult foreign law or to get state legislators to adopt "Anti-Foreign or International Law" statutes in order save their states from judges who they fear might adopt Sharia law via case law. Opponents of "wholesale" exclusion propose "guidelines for determining when [foreign law] is appropriately invoked" in deciding cases."[22] Their focus remains firmly fixed on judges making law.

B. THE ALIENATION OF CIVIL LAW

American isolation from civil law and its methods in the 21st century is remarkable.[23] In practically every field of human endeavor other than law, from medicine to marketing, Americans welcome and draw on foreign ideas. No sensible person would refuse a cure for an illness because the cure was found and used successfully abroad.[24]

Isolation from civil law and its methods is a product of the 20th century. In the Historical Part of my book *Failures of American Methods of Lawmaking in Historical and International Perspectives*, I show how until then Americans expected statutory methods. That had no fear of civil law or its methods as foreign.

America's founders and their 19th century successors welcomed civil law and its methods. In 1820 the young Caleb Cushing, later attorney general and nominee to be Chief Justice of the United States, wrote in an article "On the Study of the Civil Law," in the influential *North American Review* that "the

[21] *See* Vicki C. Jackson, *Constitutional Dialogue and Human Dignity: States and Transnational Constitutional Discourse*, 65 MONT. L. REV. 15 (2004).

[22] *See, e.g.*, Mark C. Rahdert, *Exceptionalism Unbound: Appraising American Resistance to Foreign Law*, 65 CATHOLIC UNIVERSITY L. REV. 537, 588, 595 (2016) (proposing a "mature theory of selective exceptionalism"). It is a common law approach: use rules to limit what the decision maker can consider rather than review the substance of the decision maker's decision.

[23] *See* Ernst Stiefel & James R. Maxeiner, *Why Are U.S. Lawyers not Learning from Comparative Law?*, in THE INTERNATIONAL PRACTICE OF LAW 213 (1997).

[24] *Accord*, Edson R. Sunderland, *Book Review*, 15 A.B.A.J. 35 (1929).

continental law ought to be made an important, it might almost be said, the most important, branch of elementary legal education."[25]

In the 19th century civil law was not theory: it offered best practices for American legislators to use in their laws. In 1822 the lay governor of Florida called on the newly created Legislative Council of the Territory to "combine whatever is excellent in both systems, and avoid whatever is objectionable in either, as a distinct code."[26] Serious legal journals made civil law and its methods an important part of their contents.[27]

Perceptive participants in the codification controversies recognized that civil law and common law methods need not conflict but can complement each other. As one scholar explained at century's end: "The question of Code versus Common Law is, then, not a question whether all law shall be expressed in statutory form or in case form, but whether portions of it embracing certain subject-matter shall be expressed in the form of a Statute, or in the form of a Reported Case."[28]

American law school education did not come into its own until after the Civil War, when it supplemented and then supplanted law office study. Some of its early leaders sought to take it in a direction that included rather than excluded civil law and methods. In 1879, the ABA's first committee on legal education reported: "Happily the ancient rivalry between the common law and the system of the civil law has no place in our American professional life. ... American civilization appropriates advantages from whatever quarter they may come, and discards what is not suited to it."[29] In the 1890s the Committee and the Federal Bureau of Education presented a long study of legal education, not only in the United States, but around the world.[30] The Committee recommended a course of study that

---

[25] *On the Study of the Civil Law*, 11 NORTH AMERICAN REV. 407, 412 (1820).

[26] Page 106, *supra*.

[27] *See, e.g., American Law Journal* (1808-1817), *American Jurist and Law Magazine* (1829–1843), *American Law Review* (1866–1928), and *Albany Law Journal* (1870–1909).

[28] R. FLOYD CLARKE, THE SCIENCE OF LAW AND LAWMAKING: BEING AN INTRODUCTION TO LAW, A GENERAL VIEW OF ITS FORMS AND SUBSTANCE, AND A DISCUSSION OF THE QUESTION OF CODIFICATION (1898).

[29] *Report of the Committee on Legal Education and Admissions to the Bar, in* REPORT OF THE SECOND ANNUAL MEETING OF THE AMERICAN BAR ASSOCIATION HELD AT SARATOGA SPRINGS, NEW YORK AUGUST 20TH AND 21ST, 1879 at 209, 220–21 (1879).

[30] REPORT ON LEGAL EDUCATION PREPARED BY A COMMITTEE OF THE AMERICAN BAR ASSOCIATION AND THE U.S. BUREAU OF EDUCATION (Advance Sheets from the REPORT OF THE COMMISSIONER OF EDUCATION FOR 1890–91) (1893). The Full Report is printed in 1 REPORT OF THE COMMISSIONER OF EDUCATION FOR THE YEAR 1890–91, 376–578 (1894). Only the U.S. portion was ready in time for printing in the ABA's Annual Report. REPORT OF THE FIFTEENTH ANNUAL MEETING, AMERICAN BAR ASSOCIATION HELD AT SARATOGA SPRINGS, N.Y., AUGUST 24, 25 and 26, 1892, at 317–94 (1892).

included "a careful and systematic study of the system as a whole after the European method."[31]

At the turn of the 20th century the bar still looked for a way "whereby important legislation of foreign nations affecting the science of jurisprudence can be brought to the attention of American lawyers and become available in the general study of private law."[32] The world was then and is today a civil law world of codes. In September 1904, the civil law world came to St. Louis in a remarkable trifecta of legal conferences held in conjunction with the World's Fair: the Universal Congress of Lawyers and Jurists, under the joint sponsorship of the Exposition and of the ABA, the ABA's own twenty-seventh annual meeting, and the Exposition's own international Congress of Arts and Sciences.[33]

In 1906 following the 1904 Congresses the ABA created the Comparative Law Committee which in 1908 proposed creation of the Comparative Law Bureau. It explained: "While venerating the Common Law as the traditional base of our jurisprudence, we cannot longer consider that source as all-sufficient for the needs of modern civilization but must admit the necessity for legislative limitation or extension. ... It is our mission to select from every source that which is best fitted to assure the prosperity and happiness of the American people"[34]

By the end of World War I, however, civil law and its methods were no longer under consideration in America. A new divide isolated American legal thinking from the civil law world.[35] America's legal professions saw a binary choice: We have our methods; they have theirs. We have case law and digests; they have statutes and codes. We trust judges; they trust legislators. We have an Anglo-American community built on the rule of law; they have

---

[31] REPORT OF THE FIFTEENTH ANNUAL MEETING, *supra* note 30, at 360.

[32] REPORT OF THE TWENTY-NINTH ANNUAL MEETING OF THE AMERICAN BAR ASSOCIATION HELD AT ST. PAUL, MINNESOTA, AUGUST 29, 30 AND 31, 1906, at 81 (1906). *Accord, Comparative Law Bureau. Objects,* 1 ANNUAL BULLETIN OF THE COMPARATIVE LAW BUREAU OF THE AMERICAN BAR ASSOCIATION 2 (1908).

[33] See, respectively, OFFICIAL REPORT OF THE UNIVERSAL CONGRESS OF LAWYERS AND JURISTS HELD AT ST. LOUIS, MISSOURI, U.S.A. SEPTEMBER 28, 29, AND 30, 1904 (1905); REPORT OF THE TWENTY-SEVENTH ANNUAL MEETING OF THE AMERICAN BAR ASSOCIATION HELD AT ST. LOUIS, MISSOURI, SEPTEMBER 26, 27 AND 28 (1904); and *Department IV – History of Law,* CONGRESS OF ARTS AND SCIENCE, UNIVERSAL EXPOSITION, ST. LOUIS, 1904, VOLUME 2, at 241–327 (Howard J. Rogers, ed., 1906).

[34] *Report of the Committee on Comparative Law,* REPORT OF THE THIRTIETH ANNUAL MEETING OF THE AMERICAN BAR ASSOCIATION HELD AT PORTLAND, MAINE, AUGUST 26, 27 AND 28, 1907, at 744, 745 (1907). At the outbreak of the World War I, the Bureau cut back its work; it limped along until the Great Depression. *See* David S. Clark, *Development of Comparative Law in the United States,* THE OXFORD HANDBOOK OF COMPARATIVE LAW 175, 202 (2006).

[35] *See generally,* THOMAS LUNDMARK, CHARTING THE DIVIDE BETWEEN COMMON AND CIVIL LAW (2012).

Continental bureaucracy. A general wave of nationalism that swept the nation at the time facilitated dismissing civil law as alien and even possibly subversive.

A key change in legal education that occurred at the turn of the 20th century – well known to law professors today – contributed mightily to this isolation; adoption of the case method of instruction. Enthrallment of the legal system to case law was a part of this change.

The case method makes excerpts of appellate court decisions the focus of classroom study. It turns arguing what the law is, rather than applying the law, into the focus of classroom study. Its 19th-century apostles gave no time to statutes, their drafting, their systematizing or their applying. They denigrated codification as having an "ugly sound." They trained their students "to believe that no code can be expressed with sufficient exactness, or can be sufficiently elastic to fulfill adequately the functions of our common law."[36] The professions followed their instructors. They gave up on systematic codes and turned to systems of precedents.

Adoption of case method was not automatic nor without controversy. It did not happen when Dean Langdell introduced it at Harvard in 1870. There it had a precarious existence for two decades; case method did reach beyond Harvard until 1890. But after 1890 and by 1915 Harvard conquered the American world of legal education for its case method of instruction. Its fans describe the takeover as one describes a military campaign or crusade. Harvard fought "On the Battlefield of Merit;"[37] it sent out "missionaries" to "convert" law school faculties from below and plenipotentiaries to persuade university presidents to convert law schools from above.[38]

Meanwhile, 1890s nativism facilitated the takeover. Harvard Law School fin de siècle became more English than the English;[39] the United States became "the most common of the common law countries."[40] English common law, which had been ridiculed at the beginning of the century for its claim to be the perfection of reason, was praised at the end as "Our Lady the Common Law."[41]

---

[36] SAMUEL WILLISTON, THE UNIFORM PARTNERSHIP ACT WITH SOME OTHER REMARKS ON OTHER UNIFORM COMMERCIAL LAWS: AN ADDRESS BEFORE THE LAW ASSOCIATION OF PHILADELPHIA DECEMBER 18, 1914 (1915) *reprinted* in 63 U. PA. L. REV. 196 (1915) at 1–2.

[37] DAVID R. COQUILLETTE & BRUCE A KIMBALL, ON THE BATTLEFIELD OF MERIT (2015).

[38] Bruce A. Kimball, *The Proliferation of Case Method Teaching in American Law Schools: Mr. Langdell's Emblematic 'Abomination,'* 1890–1915, 46 HIST. EDUC. Q. 192 (2006) (classifying modes of adoption as missionaries, indirect or president).

[39] *See* A.V. DICEY, THE TEACHING OF ENGLISH LAW AT HARVARD (1900), *reprinting* 13 HARV. L. REV. 422 (1900).

[40] ROBERT STEVENS, LEGAL EDUCATION IN AMERICA FROM THE 1850S TO THE 1980S, 133 (1983).

[41] *See generally* RICHARD A. COSGROVE, COSGROVE, OUR LADY THE COMMON LAW: AN ANGLO-AMERICAN LEGAL COMMUNITY, 1870-1930 (1987).

Crusaders rooted out civil law.[42] When a Carnegie study of legal education released in 1915 recommended that American law schools "apply the resources of European legal science, with its development of nearly two thousand years, to the establishment at last of a scientific system for the common law,"[43] Harvard's dean in private objected to "the very general principle of calling in Germans to pass on American instruction" and confided that "none of us are enthusiastic about the idea of an investigation by a foreigner."[44]

In 1924 when the ABA made a pilgrimage to London, the consensus of pilgrims was said to be that civil law is an attempt "to supplant the parent Common Law" and "to forsake our English heritage and follow the lead of Imperial Rome."[45] A divide between common law and civil law had been created. Civil law had been alienated.

Three years before, in 1921 the founding director of the Kaiser Wilhelm Institute for Physics in Berlin, Albert Einstein, came to the United States to discuss the laws of physics. What if Columbia University and the American Physical Association had said of Einstein's theory of relativity that it was an un-American attempt "to supplant the common law of gravity" and "to forsake our English heritage and follow the lead of Imperial Germany"? Nature would have proved them wrong. In the natural sciences, old theories are disproved by actual results. Not so in law. In law, not actual results, but the legal professions determine what works. Reformers are stymied.[46]

---

[42] *See* WILLIAM C. CHASE, THE AMERICAN LAW SCHOOL AND THE RISE OF ADMINISTRATIVE GOVERNMENT 100 (1982) (describing suppression of civil law trained legislation expert Ernst Freund); STEVENS, *supra* note 40, at 40. Llewellyn complained that "'The' case-system ... crusaders" had demanded that "'The' case system must control all courses." Columbia's curriculum had to "cast out" professors in Roman law, in comparative administrative law and in international law. Karl N. Llewellyn, JURISPRUDENCE: REALISM IN THEORY AND PRACTICE 378 (1962).

[43] JOSEF REDLICH, THE COMMON LAW AND THE CASE METHOD IN AMERICAN UNIVERSITY LAW SCHOOLS: A REPORT TO THE CARNEGIE FOUNDATION FOR THE ADVANCEMENT OF TEACHING 74 (imprint date 1914, actually released April 1915).

[44] As quoted in CHASE, *supra* note 42, at 100.

[45] J. Carroll Hayes, *The Visit to England of the American Bar Association, in* THE AMERICAN BAR ASSOCIATION LONDON MEETING 1924: IMPRESSIONS OF ITS SOCIAL, OFFICIAL, PROFESSIONAL AND JURIDICAL ASPECTS AS RELATED BY PARTICIPANTS IN CONTEST FOR MOST ENLIGHTENING REVIEW OF TRIP 9, 15. (1925)

[46] *See* Edson R. Sunderland, *The English Struggle for Procedural Reform*, 39 HARV. L. REV. 725, 726 (1926) ("Individual success in practice suffers no apparent loss from the use of a defective system;" "the lack of experience with any other technique makes it difficult for the bar to see defects in the current system"), originally published as *The Evolution of Remedial Rights*, 5 AM. L. SCH. REV. 639 (1926); Edson R. Sunderland, *An Inquiry Concerning the Functions of Procedure in Legal Education*, 21 MICH. L. REV. 372, 377 (1933); Hessel E. Yntema, *Comparative Legal Research: Some Remarks on "Looking Out of the Cave,"* 54 MICH. L. REV. 900, 922 (1956).

C. FOREIGN LAW IN AMERICAN LAW SCHOOLS

The "short and sad" report of Professor John H. Langbein in 1995 to the International Association of Procedural Law captures the fate of civil law methods in American legal scholarship today: "The study of comparative procedure in the United States has little following in academia, and virtually no audience in the courts or in legal policy circles."[47] The alienation of civil law and its methods explains why.

Litigation, not legislation, defines American law. Case law methods, not statute law, methods govern. What counts as scholarship are writings that, because of their content or because of their provenance, support arguments made to judges. Exceptionally, a social science argument qualifies for use in court; most do not. Chief Justice Roberts deprecates the latter as "largely of no use or interest to people who actually practice law."[48]

Today's foreign law controversy continues the century-long alienation of foreign law scholarship from American law. Foreign law arguments are not ordinarily legal arguments for courts to adopt in applying law in cases. They are arguments for better law; they are directed to legislatures. Foreign law scholarship, consequently, is of little moment in American law schools.

The treatment of foreign law by the American Law Institute (ALI) illustrates the fate of foreign law scholarship in America.[49] Founded in 1923 by leading judges and lawyers, the ALI styles itself "the leading independent organization in the United States producing scholarly work to clarify, modernize, and otherwise improve the law." Its stock-in-trade is not, however, a government of better laws, but a rule of judicial precedents synthesized into "Restatements of the Law." ALI's founding judges and lawyers eschewed crafting codes[50] even as contemporary comparativists hoped that Restatements might morph

---

[47] John H. Langbein, *The Influence of Comparative Procedure in the United States*, 43 AM. J. COMP. L. 545 (1995). *See* Eric Stein, *Uses, Misuses – and Nonuses of Comparative Law*, 72 NW. U.L. REV. 198 (1977); Hessel E. Yntema, *Comparative Legal Research – Some Remarks on "Looking Out of the Cave,"* 54 MICH. L. REV. 899 (1956).

[48] Chief Justice John G. Roberts Jr., *Interview*, 13 SCRIBES 37 (2010). Catalyst for many articles has been Harry T. Edward, *The Growing Disjunction Between Legal Education and the Legal Profession*, 91 MICH. L. REV. 34 (1992).

[49] In the interest of disclosure, I note that I am an ALI member and have been for twenty years. My colleagues there have patiently and politely listened to my numerous pleas that they add a foreign perspective to their work.

[50] REPORT OF THE COMMITTEE ON THE ESTABLISHMENT OF A PERMANENT ORGANIZATION FOR IMPROVEMENT OF THE LAW PROPOSING THE ESTABLISHMENT OF AN AMERICAN LAW INSTITUTE 23 (1923).

into codes.[51] Codes did not come. ALI's forays into statute drafting in the form of the Uniform Commercial Code (UCC), model codes, and principles of the law have not changed the institution's case-law method mentality. In its near hundred-year history it has hardly noted foreign law, no matter how obvious such references are.

For example, standard terms in contracts have tied the ALI in knots from its earliest days. Issues of standard term contracts were present already in the early preparation and eventual drafting of the UCC in the 1930s through the 1960s, continued into the drafting of the Restatement (Second) of Contracts in the 1970s and 1980s, and cropped up again to derail modernizing of the UCC in the late 1990s and early 2000s. Today, they are again before the ALI Council in the form of a proposed *Restatement of the Law Consumer Contracts.* The ALI Reporters state that standard terms in consumer contracts "in recent decades" have presented a "fundamental challenge" to the law of contracts particularly in controlling the incorporation and content of unread terms.[52]

Recent decades? Already in 1939 U.C.C. drafter Karl Llewelyn reviewed in the *Harvard Law Review* Otto Prausnitz's then new book, *The Standardization of Commercial Contracts in English and Continental Law.* For a half century judges, academics, and legislators around the world, including in the United States, considered the issues. It was in 1993, i.e., twenty-five years ago, not in recent decades, that Europe issued the Unfair Terms Directive. Not dispositive of all issues, it deals with the fundamental ones.[53] Yet the draft Restatement does not even note the Directive's existence. ALI's omission confirms Professor Langbein's caustic comment that "American legal dialogue starts from the premise that no relevant insights are to be found beyond the water's edge";[54] it betrays Justice Story's plea: "Let us not vainly imagine that we have unlocked and exhausted all the stores of judicial wisdom and policy."[55] Fortunately, America's physicists and physicians are not so provincial.

---

[51] *See, e.g.,* Mitchell Franklin, *The Historic Function of the American Law Institute: Restatement as Transitional to Codification,* 47 HARV. L. REV. 1367 (1934); Hessel E. Yntema, *What Should the American Law Institute Do?,* 34 MICH. L. REV. 461 (1936); Clarence J. Morrow, *Louisiana Blueprint: Civilian Codification and Legal Method for State and Nation,* 17 TULANE L. REV. 351 (Part I), 537 (Part II) (1943).

[52] Reporters' Introduction, RESTATEMENT OF THE LAW CONSUMER CONTRACTS, Council Draft No. 4, 1-2 (December 18, 2017). *See* Tess Wilkinson-Ryan, *The Perverse Consequences of Disclosing Standard Terms,* 103 CORNELL L. REV. 117, 173 (2017).

[53] *See* James R. Maxeiner, *Standard-Terms Contracting in the Global Electronic Age: European Alternatives,* 28 YALE J. INT'L L. 109 (2003).

[54] Langbein, *supra* note 47, at 546–47.

[55] Joseph Story, *Address Delivered Before the Members of the Suffolk Bar, at their Anniversary, on the 4th September 1821,* 1 AM. JUR. & LAW MAG. 1, 29 (1829).

Of foreign law research in American law schools, there is as good as none. Of legal research of any kind, in the sense of scholarly investigation to further knowledge and create better law, there is little more. A century ago American law schools kidnapped the term "legal research" from the realm of scientific understanding and used it to describe activity that a sound legal system renders simple: finding applicable law. Imagine the state of medicine today if "medical research" meant hunting through dusty old pharmacopeias for the right potion!

It is not perverseness on the part of the law schools that legal research as a term was free for the taking. American legal education did not follow the research model of medical schools that medical education took following the Carnegie Foundation's Flexner Reports of 1910.[56] Legal education did not get the public resources that medical education gets. Had it been able to do so, there would be plenty of room for foreign law scholarship. Harvard Medical School alone has more faculty members (over 11,000, according to its website) than all American law schools combined (fewer than 10,000). Nor does the United States fund any independent research institutes in law as other countries do.

If there is not much to say about the fate of foreign law scholarship, something positive can be said about the fate of teaching foreign law, now mostly done under the rubric of comparative law. Most American law schools do offer some teaching of foreign law.[57]

Why do American law schools teach comparative law when they deem foreign law to have no importance for American law?

Like it or not, Americans live in a civil law world. A century ago Harvard icon Samuel Williston reminded the bar that "practically the whole civilized world, except English speaking countries, is governed by codes; ... and that foreign expert opinion seems practically unanimous in favor of codification."[58] If only to deal with the rest of the world, some Americans for practical reasons must have some opportunity to learn about foreign law. Some Americans, such as even Justice Scalia, may for better-law reasons, be interested in learning from foreign experiences.[59] It is in large measure to the

---

[56] *See generally*, James R. Maxeiner, Educating Lawyers Now and Then: An Essay Comparing the 2007 and 1914 Carnegie Foundation Reports on Legal Education (2008); Robert M. Hardaway, *Legal and Medical Education Compared: Is It Time for a Flexner Report on Legal Education?*, 59 Wash. U.L.Q. 687 (1981).

[57] Comparative law became the preferred term for the study of foreign law or civil law early in the 20th century.

[58] Williston, *supra* note 36.

[59] *See* text at notes 17–18, *supra*. *See also*, James R. Maxeiner, *1992: High Time for American Lawyers to Learn From Europe, or Roscoe Pound's 1906 Address Revisited*, 15 Fordham Int'l L.J. 1 (1991); Ernst C. Stiefel & James R. Maxeiner, *Civil Justice Reform in the United States:*

credit of what we call the émigré generation of refugees from that we owe the stability of the basic course.[60]

Several possible approaches to teaching comparative law in law schools have stood out in American experience: (1) comparative law in every class; (2) an introductory course, mostly in comparative law, but sometimes in international and comparative law; and (3) specialty courses in particular countries or specific areas of law. The only one of these approaches that has managed to hold enduring favor is the basic comparative law course.[61] The comparison in every class approach fails for want of faculty with knowledge and interest. The specialty classes want for interested students and continuity.

Rarely is the basic course mandatory for students. It may be semimandatory, that is an optional choice of one from a selection of a wider group of "perspective" courses, such as, legal history, jurisprudence, law and economics, etc. The result is that that which Professor Langbein saw: "The vast majority of American law students graduate in complete ignorance of comparative law."[62]

Law students are not to blame. Most attend law school to prepare for professional careers in their own legal system. Career-focused students, except those who aspire to international careers, can be expected to bypass elective courses in foreign law. Surprisingly, many students do not. Some without an international interest may be enticed to take one course, either for practical reasons – i.e., everybody encounters some international transactions – or because they want to see how other systems work. Particularly students with practical experience with failures of the American system

Opportunity for Learning from Civilized European Procedure Instead of Continued Isolation? in FESTSCHRIFT FÜR KARL BEUSCH, 853 (1993), *also in* 42 AM. J. COMP. L. 167 (1994).

[60] On the Hitler era émigré generation generally, see Kyle Graham, *The Refugee Jurist and American Law Schools, 1933–1941,* 50 AM. J. COMP. L. 803 (2002); John H. Langbein, *The Influence of the German Émigrés on American Law: The Curious Case of Civil and Criminal Procedure, in* DER EINFLUSS DEUTSCHER EMIGRANTEN AUF DIE RECHTSENTWICKLUNG IN DEN USA UND IN DEUTSCHLAND 321 (Ernst C. Stiefel, *et. al.,* eds. 1993); and other essays in the Stiefel volume.

[61] *See, inter alia,* Rudolf B. Schlesinger, *The Role of the Basic Course in the Teaching of Foreign and Comparative Law,* 19 AM. J. COMP. L. 616 (1971). On the in-every class approach, see James R. Maxeiner, *Learning from Others: Sustaining the Internationalization and Globalization of U.S. Law School Curriculums,* 32 FORDHAM J. INT'L L. 32 (2008); Roscoe Pound, *The Place of Comparative Law in the American Law School Curriculum,* 8 TULANE L. REV. 161, 162–63 (1934) (arguing comparative law has no place as a course in law school, not even a place in individual classes, but "a place of the first importance in the work of the American law teacher" in considering legal methods). On the specialty courses approach, see Langbein, *supra* note 47, at 546 (seeing "a curricular Potemkin Village").

[62] Langbein, *supra* note 47, at 546.

find relief in learning of other approaches that work better. But more than one course is an unreasonable expectation of all but the wealthiest of students.

Yes, wealth. The American system of legal education burdens students more than do other systems of legal education. In many countries, legal education is tuition-free or nearly so. It is public education, after all. In many countries, practical training occurs after law school, not in it, and is compensated, rather than charged. It is, after all, training for a public profession.[63] For good reason teachers of foreign and comparative law have long spoken of challenges of the "box office." How to get enough students to come?

D. THE FATE OF AN AMERICAN COMPARATIVIST

Would an American law school hire someone as a regular faculty member for foreign law knowledge? No. There is no reason to hire someone to teach one lone course. Instead, a law school can hire an adjunct professor from practice, engage a visitor or find a faculty member with a conventional focus who has an interest in the subject.

American law schools typically find, in effect, a designated comparativist, i.e., one professor who has some knowledge or interest in a foreign legal system. Since the law school's reputation hardly hangs in the balance, and since the designated comparativist needs to know only a bit more than the students to teach a course, that person can be a draftee. The presence of the course in the catalogue sufficiently demonstrates that the school is cosmopolitan.

Faculty who are looking to teach comparative law are counseled to downplay the knowledge they acquired, and stress their willingness to teach "bread-and-butter" courses. Law schools hire professors in spite of and not because of foreign law knowledge. Colleagues do not appreciate knowledge that they do not know how to deal with.[64]

---

[63] The follow-up to the 1914 Carnegie study of American legal education was the 1921 Carnegie study by Alfred Zantzinger Reed, titled *Training for the Public Profession of the Law.*

[64] One hears this comment from many comparativists. Gerhard Casper, President Emeritus of Stanford University, recalls on arriving in the 1960s in Chicago as an émigré in comparative law being told by Professor Philip Kurland: "Gerhard, do not just do comparative law. You have to be engaged in a major field of American law because otherwise your colleagues will find it difficult to take you seriously as they will lack the expertise to evaluate your work." Gerhard Casper, *In Memoriam Philip B. Kurland*, 64 U. CHI. L. REV. 9, 11 (1997). Casper followed the advice, largely abandoned comparative law and succeeded as almost no other comparativist in America has. His judicial competitor for the honor has been cursed as "Ruth Traitor Ginsburg" for directing constitution writers to better foreign law.

Since law schools do not hire because of foreign law knowledge, and because the situation is much the same in practice for similar reasons,[65] it is fitting to ask why an American born and trained in law in the United States would go abroad to gain such foreign law knowledge.[66] Studying law abroad imposes requirements greater than studying other fields where knowledge transfers more easily. For law, one must study a different intellectual system. One must do one's work where all is in a foreign language.

An American might choose to study civil law abroad today for the same reasons Americans flocked to Europe in the 19th century to study in many areas: to learn from others what was not known at home. If the challenges of study are greater in law than in other areas of study, the possibilities of improving life in America are greater than in other areas. A dozen years ago Professor Langbein explained this in an official letter to a colleague of mine: "The German legal system is the most sophisticated exemplar of the European tradition among the major states, it supplies an endlessly interesting source of contrast with our procedures and institutions."

Professor Langbein is too modest. More than just contrast, better American law is the goal of his comparative law work. Langbein's *modus operandi* is the same as that of other of my comparative law teachers in the United States: show historical reasons for a long recognized and severe failure in our system and contrast that failure with obvious better performances of another system.[67] Learn from others how better to do it is the next obvious step. The better-law approach itself should be, but not always is, less controversial when one focuses on basic building-blocks of a legal system (e.g., knowing the law)

---

[65] *See* James R. Maxeiner, *International Legal Careers: Paths and Directions*, 25 Syracuse J. Int'l L. & Com. 21 (1998).

[66] This question does not arise for the domestic teacher who does not choose immersion abroad or for the foreign-origin comparativist. The former's choice may have been dictated by financial limitations: most Americans who have studied foreign law abroad have relied on personal resources or on foreign-sourced ones. American institutions do not seem to support such study much if at all. Without such immersion, however, criticism is almost necessarily muted.

In the case of émigrés, knowledge of a foreign system is a given. But relying on émigrés for comparative civil law knowledge has its drawbacks. If they do not have opportunity to immerse themselves in American law, as was the case with older refugee immigrants, they may hesitate in their comparisons. Younger émigrés who do immerse themselves may be reticent to criticize their host country too strenuously out of cordiality or practicality concerns. Many an émigré unleashed the sharpest criticism only after retirement.

[67] *E.g.*, Rudolf B. Schlesinger, *Comparative Criminal Procedure: A Plea for Utilizing Foreign Experience*, 26 Buff. L. Rev. 361, 362 (1976) ("I shall explore a few aspects of our law of criminal procedure that, in the light of comparable foreign solutions, appear to me to be intolerably archaic, inefficient, unjust, and indeed perverse").

rather than on specific legal choices (e.g., legality of abortion), for we all believe in the rule of law, don't we?

Failures of legal methods infect the performance of all areas of law. Preoccupation with common law methods to the point of obsession and the consequent exclusion of civil law methods is an American affliction that should have been cured long ago. What may have been unprovable in the 19th century codification debates is no longer reasonably deniable. After more than a century of experiences around the world, common law claims of superiority of case law over statute law as a general governing principle are obviously false. Americans know that they live in an age of statutes. They should realize that common law may properly supplement but cannot routinely supplant written law.

Having found a cure for common law in study abroad, the student of civil law returns home and finds a fate altogether different from that which the student had hoped for. Instead of welcome and collaboration, the student finds avoidance and quarantine. Years may be spent on the job market before anything ever comes of the effort, if something ever does come.

American law school faculty hiring expectations, perhaps unintentionally but no less effectively, work against hiring foreign law experts. Immersion in a civil law system is what comparatists should have, but what law schools expect are candidates who have had federal judicial clerkships. Clerking steals from prospective law faculty their best and likely last opportunity to learn civil law and its methods.

At a time in their careers when would-be law professors in other countries are encouraged and even expected to go abroad to confront first-hand the diversity of legal systems, America's future legal leaders are held home to make their careers clerking to develop important professional relationships to open doors. What irony: instead of being challenged to open their minds to alternative civil law methods, future legal leaders are indoctrinated in common-law methods.

Still, the acceptance of the comparative law course provides a modest opportunity for the American who has studied foreign law abroad. United States Supreme Court clerks are not sufficiently numerous to occupy all faculty positions. If the comparativist convinces the hiring committee of interest in teaching bread-and-butter courses, the faculty might make a deal.

The newly hired comparativist likely is naïve. The hire may be anxious to administer the civil law cure for common-law ailments. The new hire teaches the comparative law course, adds an international course and offers modest comparative law insights in bread-and-butter courses. The new hire pursues better law in scholarship. The new hire thinks that colleagues will welcome the knowledge the comparativist brings that can help solve the problems they face.

The naïve new hire has forgotten that foreign law has no place in American law. The new hire has misunderstood the allotted role. Even at Yale, according to Professor Langbein, "Like a child in Victorian England, the comparativist on an American law faculty is expected to be seen but not heard."[68]

Professor George P. Fletcher, at Columbia, explains why: comparative law is "subversive." Of course, that is "the advantage of comparative law." "It enables us to get beyond ourselves to look back, with slightly alienated eyes, on the assumptions that American lawyers simply accept without reflection."[69] But colleagues do not want that. For them, in Professor Fletcher's words, these "options are simply off the table. Some solutions are out of range. They are not 'thinkable.'" The new comparativist does not realize that for many colleagues that is the way things should remain.

Comparativists find that most colleagues on the faculty, however well intentioned, believe and even preach Chief Justice Roberts' uninformed patriotic prattle that our system "is the model for justice throughout the world."[70] Why shouldn't they? Most graduated law school in complete ignorance of comparative law.[71] Ignorance is bliss.[72]

America offers comparative law scholars a Faustian bargain. Stay out of the mainstream, write only for each other, and we will leave you untouched. Chief Justice Roberts – not an academic – stated the choice explicitly: "You can decide whether you want to be an engineer or a theoretical mathematician or a theoretical physicist, and those are two different lines of work. But don't expect, if you're going to be a theoretical mathematician, to have an impact on how people build bridges. And if you want to have an impact on how they build bridges, you need to become more of an engineer."[73]

Chief Justice Roberts' choice reveals his common-law addiction. There is a choice he did not offer that is the first choice of every better law comparativist: inform lawmakers how they might make laws better. That is, helping lawyers

[68] Langbein, *supra* note 47, at 546.
[69] George P. Fletcher, *Comparative Law as a Subversive Discipline*, 46 AM J. COMP. L. 683, 695–696 (1998).
[70] John Roberts, Chief Justice, 2010 Year-End Report on the Federal Judiciary 3 (2010). *Accord*, John Roberts, Chief Justice, 2013 Year-End Report on the Federal Judiciary 3 (2013). Judge Posner calls the claims of the Chief Justice "nonsense." Richard A. Posner, *What Is Obviously Wrong with the Federal Judiciary, Yet Eminently Curable, Part I*, 19 GREEN BAG 2D 187, 188 (2016).
[71] Langbein, *supra* note 47, at 546.
[72] Ernst C. Stiefel & James R. Maxeiner, *Civil Justice Reform in the United States: Opportunity for Learning from Civilized European Procedure Instead of Continued Isolation?* FESTSCHRIFT FÜR KARL BEUSCH, 853 (1993), *also in* 42 AM. J. COMP. L. 167 (1994).
[73] Roberts, *supra* note 70.

and judges wholesale. The Chief Justice's failure to see this choice for procedure is unforgivable. In its responsibilities for rules of procedure, the Supreme Court is the legislature.

Comparative law as an institution in the United States apparently accepts the Faustian bargain offered by Chief Justice Roberts: academic theory over practical impact.[74] Recent editors of the *American Journal of Comparative Law* seem to me to have been less interested in using comparative law "in considering proposed legislation and legal reform in the domestic scene,"[75] and more interested in establishing comparative law as a "coherent and intellectually convincing discipline."[76] What a contrast there is between the first *Journal* editor's own, *Comparative Legal Research: Some Remarks on Looking Out of the Cave*, and the *Journal's* recent 255-page special issue centered on an 132-page article titled *Jameses at Play: A Tractation on the Comparison of Laws*. The former is a vigorous call for better law; the latter, as its title suggests, is a "dizzying torrent of wordplay."[77]

The 2015 Annual Meeting of the American Society of Comparative Law considered a resolution that the Society "Affirms that academic freedom extends to recognizing and teaching that foreign law and foreign legal systems *may work better* than their American counterparts." With controversy, it passed the motion by voice vote, however, subject to reformulation by the Executive Committee. In Committee, it turned into mush: teaching other systems may *work better*, became "*we may draw useful lessons for the law in the United States.*" The Committee accepted that the modern American comparativist is to be the Caspar Milquetoast of the 1920s, to speak softly or be hit with a big stick.[78]

And getting hit with the big stick is a shock for the better-law minded American comparativist. He or she might have been anticipated loneliness,[79]

---

[74] To be sure, individual comparativists have different views both as to the proper role of comparative law and as to what goals are in reach within different environments. Most are not dogmatic in their choices. There is no one right use of comparative law. I do not intend to suggest that there is. Notwithstanding this diversity of views, I feel more welcome in an ASCL meeting than just about anywhere else in the American academy.

[75] Hessel E. Yntema, *The American Journal of Comparative Law*, 1 AM. J. COMP. L. 11, 12 (1952).

[76] Mathias Reimann, *The Progress and Failure of Comparative Law in the Second Half of the Twentieth Century*, 50 AM. J. COMP. L. 671, 673 (2002).

[77] James Q. Whitman, *The Hunt for Truth in Comparative Law*, 54 AM. J. COMP. L. SPECIAL ISSUE 181 (2017)

[78] Jedidiah Kroncke takes a still-bleaker view: comparative law turned from finding better law, to asserting our law is better for others. It became a kind of anticomparative law. Jedidiah Kroncke, *Law and Development as Anti-Comparative Law*, 45 VANDERBILT J. TRANSNATIONAL L. 477, 510–12 (2012).

[79] *See, e.g.*, JOHN HENRY MERRYMAN, THE LONELINESS OF THE COMPARATIVE LAWYER AND OTHER ESSAYS IN FOREIGN AND COMPARATIVE LAW (1999).

but punishment for pointing out better law and legal methods? Yet that is the fate of the impatient comparativist: to be told that advocating better law "in your scholarship is fine, but using it in a comparative law class does not pedagogically advance our students' education."[80]

At higher scholarly planes, suppression consists of attacks on better-law work.[81] At operational levels, suppression includes denial of promotion, salary adjustments, course assignments, summer research support, sabbatical leaves and perhaps even tenure.

The subject of academic freedom is beyond the scope of this essay,[82] but it suggests a provocative question: Is foreign law scholarship outside the bounds of academic freedom protection? Has promoting civil law and its methods become in an American law school like promoting creationism in a biology faculty? Have civil law methods become what academic freedom experts call law an "alternative framework," that is, an approach to study that lies outside the accepted confines of the discipline and thus is not protected?[83]

The fate of better law scholarship might make it seem so. I know of no American institution that has stepped up to protect a comparativist in exercise of the academic freedom to espouse better laws and legal methods *for America.*

---

[80] These words were written by a professor of civil procedure, co-authored by colleagues and in effect approved by faculty and university. What is to explain this? What Professor Langbein wrote in another context has application here: "The real explanation for the tenacity of our deeply deficient system of civil justice is not culture, but a combination of inertia and the vested interests of those who profit from the status quo." John H. Langbein, *Cultural Chauvinism in Comparative Law*, 5 CARDOZO J. INT'L & COMP. L. 41, 49 (1997).

[81] Responding to such criticisms, see, e.g., John H. Langbein, *Trashing 'The German Advantage,"* 82 NW. U. L. REV. 763 (1988). Already in 1936 Karl Llewellyn warned Stefan Riesenfeld that "to identify in America the foreign origin of a legal idea is to give it the kiss of death, the kiss of death, the kiss of death." Stefan Riesenfeld, *The Impact of German Legal Ideas and Institutions on Legal Thought and Institutions in the United States*, in MATHIAS REIMANN (ED.), THE RECEPTION OF CONTINENTAL IDEAS IN THE COMMON LAW WORLD 1820–1920, 89, 90–91 (1993). Llewellyn practiced what he preached. Although he himself visited as a professor at Leipzig and published some of his best work in German, he never let on that in drafting the Uniform Commercial Code he drew on German law and legal methods.

[82] It may be too much to hope for universities and their faculties to police themselves. The question arises in a current ALI project: Student Sexual Misconduct: Procedural Frameworks for Colleges and Universities. It is common to criticize campus legal systems for not living up to legal system requirements. My observation is that campus legal methods *all too well* mirror the American system: poorly executed process and poorly crafted statutes. *See*, e.g., "The Red Book," AMERICAN ASSOCIATION OF UNIVERSITY PROFESSORS, AAUP POLICY DOCUMENTS AND REPORTS (11th ed., 2015).

[83] Akeel Bilgrami, *Truth, Balance and Freedom*, in WHO'S AFRAID OF ACADEMIC FREEDOM 10, 18–21 (2015).

University guardians of academic freedom do not safeguard civil law studies, but defer to colleagues' actions that blatantly deny academic freedom. I know of deans joining in suppression, provosts washing their hands of the issue and presidents taking ineffectual action that changed nothing. Some regret it; others do not.

The institutional police of academic freedom, i.e., associations of professors and the accreditation authorities, would rather not think about civil law teaching at all. I know of nearly half-a-dozen such police that have sung the praises of academic freedom, yet did nothing of significance to protect teachers' freedom to teach better law and methods when called upon to do so.

E. CONCLUSION

The fate of civil law and its methods in American law schools is ignorance at best and suppression at worst.

When I went off to law school in 1974, I would never have thought that. Law schools, I thought, have a mission of making law better. Surely, they would welcome cures for America's legal ills wherever found.

I was wrong.[84]

---

[84] *Compare* James R. Maxeiner, *Bane of American Forfeiture Law – Banished at Last?*, 62 Cornell L. Rev. 768 (1977) and James R. Maxeiner, *Constitutionalizing Forfeiture Law – The German Example*, 27 Am. J. Comp. L. 635 (1979) *with* Caleb Nelson, *The Constitutionality of Civil Forfeiture*, 125 Yale L.J. 2182 (2016) and John Oliver, Civil Forfeiture: Last Week Tonight with John Oliver, https://youtu.be/3kEpZWGgJks (2014). *Cf.* Memoirs of Jeremy Bentham; Including Autobiographical Conversations and Correspondence. By John Bowring. Vol. X, The Works of Jeremy Bentham at 66 (1843) ([When I was younger I] "never suspected that the people in power were against reform. I supposed they only wanted to know what was good in order to embrace it.")

Index